HOMER FOLKS
PIONEER IN SOCIAL WELFARE

HOMER FOLKS

PIONEER IN SOCIAL WELFARE

WALTER I. TRATTNER

COLUMBIA UNIVERSITY PRESS

NEW YORK   1968   LONDON

Walter I. Trattner is Associate Professor of History and
Social Welfare at the University of Wisconsin-Milwaukee.

FOR MY MOTHER
MINNIE TRATTNER

PREFACE

ALTHOUGH concern for needy members of the community has been expressed in some form for many centuries, the terms *social work* and *social welfare* are of recent origin; they came into existence in the twentieth century. These terms, as we know them today, differ in their content and values from *charity, philanthropy,* or *correction,* terms which preceded them historically. Whereas the older philanthropy was, on the whole, characterized by private or voluntary care for those in need, the newer social work or social welfare includes also public action, preventive efforts to eliminate the causes of distress, and constructive measures to create a freer, more secure, and fuller life for all citizens. In other words, social work and welfare contribute to the building of a sound social structure as well as the remaking of lives, to the improvement and reconstruction of not only individuals and families, but also the neighborhood.

In enlarging their services and placing a new emphasis upon the interdependence of the well-being of the individual and the welfare of society, social work and social welfare underwent many changes during the late nineteenth and twentieth centuries. Some of the more important ones included the reform of the almshouse and the removal of children and the insane from this catchall of social refuse; the adoption of foster homes rather than institutional care for dependent, neglected, and delinquent children; the removal of children from the jurisdiction of criminal law and punishment and the establishment of children's courts and probation systems; the condemnation and reduction of child labor; public aid or "pensions" for dependent mothers; the introduction of decent standards of living for the recipients of relief; the introduction of prenatal and postpartum care, visiting nurses and health education for expectant or recent mothers; the prevention of mental illness and the promotion of mental hygiene; and the infusion of social work into medical treatment and public health, including the great movements for combating communicable diseases, especially tuberculosis. Homer Folks was in the forefront of most of these major advances.

From his early work with dependent, neglected, and delinquent children Folks learned that in most cases dependency and delinquency resulted from the breakdown of family life, which in turn was caused by poverty—poverty rooted not in personal failure, but in social and economic conditions, especially sickness, invalidism, and the premature death of the family breadwinner. He was certain, therefore, that health and welfare were inseparable and that the solution to most social problems involved the abandonment of the false dichotomy between them in favor of a vigorous and whole-hearted cooperation among all citizens interested in the public welfare. Folks was one of the first social workers (1) to realize that the social well-being of children depended upon the foundation built for the preservation of the family and the community through reducing all preventable hazards to life and good health, and (2) to recognize the vital importance of mobilizing the entire community—public officials and private citizens, health officers and social workers, physicians and laymen—in the war against illness and insecurity. As a result, he turned from his narrow interest in the protection of needy children through foster homes as opposed to institutional care, to the larger and more important concern for maintaining the family and the home in its totality.

Keeping abreast of progress in all fields, and working alone or with others through many public and private organizations, Folks repeatedly brought to public and official consciousness practical ways to help those in distress. In addition, he helped draft and promote sound public health, mental health, and social welfare legislation, creating new machinery to alleviate and prevent human suffering. Folks, therefore, not only communicated to many the great need for reform, but also played a large part in the practical task of getting bills passed in the New York State legislature in Albany and elsewhere to fill that need. His eminently successful efforts to prevent tuberculosis and other communicable diseases, improve the administration and expand the range of public health services, and fuse the public and private benevolent forces of society into a working team, helped to make the fruits of scientific medicine a common possession and to bring preventive medicine into the organized social welfare crusade of the era. He also helped to extend the scope of social work, thereby making it a valuable addition to the economic and political machinery organized for the improvement of the entire community.

Folks was modest and unobtrusive but knowledgeable in the ways of practical politics. As a result, he attained a unique position of confidence and influence in matters concerning public and mental health and welfare. In fact, gifted with a fertile mind and a heart dedicated to humanity, he became somewhat of a legend even while he lived. No mere follower, but a leader who shaped events, Folks occupied a broad stage. Though primarily concerned with conditions in New York State, he gained national and even international influence as a social statesman devoted to the public welfare. Recent generations, to whom his name is unfamiliar, live happier and healthier lives because of Homer Folks.

This, then, is basically a study of the life, thought, and achievements of a humanitarian whose wide-ranging social work, although of great significance, has been neglected. While it is mainly an effort to paint a clear picture of one reformer and thus concentrate on the broad process of social change concretely, it is, to a degree, both biography and history; the two cannot be entirely separated—personality cannot be divorced from history and history cannot be divorced from personality. For that reason, I have on occasion mentioned the major political and social developments that Folks's long, productive life spanned. However, mindful of the fact that such words as *Progressivism* and *New Deal* have been used in so many different ways that they, and others, have lost all clear meaning except as a designation for a particular time period (and even that is debatable) or a particular political program, I have used these terms sparingly. Nevertheless, as this study shows, in advancing—sometimes along with his colleagues and often ahead of them—from the negative policy of relieving distress to the more generous one of preventing it, and finally to the more constructive and positive task of creating possibilities for a more secure, abundant life, Folks made immeasurable contributions to the central program that most Americans wanted, and have accepted, since the 1930s, including the present so-called Great Society.

Also, while by virtue of Folks's wide variety of interests and activities this work covers a large part of the development of modern social work and the "welfare state," it is not a history of either. Hopefully, however, it enlarges an understanding of these, as well as the reform process, by presenting within the context of both an account of one of the major figures in America's social experience. By so doing, perhaps it can along with similar studies begin to serve as a jumping-off point for more insights, interpretations, and generalizations about the dynamics of reform in twentieth-century America.

WALTER I. TRATTNER

Milwaukee, Wisconsin
August 1967

ACKNOWLEDGMENTS

SINCE this book grew out of my doctoral dissertation completed at the University of Wisconsin in 1964, I refer the reader to that study for a list of the many libraries, schools, public departments, and private agencies to which I am indebted for making their resources and facilities available to me. I would, however, like to acknowledge once again the unfailing courtesies and helpfulness shown me by the staffs of the Columbia University School of Social Work Library and the New York State Charities Aid Association. Mrs. John M. Bermingham and Mrs. Jacob B. Hoptner of the Columbia University School of Social Work provided me with countless bibliographical suggestions, more than ample work space, and allowed me the freedom of the school's library. The same is true of Gordon E. Brown, executive director of the New York State Charities Aid Association, which, on May 3, 1967 changed its name to the State Communities Aid Association. Not only did he put at my disposal the entire agency, but he also gave me the benefit of his rich knowledge in discussing the problems involved in my research.

In addition, many people who knew Mr. Folks were kind enough to grant me interviews. They patiently endured questions and generously shared their valuable information, thus making vital contributions to this study. Their names can be found in the bibliographical essay at the back of the book.

I owe a special debt, however, to Mr. Savel Zimand and the late Mrs. Zimand, and Mr. and Mrs. Lawrence M. Orton, Folks's daughters and sons-in-law. They answered frankly innumerable questions, shared their knowledge of Mr. Folks and his many activities, and provided much personal material unavailable elsewhere. In addition, they opened their homes to my wife and me so that we could meet and talk with their ailing father before his death on February 13, 1963. In these, and many other ways, they made the task of research and writing an enjoyable experience.

Grants from the Russell Sage Foundation, the History of American Philanthropy Project, the University of Wisconsin Graduate School, and Northern Illinois University provided funds for conducting the original research and completing the book. For this financial aid I should like to thank Dr. Donald Young and Dr. Orville G. Brim, Jr., former president and current president, respectively, of the Russell Sage Foundation, Professor Merle Curti and Professor Irvin G. Wyllie, directors of the History of Philanthropy Project, the Summer Fellowship Committee of the University of Wisconsin History Department, and the Council of Academic Deans, Northern Illinois University.

For reading one or another version of the manuscript and making valuable suggestions I am grateful to Tom K. Barton, the late Mrs. Savel Zimand, Marvin H. Trattner, Alfred E. Young, and Freeman Cleaves.

I owe my greatest debt to Professor Merle Curti of the University of Wisconsin, under whose supervision this work was originally conducted. It was his suggestion that gave rise to the study, and the advice, constructive criticism, and encouragement he gave me throughout the work cannot be fully acknowledged; they went far beyond the bounds of a teacher.

Parts of Chapter 2, Chapter 4, and Chapter 9 appeared, respectively, in *The New York Historical Society Quarterly,* in *The Journal of American History,* and in *The Social Service Review*. I wish to thank the editors of these journals for allowing me to use this material.

Finally, I am deeply obligated to my wife, Joan D. Trattner, who in so many ways gave her patient help. Her confidence and good cheer, as well as editorial assistance and typing and retyping of the manuscript, added much to the production of this study.

W. I. T.

CONTENTS

HOMER FOLKS
PIONEER IN SOCIAL WELFARE

1

EDUCATION

IN the spring of 1853, James Folks, the twenty-three-year-old son of a Methodist minister, accompanied by his young wife and their newborn baby, boarded ship to cross from England to America. Unhappily, the child died at sea, and Mrs. Folks, after being hurried to a hospital as the ship reached New York, also died, a victim of grief and fatigue. Alone and bereaved, James headed west to join a group of English immigrants who already had settled inland. The tiresome journey had its end in Jackson County, Michigan, where, in southwestern Hanover Township, James Folks staked out his frontier homestead.[1]

Inhabited by settlers from Massachusetts, Vermont, and New York, Jackson County had been organized by the Governor and the Council of the Territory of Michigan in June 1832. The Township of Hanover, in the western part of the county, came into existence in 1836, a year before Michigan gained statehood and only four years after its first white settler arrived. Situated in the highest portion of southern Michigan, this excellent grain-producing area was one of the finest agricultural sections of the county which, by the 1840s, along with a steady growth in population, boasted of brick homes, a railroad station, large church structures, and many other signs of urban life.[2]

It was within this township, on the site that in 1870 was to become the village of Hanover, that James Folks settled in 1853. And the village of Hanover, wrote an historian in 1881, was "deserving of particular notice on account of its rapid growth and the enterprise of its citizens."[3] Within ten years the ground on which it stood went from a cultivated field to a wide street lined with numerous stores and fine dwellings, a brick schoolhouse, Methodist and Universalist churches, and a Quaker meetinghouse, as well as many prosperous commercial firms.[4]

Hanover became a large center of trade when it captured the Fort Wayne division of the New York Central Railroad in 1870. Its ambitions for a second railroad were fulfilled when the Cincinnati and Mackinaw line was extended to Hanover, but instead of benefiting the village the new road ushered in its decline. The railroad established trading points east and west that soon absorbed most of Hanover's trade, and when a fire destroyed about half the village in 1884 it never recovered from the disaster. At the turn of the century, aside from its schoolhouse, Hanover's attractions were a few residences, a weekly newspaper, two grain elevators, and but a dozen stores.[5] By the middle of the twentieth century Hanover could list a population of only 377. The village was maintained by its enterprising farmers rather than, as predicted earlier, its commercial firms.[6]

Unlike his preacher-father, James Folks maintained the farming tradition of most of his forebears. The hardships of frontier life and the burden of caring for his dependents, including his elderly parents who left England in 1857 to join him, allowed little time for educational opportunities for this quiet, thoughtful, steadfast believer in the Christian religion who "exhibited in his life the fruits of the spirit." Despite his lack of formal education, however, James, one of Hanover's pioneers, became one of its most highly esteemed citizens. By his industry and foresight James Folks, always spoken of by his neighbors as a man of "good judgment," rose to a position of responsibility in the community. It was said that "his name," would be remembered as "a synonym for absolute uprightness and fair and honest dealing." Cast in the role of counselor to an unusually large circle of relatives, friends, and neighbors in need, he gave freely both of his time and aid. But it was always as a friend, never simply as a giver, that James Folks's memory lived in the community.[7]

On June 1, 1855, two years after settling on his land, James Folks married Esther Woodliff, daughter of a farmer in an adjoining township. Esther, third in a family of fourteen children, was born in 1836 at Grimsby in Lincolnshire, England. She was a young girl when she and her family arrived in this country; five years later, at the age of nine-teen, she married.[8] This tall, good-looking young woman, like her husband, was known to be a kind and helpful neighbor. Some fifty years later one of her sons fittingly recalled the heritage his good-Samaritan mother had left him: "I have never been at a loss to account for my own interest in social work whether it be an inheritance or the result of early training, or both." [9]

James and Esther Folks enjoyed life on their farm. Hard work, fertile soil, and good weather usually, although not always, brought abundant crops. The Folkses, like a majority of rural Michigan's inhabitants after 1854, took their Republicanism as well as their religion seriously. Abolitionism and Methodism were well entrenched in the area. Han-over, however, a tolerant and broad-minded community noted for standing "foremost against slavery, the saloon, and for all sane re-forms," welcomed all comers regardless of their beliefs. The social responsibility of the church, not theology, was emphasized by its residents, whose creed was simple and whose gospel was one of love, "right living," and charity.[10]

It was into this community that Homer, the fourth of James and Esther Folks's seven children—all boys—was born on February 18, 1867. Young Homer lived the busy and rugged life of a small farmer's son. When the rural one-room ungraded school was not in session he helped with the household tasks and farm chores, and there was the usual play, between school, work, and church. At the age of twelve, having never been absent or tardy for five consecutive years (an amazing feat since he had to walk three miles to school), Homer finished his elementary education in 1879 as a "model scholar." [11]

Young Folks entered Hanover High School and fell under the influence of its principal, A. Frank Burr, a man of Christian character and a devoted teacher. Burr, whom Folks later called "A Modern Michigan Saint," seemed at home in all subjects. An innovator in education, he introduced his young students to "heresies" not found in textbooks. Often paying for school equipment out of his own money, Burr "began a lab for teaching chemistry, insisted that botany had to do with growing plants rather than books, and that geology was to be studied in the fields." [12] Burr was a man of exceptional endowments —moral, spiritual, and pedagogical—and in his hands the Bible and education came to life. He was to have a great influence on the maturing but still impressionable Folks.

Homer Folks was a model scholar in high school too, where he earned excellent grades in a wide variety of subjects. More significant than grades, however, were Homer's high school compositions, which showed a remarkable degree of thoughtfulness and social consciousness for his age. "Liberty," which is "founded on equality," he said in one essay, "is an inherent right of every man." In another paper on the "Evils of the Age," young Folks questioned the prevalent belief of inevitable progress. "The state of society on the whole," he declared, "is little if any better now than it was in the primitive Oriental nations." [13]

Ranking above all his other early themes, however, was a brilliant essay on the "Sources of Happiness," written at the age of fifteen. At a time when the twin gospels of wealth and individualism were thought to be sacred by most Americans, this paper testified to Homer Folks's feeling for mankind and his early awareness of man's social responsibility. Happiness, defined by Folks as a feeling of satisfaction and enjoyment, comes not to those who sit idly by and do nothing for themselves or others. It is achieved, rather, through work and education, including the study of nature, where the mutual dependencies and the complete gradation from the lowest to the highest forms of life are clearly seen. Another source of happiness, he wrote, is a consciousness of having done right. But by far the greatest source of happiness "is doing good to others." Folks continued, "He who, taking little thought of his own welfare, is constantly seeking for opportunities to do good to others, giving liberally according to his means even though he is not searching for happiness is sure to find it." Sensitive and thoughtful, he ended by asserting that "all the riches of this world cannot purchase happiness, it comes only through doing good." [14] Giving and helping others were means of achieving contentment and personal fulfillment to this young boy reared in a home where charity was not only preached, but practiced. He reasoned and felt that the individual who has no desire to help his fellow human beings remains isolated. From this fountainhead of idealism would flow Folks's devotion to the public good and his desire to correct whatever injustices he might see.

As each of James Folks's boys finished high school, he offered them the choice of a piece of land to farm, or tuition for a college education. Homer (and one other, his youngest brother) chose college. He did not, however, continue his schooling immediately. College was put off for two years while he taught school to earn extra expense money, returning home several miles by foot each weekend to help on the farm.[15]

Although the age in which Folks grew to maturity was characterized chiefly by business and laissez faire, it was also an age of farm agitation and, to an extent, radical upheaval.[16] Frequent and prolonged depressions and financial panics provided the ingredients that produced various philosophies and programs that promised many a better life. Jackson County, whose farmers suffered a great deal as a result of the depression of 1872 and the panic of 1877, was not immune to these developments. The community ultimately remained loyal to the Grand Old Party, but Greenbackism and Free Silver, for example, had their day there.[17] As a youngster, then, Folks witnessed, and no doubt later remembered, desperate farmers casting aside their long-professed reliance on self-help in an attempt to attain security through organization.

It is also worth noting that Jackson County's first historian saw fit to describe the poorhouse which, he related, "exists in this prosperous county." The fact that the maintenance of the poor cost the residents of the community over $3,000 a year clearly indicates that many in the area did not share in any prosperity. Equally important is the fact that the "inmates [of the poorhouse] are healthy and appear well fed and contented, and differing in no particular respect from those outside [the institution],"[18] suggesting that perhaps Jackson's citizens, unlike most nineteenth-century Americans, did not view idleness as a sin and pauperism akin to crime. Folks was reared in a community that seems to have softened the harsh but prevalent notion that in America, where labor was scarce and land cheap, poverty was evidence of improvidence, shiftlessness, or criminality—a myth to be exposed only several decades later.

In 1885 Folks entered Albion, a Methodist college seventeen miles from his home. Years later Folks recalled that he "went to Albion on the general principle of getting further education after high school, but for no particular kind of work." [10] Founded by a Methodist minister in 1843 as Albion Wesleyan Seminary, it became a college of liberal arts sometime between 1854 and 1864. President George B. Jocelyn, Albion College's second of a long succession of Methodist minister-presidents, aptly described the educational plan of the small liberal arts college when he said,

It is not the design [of Albion] to . . . prepare students for any specific destination in life. It is designed, however, to require students to prosecute a thorough and systematic course of study—such as is approved by the best educators of the country—to secure that mental discipline and development which alone are worthy of the name of a collegiate education.[20]

Sixty years later one of its most distinguished graduates unwittingly attested to the fact that Albion indeed did hold true to its design when he remarked, "I finished four years at Albion without having clearly seen exactly what would interest me most. It was a general liberal education that I had." [21]

Actually, the four years that Folks spent at Albion were more profitable than he realized, for the small midwestern college was gifted with an unusual number of outstanding scholars and teachers. The presence on the faculty of such men as Samuel Davis Barr and Delos M. S. Fall spoke well for Albion. Barr, a graduate of Williams College and professor of mathematics, came from the East to Albion with a distinguished reputation as an educator. Before serving as deputy superintendent of New York State's Department of Public Education, where he progressively reformed the state's entire educational system, he originated and developed several new mathematical theories and formulae. The professor of chemistry, Delos Fall, was a frequent contributor to the scientific literature of the country. In addition, after coming to Albion in 1878, he was an active member of both Michigan's

State Board of Health and the American Public Health Association.[22] A tradition of public as well as private service was therefore well entrenched at Albion.

Other faculty members helped mold Folks's development. Ransom Lewis Fiske, Albion's fifth president, was both a minister and a natural scientist, an unusual combination for a nineteenth-century rural sectarian college president. A graduate of the University of Michigan and of a theological seminary, he also attended the Lawrence Scientific Institute at Cambridge. It was written of President Fiske that he was "a ripe scholar, a polished writer and speaker, a safe counselor, a popular college president and a gentleman of wide influence and extended usefulness in every department of life." [23] Frederick Lutz, a man of German lineage who came to America in 1870, was another notable member of Albion's faculty. In 1876, after graduating from Baldwin-Wallace College in Ohio, he entered Harvard and then stayed on there for seven years to serve as an instructor in German. He was called to Albion as a professor of modern languages in 1885. Besides publishing some scholarly pamphlets Lutz was an enthusiastic and successful teacher.[24]

Folks's college essays, like those written in high school, reveal the wide range of his interests, his religious feelings, and his idealism couched in realism and practicality. It was Fiske's influence (and perhaps Barr's too) that led Folks to conclude that "the inevitable law of change will bring . . . new problems, whose like is not found in history, books, etc., but is only to be reached by original investigation pushed by the highest powers of the human mind." The fact that Folks was aware of and friendly to the higher biblical criticism, maintaining that it only "leads to a grander view of spiritual truths," also speaks well for Albion and its minister-natural scientist president.[25]

Folks had a keen awareness of reality. He knew that man must take the sad along with the pleasant, the wrong with the right, for he felt, "He who looks only upon the bright side sees little more than half of life." [26] But he still reminded his classmates in the pages of an essay, one that scarcely could be improved upon later in his life as a statement of the values he held to be essential, that "the only successful life is that which raises the fallen, sympathizes with the unfortunate, relieves the toiling, cheers the disconsolate, and by so doing fulfills the will of its great Creator." [27]

Homer worked hard at college, where his courses included Latin, Greek, chemistry, history, English, philosophy, biology, and political science. It was not all study, however, as a glimpse at his diary reveals. Such notations as "Invited to leap year party," "practice Shakespeare, Henry IV," and "Go for sleigh ride," abound throughout its pages. Folks played tennis and baseball, debated, read a great deal, was a member of the choir, and so enjoyed a varied life at Albion.[28]

Religion occupied much of his collegiate career. He attended prayer and missionary meetings and preached evening sermons. "Attended a revival meeting tonight" was frequently noted in his diary along with "Elected a delegate to the Y.M.C.A. State Convetion" and "Just five years ago today I was converted." He also was an active member of the Prohibition Club and, no doubt, one in good standing: "Ride to Hanover and put in my first vote for Fisk and Brooks and a straight Prohibition ticket." [29] He endorsed Prohibition, however, not on moral grounds, but as a measure aimed at eliminating the poverty, insecurity, and family troubles, which he felt resulted from alcoholism.[30]

During his junior year in college Homer met a girl student, Maud Beard, an Albion resident and the daughter of a Methodist minister. Frequent dates and visits to the Beard home followed, and a year and a half later, just prior to commencement, Homer could write in his diary: "I visit Maud. In the twilight I ask her to share my lot in life and she consents. . . . I am a happy boy." [31]

On the other hand, there was little happiness at home on the farm during school vacations. Homer's aversion to farm work could not have been been stated any more explicitly than by the following succinct phrases:

June 25, 1887—Mowed and drew hay all day, Hard work, tired and sore. Awful glad that tomorrow is Sunday.

June 27, 1887—Mowed all day. Sore. *Ah me.*

June 29, 1887—Drew hay all day, tired more and more. Thermometer 90 in the shade. Finished the 47 loads from the 20 acres at noon. *Awful glad!*

June 30, 1887—Dragged all day again in the same field in the same way with the same sameness.[32]

Back at Albion during his senior year, Folks's thoughts turned to the future, and the ministry. It is, of course, not surprising that Folks considered entering the pulpit. His more secular-minded instructors, however, whom he greatly respected, felt he could be more useful to society in an academic rather than a priestly position and strongly suggested teaching as a profession. This idea he felt was at least worthy of consideration, especially when they hinted that a position as an instructor of modern languages at Albion might be available to him. Professor Lutz suggested that another year's preparation, at Harvard, would be invaluable for a future career in teaching. He even offered to lend Homer the necessary funds when his parents were not fully sympathetic to the idea of their son's enrolling at Harvard for further study.[33] More education would not only be expensive and further postpone employment, but eastern urban life might corrupt the morals so carefully inculcated in rural Michigan.[34] His parents, however, finally consented and at the end of his senior year agreed to advance him a loan of $200, which, with the small scholarship he won, would allow him to enter Harvard in the fall.[35] Content with his future plans, Homer returned home after graduation to work on the farm, visit Maud, become engaged, and prepare for his trip to Cambridge.

On Monday, September 16, 1889, after the usual parting sorrows, Homer Folks left home for the uncertainties of Harvard and Cambridge. The journey from Hanover to New York (Jackson–Ypsilanti–Detroit–Erie–Buffalo–New York City), from where he proceeded to Cambridge, was carefully recorded in his diary: four days after leaving home he wrote, "The trip down the Hudson [is] the most magnificent thing I have ever seen." [36] After spending several days in New York City and Connecticut, Folks finally arrived at Harvard on September 24, and immediately recorded approval of his new home: "I am very much pleased with Cambridge." A day later, however, he would write, "Have a little cry, P.M.," and, he went on, "am very homesick some of today." [37]

That the shy and reserved lad from rural Michigan was both scared and homesick during his first days at Harvard is easily understandable. The difference between Harvard and a smaller college, in a small town, at that time, was the difference between living in a big city and living in a small town; and in 1889 that difference was great. Harvard was the reflex of Boston society, and Boston was a far cry from Hanover: "Harvard only reinforced the influences of my Boston upbringing," remarked one of its graduates, for, "after all, Harvard is stamped with Boston." [38]

Harvard's leadership in the collegiate world in the 1890s was clearly established. With such eminent teachers and *savants* as Royce, James, Norton, Channing, Hart, Taussig, Shaler, Palmer, Peabody, and Santayana, a body of scholars known throughout the world, no other undergraduate institution could compete with its fame and prestige. Moreover, in President Eliot Harvard had the undisputed leader of American education.[39]

Cast in a strange environment, and in many ways an intruder in a place to which others were born, Folks became homesick. Little did he, at that time, imagine that many years later the class secretary would write: "We had many men of eminence in their varied professions. I think that in the opinion of the majority of our class members, the name of Homer Folks would head the list." [40] In any event, from the start, he made it plain that he had come to Harvard for an education, not to have it serve as the vestibule through which he could enter society. It is revealing that one young man who attended Harvard with Folks would, in retrospect, write of the venerable President Eliot, "We were awed by him and his rectitude." [41] Folks, on the other hand, only a few days after arriving at Harvard, confided to his diary, "Attend lecture . . . by President Eliot. A forcible talk. He does not recommend total abstinence to all. Some very good sense and some very bad." [42]

Harvard, Cambridge, Boston, and the surrounding area offered opportunities to Folks that Michigan was unable to provide. Taking to foot a great deal, he made the most of them, despite the fact that after the first day of classes the Harvard senior recorded that his professors "give out very much work." [43] As his diary indicates, Folks, among other things, "went through Aggasiz and Peabody museums"; "visited Botanical gardens"; "visited Commons, Tremont Temple, Bunker Hill monument"; he went "to Trinity Church and hear[d] Phillips Brooks preach"; he "hear[d] Lyman Abbot preach again"; he heard Richard Henry Dana speak on "Political Reforms and How Obtained," "watch[ed] Harvard-Princeton football game," "attended opera Faust," "visited the Longfellow house," "State capitol, Faneuil Hall," and so on. Folks attended many lectures, visited the theater often, exercised frequently in and out of the gymnasium, read a great deal, and managed to get mostly A's in his courses.[44]

Folks took four courses at Harvard. In preparation for his future profession, two were language courses. Two others he "took because they sounded interesting." It was the latter two, a course in the philosophy of ethics, taught by Geroge Herbert Palmer, and a course in the ethics of social reform, under Francis G. Peabody, that proved the more valuable. These two courses and the influence of these two brilliant minds, as much as anything else, led Folks to abandon his earlier plans and choose a new kind of teaching career—social service, where he would teach a way of life rather than foreign languages.[45]

Francis G. Peabody, "Harvard's Theologian of the Social Gospel," was a lecturer in ethics and professor of theology from 1880 to 1912. An educational as well as a social reformer, he was the first American theologian to introduce the subject of social reform into a divinity school curriculum. Preferring to deal with facts and experiences based upon observations rather than the subtleties of metaphysics, Peabody made his students keenly aware of the problems raised by industrialism, teaching them that every citizen had a moral duty to himself and to his community to contribute to the common good by helping to soften the evil effects of the new order. For him, in the last analysis, the social question was a question of ethics, and its solution lay in charity and Christian cooperation.[46]

Although an optimist and reformer, Peabody was never able to rid himself of the social conservatism of his Boston upbringing. "Go slow in social reform" was his message; gradualism was his byword.[47] Peabody emphasized the conservative approach to reform, and he tried to show his students the limitations of utopian and revolutionary answers to social problems. The gradual but persistent efforts of education, legislation, and, above all, spirituality were the agents of social progress, an inevitable but slow process.[48]

It was in Professor Peabody's famous philosophy course that Folks "began to hear about things that were going on that people might get a hand in," and which, he recalled at the age of eighty-two after a distinguished career,

appealed to me very much as things that I'd like to know about. . . . We heard about Charity Organization Societies, the Settlement houses, improved housing, and things that were practically being done to make life more comfortable and possible for people with small means. It seemed to make a very strong impression on me as an attractive thing to have a hand in.[49]

Philosophy 11, described in the Harvard catalogue as "The Ethics of Social Reform; The Questions of Charity, Divorce, the Indians, Labor, Prison, Temperance, essays and practical observations," but known among the undergraduates as "Peabody's drainage, drunkenness, and divorce," was the inspiration that directed many young men into the path of social work. In fact, it produced many of the profession's outstanding leaders. At least seven men who assumed leading roles in social work came out of Harvard and its Philosophy 11 course in the short period between 1885 and 1893: Dr. Richard C. Cabot, Homer Folks, Sherman Kingsley, Robert Woods (all of whom became presidents of the National Conference of Charities and Correction), Charles Birtwell, William H. Pear, and Harvey Baker.[50] One could add the two political-social reformers, W. E. B. DuBois and Roger N. Baldwin, to that list, along with countless others.[51] Apparently Peabody's students responded to the challenge their professor issued when he ended his course with the exhortation, "Putting to practical service the principles here laid down is the happiest result that could be wished for by your instructor or the university that sends you out." [52]

Peabody frequently arranged evening meetings for his class, bringing in speakers from Cambridge and Boston to talk on such topics as charities, child welfare, housing, and social legislation. On one occasion, the great public servant-philanthropist and one-time president of the National Conference of Charities and Correction, Robert Treat Paine, addressed Folks's class. Another speaker was a gentleman who later became one of Folks's most intimate friends and stimulating influences, Charles W. Birtwell, executive secretary of Boston's Children's Aid Society. These were evenings Folks never forgot. Greatly interested in what these men were talking about and impressed by their sincerity and concern for those in need, he already began to decide against inflicting French and German upon students at a little fresh-water college. In addition, as a result of an essay he wrote in Peabody's course—"Homes of the Poor"—for which he spent many evenings visiting the Boston tenements, Folks began to find classroom work no substitute for first-hand studies.[53]

George Herbert Palmer, professor of philosophy at Harvard, was another long-lasting, constructive influence. Palmer's course on ethics, known as Philosophy 4, was officially announced as "A Theory of Ethics Considered Constructively—Lectures, Theses, and Private Reading."[54] This course, which Palmer taught to Harvard students for more than twenty-five years, was devoted not to metaphysics and epistemology, but to a critical analysis of human conduct. Palmer, who liked to refer to himself as a "moderate idealist," taught that morality had no meaning apart from society, a society whose claims were paramount. Man is essentially a social being and a single isolated individual is an empty fiction, wholly abstract and unreal. The real man is only he who stands in living relationship with his fellows. Self-sacrifice, then, for Palmer, was simply the effective affirmation of the supreme worth of selfhood, and was, therefore, the highest form of rationality. Service to the social and infinite self became, by definition, virtue. It was also the supreme principle of rationality in the realm of deeds, for it brought order out of the chaos of conflicting aims.[55] At his death it was agreed that "Palmer's chief contributions were written in the souls of men, wrought in the lives of the thousands of students whose eyes he opened to the meaning and the possibilities of life."[56] George Herbert Palmer could, without doubt, list Folks as one among those thousands.

The new year found Homer Folks "A Senior at Harvard studying French, German, Ethics-pure and social reforms. I am enjoying it fairly well here," he wrote, "but waiting for the time to return to Michigan." [57] But loneliness and thoughts that turned to a fiancée a thousand miles away did not slow Folks's busy life. He visited the birthplace of Margaret Fuller, the Transcendentalist, attended more ballgames, won a prize in a bowling tournament, saw performances of *Hamlet* and *Romeo and Juliet,* heard lectures by Fiske, Channing, and Theodore Roosevelt, and avidly read through Wordsworth, Carlyle, and George Eliot.[58] Most of the time, however, his thoughts confronted the future. After turning down a teaching position at Albion, he was faced with the matter of finding a job.

A position at the Children's Aid Society of Pennsylvania came to Folks's attention and although he immediately turned for advice and counsel to Palmer, Peabody, and Birtwell, the outcome was inevitable. His youthful altruistic instinct possessed him, and on the way home to Michigan after commencement Folks stopped for an interview at the society's central office in Philadelphia.[59] In the meantime, Professor Peabody addressed a letter to Mrs. James C. Biddle, president of the Children's Aid Society, in which he wrote of his student's "high distinction" at Harvard. "He is a serious, vigorous and scholarly man," the letter continued, "and I should expect of him the best of results in such work as you propose." [60]

Palmer, known for being especially "gifted in the capacity of reaching objective estimates of personal ability," [61] joined Peabody in recommending Folks for the job. His letter is worth quoting at length:

Of course I have no knowledge of his special qualifications for such a post [as general agent for the Children's Aid Society of Pennsylvania]. But I should like to testify to the universal excellence of his work with me in an advanced course of study in Ethics and at the same time to my admiration of him as a young man of power, modesty, industry and intelligence. I am confident he will succeed best in work where he has sacrifices to make and needs of others to consider. There his peculiar nobleness will be discovered. And I believe one so intelligent as he will quickly acquire a mastery of the details of a subject with which he has previously had no acquaintance, if by so doing he can help those who require help.[62]

Impressed with Folks's "earnestness" and "with the remarkable testimonials from the Harvard professors," Mrs. Biddle offered him the position. He wired his acceptance at once, to which she replied, "I am profoundly thankful that you are coming [to Philadelphia]. You won't regret the venture." [63]

There were many reasons why Homer Folks accepted the call to Philadelphia and entered into the venture he indeed was not to regret. Folks's family tradition of doing good and his formal training under a series of exceptionally able and devoted teachers, whose doctrines fired their students to constructive labors, help in large part to explain that decision. No doubt his agrarian heritage also played some part in Folks's choice of a career. Hard times on the farm, which occurred despite diligent work, acquainted Folks with the impersonal causes of poverty and probably helped lead him into organized charity work aimed at ameliorating the conditions of those in need. But there were other reasons as well.

Folks's visits to Boston's slums, where he discovered firsthand the poverty, wretchedness, and human misery attacking the nation in the wake of industrialization, urban growth, and large-scale immigration, also helped him decide on a career in social service. He developed a compassion for the unfortunate, thus strengthening the emotional as well as the intellectual bases of his convictions. After seeing people so desperately in need, he found it impossible to turn his back on their problems and retreat to academic life.

And, as Reinhold Niebuhr once pointed out, many Americans entered social work because it seemed a logical way to express a sense of mission to mankind which had been nurtured by the religion of their youth.[64] Social work offered to many a practical substitute for a religious vocation, one that was void of theological doctrines and ritualistic practices; a life of practical helpfulness to the needy gave them more satisfaction than was afforded in the often vague and not generally applied idealism of religious devotion.

This was certainly true of Folks, who was acutely conscious of the paths which lay before him and the reason he chose one rather than the other. "It was the appeal of the subject matter," as he recalled it, that led him into social work. "It had a quality of definiteness. Somehow it appealed to me, whereas the ministry itself seemed a shade vague. I was a person," he continued, "who wanted to see how a thing worked; if you could get somewhere, if you could measure results in some way or other." [65] He would not be happy as a minister or a college professor, for he wanted to do things rather than talk about them. Searching, then, for a meaningful religion and a way to satisfy his sense of responsibility through service, tired of theory and eager to experience the real world, Folks found social service irresistibly attractive.

Evangelical religion, nineteenth-century faith in progress, and the democratic belief in the right to be free, all coalesced to produce a crusading zeal which swept a large number of Americans into various reform movements designed to perfect their country's institutions.[66] Some of these sensitive men and women decided to attack the social evils created by the new industrialism by becoming social gospellers, or university teachers, or muckrakers, while still others chose the path of political radicalism. Folks decided upon social service as a career because of a passionate belief in the obligation of society to help those in need, a social mindedness which was the product of inheritance and formal education, and an interest in action rather than speculation. The newly emerging field of social work seemed to be the best area in which those passions might, for him, find their most worthy outlet.

On August 14, 1890, Folks, at the age of twenty-three, once again prepared to leave Hanover for a trip eastward. To paraphrase the words of one who knew him well, Homer Folks, brought up with a Methodist background of the straight and narrow, was about to begin his efforts to keep the straight but widen the boundaries of the narrow.[67]

2

CHILD WELFARE—THE
APPRENTICESHIP

WHEN Homer Folks arrived in Philadelphia on August 15, 1890, to assume his duties as general superintendent of the Children's Aid Society of Pennsylvania, the city, bounded by the Delaware river on the east and the Schuykill on the west, had outgrown its limits and a number of suburbs had sprung up around it. With about one million residents in 1890, Philadelphia was outranked in population by only New York and Chicago.[1]

The City of Brotherly Love was a quiet place. In spite of its large and growing foreign element the early Quaker influence still prevailed. Unlike most American cities, Philadelphia was known for its extremely regular streets and neat brick houses with white wooden shutters and marble facings and steps, which gave the city a look of primness. The tenement houses and cheap flats already characteristic of New York and Boston were notably absent. As an early urban historian wrote, Philadelphia was not without the squalor, misery, and crime that is found in all large cities, "but the proportion is smaller than in some other cities, and the aggregate amount of domestic content, owing to its many comfortable homes, much greater." Nevertheless the city had more than 800 agencies and countless persons engaged in aiding its poor and unfortunate.[2] Homer Folks now joined the ranks of the many engaged in this work.

The Children's Aid Society was one among the city's 109 child-caring agencies.[3] Unlike most of Philadelphia's other private social agencies, however, the Children's Aid Society was not engaged in alms-giving, nor was it attached to any institution that housed and cared for youngsters. Devoted entirely to dependent, neglected, and delinquent children, the Society consisted of little else than a couple of office rooms and a small but devoted staff. Yet this group of people was in the midst of an interesting experiment, which, under its new leader would help revolutionize the care of dependent children in the United States.

Many Americans in the nineteenth century were suspicious of charity and public relief. Because of the supposed "pauperizing influence" upon recipients (adequate aid would encourage idleness) as well as the widespread opportunities for corruption in its distribution, assistance was thought to be more harmful than good. This distrust, especially of public relief, went back to the English experience—there, the "upper classes," who were also the governing classes, believed that public relief was the root of many evils and that such assistance, especially when given in the home ("outdoor relief"), should be abolished entirely. This theory was accepted by large numbers of competent and generous people who belonged to the well-to-do classes in America. Wanting to be givers and to help the poor, but concerned with corruption and alarmed over the possibility of pauperizing the needy, they preferred offering advice, private charity, and, at best, public relief on an institutional basis. Because of the insufficiency of wise words, the uncertainty of private charity, and the argument that home or outdoor relief was expensive, pauperizing, and corrupting, an era of building poorhouses followed. By the 1830s many state legislatures had passed acts making it the duty of each county within their jurisdiction to support its dependents, erect a poorhouse, and create a new body of relief officials, county superintendents of the poor, to manage the institution. With the creation of poorhouses (or almshouses) and county responsibility, the general trend toward "indoor" or institutional relief as opposed to "outdoor" or home relief was established firmly.[4]

For various reasons, in part financial and in part the prevalent belief that the destitute were a disgraceful and even a criminal class of people who solely through their own sloth and lack of far-sightedness were in need, the poorhouses soon became vile catchalls for victims of every variety of misery, misfortune, and even misconduct. As Robert Bremner properly summed up the situation, the "old and the young, the vagrant and the abandoned, the feeble-minded, insane, and disabled, were all herded together in buildings that were poorly constructed, foully maintained, . . . wretchedly furnished," [5] and, making matters worse, run by officers usually appointed for their political affiliations rather than for their ability or concern for the needy inmates.

By mid-century the shocking abuses resulting from the indiscriminate herding of dependents in almshouses led to pressure for the proper classification and segregation of different types of destitute persons. This demand for better care of the almshouse poor received great impetus with the creation (beginning in the 1860s) of State Boards of Charities, whose functions were to inspect, report upon, and make recommendations for improving public welfare institutions. And although unsegregated almshouses still existed in parts of the country at the end of the century, most of their glaring abuses were remedied before that time.[6]

Child welfare was the first, although perhaps not the most successful, focus of the movement to reform the poorhouse. Humanitarians long had demanded special institutions for dependent, neglected, and wayward youths. During the 1860s the first of a series of laws for the removal of children from almshouses was passed. Nevertheless, by the turn of the century only one fourth of the states had passed such laws, and even in these states they were not fully enforced.[7]

A natural result of removing children from poorhouses, where that did occur, was the encouragement and growth of child-caring institutions. These institutions, often large and of the congregate (as opposed to the cottage plan) type, were mostly private and sectarian in nature. Quite commonly they were aided by public funds, but public officials had little or no control over them. Although they were, on the whole, superior to the almshouses as a place for child care, they too had many defects and limitations.[8]

As a result, the growth of child-caring institutions dismayed some reformers who preferred family care to institutional treatment. The first child-placing agency in America was the Children's Aid Society of New York City. Founded in 1853 by Charles Loring Brace, a twenty-seven-year-old minister who opposed institutional care, its avowed purpose was to rescue children from "the haunts of vice and crime" and provide homes for destitute and neglected children. Convinced of the futility of "saving" many of the children except by transplanting them to new environments, Brace began his placing-out work in 1854 when he transported a party of forty-six children from New York to new homes in Michigan. A controversial figure, Brace nevertheless popularized home care for dependent children.[9]

Despite its obvious potential advantages over institutional care, placing-out had gained little ground before 1890. Except for a few notable exceptions (like the Children's Aid Society of Pennsylvania and the Boston Children's Aid Society, under the leadership of Charles W. Birtwell), most charity workers opposed child placement because of the inadequate attention usually paid to the foster homes and the "placed-out" children. Supervision of the children was haphazard and left largely to volunteers living in the vicinity of the foster home: very few of the children were properly safeguarded. Moreover, when practiced even on a limited scale, placing-out was confined almost entirely to the dependent and neglected, ignoring other types of disadvantaged children, as the noted Dr. Samuel Gridley Howe pointed out as early as 1864.[10] It was not until the 1890s, when young reformers, led by Homer Folks, started to concentrate on the question of method and administrative technique of family care, that many others rapidly began to see its value—not only for neglected and destitute children, but also for those in need of correctional care.

After 1883 Pennsylvania children were forbidden by law to be placed in almshouses: the county was charged with providing for the care and support of these dependents. The Directors of the Poor, usually three in each county, had charge of dependent minors as well as the distribution of outdoor relief and care of almshouses. County supervision of dependent children in Pennsylvania was, on the whole, haphazard and poorly administered except in the counties where the "Pennsylvania Plan" developed. This Plan, a cooperative effort between the state's Children's Aid Society and the Directors of the Poor, included the placing-out of children in private families under the Society's supervision.

The Children's Aid Society, the largest child-caring agency in Pennsylvania, was organized in 1882 solely to provide for homeless children by placing them in foster homes. Most of its work had been in cooperation with the county Directors of the Poor, who, it recognized, were unaccustomed to child care and not fitted for their task. The Society conducted a responsible placing-out system by taking children out of the many institutions throughout the state and putting them in private homes.[11]

In 1890, however, just before Folks joined it, the Society began a unique experiment in child welfare. While it and a few other agencies had been active in placing-out dependent and neglected children, no agency had successfully implemented Samuel Gridley Howe's idea of extending the system to delinquents and defective children. The Pennsylvania Society now pioneered in the placing-out of children convicted in courts of crimes; children who had gotten themselves in trouble were rescued by the Society before they were committed to correctional institutions and were placed instead with private families in the hope that a home atmosphere might be more conducive to good behavior than a penal institution. The Society, however, suffered from a lack of financial resources and leadership, which threatened to end its useful services.[12]

From the start, Homer Folks's days in Philadelphia were busy ones. He had little time to prepare for his first professional job, as his diary makes clear. "See Mrs. Biddle, Pemberton and Hancock. Run out to Germantown. Visit County Prison with Miss Pemberton. Interview 5 boys. Visit office of the press and YMCA rooms." All this, and more, amounted to a hectic initiation into social service for the recent college graduate. Looking through the Society's files, reading back correspondence, meeting many people, and keeping track of 330 children under the Society's care kept Folks busy into the late hours of night. He often took work home from the office and found it necessary to work all day on holidays. He came in touch with the city administration, police, and courts, and other public and voluntary welfare groups. He ran the office, visited various child-caring institutions, called on children the Society had already placed-out, wrote an endless number of reports and newspaper articles, and attended innumerable board meetings.[13]

Despite his lack of experience, from the start Folks made a most impressive manager. He tirelessly concentrated with a definite, clear, and methodical earnestness upon the problem of looking after the children in the Society's care. He and several members of the society's staff traveled almost constantly. He insisted that the Society not only consider each child but also keep track of his relation with the foster parents, who also needed training and supervision. As a result, they investigated families who applied for children, took the children to or from their new homes, and then reinvestigated both the children and families involved. From one to five personal and unannounced visits each year to such homes became standard practice. No task was spared for the welfare of the children. As one entry in Folks's diary indicates, regardless of the circumstances, contact had to be maintained with those who either accepted children from, or gave their children to, the Children's Aid Society for disposition: "Look up Riley case. . . . Call on Mr. Riley at a 'speakeasy' in eve." [14]

The Society's experiment with delinquent boys was not always successful. Only a week after he began work Folks was informed that two of the "model boys" placed-out by the Society stole money and ran away from their new homes. In his own travels he experienced similar cases. These, however, were the exception rather than the rule, and they did not discourage Folks, who as a boy had written an essay on the need to accept some bad along with the good. The few failures only seemed to convince him of the need for more thorough investigation and supervision of the children and the homes in which they were placed. The real work of the Society, he was convinced, was out in the field. Conscientious in his attention to the business of his office and wards, Folks quickly won admiration for the way in which he conducted the Society's affairs. Only five weeks after he arrived, Folks had so impressed his co-workers and superiors that none other than the Society's president, who usually spared her compliments, expressed the sentiments of all when she wrote in gratitude, "I send you my sincere congratulations, as well as my hearty thanks, for your services. . . . You can scarcely imagine the feeling of peace your presence in the work gives me,—in strange contrast to the dread anxiety I have suffered for so long a time." [15]

Engrossed though he was in his work, life wasn't all toil. Folks did not forget his other interests. For the time being, at least, he pursued the pleasures Philadelphia offered to a young bachelor with some money to spend. The city's theaters, its newspapers, libraries, churches, and colleges provided opportunities he could not neglect. He went sailing. He bought a ticket for a YMCA concert series, he attended a performance of the Boston Orchestral Club, went to various glee club recitals, heard Phillips Brooks and Josiah Royce each lecture several times, saw *Othello* ("The best play I have ever seen"), chatted with University of Pennsylvania professors, and shopped often in Philadelphia's big stores. He studied German, read a great deal, wrote many letters to those at home whom he missed, and continued to attend church, although not as regularly as before.[16]

Early in 1891 Dr. John H. Finley, secretary of the New York State Charities Aid Association, came to Philadelphia and invited Folks to speak at the National Conference of Charities and Correction. The Conference, established as an independent organization in 1879, was a child of the American Social Science Association and the Conference of (State) Boards of Public Charities, which since 1874 had been meeting together "to better get acquainted, to discuss questions of common interest [and] . . . mutal benefit." The Conference met annually, published its proceedings, and served as a national clearing-house of ideas and experiences. It was, in the words of its official historian, "a national medium of exchange of opinion, a national forum in which to debate and appraise different themes, policies, and practices; a platform from which could be presented fresh information on social problems and methods of dealing with them as the frontiers of knowledge were moved forward." [17]

Like its parent organizations, the National Conference of Charities and Correction embodied the conviction that the application of science to the social problems of the day would result in new discoveries and improvements in the field of human relationships. Its members believed it was possible to subject social ills to study and experimentation, and thereby eliminate such things as sickness, insanity, crime, and poverty and thus create a better society. They were anxious to hear about the Pennsylvania experiment in placing-out delinquent children in family homes.

Seated in front of a large gathering of social workers in Indianapolis, Folks nervously listened to John Finley's talk on the problem of children in cities as he waited to address a national audience for the first time. Although he spoke readily and easily and had a prodigious memory, he had been and would always remain careful in preparation. When he finally rose to speak, this tall, slender young man conveyed complete authority. Using the facts and figures he had carefully recorded and studied, Folks summed up a year's work on "Home Care for Delinquent Children" by proclaiming that the results of the Society's experiment had been "more encouraging than most of us had dared to hope." He pointed out that his investigations showed that contrary to popular belief not all so-called delinquents were from the pauper class; most of the children convicted of crimes were little different from ordinary children. The causes of their delinquency, which could be determined only through careful, individual study, were attributable to many factors. A frequent cause of the trouble was physical defect. Most often, however, delinquency was caused by "a lack of parental oversight due to the loss of one or both parents." Turning once again to placing-out, Folks attributed the Society's success to its careful and painstaking methods of placing-out, as well as its willingness to pay a fee for the child's care when free homes were not available, an expense entirely justifiable, he felt, for reformatory care of the same children would cost the community a much greater sum. Many of the best homes in any community were willing to take in so-called delinquent children, and the fear that they would run away, he maintained, was unfounded. "We have proven," he went on to say, "that we can hold the children by our methods." [18]

While some remained skeptical, Folks was heartened when Charles

D. Kellogg, vice-president of the famed Charity Organization Society of New York, told the audience that in his opinion, "The experience of the Children's Aid Society of Philadelphia [*sic*] . . . proves not only that this suggestion [of placing-out delinquents] is easily practicable, but goes far to show that institutions . . . are not only unnecessary, but of very questionable utility." [19]

A year later Folks was more firmly convinced than ever that the best place for a homeless child—delinquent or not—was in a good family home. Institutions dulled and blighted their inmates. Only in families, he maintained, "can we give full play to those natural forces which were intended to shape the development of the child." In another address before the National Conference he concluded that the care of delinquent children, "undertaken two years ago with much hesitation, became in the light of . . . [the Children's Aid Society's] results, an established and important branch of the Society's work,—a work which is worthy of its best efforts, and promises for the community the most fruitful results." [20]

In 1893, in connection with the Columbian Exposition at Chicago, a special conference on child-saving was held under the auspices of the National Conference. Once again Folks appeared before a distinguished group of his peers when, at the request of his friend Charles Birtwell, he spoke to those assembled there—leading representatives of the different types of children's agencies and institutions—on "Family Life for Dependent Children." He covered much the same ground of his earlier papers—how family life "may be secured for the greatest proportion of dependent children . . . and how the plan may be made safe and efficient." At Birtwell's insistence Folks again emphasized one of the themes for which he rapidly was becoming known: the major importance of sound administration in family placement and the need for careful investigation and supervision of both the foster home and the child.[21]

However, he also stressed another theme which, like placing out, he did not originate but which he, more than anyone else in this country, would popularize—boarding-out, or the family plan with payment of fees, if and when it was necesssary. He recognized that the legal adoption of dependent children was the ideal, but he also knew that it was both undesirable and unfeasible when applied to certain classes of dependent children. As a child increased in age likelihood of adoption decreased. Physically and mentally handicapped children rarely were adopted. Moreover, a large number of dependent and neglected children were unsuitable for legal adoption because of a living parent (or parents) who might have temporarily forefeited a right to them as a result of neglect or misfortune, but who might reclaim that right under different and improved circumstances. These children, however, Folks felt, should not be deprived of family care and be herded into institutions where their natural development would be stunted by unnatural conditions. When it was a question of family versus institutional life, boarding-out was the only choice, for that system secured for the child the benefits of home life and of a normal community environment, without depriving worthy surviving parents of the opportunity to visit their children from time to time, and without impairing their right to reclaim them if the circumstances made that possible and desirable. Orphanages, then, weren't good for the child, the mother, and, because of their expense, society. The successful work of the Children's Aid Society proved that the plan was good in theory as well as in practice. "If we believe in the divine developing power of the family," he asked rhetorically, but passionately, "shall we not be willing to lay upon its altar as much of our gold as we do upon that of its artificial limitation [institutions]?" [22] Folks's youthful instinct had grown into a passion for service which would lighten the burden of children who were neglected, dependent, delinquent, or in any way handicapped; he wanted to make available to them the opportunities he felt should be the heritage of all children.

Lastly, Folks talked at length on a new but related idea. He called to the attention of his audience, an audience still comprised mainly of well-to-do volunteer workers, the need for experienced and trained agents to administer the investigating and supervising of placing-out. In his estimation, the most desirable results could not be attained otherwise. Child welfare work imposed demands upon social workers, in terms of time, skill, and training, that the volunteer could not usually satisfy; training and skill were more important in child welfare work than good will. Anticipating criticism from well-meaning moral-minded amateurs, he remarked, "There is no more dangerous enemy to the family plan than he who administers it carelessly." Efficient supervision of placed-out children, an absolute necessity for the child's well-being, he felt, could be accomplished only by an expert agent—a carefully selected, well-paid person "given large freedom in his work and retained except for cause, for a term of years." [23] One of the first to call this dire need to his colleagues' attention, Folks thus anticipated by many years the professionalization of social work.

By 1893 Homer Folks had traveled a long way. From an inexperienced young man he had developed into an authority on child welfare and a seasoned speaker before large audiences.[24] While his entire professional career with the Children's Aid Society had been nothing more than a practical social experiment to solve one question—how far the family plan could meet the problem created by dependent, neglected, and delinquent childhood—it is important that Folks concluded, before most of his collegues, that the plan, broadly defined, was in itself able to meet the whole of the problem.[25] It is noteworthy also that he pioneered in developing a sound system that enabled others to accept the family plan. Concerned thus far solely with institutions and foster homes, palliatives, later he would turn to the more important problem of eliminating the causes of child dependency and delinquency: physical and mental defect and premature death of one or both parents.

After a year in Philadelphia, Folks's salary was increased from $600 to $1,000 a year, an amount he felt that would allow him to support a wife. On December 22, 1891, he married Maud Beard, who (in the words of their future son-in-law) "profoundly influenced his success as a parent, citizen, and public figure." [26] A gracious and charming woman, Maud Folks proved to be a genuine help to her husband. While rearing their three children—Lalitha, Gertrude, and Evelyn—she also took an active interest in his work. In both good times and bad, Folks came to rely heavily upon her for advice and guidance.

Shortly after his marriage, Folks wrote a few lines to his old friend

Birtwell in Boston: "I hardly know how to introduce the subject," he
began, but the "simple fact is I think my connection with the society
may soon end. I do not know why," he continued, "but as I read the
signs of the times, the attitudes of the committees and officers of the
Board, I feel that is probably the inevitable outcome." [27] To those
familiar with the situation in Philadelphia this came as no surprise.
While outwardly all seemed well, almost from the start of his work
there had been many complications and differences of opinion between
Folks and some members of the Society. In particular, Folks and Mrs.
Biddle, the Society's president, apparently a temperamental person,
simply could not get along.

In spite of her earlier compliments, Mrs. Biddle almost always sided
with the Society's conservative Board of Directors in its differences
with Folks. His suggestions for reorganizing the Society's office work
and increasing its efficiency were jealously opposed by one fearful of
innovation and resentful of the growing authority of the Society's
young general agent. Moreover, Mrs. Biddle's insistence that the
Society reduce its expenditures despite the fact that its activities were
expanding rapidly made it impossible for Folks to operate as he would.
And when she repeatedly reprimanded him, even in public, for being
uneconomical with the Society's funds, Folks knew the end of his stay
in Philadelphia was near.[28]

Actually, the root of the trouble lay in one basic matter: the question
of the duties of a paid executive head of an organization, and his
relation to the staff on the one hand, and the Board of Directors on the
other, a problem that still plagues all such agencies. Nothing could
have more disturbed the young but already knowledgeable chief
executive than Mrs. Biddle's revealing statement to him that he was
"employed by the Board of Directors to take a general supervision of
the *work of the society that proceeds from the office,* and all else . . .
are outside of your duties." [29]

For Folks, an all-powerful and controlling Board that left nothing
but routine work to its paid officials was bad. Equally bad was a Board
that sat back, did nothing, and merely acted as a rubber stamp for the
agency's executive. For him, the answer lay somewhere between these
two extremes:

The proper and harmonious working relation which shall utilize all the judgement and devotion of the managers, all the experience of the officials, tending to make them work with the spirit of volunteers and altogether issuing in the closest, kindest and most thorough execution of such an immense work as ours is altogether too living, too organic a thing to be formulated in words and phrases. It will be found if found at all by persistent efforts at adjustment, by experiment if necessary, by a conviction that we all *want* to do the same thing and there *must* be some way of working together to secure it. In other words we can *learn how* to work together only by *working together*.[30]

The Board, and more particularly one member—Mrs. Biddle—insisted on remaining the moving spirit of the Society; she would stand for no initiative on the part of the general agent. Endless friction and frustration were inevitably in store for the young man who had always displayed a tendency toward independent thought. He was thus forced to resign.[31]

Because he felt the work of the Children's Aid Society was important, Folks was sorry to leave. He expressed his feelings succinctly, but tenderly, when he wrote to a prospective successor, "In my opinion *no* other work comes with such directness and such *intensity* to the very heart of human life. Upon no other body of benevolent people have been placed problems of such magnitude, of such virtue and import to society." [32] Nevertheless, he searched for another job, and in the process he may have recalled Mrs. Biddle's "profound thanks" for his decision to come to Philadelphia. In spite of all the misunderstandings and differences of opinion he had not regretted the venture. Nor had Mrs. Biddle, whose Children's Aid Society, under its departing general agent, had grown and prospered as never before.[33]

In the meantime, Folks was informed that his friend the noted child welfare worker, John H. Finley, secretary of the New York State Charities Aid Association, was about to leave his position in favor of a career as an educator; he had just accepted the presidency of Knox College. Folks immediately offered himself as a candidate for Finley's position. An exchange of letters and a trip to New York followed.

Coincidentally, at that time the State Charities Aid Association was planning to develop further its work with New York's needy children. The Board had just resolved to urge the free placing-out of dependent children whenever possible, and also recommended "the temporary boarding of such children in private families under careful supervision until a desirable free home can be found, rather than placing them in institutions, believing that in the large majority of cases, family life is preferable to life in an institution."[34] Among the applicants for the job, Homer Folks, well trained by practice and conviction to lead an organization devoted to those principles, seemed to have the best qualifications. Accordingly, on December 5, 1892, Gertrude Rice, chairman of the Committee on Finding a New Secretary, offered Folks the position on a one-year trial basis at a salary of $1,600, to be increased to $2,000 if rehired for a second year. To allay any fears Folks may have had for his future, she added, "Should the arrangement prove entirely satisfactory, the position would probably be of some permanence."[35] When a day later Folks advised Mrs. Rice that he gladly accepted the challenge, he did not realize the prophetic nature of her statement. He did not know he was assuming a task that would last the rest of his active life, a fifty-four year partnership with an association that would so enrich and intertwine their lives that they would always be thought of as one.

Five and a half decades later, Emma Lundberg, reformer and first head of the Social Service Division of the United States Children's Bureau, wrote that the New York State Charities Aid Association had activated community efforts throughout the nation in the fields of social welfare and health protection. And, she went on to say, "The history of the Association is the history of the man [Homer Folks] under whose guidance this agency . . . developed its progressive program of pioneer services wherever the need was greatest for the initiation of social welfare or health measures."[36] The same sentiment was echoed by one of Folks's successors when in 1957 he remarked that his "foresight and . . . high degree of statesmanship made the State Charities Aid Association what it is today."[37] Countless others, including the present executive director of the Association, have repeated the same thought.[38] Because it is also true, however, that Folks would learn a great deal from the agency he was called to lead in February 1893, a brief history of the organization is in order.

The nineteenth-century history of the New York State Charities Aid Association is the history of its humanitarian founder and organizer, Louisa Lee Schuyler. Miss Schuyler (1837–1926), a descendant of General Philip Schuyler and Alexander Hamilton, from girlhood displayed an inherited interest in the public life of New York State and the nation. The Civil War provided the first significant outlet for this young lady's benevolent energies.

When the war broke out Louisa Lee Schuyler was a member of New York's All Souls Unitarian Church, whose pastor, Dr. Henry W. Bellows, recognized the need of providing relief services to the Union soldiers. He therefore sought to organize a citizen effort to give comfort and aid to the men at the front and to establish communication between them and those at home. In setting up a committee to carry out his plans he turned to a twenty-four-year-old girl in his congregation. Thus Miss Schuyler helped organize and then became secretary of the Women's Central Relief Association, which, along with other "aid" associations, gave birth to the great and well-known United States Sanitary Commission, America's first nationwide voluntary health organization.[39]

The Sanitary Commission's primary purpose was to provide medical supplies and nursing care to sick and wounded soldiers. Organized in 1861, privately financed and directed, it united local relief societies into a national body that supplemented the work of government agencies in meeting the physical and spiritual needs of the fighting men. It sent bandages, clothing, and food to battlefields and encampments; it arranged hospital units, established lodging houses for men on furlough, provided receptions and meals to soldiers at railway stations; and in general it used its money, influence, and knowledge to improve conditions in military camps and hospitals in order to prevent needless suffering and loss of life through disease.[40] The Sanitary Commission thus demonstrated that a well-planned and well-organized coordinated effort by small voluntary groups in various communities, with the support of a central organization, can influence public opinion, educate masses of people, and bring about important reforms.

When in 1871 Miss Schuyler became active again after a long illness resulting from her four years of grueling work on the Women's Central Relief Association and the Sanitary Commission, she had not lost sight of the lessons that the war had taught her. The success of the Sanitary Commission opened her eyes to the great value and power of voluntary organization in promoting public welfare. As a result, she was convinced that "given a good cause to work for and a well organized, educated public opinion, . . . no reform is impossible." [41]

Reports of the New York State Board of Charities made Miss Schuyler aware of the deplorable condition of the poorhouses and almshouses throughout the state. Her visits to the Westchester County poorhouse, one of the largest, confirmed her worst fears; everything she had read about, and much more, was true. To remedy the situation, she planned to organize volunteer visiting committees for the poorhouses and almshouses of each of New York State's sixty counties. The committees, to be known as visiting committees of the State Charities Aid Association, would be composed of men and women willing to visit these public institutions in an earnest desire to better their conditions by keeping them under constant surveillance. Surely, she argued, as taxpayers and citizens, individuals had the right of visitation and the duty to insist upon proper management of public institutions. [42]

The county visiting committees would report to a central association of the State Charities Aid Association, whose headquarters would be located in New York City. The central association would be composed of men and women recognized as authorities on different subjects: the care of children, the construction and management of hospitals, sanitary science, poor law, and the like. Therefore, when the visiting committees would apply to the central association for assistance concerning various problems confronting them, they would be advised accordingly by those competent to do so. The force of public opinion was counted upon to bring about all necessary reforms, whether local or statewide.

The first visiting committee of the State Charities Aid Association was organized on January 9, 1872, in Westchester County, with the understanding that it was to report to and work under the direction of the central association, to be organized a few months later. [43] Shortly thereafter, at the invitation of the president of the New York City

Commissioners of Charities and Correction, Miss Schuyler visited the wards of New York's Bellevue Hospital. Familiar with the clean and well-organized Civil War hospitals, she expected to find the celebrated and renowned Bellevue Hospital a picture of cleanliness and perfection. She was deeply dismayed to find the opposite true; she recalled how her "heart sank within her" as she went through the wards and found that many of the "helpers"—nurses and orderlies— were ignorant and even degraded inmates of the city's poorhouses (tramps, drunkards, etc.) who had been taken to the hospital to work, where their inefficiency, wastefulness, and thievery resulted in incalculable suffering. She found the hospital lamentably deficient in its construction, its equipment, management, service, food, and just about all else. "At every turn," she recalled,

I found myself more and more depressed, more and more hopeless. What could be done for such a place? What could the visitors do? Suddenly it came to me: "We must have a training school for nurses in this hospital," I said to myself; it is the only thing that could regenerate it; and the visiting committee shall be organized with this in view. And so it was.[44]

Another of the Association's committees, the Visiting Committee for Bellevue and Other (New York City Public) Hospitals, was organized at Miss Schuyler's father's home in New York City on January 26, 1872. About sixty men and women, some of whom had served on the Sanitary Commission with Miss Schuyler, were summoned by her to undertake periodic visits to New York's hospitals and to create a training school for nurses at Bellevue.

At that time there were no nursing schools in this country, but this did not discourage Miss Schuyler's earnest and active group. They knew of the training school for nurses Florence Nightingale had established in London—the first of its kind in the world. A member of the committee immediately sailed for London to observe that school and talk with its founder. He returned with a letter from Miss Nightingale which counseled and encouraged the Association.[45] After fifteen months of constant agitation, during which time strong opposition from the medical profession—the same fight that Miss Nightingale had in London—and Bellevue's own physicians had to be overcome, the Bellevue Nurses Training School opened its doors on May 1, 1873.[46] Improvement in the care of patients and in ward conditions immediately followed. By 1879 several of Bellevue's wards employed trained nurses only. Dr. Charles V. Chapin, future Health Commissioner of Providence R.I., noted that "the trained nurses had 'worked wonders' in the wards while untrained nurses provided a horrible contrast with their slovenliness and general lack of method." [47]

In New York City on May 11, 1872, the central association of the State Charities Aid Association was organized, as was stated,

To promote active interest in the New York State Institutions of Public Charities, with a view to the physical, mental and moral improvement of their pauper inmates. 2nd. To make the present pauper system more efficient, and to bring about such reforms in it as may be in accordance with the most enlightened views of Christianity, Science and Philanthropy.[48]

The central association was divided into three standing committees: (1) for children, (2) for the sick, aged, and infirm, and (3) for vagrants—corresponding with similar divisions within the county visiting committees as they were being formed throughout the state. The chief functions of the New York central headquarters were to organize the county visiting committees, to recommend to the proper authorities from time to time improvements in public welfare that might seem desirable on the basis of the reports received from the local committees; and to disseminate useful information on matters pertaining to public welfare. The active interest of social-minded citizens was to be enlisted as a nucleus for the mobilization of public opinion in favor of the desired reforms.

A stronger or more influential group of people could scarcely have been named in the city of New York for the purpose of forming the central association and fulfilling its stated function. The Association's success was all but assured by the roll call of its earliest members: Charles Loring Brace, Professor Theodore Dwight, Henry Fairfield Osborn, Theodore Roosevelt, D. Willis James, Professor Charles Chandler, Doctors Stephen Smith, Abraham Jacobi, and W. Gill Wyllie. Also, Mrs. Josephine Shaw Lowell, Miss Abby Woolsey, Mrs. Joseph Hobson, Miss Grace Dodge, Joseph H. Choate, and Mrs. William B. Rice.[49] These men and women were, as a group, blessed with enlightened views, benevolence, experience, and wealth.

The New York Board of State Commissioners of Public Charities (later called the State Board of Charities), which was established in 1867, welcomed the founding of the State Charities Aid Association, whose express intent was to cooperate closely with the State Board; the Association's constitution specified that annual reports should be submitted to that body. The election of Theodore Dwight, vice-president of the State Board, as the Association's first president symbolized the cooperative effort and approach of the new society.[50]

In 1875 the State Board took a leading part in what has been called the "greatest single achievement in child welfare during the years 1865–1895"—the removal of children in New York State from the poorhouse through the instrument of the Children's Law of 1875. In its successful campaign to remove dependent, neglected, and wayward youths from those wretched institutions the State Board's strongest ally was the State Charities Aid Association, whose first annual report had called for the removal of children from public almshouses as one of the most urgently needed public welfare reforms in the state.[51] By 1875 the State Charities Aid Association, through its visiting committees, mobilized so much effective support in favor of the Children's Law in the various localities of the state that the measure was secured. Thereafter the Association's committees constantly kept a watchful eye over the state's poorhouses to make sure the law was obeyed.[52]

Six years later the Association won another, and one of its most important victories—the "right of entrance law." Despite its evident usefulness, and perhaps because of it, the Association had to overcome extremely strong opposition from managers of public institutions who preferred not to have interested citizens "looking around." Finally, however, in 1881 the New York State legislature conferred upon the State Charities Aid Association "the power to visit, inspect, and examine any of the County Poorhouses and Town Poorhouses and City Almshouses within the State." [53]

With the Association's earliest aims achieved, Miss Schuyler searched for the next most pressing need. Her visits to poorhouses confirmed the notes of other Association visitors which told of the unbearable suffering and unbelievably poor treatment of the insane in almshouses. Mentally ill men and women were often chained naked in outhouses, put in unlighted rooms too small to walk or stand in, and, in general, treated brutally. Better care for the insane must be attained, she inevitably concluded, and she immediately began work to secure reforms on their behalf.[54]

With assistance from others, she studied care for the insane in other countries. She thought about the most practical system for this country and concluded that only through a system of complete state care could the lot of the insane be fundamentally improved. Turning aside all compromises, offers of mixed systems of public subsidies to private institutions, Louisa Lee Schuyler steadfastly pursued the goal of a single, unified, unqualified system of state care for all the insane, a system thought to be visionary by some and socialistic by others.

Experienced legislators at Albany merely smiled at the Association and Miss Schuyler's scheme; they realized fully all the political implications involved: in many cases this would mean the closing of small, wretched institutions where the officers and other local residents reaped large financial rewards from supplying and maintaining them. But then the process of education began. Miss Schuyler collected data, verified reports, constantly informed the public of the facts, and aroused public opinion. By 1888 enough support for the idea had been mustered to secure the drafting of a bill and its introduction into the state legislature. The bill was not reported out of committee the first year, but the progressive forces behind the measure reintroduced it in 1889. Although taken a little more seriously, it still failed to pass.

The State Charities Aid Association kept up its campaign. Miss Schuyler, an astute tactition, was not unaware of the state's political organization and operation. Nor, however, was she unaware of the fact that, unlike other voluntary social welfare organizations, the State Charities Aid Association had a good deal of its own political power. Although operating on a tight budget with a limited staff, it represented organized blocs of voters in the constituencies of the state's legislators. Continuing to rely upon an informed public opinion and this political pressure, the county visiting committees popularized the idea of state care for the insane throughout New York until finally, thanks to its efforts, the measure became law in 1890.[55] And, as Albert Deutsch, the leading authority on care of the mentally ill in America, has noted, this statute, the New York State Care Act, embodied "the most sweeping legislative provisions in behalf of the insane ever enacted in the United States." This, then, marked the beginning of a new period in the care and treatment of the most unfortunate citizens of New York and many other states.[56]

So it was that the postwar era witnessed some impressive accomplishments in all fields of philanthropy. The "Gilded Age," which in Robert Bremner's words, was characterized by as much "generosity and altruism" as "acquisitiveness and self-seeking," [57] saw reform, like so many other things in America, become highly organized: agencies devoted to alleviating misery and combating disease, pauperism, ignorance, and crime, multiplied endlessly as reformers, freed from the stranglehold of slavery and with it, presumably the race question, attacked many of the "lesser" evils so long neglected.

But in an era when many Americans were hypnotized by laissez faire and appalled by the prevalence of graft and dishonesty in public life, which led to widespread corruption in the distribution of public relief, most charity workers continued for many years to follow the English tradition of thinking that private charity was the only wise method of relief. They believed that a system of voluntary organization could, and indeed was, the best way to solve the problem of need. As a result, practitioners of benevolence disassociated themselves from public service and, in the words of one authority, "except for the [state] boards of charities . . . and an occasional other agency, social work was exclusively identified with the voluntary forces in the community." [58]

The New York State Charities Aid Association, only one among many organizations created at the time to kindle support for humanitarian endeavors, in part conformed to the prevailing attitude among those engaged in charity and relief work. Certainly some of its early aims, "the physical, mental and moral improvement," of pauper inmates of institutions could hardly be distinguished from those of other agencies. True, the Association dispensed no direct aid itself, but other agencies, such as the Children's Aid Society of Pennsylvania, followed the same pattern. Its tradition of voluntarism and its reliance on the prestige of the "better classes" were not novel. Furthermore, its emphasis upon visitation, inspection, and advisory functions sounded familiar. And, finally, its reliance upon education and public opinion meant, at best, slow change.

Yet, in at least one extremely important way, the State Charities Aid Association differed from other charitable organizations; it did not divorce itself from public service. The title of the organization, unfortunately, did not fully reveal its uniqueness—to aid in the direction of public charities. It was in part, like other voluntary agencies, an expression of the prevalent distrust of political control of the agencies for aiding the unfortunate. At the same time, however, it was an admission of the need for and a reliance upon public support in the care of the needy. The State Charities Aid Association unfortunately was regarded often as an intrusive critic when, in fact, it should have been looked upon as a trusted ally of public administration. Unlike other voluntary agencies, the founders and those associated with the State Charities Aid Association, whatever their convictions about the inherent value of private as opposed to public relief, nevertheless from the start maintained that private philanthropy was not sufficient to solve the social problems of the state and nation: both private charity and public relief were needed to deal with poverty and dependency, deeply rooted consequences of America's social and economic life too complex to be affected by any single form of relief.

The long list of victorious battles that the organization could point to after its first few years of existence bore testimony to the value of its founder's vision.[59] It also laid the foundation for a trust and a tradition in "united helpfulness" and cordial cooperation between private citizens and public officials from which future leaders of the Association would not depart. Its importance was this: armed with a method and an organization that demonstrated startling results, under proper leadership the State Charities Aid Association had enormous possibilities for the future.

3

CHILD WELFARE— MATURITY

NEW YORK, the nation's largest city in the 1890s, was a place of contrasts. Comprised of red brick business buildings and brownstone homes, office structures, and shops, the city also had its Mulberry Bend and Five Points sections—congested centers of squalor and sordid poverty. Fifth Avenue, lined with trees and palatial homes, wasn't far from the teeming hive of pushcarts, paupers, and the chronically ill. New York was a paradox—beautiful and ugly, cosmopolitan and provincial. Perhaps the only thing that could be said with certainty about the city was that it offered everything in the way of business and entertainment.[1]

Like Philadelphia, New York had its large share of charitable enterprises, whose capabilities were being taxed to the limit in 1893. The depression that year reduced thousands to poverty, creating relief problems of great magnitude. In fact, conditions were so bad that charity organizations were unable to keep pace with the growing need; in the face of increasing unemployment, thousands of New Yorkers struggled for subsistence.[2]

When Homer Folks arrived in New York on February 1, 1893, to assume leadership of the State Charities Aid Association, its offices consisted of two small rooms and it had a paid staff of three. Its expenditures for the preceding fiscal year totaled $5,127.[3] But because the Association could list among its members some of New York's leading citizens, it had far more potential for doing good than its meager resources indicated. Charles F. Chandler served as president of the Association. Professor of chemistry at Columbia University and a

member of the faculty at Physicians and Surgeons Hospital, Chandler
greatly influenced the Association's new executive secretary. The State
Charities Aid Association's limited funds were in the safe hands of
Charles S. Fairchild. A banker and lawyer, Fairchild had served suc-
cessively as New York's Attorney-General, U.S. Assistant Secretary of
the Treasury, and Secretary of the Treasury under President Grover
Cleveland. Louisa Lee Schuyler and Gertrude Stevens Rice, however,
served as the Association's real guiding lights.[4] These two remarkable
women of high social standing already had demonstrated they knew
how to get things done; public-spirited citizens and able administrators
with "a good understanding of government," they remained persistent
in pursuing their objectives. Armed with a vigorous philosophy, which
was embodied in the organization of the Association, Miss Schuyler
and Mrs. Rice set a stimulating example, a call to action to which their
young protégé would respond.

However inadequate their resources, New York's charitable societies
at least attempted to help the city's adult poor in the face of the nation's worst depression. On the other hand, the city's long-neglected
dependent children continued to be ignored. Increasing in numbers as
the depression deepened, their problems required immediate attention;
as a result, the State Charities Aid Association under Folks's leadership
turned first to child welfare work.

While juvenile delinquents were maintained in state institutions,
New York had no well-coordinated plan for helping its dependent or
neglected children. In 1874 a constitutional provision abolished state
aid to private institutions, except for the education and support of the
blind, deaf, dumb, and delinquent. A year later, with the passage of the
law removing children from poorhouses, cities, counties, and towns,
through the contract or subsidy system, assumed financial responsibility for needy children. They placed dependent and neglected children
who were public charges under the care of private agencies and
institutions, reimbursing them on a per capita basis. The payments to
these private (and sometimes profit-making) institutions continued
as long as the children remained in them, a situation that often led to
poor and protracted institutional care. Most of New York's dependent

and neglected children, and all its delinquents, were in institutions; only a few were provided foster family homes.[5]

Children either were committed to institutions by magistrates or received from parents by surrender. In New York City, where the process was typical, the commitments by magistrates usually were made upon the recommendation of the city's Society for the Prevention of Cruelty to Children, popularly known as the "Gerry Society," after the name of a founder and long-time president, Elbridge T. Gerry. The institutions and child-caring agencies had no uniform plan, policy, or method of operation. The retention of children was legally in the hands of the managers of the institutions but this power was exercised in many cases only upon the recommendation of the Gerry Society. By 1890 the Society, a private corporation, controlled the reception, care, and disposition of destitute, neglected, and wayward children in New York and other cities throughout the state.[6]

The influence of anti-cruelty societies, many of which received generous public subsidies as well as private contributions, encouraged institutionalism. The societies did not cooperate with placing-out agencies and they rarely undertook the continued care of the children they had committed to institutions. Under this system the number of children supported by New York City increased 133 per cent during a twenty-year period (1875–1895), while the population of the city increased only 73 per cent during the same time.[7] Private institutions obviously found it profitable to keep children behind their walls as long as possible, while many parents found it to their liking to deposit their young ones in nearby institutions and not be bothered with their care or support. For Folks, New York State's system of child care clearly left much to be desired; he undertook to utilize the State Charities Aid Association's resources to change it.

Folks, of course, firmly believed the family was the natural and best home for dependent (and delinquent) children. Many of the features of family life that played a large part in the development and growth of children were lacking in institutions. For example, the ever-changing activities of family life sharply contrasted to the monotony of an institution. The family could not be duplicated in an institution.

The progression from a dependent infant in a family to a free and independent adult was denied by institutional life, which offered only continued restraint and repression. The opportunity to learn the value of money and to develop a consciousness of the need to "make both ends meet" was not present in institutions. But perhaps the most important feature of family life, and that which provided the sharpest contrast to institutional life, was in the development of affections. For this, young ones needed fathers and mothers. Thus, an institution in many ways was inferior to the outside world; it was artificial, no microcosm of the real world. In general, then, as Folks pointed out, "Good judgement is impossible without experience, and it is precisely the line of experience which would teach a child to judge wisely in the ordinary affairs of life, that is . . . lacking in an institution."[8] It is worth mentioning here that in expressing these ideas Folks anticipated psychological principles of human learning that would become popular later; students need to be taught in environments similar to those in which they will later be required to perform.

Although his special interest was in the development of good foster family care for children who were deprived of the protection and care normally given children in their own homes, Folks now engaged in his first service aimed at preventing the separation of children from their own parents. From his earlier work he knew that the death of the family wage earner frequently forced mothers to give up their young children. Unable to support their children without working or to care for them while earning a living, many mothers had to place their children in institutions. The same was true for illegitimate children. To help remedy this situation, Homer Folks suggested that the State Charities Aid Association create a Sub-Committee on Providing Situations for Mothers with Babies. The organization immediately formed the committee, the first such undertaking in New York State. It worked to find positions for women where they could keep their children with them, rather than send them to boarding homes or institutions. Most women were placed as servants in homes outside the city. The Association not only worked out a careful system to investigate the homes to which the women and children were sent, but also kept in constant touch with those so placed. At the end of the first year 113 mothers with young children had been provided suitable jobs. The service was so successful that by September 30, 1901, less than eight years after the experiment began, the committee had placed the amazing number of 2,627 mothers with their children.[9] Thus thousands of New Yorkers were kept off the charity lists; children were kept out of institutions and given the advantage of their mother's care; and mothers in turn received the benefit of keeping and caring for their own children.

In 1894, with the launching of another successful experiment, Folks again proved he could initiate and organize as well as administer new programs. In that year the residents of Newburgh, N.Y., proposed to spend a large sum of money to enlarge their children's home. As an alternative, Folks suggested to the chairman of the Newburgh visiting committee of the State Charities Aid Association that instead of enlarging the institution, the committee volunteer to cooperate with the local poor law official in the placing-out of children. Realizing that most local officials were not trained in child-saving work and that they often were busy with "other" jobs, he further suggested that the committee employ an agent to look into the circumstances surrounding the commitment of each child to the institution, place-out those children for whom homes could be found, and undertake periodic examinations of foster homes. The public officials consented to try the idea and it was put into operation. Within two years the population of the municipal institution had been cut in half, partly by returning children to their own homes, partly by placing some with relatives, and partly by placing many of the children in foster homes; a large child-care institution was no longer needed. The Newburgh experiment proved to be a valuable lesson of far-reaching significance: it gave birth to "one of the major events in the history of social services for children destined to have an enduring influence upon public social welfare agencies and activities" throughout the nation—the County Agent System.[10]

In cooperation with its local committees and the local public officials throughout the state, the State Charities Aid Association formed county agencies for dependent children. Under the county agent system the public officials contributed a stated sum per month and the local committee of the Association secured through voluntary contributions any additional sums needed to employ a trained paid agent who then devoted his or her entire time to the county's destitute children. Recognizing that untrained service often resulted in cruelty, and that politics and child care usually had little in common, the program laid special emphasis upon the employment of trained child welfare workers, who then dealt with individual children according to their separate needs.[11]

The duties which the local committee and the trained agent undertook to perform for the county authorities included the following: to investigate families of children who were public charges; to assist local authorities to return children to families when possible; to help local authorities collect funds for the partial support of children from families who could afford to contribute to the care of their children; to investigate all applications for public care; to investigate potential foster homes; and to supervise the placing-out of children. The agents, under Folks's tutelage, also introduced to New York State the boarding-out system.[12]

The agents worked as assistants to the county superintendents of the poor, but under the general supervision of the county visiting committees and the central association. In 1898 the central association established a child-placing and adoption committee, which served as a clearing house for finding homes and placing children throughout the state. Under Folks's leadership this committee placed 6,685 dependent children in permanent homes.[13] In addition, the New York office employed two people who gave their entire time to the establishment of county children's agencies and the supervision of the work of the county agents.

Like the Sub-Committee on Providing Situations for Mothers with Babies, the establishment of the county agencies and the central association's agency for providing homes for needy children throughout the state greatly reduced the number of children that became public charges. Equally important, it also secured much wiser and more effective care for those who remained dependent. After more than forty years of operation, during which time nearly 50,000 children came under the care and direction of the county agents, the State Charities Aid Association's services for children were taken over by the State Department of Social Welfare.[14] Today the county agent system for dependent children, under public auspices, is standard procedure throughout the United States.

In 1895 Homer Folks ignited a discussion that raged for many years. In an address before the National Conference he advocated the novel idea that the states be given broad supervisory powers over all child-caring agencies and institutions, public or private. The state, he maintained, should have the authority to set standards for all such agencies, to make regular inspections of their work, to remove improperly cared for children, to give publicity to their findings, and, if necessary, to revoke the charter of any agency or institution that did not adhere to the announced regulations. Folks believed that such state supervision should be in the hands of a staff of paid experts working under the direction of a special children's bureau, apart from the State Board of Charities. The creation of a children's bureau was necessary because "the intimate acquaintance with the subject which the performance of such duties presupposes" seemed to Folks, "to be all but incompatible with an equal familiarity with all the other divisions of the great fields of charities and correction." [15]

Folks maintained that such supervision would serve various purposes. In New York, for instance, it would correct many of the evils in the existing system by bringing order to the state's chaotic and backward child-caring policies. Also, the state could serve as a fact-finding and information-dispensing agency and thereby make the experiences of each agency and institution available to all. Finally, and most important, only the state could serve as a body that would oversee child care work as a whole, thereby transcending individual and local loyalties and prejudices. The state, Folks implied, was a more intelligent, resourceful, impartial, and efficient administrative unit than local political divisions. It commanded a better grade of talent, had more ample resources, and, as a rule, was subject to less partisanship than the smaller administrative units. It should therefore be made into an effective and positive instrument of social progress.

Folks's statement on state regulation and supervision of child-caring institutions is significant because, as Frank Bruno has pointed out, it was the first to be made on the subject.[16] Moreover, the plea came from an executive of a private agency that would come under the official scrutiny he called for. More important, it represented a plea for an end to the era of laissez faire in regard to the child welfare problem. In this respect, Folks expressed the regulative ethos that progressives would, a few years later, insist upon; he voiced a desire for a planned and orderly development of child welfare work. State supervision was in agreement with the progressive outlook in its collectivist emphasis. Folks, like the bands of determined progressive insurgents throughout the country who soon would begin attacking the selfish and corrupt "interests" in control of the political and economic orders, felt that a "hands-off" policy resulted in disaster and that the interests of the individual must be subordinate to the welfare of the group. Both were willing to restrict personal liberty for the sake of the corporate good, and both turned to the state as an instrument of reform.

When a constitutional convention was called in 1894, Folks was given the opportunity to implement his ideas. The State Charities Aid Association received a request from Edward Lauterbach, chairman of the Committee on Charities of the Constitutional Convention, to prepare any amendment it wished to see incorporated into the state's constitution. Folks took advantage of the opportunity to press for a comprehensive system of state supervision—not only of child-caring institutions but of all charitable societies. He and Miss Schuyler drafted an amendment which the Association submitted to Lauterbach's committee. The amendment provided for constitutional recognition of the State Board of Charities and state supervision over all charitable, eleemosynary, correctional, and reformatory institutions, both public and private.[17]

In addition to vastly extending the State Board's power of visitation and inspection, the Association's "Charities Article" had other important provisions. Contrary to the Board members' wishes, the amendment took away existing power of supervision over adult reformatories and institutions for the epileptic and feeble-minded. Reflecting Folks's penchant for *expertise* in public service, the amendment called instead for the creation of a constitutionally recognized State Commission in Lunacy and a State Prison Commission, each with its own supervisory functions. When the article was finally reported to the convention, however, institutions for the epileptic and feeble-minded were to continue under the supervision of the State Board of Charities, but the power of visiting and inspecting institutions for the insane was given exclusively to the proposed State Commission in Lunacy.[18]

From June to October 1894 Folks devoted all his time to the proposed new Charities Article of the constitution. He remained in Albany throughout the summer months working on its behalf, never relaxing in his efforts to secure the coordination of social welfare activities through state control. He explained the measure to legislators, members of the convention, and others. A man of unusual charm with an excellent sense of humor, always tactful and yet forceful, Folks pointed out the shortcomings of the existing system and the need for the amendment. His hard work and mastery of the subject brought results. The Charities Article, substantially as prepared and submitted by the State Charities Aid Association, was adopted first by the convention and then by the people of the state in the November election.[19]

At least two other provisions of the new Charities Article were important for their effect on child welfare. The first prohibited the state legislature from compelling any county, city, town, or village to make any payment of money to a charitable or correctional institution that was wholly or partly under private control. More important, however, was the provision that no payment be made by any county, city, town, or village, to any charitable or correctional institution wholly or partly under private control for any inmate who is not received and retained therein pursuant to the rules established by the State Board of Charities.[20]

The power of the State Board of Charities was thus purely restrictive. It could not authorize increased appropriations not already sanctioned by law, but it could limit all appropriations to the extent it wished by imposing restrictions on the reception and retention of inmates; that is exactly what it did.

In January 1895 the State Board adopted a rule that every institution under its jurisdiction had to make a full report to the Board concerning each inmate received. Consequently, a complete register of all the state's children who were public dependents was established in the office of the State Board. The following year the State Board ruled that no person was to be maintained as a public charge unless accepted in writing as such by the local authorities charged with the relief of the poor. Each application was to be renewed yearly to prevent managers of private institutions from keeping their inmates too long. As a result, some of the gravest abuses of the New York State system that Folks set out to attack were removed. Finally, when in 1897 the State Board divorced politics from child care by extending the merit system to include the appointment of inspectors of public institutions and child welfare workers, Folks's plea for the control of child welfare by trained experts was all but fulfilled. To assure the proper results, Folks prepared and graded the civil service examinations for the State Board in the fields of charities law and institutional inspection and management.[21]

Next, Folks turned his energies to another abuse touched on in his epoch-making speech on state supervision of child-caring agencies. Evils in child-care work, he had told his audience, were not limited to institutions; those "who have seen much of placing-out work as it is usually done," he had gone on to say in his familiar manner, "will, I am sure, agree with me that there is fully as much need that the protecting care of the state should be extended to children who are in families as to those who are in institutions."[22] In 1898 that need was met when at Folks's suggestion the State Board recommended and the legislature passed "An Act to Prevent Evils and Abuses in Connection with the Placing Out of Children." This act, drafted by Folks, prohibited any individual or agency, not incorporated under the laws of the state (other than poor law officials) from placing-out children without a license from the State Board of Charities. The Board was also given the power to revoke these licenses after they were issued, as well as the right to visit children placed in foster homes.[23] In other words, all child welfare work in New York State was henceforth to be carried out under the aegis of the state.

Folks's contemporaries appreciated the skills he had applied to the task of solving the state's child welfare problem, and he received their praise. Miss Schuyler, a veteran of many legislative battles, congratulated Folks. New York's Children's Aid Society passed a resolution "extending its hearty and appreciative thanks to Mr. Homer Folks for his efforts in shaping legislation" on behalf of dependent children. No congratulatory message was appreciated more, however, than the one he received from the son of the dean of placing-out, the late Charles Loring Brace.[24] Folks had become the pivotal figure in the child-care movement. He was not only the prophet who more than anyone else had aroused men's thoughts to the advantages of placing-out and state supervision, but his technical skill, political resourcefulness, and administrative abilities had transformed ideas into legislation.

Nearly every extension of state supervision over welfare institutions and agencies encountered active opposition on the part of some local authorities and/or other "interested" individuals and groups. The State Board immediately found itself engaged in open warfare with various public or private agencies over its supervisory rights and powers. In 1897 the New York Institute for the Blind unsuccessfully challenged in court the Board's constitutional powers. In 1898, however, the issue was again brought into the courts. The New York Society for the Prevention of Cruelty to Children contended that it was not subject to the Board's supervision. In a four-to-three vote the Court of Appeals ruled that the Gerry Society was not a charitable, eleemosynary, correctional, or reformatory institution and therefore was not subject to the Board's jurisdiction. More important, however, was the court's ruling that the Board's powers extended only to institutions in receipt of public funds. The decision was a serious blow to the progress of state supervision of welfare activities. The State Board was forced to relinquish jurisdiction of more than half the private agencies under its supervision.[25] Despite this reversal, a substantial advance had been made. At least all of New

York's public and quasi-public institutions and agencies had to account to a centralized body and adhere to decent standards, which meant better treatment for thousands of dependents throughout the state. The anti-cruelty societies' victory simply meant that the people of New York were not yet prepared to admit that the care of its dependents was a legitimate community responsibility and thereby justified limited restrictions on the use of private property. The right of state supervision over private welfare institutions not in receipt of public funds was finally achieved in the midst of the nation's great depression. Thus, more than thirty-five years later, the thinking of most New Yorkers finally caught up with that of the State Charities Aid Association's far-sighted secretary.

Folks's efforts to brighten the lives of dependent children stemmed from a larger sense of humanity. Convinced of the inherent worth of all human beings, his goal was to secure for every individual the right to a normal life. This desire to give every man an opportunity to attain his maximum physical, mental, and cultural development led Folks and the State Charities Aid Association into various endeavors; they did not confine their activities to New York State's child welfare problem. The Association and its secretary were equally active, and perhaps more successful, in their labors on behalf of improved charity legislation for New York City.

For many years New York City denied that there was a difference between poverty and crime. The city placed its poor wards and its prisoners in one department and made common appropriations for their support. There was one Board of Commissioners in charge of the city's public hospitals, prisons, almshouse, and workhouse. People convicted of disorderly conduct, intoxication, petty larceny, vagrancy, cruelty to children, and other offenses were committed to the workhouse. Hundreds of destitute people, not convicted of any crimes, were also sent there. Thus, in effect, many of the poor were being sent to prison.[26]

In 1894 with the advent of Mayor William L. Strong's reform administration Folks saw an opportunity to remedy the horrible abuse. He drafted a bill under which the sick, the destitute, and the children would be in a single department, and the vagrants and criminals in an entirely separate one. Not only did Folks draft the legislation, but he accepted the burdensome task of steering it through the legislature. First he took the measure to Mayor Strong who, with little urging, approved it. Folks then traveled to Albany, where he successfully maneuvered it past the obstacles at the Capitol.[27]

In 1897 Folks demonstrated that he and the Association could function effectively in still other ways, including the prevention of what appeared to be undesirable legislation. A notable example was a bill sponsored by State Senator John F. Ahearn, known as the "destitute mother's bill." The measure would have been placed upon the state's statute books if Folks had not almost single-handedly mustered enough support to defeat it. It is worth examining this episode in detail, for it illuminates the political dynamics of pressure politics, a process Folks quickly mastered.

New York City had abolished public outdoor relief in 1876. At that time it was voted that no public funds be used "for distribution to the poor"; outdoor grants, with the exception of cash grants to the adult blind, were restricted to the provision of coal. The destitute mother's bill was intended to prevent the separation of destitute children from their parents simply for reasons of poverty, a sentiment with which Folks obviously agreed. The bill provided that any child who had been committed to an institution might be returned to its parents by the Society for the Prevention of Cruelty to Children, and that thereafter the City Comptroller should pay the Society the same amount of money that the institution had been receiving from the city for the child's care. The Society for the Prevention of Cruelty to Children was then to hand the money over to the child's parents. The Gerry Society was also empowered to take the child away from its parents and return him or her to the institution whenever in the Society's judgment this would benefit the child.[28]

Folks objected to this proposal for several reasons. He opposed the measure on procedural grounds. The bill left the entire administrative responsibility for carrying out its provisions in the hands of the Gerry Society, a private corporation with no direct responsibility to the taxpayers, an agency which, it will be recalled, had in the courts defeated the principle of state regulation. He also opposed Senator Ahearn's bill because it would re-establish public outdoor relief in New York City, "a system which in large cities," he maintained, had "been found to promote pauperism, to discourage self-reliance and thrift and to be especially liable to flagrant abuses." [29]

At this time Folks shared the nineteenth-century charity worker's fear of public outdoor relief. Contending that it was difficult to administer public home relief honestly, efficiently, and economically, he felt that private societies were vastly superior to public agencies in the dispensing of relief. Folks also believed that public funds for outdoor relief tended to diminish and discourage private charity. More important in his mind was the conviction that appropriations for such relief would prevent adequate provision being made for the public hospitals and almshouses maintained and controlled directly by the city. Finally, Folks also believed that public outdoor relief was not necessary for the humane care of New York's poor: "The private agencies for the relief of the poor in their homes," he contended, "were fully . . . equal to their task." [30] To his credit Folks realized that pauperization by alms was no worse than pauperization by neglect. As a result, when he soon realized that private societies maintained a very low standard of relief, he changed his mind. He came to understand that adequate standards of assistance could be maintained only by means of public funds and a system of public aid. In a few years Folks would be among the earliest of social workers to support, for instance, widows' pensions—public aid for dependent children in their own homes.[31]

On April 8, 1897, the destitute mother's bill passed the state Senate and the following day it passed the Assembly without a hearing. Folks traveled to Albany but his protests and demands for a hearing went unheeded. A provision in the state constitution stated, however, that all special laws pertaining to cities of the first class (250,000 or more population) had to be approved by the mayor within fifteen days or, if disapproved, reconsidered and passed by the legislature over his veto. And since the destitute mother's bill dealt only with New York City, it had to come before Mayor Strong for approval. Folks returned to New

York and immediately drafted an appeal to the Mayor. After reviewing the bill's history for Strong, Folks went on to denounce its provisions as "so extraordinary, that one could hardly believe it was seriously
proposed. I am confident," he added, hopefully, "that many organizations and individuals will desire to be heard before you in opposition to
this bill, and I am writing to you to ask you to fix . . . [a] hearing at
such a date as to give us ample time to prepare for [it]."[32]

Next, he exhibited an adroitness as an organizer of public sentiment
and strategist of pressure groups which would typify all his work. On
April 10, 1897, Folks sent to the various relief-giving agencies of the
city, the institutions affected by the measure, and to New York's
leading citizens, a circular he drew up which outlined the destitute
mother's bill and his objections to it. He urged all involved to pass
resolutions against the bill and to volunteer their time and energy to
assist in the drive to defeat it. They were summoned to the hearing set
for the bill on the twenty-first of the month. Many of the city's
nonpartisan political organizations passed such resolutions and sent
representatives to speak against the measure at the public hearing.
Seldom had so much opposition to a bill been expressed in public. The
hostility aroused by Folks's tireless educational efforts persuaded
Mayor Strong to veto the measure. The destitute mother's bill never
became law.[33] The incident provided Folks with a valuable lesson:
converting individual efforts into an organized force was a sound
method not only for effecting reforms, but also for preventing the
passage of undesirable legislation.

Folks had the loyalty of his staff; his leadership was unquestioned.
Most of those who worked for him believed in the reforms they
worked for and the programs they administered, but even more they
believed in and admired Folks. His radiant good humor kept the office
sparkling. More important was his ability to communicate to those
around him a sense of the importance of their efforts. He instilled
devotion to the job, which many administrators never develop in their
subordinates. As a result of this, as well as by virtue of its organization,
the State Charities Aid Association was instrumental in both the
passage and the defeat of many bills that affected the entire welfare

structure of New York State. According to Frank J. Bruno, through its relationship with the executive and legislative branches of the state government, the State Charities Aid Association had become "the most successful non-official adviser on matters of social welfare in this country."[34] Folks had demonstrated that leadership in public affairs can be effectively exercised by a nongovernmental organ; despite a limited staff and budget, the State Charities Aid Association was not merely a forum for discussion, it was a vigorous instrument of reform.

A man of tremendous energy and drive, Folks was extremely active throughout his early years with the State Charities Aid Association. He gave countless lectures on various topics ranging from private child-care work to municipal charities. He talked before the National Conference several times, he was chairman of its section on municipal and county charities, and soon was to be elected the Conference's next general secretary, a position he would resign a year later when he became New York City's Commissioner of Public Charities. He lectured before college and university classes, as well as numerous civic groups. Under the auspices of New York's Board of Education he gave a series of public lectures on "The Public Charities of New York City."[35]

In addition, Folks served on the governing board of many of New York's leading charitable societies. He helped establish the New York State Conference of Charities and Correction. One of his addresses on "Annual Reports of Child-Caring Agencies" was printed in pamphlet form and distributed to all the child-caring institutions in Massachusetts and New York, where it served for years as a guide to secretaries of such organizations.[36]

A recognized expert on state and municipal charities, Folks appeared in the first (and during his lifetime every subsequent) edition of *Who's Who in America*. A few years later his biography was included in W. D. P. Bliss's famous *Encyclopedia of Social Reform,* which, in the editor's words, treated "only those [reformers] having national recognition." In 1899 New York's governor, Theodore Roosevelt, felt he needed Folks's support to get Senate confirmation of one of his appointments in the welfare field. And although not in the public eye as much as others, Folks was the leader of the so-called "charities trust," a small coterie of social workers whose approval was almost always needed to get charity legislation placed on New York's statute books.[37]

Because of his widening scope of interests Folks increasingly became involved in countless "movements," but it is impossible to understand his life merely by listing his activities. He remained direct and personal, never ceasing to be a devoted husband and loving father. During these hectic years, for example, when the legislature was in session Folks went to Albany each week. When he returned he always brought with him a box of candy—one special kind—and his children ritualistically combined their welcoming kisses with a grab for his suitcase. Despite his herculean schedule, Folks never forgot the candy.[38]

Numerous organizations throughout the country tried to entice the popular chief executive of the State Charities Aid Association away from his job. Such well-known reformers as Julia Lathrop, Professor Albion Small, and Dr. Graham Taylor asked Folks to come to Chicago to create and head a Chicago Bureau of Charities. The famed Civic Federation of Chicago was to sponsor the new venture and its members felt that Folks was just "the person to make a really great success in the undertaking." Others sought to make him the general manager of Chicago's Children's Aid Society, superintendent of a state child-caring institution in Michigan, secretary of the New York State Board of Charities, and secretary of the newly created New York State Prison Commission.[39] To all who sought his services the answer was the same: his work at the State Charities Aid Association was congenial, his relations with the Association's Board of Managers were extremely pleasant, and his salary was good enough. Most important, he informed them, his work was "full of opportunities for research and effort in connection with . . . [his] special interest, the care of destitute and wayward children." [40]

One call for his services, however, did not go unheeded. After the Spanish-American War when General Leonard Wood, United States Military Governor of Cuba, began to reorganize the charitable and correctional institutions and establish a Board of Charities for that devastated island, Folks was summoned for the job. "The need is urgent and the opportunity large," one of Wood's aides wrote.[41] Another adviser to the military governor informed Folks "that the time will never come when your skill will accomplish such far reaching results as it will here. If you can get a short leave of absence, of only a few months," she continued, "you can put things on their proper basis and train into the work those who will have to carry on later." [42] Further appeals prompted Folks to accept the offer.

The opportunity was indeed great. Two years after the war ended, Cuba was still badly devastated. Years of fighting between the Spaniards and Cubans had taken their toll: much of the country was ravaged, there was a large dependent population, and most of the island's charitable agencies and institutions were thoroughly disorganized and chaotic.[43] Given the authority to create a State Board and reorganize the island's charities, Folks could use Cuba as a testing ground for all his ideas.

The thirty-three-year-old Folks, as lean as he was at twenty and now sporting a long brown handle-bar mustache, arrived in Cuba in mid-April 1900. Although he was comfortably settled on the seashore, the days were long and full of work, the evenings short, hot, and humid. Matters could have been worse however, for, as he related with pleasure in his first letter to the States, General Wood opposed the establishment of any more child welfare institutions; he strongly favored the placing-out system. Folks's dynamic driving energy and tremendous capacity for work were never better revealed than when, only four weeks later, he informed his friends at the State Charities Aid Association that he had "drawn up a proposed decree [reorganizing the island's charities] . . . which is now being put into Spanish. The placing out work has taken a good firm hold, I think, and, on the whole," he ended, "I am very much pleased with what I have been able to do here." [44]

On July 7, 1900, General Wood promulgated Folks's decree. Effective the first of August, it created an insular Department of Charities and provided for a Board of Charities with specifically defined powers and duties. It also reorganized several local and state institutions and established a Bureau for Placing Out Children under the Department of Charities.[45]

Folks considered the article dealing with the welfare of children most important. According to its provisions, all destitute and delinquent children in need of public funds were to be cared for by the state. Such children were to be dealt with in families, training schools, or reformatories, according to their respective individual needs.[46] Four state institutions were provided for children in need of special training (who therefore could not be placed-out); one each for destitute boys and girls (special training schools) and one each for criminal boys and wayward girls (reform schools). After the children received the needed training from these various institutions, they were to be placed with families by the child-placing bureau. The provisions governing the two reform schools were very progressive. They provided for indefinite commitment, a system of rewards, and discharge upon parole to be earned by good conduct. Delinquent children were to be committed to reform schools by the courts, while destitute youngsters were to be handled by the Department of Charities.

In regard to the insane, New York's system was adopted. They were to be cared for at public expense in state institutions. Hospitals for the destitute and sick, which were put under the management and support of municipalities or districts, were subject to the Department of Charities, which was given full power of inspection, inquiry, and recommendation of all the island's public and private charitable agencies and institutions.[47]

Folks's experiment in the Cuban laboratory was eminently successful. Major E. St. John Greble, appointed by General Wood to head Cuba's new Charities Department, expressed the feelings of a good many others when he wrote to Folks after he left, "I do not believe you have ever put in a better month's work." [48] Years afterward others continued to express their appreciation of Folks's Cuban work.[49]

By the turn of the century Folks was the leading evangelist among those preaching the gospel of placing- and boarding-out. And, in large measure due to his efforts, the major differences of opinion among

charity practitioners in regard to child welfare work were rapidly dis-
appearing. Placing-out of dependent and delinquent children was becoming increasingly popular. Where institutions remained, the congregate type were being replaced by the colony or cottage plan, which
facilitated individualized treatment and improved classification. The
principle that no child should be removed from his family because of
poverty was gaining popularity.

Evidence that the long argument over the best methods of caring for
children in need was being resolved was provided by the Report of the
Committee on Children, the first careful statement of methods and
principles upon which national representatives of various child-caring
agencies agreed. Read before the National Conference of Charities and
Correction in 1899 by committee chairman Thomas M. Mulry, head of
the Catholic Society of St. Vincent De Paul, long the leading advocate
of institutional care for dependent children, the report urged the paramount necessity of preserving the home wherever and whenever possible. For those children without relatives to claim them, however, the
committee recommended placing-out, after careful investigation and
with constant supervision.[50] Although the report did not mention
boarding-out, it was not long before that too was widely adopted.[51]
Folks's ten years of effort on behalf of dependent, neglected, and delinquent children were bearing fruit: the revolution in child care was
beginning.

The revolution certainly was not a violent one, however. Its aim was
modest—to provide the best possible care for neglected, dependent, and
delinquent children. The weapons were restrictive control legislation,
and placing- and boarding-out. Nevertheless, to achieve even these limited aims Folks had to overcome a great deal of opposition from the
entrenched interests in the orphanages, who, the story goes, used to
pray that the Lord would send them many more orphans the following year so that they might add a new wing to their institution.[52]
Folks not only helped change the course of child-care development in
New York, but he influenced its history throughout the nation.[53]

It is true that Folks didn't always present original ideas. He bor-
rowed extensively from others, always, however, acknowledging his

debts to them. Folks's importance in the history of child welfare work lay not so much in his creative capacity, but in his synthesis and elaboration of older thought, and especially in his practical and realistic application of that thought to the current situation. Through his experiments, propagandizing, and proselytizing Folks left as a permanent legacy to the nation not so much the principle that dependent, neglected, and delinquent children should be cared for in families, but that it was practical to do so.[54] In this respect he emerges as a figure of major significance; from 1891 until 1947 no man was more active than Folks in advancing that idea.

4

PUBLIC OFFICE

IN 1888 a foreign observer of American affairs, James Bryce, declared that the nation's "one conspicuous failure" was the government of its cities.[1] Two years later an astute American agreed: "Without the slightest exaggeration," Andrew White, the noted reformer and educator, maintained, "we may assert that with very few exceptions, the city governments of the United States are the worst in Christendom—the most expensive, the most inefficient, and the most corrupt."[2]

These deplorable municipal conditions were due, for the most part, to swift growth, an unprecedented need for new municipal services, and a citizenry more concerned with its own desires than with the community's social welfare. In the midst of profound economic and social changes, Americans were unprepared for and unconcerned with the complex problems of city life. By the last decade of the nineteenth century, however, the forces of reform and reconstruction had been set in motion. The period that witnessed the triumph of the party machine and municipal corruption also saw the genesis of the municipal reform movement.[3]

Municipal reform was related to a larger movement for social justice. The 1890s and early 1900s were decades of confidence characterized by an aggressive optimism and a belief that social evils could be eradicated and more wholesome society achieved. "If I had ever needed assurance of the merits of a reformer's career," wrote Roger N. Baldwin recollecting his meeting in the early twentieth century with some reformers in New York, "I got it with these bright and busy saviors, who struck me as living not only significantly but with unexpected gayety of spirit and a buoyant optimism."[4] Political reformers and pioneer social workers often joined hands as they moved with great facility from one cause to another in their attempts to remedy political and social evils. A belief in the right of all citizens to a healthy, productive life was a goal that linked many of the seemingly disparate reform crusades of the era into what has been called the progressive movement.[5]

For years Tammany Hall held New York City firmly in its grip. Political corruption and police collusion with gamblers, prostitutes, and criminals ran riot in the metropolis. By the 1890s, however, New Yorkers were awakening to the degraded condition of their city. Reverend Dr. Charles Parkhurst, famous clergyman and anti-vice crusader, delivered his memorable sermons that led to the popular Lexow Committee investigations. Some members of the "better classes" turned their attention to public affairs and numerous nonpartisan political organizations devoted to "good government" appeared. In short, a social and moral concern began to replace self-interest.

Unlike some humanitarians and social workers, Folks attached tremendous importance to political action. He did not share some of his colleagues' contempt for and distrust of politicians. His formal training had reinforced his parents' conviction that public service, including politics, was a noble calling. Professor Peabody, his Harvard mentor, had taught that in politics beneath "the operation of self-interest and intrigue a moral purpose may be fulfilled." [6] In addition, as a taxpaying citizen with a keen sense of civic responsibility and a concern for social welfare, as well as head of an organization devoted to raising standards of public service through citizen interest in the fields of public health and welfare, it was inevitable that Folks would be interested in New York's political renaissance; public charities, unfortunately, were not exempt from partisan politics.[7]

The City's Republican Party, sustained by the national organization, was feeble and accomplished little. It was completely controlled by a ring of professionals who manipulated it for their own use as a medium for securing and distributing federal patronage and bargaining with Tammany for local offices in exchange for election favors. But since an affiliation with Tammany was out of the question, Folks, a Republican by upbringing, remained Republican only by default, like many others in New York at this time.

By 1894, however, more than a dozen reform groups had arisen, all anti-Tammany and devoted to the common aim of securing good, clean, economical municipal government.[8] It was to these groups that Homer Folks devoted most of his political energy; he became a leading member of one of the most important—the City Club of New York. Incorporated on April 4, 1892, the City Club set the pattern for countless similar groups. Restricted to nonpartisan action, the Club's members sought to sever municipal from national politics. Maintaining a public information bureau, which issued literature on municipal government and reforms, the City Club, in the words of one member, "was the Tammany Hall of the reformers of New York." It was "a sort of exchange where we came together to share our hopes and our fears, our gossip and our truth."[9]

The City Club's chief accomplishment was the creation of twenty-four Good Government Clubs throughout the city (Good Government Club "A," "B," "C," etc.), one of which Folks served as secretary. Six thousand New Yorkers were organized into these clubs stigmatized as "Goos Goos" because, as one member explained, "to be good, and to think of good government as something achievable in Tammany-ruled New York was in those days so highly fantastic as to merit derision and satire."[10] The Good Government Clubs stood for the same objectives as their parent organization. They served as local social and political centers where citizens met for serious discussion or for spending leisure time. Advocating various reform measures, they claimed as their accomplishment a general awakening of public reform sentiment and the nomination of better men to public office.[11]

Finally, in February 1897, Folks helped form the Citizens' Union—a permanent municipal reform party. Headed by R. Fulton Cutting, president of New York's Association for Improving the Condition of the Poor, it was composed of such notable New Yorkers as Elihu Root, Charles Fairchild, James Carter, James B. Reynolds, Nicholas Murray Butler, and the social-economist Henry White. The most active of all the nonpartisan associations, the Citizens' Union became known as "the people's lobby."[12]

After years of debate, in 1897 a new charter for a "Greater New York

City" was adopted. Effective as of January 1, 1898, it added to Manhattan and the Bronx the city of Brooklyn and the areas known as Queens and Richmond. With the patronage of the newly consolidated boroughs at stake, the enlarged city's first election took on added importance. In the opinion of Dr. Albert Shaw, editor of the liberal *Review of Reviews,* there never had been a "time in the history of any great city, whether in the United States or in any other country, when so much was at stake for the cause of good municipal government at one single election." [13]

The Democrats nominated for mayor Robert A. Van Wyck, an obscure judge who promised Tammany he would do as he was told. Refusing to form a fusion ticket with the reform element, the Republicans nominated General Benjamin Tracy on a platform that advocated administering city governments on national party principles. Seth Low, wealthy merchant and former mayor of Brooklyn, was called to head the newly created Citizens' Union ticket.

On September 30, 1897, C. H. Strong, chairman of the Citizens' Union Campaign Committee for the 29th Assembly District, asked Folks if he would consider running for the Greater City's first Board of Aldermen. "The voters of the district last night cast a large number of ballots for you as their first choice," Strong informed him. [14] Folks hesitated to accept the nomination. Central to all his interests was the State Charities Aid Association. No matter how far afield other activities took him, he found it difficult to think of leaving the Association. But when Gertrude Rice and Joseph H. Choate, the Association's new president, advised him to seek election, and when the Board of Managers assured Folks that he could continue his work with the Association even if elected, he decided to enter the race. [15]

After a strenuous campaign, reform advocates were disappointed with the election results. As usual, the Tammany Tiger captured the spoils; the Democrats were swept into nearly every elective office in the city. Only Homer Folks and a handful of other reform candidates won seats in the Municipal Assembly. Folks received many congratulatory messages on his stunning victory. Robert Hebberd, secretary of the State Board of Charities, reflected the sentiments of many when he expressed "the hope and prediction that it is but the first rung of a ladder that may reach dazzling heights." [16]

Although the city's legislative authority was vested in the Assembly, composed of a City Council and Board of Aldermen, to most New Yorkers these, especially the Board, were nothing more than labels for misrule and corruption. In 1851, when it "gave away" the city's first trolley franchise, the Board began its long career of spoliation. Consequently it became known as the "Boodle Board." Boss Tweed, who served his apprenticeship on the Board, once said there "never was a time when you couldn't buy the Board of Aldermen." [17] And when a mayor of New York was asked by a delegation of medical men, alarmed by an approaching cholera epidemic, to summon the Board, which also was the Board of Health, he replied, "I will not call the Board, for I consider it more dangerous to the city than cholera." [18] Despite the perennial pleas of civic-minded reformers, unprincipled aldermen continued to barter away public property for private gain. Although not all aldermen could be classified as disreputable, for on rare occasions "respectable" wards sent honest, intelligent men to City Hall, few men of substance and integrity ran for the office. The Board was dominated by saloon keepers, gangsters, and petty politicians who were in most cases merely the puppets of local Tammany ward bosses. As late as 1890 one of the city's leading newspapers suggested that the word "alderman" be blotted from the dictionary and eight years later a foreign observer visiting the Aldermanic Chamber found it composed of an "inconceivably low-looking set of men . . . [with] one face more repulsive than another in its cynicism, sensuality or greed." [19]

Because "boodling" had become such a well-organized and large-scale business, the Board had been stripped of most of its powers. On the whole, by 1898 the aldermen did little more than grant permits for street stands and confirm the tax rate computed by the Comptroller. The city's new charter stated that most local ordinances could be initiated only by the administrative departments whose work they affected, and the Municipal Assembly could merely ratify or reject the proposals without amendment. In any event, charter provisions mattered little, for when one conscientious alderman discussed a section of the charter before the Board he discovered that not more than half a dozen of its members had ever heard of it.[20]

In 1898 the Board was composed of forty-seven Democrats, two Republicans, three representatives of the Citizens' Union, and eight members elected on a Citizens' Union-Republican fusion ticket. The minority members regarded their position on the Board as the only check upon Tammany and almost always acted as a single party. At times they were joined by fourteen Brooklyn Democrats whose insurgency grew out of ill feeling toward consolidation of the city.[21] With or without the Brooklyn Democrats' support, however, the thirteen minority members often managed to "hold up" financial measures, which required the consent of three-fourths of the members elected to the Board. To assemble at one time forty-five out of sixty aldermen was a difficult task. With dull meetings, a calendar filled with trifles, onerous nonlegislative duties, a meager salary, and difficult transportation, absenteeism was common. As a result, a cohesive minority could at least delay the passage of suspicious financial matters.

In the chamber Folks spoke frequently but seldom at length. More often, he listened to majority members introduce and endorse poorly drawn up resolutions which had been handed to them by the political bosses. He was also occupied with the usual petty aldermanic affairs —obtaining for his constituents permits for street parades and displays, for news, fruit, and peanut stands, and for all building projections, signs, awnings, horse troughs, lampposts, and the like. He also performed personal services (marriage ceremonies) and secured patronage (appointments as Commissioners of Deeds) for the residents of his district. But while some legislators used their limited power and privileges to garner "extra" sources of income, Folks refused to accept any payment for his official services while a member of the Board. To the consternation of some of his constituents, he even steadfastly refused to comply with the traditional aldermanic function of securing for them free railroad passes.[22]

During the session only two important financial measures came before the Board. Both were appropriations for celebrations. One was an appropriation of $175,000 for a celebration in honor of the return of

Admiral George Dewey from Manila. Folks voted in the minority against it.[23] The other financial measure was a proposed appropriation of $50,000 to celebrate under the name of Charter Day the anniversary of consolidation. Although Mayor Van Wyck earlier had refused to favor an appropriation of $150,000 for a new public library on the ground that the city's constitutional debt limit had already been reached, the Charter Day appropriation passed the Board.[24] Folks, a member of the Celebration Committee, voted against it. Good Government Club "A" lauded Folks's action and passed a resolution in his honor, which read: "Whereas our representative in the board of aldermen, Homer Folks, . . . was the only Manhattan member that voted against the charter day appropriation, Resolved, that we commend him for his action in this matter." [25] Two weeks later a widely distributed Citizens' Union circular discussed Folks's "unassailable" official record and mentioned that it "is said on all sides that the work [he has] . . . done . . . in the City Hall is ample return for all our labor and expenses in the last contest." [26]

The Board of Aldermen did however have one important function. The new charter contained a provision, Section 647, which called for the appointment by the Municipal Assembly of a commission to revise the city's building code.[27] Its work, of course, would have a great effect upon the health and safety of the vast population of the five metropolitan boroughs, especially the unfortunate residents of the city's slums. This power to enact a code of building ordinances was by far the greatest legislative power granted to the Assembly, and it also represented its greatest opportunity for graft; the majority lost no time in trying to make use of it. Because of its importance the incident deserves detailed study.

New York's speculative builders were organized in an association known as the Builder's League. This "building ring," according to Lawrence Veiller, professional housing reformer, was probably "the most corrupt 'ring' that was ever known in New York City," and its "affiliations with Tammany Hall were indeed close." [28] In anticipation of the Municipal Assembly's action, the League appointed a committee to confer with it on the provisions of the new building law.

When the matter (Section 647) came to the Assembly's attention in September 1898 a long war began between Tammanyites allied with the city's speculative builders in demand of a "practical law," and architects, engineers, and reformers who were opposed to cheap, flimsy, poorly ventilated, and highly inflammable buildings. The initial, and in many ways the most important, battle for tenement house reform centered around appointing the commission to revise the building code.

A resolution drawn up by the "building ring"–Tammany alliance was hurried through the City Council. Then, in accordance with a prearranged scheme, it was introduced in the Board without previous announcement. The resolution called for the creation of an eight-man paid commission composed of one carpenter, one iron worker, one plumber, one mason, one engineer, one architect, one representative of the Board of Fire Underwriters, and one ex-officio representative of the Corporation Counsel. This commission, appointed by the Assembly, was to draw up the new building code. This maneuver, however, did not go unopposed, for Folks was well acquainted with the subtleties of Tammany politics. The newly elected, impressive thirty-year-old "city father," immediately rose to object to the measure on the grounds that the building interests were too largely represented on the proposed commission. In his opinion, the "manifest unwisdom of asking the building interests to frame laws for the regulation and restraining of their own business for the sake of the public health and safety . . . [was] apparent." [29] The proper parties to make such laws were the persons who naturally desired to see their enforcement, not those who as a rule were always trying to evade them. Although the boodlers jeered and tried to shout him down, Folks succeeded in postponing action on the measure.

From the start, Folks saw the importance of the Municipal Assembly's power in regard to legislation regulating the construction of tenement houses. As a student at Harvard he had spent evenings in Boston visiting the slums, seeing firsthand urban poverty and human wretchedness. Thus he had been provided with the evidence needed to champion the cause of those who lived, worked, and died in those venemous structures. He was all too aware of the slum's spiritual, mental, and physical destructive power: poorly constructed, unsanitary, crowded tenements were breeders of disease and consequently caused illness, unemployment, and reduced earnings; this in turn produced poverty, suffering, vice, crime, and often premature death.[30] Folks could not permit the profit motive to rule without raising his voice in protest.

Folks was certain of one thing: "the importance of securing a proper commission of *experts* to prepare a building code [could] . . . hardly be overestimated." [31] Only such a commission would bring relief from corruption and thus cleaner, more healthy tenements. Accordingly, he recommended to the City Club that it form a committee to study the revision of the building code and assist the Assembly in formulating a proper ordinance. He corresponded with the city's leading architects surveying their opinions in regard to the appointment of the commission. Hoping also that something might be accomplished by the constant pressure of an organized and enlightened public opinion, he addressed letters to and personally canvassed most of New York's leading citizens, humanitarians, and heads of charitable societies and social and civic clubs to prepare them for action in behalf of humanity.[32]

Folks, however, realized that mere obstruction was not enough to solve the problem; a constructive alternative was needed. He began to formulate his own proposal, which would rest upon the principles he believed necessary for sound and scientific housing legislation. He again consulted with leading technical authorities and lay housing reformers, including the prominent and well-informed Richard Watson Gilder, editor of *Century Magazine* and chairman of the 1894 Tenement House Committee, which had written the existing building laws after an exhaustive study of New York's housing conditions and needs.[33]

When completed, Folks placed before the Board of Aldermen an alternative resolution that he felt was "distinctly representative of the interests of the public, as opposed to the interests of a small class of builders, real estate owners, and others directly and pecuniarily involved." The measure, which gave fair representation to the municipal administration, scientific experts, and philanthropic and business interests, called for an unpaid commission composed of six ex-officio representatives of city departments, two members of the Tenement House Committee of 1894, six professional experts (one engineer and five architects), and five representatives of business interests (one of insurance and four builders). "Does it not appear that a commission so constituted," Folks asked Mayor Van Wyck, "is more likely to give due regard to the interests of the public and tenement house dwellers, than a commission in which the building interests predominate?" [34]

On October 21, 1898, the two proposals were discussed at a public hearing that Folks almost singlehandedly secured. His wide contacts throughout the city and his urging of interested citizens to attend the session paid handsome dividends. The Aldermanic Chamber overflowed with spectators and participants. The city's leading architects, engineers, housing reformers, and representatives of charitable societies assured the assembled that their support was behind Folks's measure. Some of his more prominent supporters present at the hearing were Jacob Riis; Frank Tucker, general agent for the Association for Improving the Condition of the Poor; Richard Watson Gilder; George B. Post, president of the American Institute of Architects; John M. Carrere, president of the New York chapter of the American Institute of Architects; F. Delano Weekes, president of the Architectural League; Alfred T. White, housing reformer, chief spokesman for the "model tenement" ideal, and president of the Brooklyn Bureau of Charities; and E. R. L. Gould, well-known housing reformer and president of the benevolent City and Suburban Homes Company. Only three speakers opposed the measure, and all three, representatives of the building and real estate interests, were paid members of the notoriously crooked Board of Examiners in the Buildings Department of Manhattan and the Bronx.[35]

Several weeks later the Assembly's Joint Committee on Law, Public Buildings, Lighting and Supplies, and Public Health met in executive session to consider the two measures in light of the testimony received at the public hearing. Folks, however, knew what to expect, for as another Board member pointed out, "if . . . measures were so important as to arouse the interest of the party organizations, the decisions of

Tammany Hall were [always] reported [out of committee] regardless of the merits of the matter as brought out at the hearings." [36] As Folks expected, his resolution died in executive session. But, instead of recommending the original proposal, without prior knowledge or consideration, Alderman John T. McCall, Tammany chieftain in the Assembly, sprang an entirely new measure on the Board. Pandemonium broke out in the chamber when Folks objected to the new resolution, denounced the venal gang of aldermen behind it, and introduced a motion to adjourn. All parliamentary law was ignored, however, and under gag rule the Tammanyites lined up behind the new proposal and managed to "railroad" it through the Board without discussion. [37]

The new measure appeared to be much better than the original one. It stated that the Building Code Commission was to be composed of a representative of the Corporation Counsel, the three City Commissioners of Buildings, and seven unspecified "experts." Unlike the original proposal, therefore, the measure did not limit the appointments to representatives of specific building trades; rather, the way was at least left open for men of experience in building operations who would consider the public interest. E. R. L. Gould congratulated Folks for the "achievement of a very substantial victory. You have undoubtedly rendered an important public service," declared the well-known housing reformer. [38]

Unlike Gould, however, Folks realized that the battle was far from over, for there was no assurance that the commission would be staffed in the public's interest. The next maneuver was obvious. Folks urged architects and engineers to suggest to the Assembly leaders names of the members they wanted on the commission and to then "use whatever influence they . . . [could] to secure their appointment." [39] In the meantime Folks did not remain idle. He took an active part in creating what proved to be the extremely important Tenement House Committee of the New York Charity Organization Society. He not only conferred with Robert deForest, the society's president, and Edward T. Devine, its secretary, about the wisdom of forming such a committee, but he also helped to select its members. This Tenement

House Committee, formed in December 1898, was manned by outstanding authorities on the housing problem and represented a triumph for effective organization and expertise in housing reform. Long after the battle in the Municipal Assembly ended, this committee continued to serve successfully as a permanent pressure group and lobbyist for housing reform.[40]

Folks's worst fears were confirmed when Assembly leaders appointed the members to serve on the Building Code Commission. The positions were filled by stooges of the "building ring." Except for one obscure architect, all were contractors and there was not a single engineer placed on the commission. Referring to the Assembly's action, the New York *Times* reported that "as usual in Tammany proceedings, character, public spirit, and expert ability went for nothing."[41] Finally, after five months of feverish effort by a determined opposition, on January 10, 1899, the majority succeeded in creating a commission controlled by the building interests to revise and codify Greater New York's building laws.

In September 1899 the Building Code Commission presented its recommendations to the Assembly, which in the words of Lawrence Veiller, who by now had emerged on the battleground to assume command of the reform forces, moved the building code "a distinct step backward."[42] In brief, the new building code virtually abolished all the laws governing the building of tenement houses and gave Tammany Commissioners the authority to allow flimsy and unsanitary structures to be erected. As one of Folks's colleagues maintained, the new code meant that "an architect or builder whose relations with Tammany Hall . . . [were] 'satisfactory' . . . [was] now subject to few practical restrictions as to the character and quality of his building."[43] Although it was severely arraigned at a public hearing, the new code promptly passed both houses of the Assembly and was immediately signed by Mayor Van Wyck. The New York *Times* once again properly summed up the deplorable episode when it informed its readers that the "code was pushed through the Municipal Assembly by the order of [Tammany Boss] Richard Croker."[44]

Although it was not until later that clear advances for tenement house reform were achieved, Folks's struggle for better housing in New York City was not in vain. The support he mustered for his resolution and the protracted Assembly fight he led probably resulted in at least a slightly better commission and building code than would otherwise have been secured. In addition, in the person of Homer Folks, a social worker by profession, the struggle testified to the close relation between political reform, housing reform, and other crusades for social welfare during the era. Moreover, for his leading role in the dramatic Assembly fight Folks deserves recognition heretofore denied him in the history of the tenement house reform movement. One of the earliest, if not the first reformer, to insist upon the idea of expertise in housing reform, the fire of controversy he started and the attitudes he expressed marked all later thinking on the subject.

More important, the incident not only performed a valuable educational service, but soon produced extensive improvements. Thanks to Folks and his colleagues dirt paths were already becoming well-paved roads; the fight over the composition of the Building Code Commission planted the seed basic to the growth of housing reform and the establishment of adequate machinery to administer progressive housing regulation. As a result of this skirmish reformers began to realize that since they could not defeat a corrupt Municipal Assembly, the next logical move was to bypass it. They became convinced that to be effective, to defeat the enemy, they had to extend the battleground to the state level. This was done by the Tenement House Committee of the Charity Organization Society. The result was the establishment of the famous New York State Tenement House Commission of 1900 and the New York City Tenement House Department. And, as the leading student of the subject has recently pointed out, the creation of these agencies finally led to the recognition of the professional technician of housing reform, and "insured that high standards of restrictive housing legislation would be accepted . . . as basic to the safety and welfare of an urban society." [45]

Finally, and perhaps most important of all, was the broad significance of the incident. As more than one authority has attested, the movement for better housing at the turn of the century was foremost among the new developments in social work, for through its various committees and commissions housing reform exerted a great influence on later developments in other fields of social welfare by teaching the lesson that the path to reform lay in research and expert knowledge.[46]

In an effort to defeat Tammany, the Republican and Citizens' Union parties of the 29th Assembly District decided in June 1899 to unite forces in support of a fusion candidate. Members of both parties agreed Homer Folks should be the candidate. Since no one else was acceptable to the fusion forces, Folks reluctantly accepted the nomination, for he did not want to end what was considered the "most significant action taken toward the amalgamation of the anti-Tammany political forces" which promised to start a movement "looking toward the nomination throughout New York City of a good, clean ticket . . . [that] would attract the combined anti-Tammany vote." [47] Folks's decision was hailed with delight by many independents and Republicans throughout the city.

Most people, including Folks, thought he would have little difficulty capturing the Republican district. His opponent in the hotly contested race was Moses R. Ryttenberg, lawyer and Johns Hopkins University graduate who had been defeated in his bid for the post during the previous election. Governor Theodore Roosevelt favored Folks's election. The Independent Labor Party publicly endorsed Folks and obtained enough signatures to have his name appear on its ticket. A prominent group of independent Democrats led by Carl Schurz came out in support of Folks's candidacy. So did such other leading New Yorkers as Felix Adler, founder of the Ethical Culture Society, ex-Mayor William L. Strong, Seth Low, Edward Lauterbach, and Chauncy Depew.[48] Yet, when the returns were counted they showed that Folks lost by about 150 votes; more than 7,000 had been cast. Folks lost the Assembly race for several reasons. Most important was a factional fight within the Republican party. During the campaign the reformers refused to endorse the Republican candidate for the aldermanic seat Folks vacated. As a result, many Republicans in the district did not support Folks. In addition, when fusion was decided upon, the Assembly seat was held by Frank Bulkley, a straight Republican who

had become obnoxious to the party. When Bulkley was discarded by
his party in favor of the fusion candidate, his supporters refused to
support the ticket.[49]

Still another incident played an important part in ending Folks's
legislative career. After the 1897 municipal elections, captured by
Tammany, the Republican-controlled state legislature sought to em-
barrass the Democrats by creating a special committee to investigate
New York's administrative affairs. Although the Republican-domi-
nated committee, known as the Mazet Committee, disclosed the
existence of maladministration, its investigation was inefficient and
unduly partisan. As a result, the Citizens' Union succeeded in defeat-
ing Mazet's bid for re-election.[50] As one well versed in New York
politics testified, this too hurt Folks: "In New York City, the Citizens'
Union actually turned in with Tammany to beat Mazet. This was
not only bad in itself," explained Governor Roosevelt, "but it irritated
machine Republicans to turning in and beating Homer Folks."[51]
Folks's career as a public official seemed to be at an end.

In 1898 Van Wyck had become the first mayor of Greater New York
because in part, at least, Boss Platt and the Republican machine refused
to unite behind Seth Low's reform ticket. Most people agreed that the
record of the Van Wyck administration, even when tempered by the
most conservative estimates, remained an unsavory one. The police department scandal involving the notorious Commissioner Devery was
only one among many similar incidents. Popular disapproval of
Tammany rule was at a high point. As a result, when Seth Low was
renominated by the Citizens' Union in the fall of 1901, the Republicans
and all anti-Tammany forces united behind him on a platform which
"subordinated every purely partisan interest . . . in the belief that the
government of a great municipality should be conducted on purely
business principles."[52] After one of the most exciting campaigns in
New York's history, Low's victory ended Tammany rule—temporarily.

Early in 1901 a Revised Charter for New York City had been
adopted, which in the interests of centralization, efficiency, and economy replaced the city's three Commissioners of Public Charities by a

single commissioner. Commenting on that change, Folks wrote in September 1901 that "given a competent commissioner, without doubt important economies and improvements will result from such consolidation."[53] Two months later John W. Keller, a Democrat and president of New York City's three-man Board of Commissioners of Public Charities, confided to Josephine Shaw Lowell "that [since] the election is over and all my efforts to defeat Mr. Low have [failed,] . . . I want to say that . . . the best man to succeed me as Commissioner of Charities is Homer Folks." In his opinion Folks was "competent, honest, and better acquainted with the condition and need of the Department of Public Charities than any other man" in New York.[54]

Many others agreed with Commissioner Keller and a move was immediately launched to present Folks's name to Mayor-elect Low "as the man peculiarly fitted by education, character, and experience and by very great ability to make an admirable Commissioner of Charities."[55] Carl Schurz, Charles S. Fairchild, Mrs. William B. Rice, Louisa Lee Schuyler, Joseph H. Choate, Robert Fulton Cutting, Robert W. deForest, Jacob Riis, and Alfred T. White were only a few among many of New York's leading citizens who favored Folks's appointment, and either wrote to or personally saw the Mayor-elect on his behalf.[56] It was, therefore, no accident, especially in light of Folks's work for the needy and his great knowledge of the subject, that several weeks later Low decided upon him for the position.[57]

The appointment was widely applauded. Folks received hundreds of congratulatory messages from all over the city, state, and nation. Alfred T. White and Felix Warburg were just two among many others who agreed with Carl Schurz that the "city must be congratulated" rather than Folks, for choosing "conspicuously the best man for the office." New York's press also welcomed the appointment. An *Evening Post* editorial reflected the general feeling when it maintained that "of the many good appointments Mr. Low has made, none is more preeminently proper and fitting than the selection of Homer Folks as Commissioner of Public Charities." *Charities,* the official organ of the social welfare movement, summed up in the following manner the reaction of the nation's periodicals to Folks's appointment: "The appointment of Mr. Homer Folks . . . is a conspicuous instance of a recognition of expert ability in a field in which experts are still few in number." [58]

Folks faced an enormous task. He was in charge of hospitals, almshouses, and other institutions that contained over 9,000 inmates, had more than 2,000 employees, and expended more than $2,000,000 annually. He not only had to overcome the usual inertia of a municipal department, but under Tammany the city's public charities, neglected, inadequately supported, and used for political purposes, had fallen into terrible disrepair. Cruelties and abuses in the department were well known and administrative details would necessarily occupy much of his time. But in outlining his proposed policy Folks made it clear that the Department of Public Charities was not solely a "matter of business." It was, in fact, as he made plain, "primarily a matter of charity"; it was securing kind and intelligent treatment for every recipient of city aid.[59]

Folks's reforms began the day he assumed office. He dismissed employees for violating the department's rules and also removed from the payroll several "extra" persons hired by Tammany for political purposes. The department's books, in extreme confusion, were audited. He discovered that a great deal of money, especially funds belonging to the inmates of various institutions, had been embezzled. Folks immediately placed the funds on a business basis and instituted a new system of receiving and accounting. Several months later the bookkeeping, auditing of bills, and preparation and awarding of contracts were centralized in the main office under the immediate direction of the commissioner. Irregularities in furnishing supplies to the city's charitable institutions were ended. He had no desire to save money at the expense of worthwhile activities, but he insisted that every dollar appropriated be spent wisely.[60]

Next, Folks attacked the old abuse of transferring dying patients from one hospital to another. This grew out of the staff's desire to keep the death rate of their institution as low as possible. As a consequence, critically ill patients often were shuttled from one hospital to another, resulting in cruelty, danger, and premature fatality to many patients.

Simply by issuing an order that required a full report to be made to him by the superintendent of any hospital receiving from any other hospital a patient who died within three days after admission, Folks succeeded in reducing the number of transfers and thus prolonging many lives.[61]

Another abuse Folks quickly ended was the "undertakers' trust." A small number of undertakers situated near the city morgue maintained mutually profitable relations with some employees of the Charities Department. Upon the death of an inmate at a public institution, one of the undertakers would immediately be notified by the city employee in his pay. The undertaker would then call upon a relative of the dead person, often at unseemly hours of the night, and sometimes even before the official notification of death; undertakers also forged death certificates and removed bodies from the morgue, charging poor families extortionate prices for burials. In addition, they charged the city for the burial of Civil War veterans when, in many cases, they had already received payment for the service from relatives or friends of the dead person. Through a simple system of tags and receipts Folks eliminated most of these abuses.[62]

Shortly after taking office Folks began to investigate the various institutions' food supplies. In most cases he found that inmates received an insufficient quantity of food. Throughout 1901, for example, breakfast in the almshouse consisted of coffee with a little sugar or milk and bread without butter. Lunches were a bit better, but the food was of bad quality. Supper was the same as breakfast, with tea substituted for coffee. Folks increased the supply and provided a choice of foods for the inmates. Moreover, through better purchasing and distributing methods and by hiring a dietitian for the first time in its history, the department was able to provide food in a more wholesome and attractive manner without increased expenditures. In addition, chairs with backs were substituted for stools, while knives, spoons, and forks were supplied in sufficient number and crockery was substituted for the tin dishes that had always been used in the past.[63]

Because none of the department's employees wore uniforms and many of them were of questionable character, on his inspection visits

Folks often had difficulty distinguishing the employees from the inmates. As a result, uniforms were adopted for officers and employees, raising the department's standard of discipline. Moreover, to decrease the number of incompetent and untrustworthy staff members, Folks employed an agent to hire more qualified help.[64]

Folks reorganized the Department of Outdoor Poor, which in the past had been terribly mismanaged. He changed its name to the Bureau of Dependent Adults and gave orders that all applications for relief were to be examined carefully and impartially with due consideration to the feelings of the applicants. The names of numerous institutions were also changed so that all terms of reproach were removed from them. He issued an order to the interns, orderlies, and all other personnel of the various institutions prohibiting them from referring to the inmates as paupers. At all times the inmates were to be treated respectfully; they were not to be reminded that they were dependent upon the city.[65]

The Bureau of Dependent Children was reorganized. It investigated cases of children brought before it for commitment as public charges to a city or private institution. Formerly the bureau had been attached to the Department of Outdoor Poor, but Folks made it a separate agency, the head of which was directly responsible to the Commissioner. A complete card system of records was adopted. A list was kept of children under eighteen years of age who had been placed by the department in family homes, and a plan was adopted for visiting and overseeing these children. The bureau, working in close cooperation with New York's private charities, placed- or boarded-out a great majority of the city's dependent, neglected, and foundling children. More examiners were hired to ensure that the State Board of Charities' rules were carried out by the city's private child-caring institutions.[66]

The public institutions on Randall's Island were reorganized and improved. These included hospitals for the care of destitute, sick, and crippled children; hospitals for the care of sick and abandoned infants; institutions for the training of the feeble-minded; and institutions for the custodial care of the idiotic. Folks appointed the Island's first visiting dentist, and for the first time toothbrushes were provided.

Convalescent wards for skin and eye cases were established. A clinical and pathological laboratory was opened. More attention than before was given to educational work among the children on the Island.[67]

The new Commissioner of Charities improved the physical plant of the city's institutions, especially its hospitals. Fire escapes and sun parlors were added to the buildings, many of which were repainted and provided with more and better furniture and equipment. The Metropolitan Training School for Nurses, which supplied nursing service to the city hospitals, was reorganized and provided with increased facilities. Antiquated and insufficient heating systems were replaced. Additional quarters to replace the existing overcrowded and unsanitary ones were provided to the hospitals' medical staffs. Care of feeble-minded, epileptic, and insane patients was immensely improved through better classification and segregation and the hiring of well-trained and competent employees.[68]

When Folks assumed office there was no separate city hospital for tuberculosis patients. Over three hundred were scattered throughout the city's hospitals, and about half of them were in wards occupied by other patients, thus inviting constant danger of contagion. The remaining ones, isolated in separate wards, were nevertheless in buildings that housed other patients. By taking advantage of three vacant public buildings on Blackwell's Island, Folks remedied this situation. Only a month after becoming Commissioner, he opened one of the buildings as a hospital for consumptives, thus establishing the nation's first municipal tuberculosis hospital. Within a week all the tuberculosis patients not in isolated wards were transferred to the new tuberculosis infirmary. Soon the second building was opened for the remaining consumptives. Other facilities such as cottage tents, solariums, and wards for convalescents were also provided. Consequently, for the first time the city's tuberculous wards were able to have surroundings well adapted to their needs, a special diet, and, most important, appropriate sanitary precautions which minimized the chances of contagion.[69] For this innovation, which Folks considered his "most important achievement," he received the highest praise from medical as well as lay men. To cite one example, the *Medical Times* declared that the establishment of the Tuberculosis Department of the Metropolitan Hospital is "the most important advance in the general care of the city's sick poor which this generation has been privileged to see and which will distinguish for all time Mr. Folks's administration in the annals of the Department of Public Charities." [70]

On a city-owned Staten Island farm of 114 acres Folks established the New York City Farm Colony. He sent there all able-bodied dependent men, including epileptics, who successfully grew and supplied fresh vegetables to the city's various charitable institutions. The farm not only saved the city thousands of dollars each year, but it provided work and pleasure to its inmates. In addition, Folks built a cottage colony on the farm, which provided accommodations for the aged and infirm not requiring hospital care and, for the first time in history, allowed indigent husbands and wives to live together. "To say that there is joy among the inmates of the almshouse is putting it mildly," a New York paper reported in commenting on this innovation.[71]

Folks also improved the city's lodging house and increased the department's ferry boat service, which made it easier for physicians, relatives, and friends to visit inmates at many of the city's institutions. Classes in vocational training for the blind were instituted, the products of which were used by the department. Folks provided week-end band concerts during the summer for the inmates of the Home for the Aged and Infirm and carried out a host of similar "minor" reforms. Officials from all over the country came to New York to tour its public institutions and meet its indefatigable and efficient Commissioner of Public Charities.[72]

In the fall of 1903 when John S. Clark, the Mayor's campaign manager, made public a letter that had been sent to Low by a former patient of the municipal tuberculosis hospital, Folks inevitably became a key figure in Low's bid for re-election. The letter testified to the appreciation felt by those who actually came in touch with the improvements Folks initiated. The writer appealed to the friends of the poor to "vote and do all in their power to elect Mayor Low again, so that the good man and humanitarian, Homer Folks, . . . can continue in office and keep on the noble work he is doing." [73] In an editorial the *Outlook* also pointed to Folks's "brilliant" record as one reason Low should be re-elected.[74]

Although Low's administration was not perfect, it was honest, able, and in Lincoln Steffens' words, "undeniably one of the best in the whole country." [75] Yet, for several reasons, Tammany returned to power in 1904, with the election of George B. McClellan, Jr. Low's cold, austere, and aloof personality alienated many of his earlier followers. Other backers left the reform forces when they failed to place a Democrat at the head of the ticket in 1903. In addition, because of his political naïveté and pledge to disregard patronage, Low never managed to rid the government of hundreds of Tammany officeholders. Consequently, many New Yorkers were disappointed in the administration and the fusionists never built up the machinery needed to stay in power. Unlike in the previous election, there were no sensational scandals to excite the voters. Moreover, the Tammany boss, Charles F. Murphy, Croker's successor, healed the party rift and reunited the Hall, taking many disaffected Democrats back into the fold. Finally, and most important, however, was the nature of the administration. Honest, efficient, and economical government proved no substitute for the favors Tammany provided to the working class.[76]

Low's defeat did not mean that Folks's efforts were unappreciated. Not only did medical and lay authorities pass many resolutions expressing their appreciation for the "unusual services" rendered by Folks,[77] but the president of the Medical Society of the County of New York along with representatives of the city's leading charitable societies began a movement to get Mayor-elect McClellan to retain him in office. Despite the support of newspapers and periodicals, McClellan refused and Folks resigned.[78] Of the many editorials and letters of regret that poured into Folks's office, the one from Josephine Shaw Lowell, a woman well versed in charitable affairs, was the most fitting: "It is the greatest disappointent to me that you are no longer to act as friend and protector for all those helpless human beings," she wrote, "but it is a comfort to think that much you have done for them can not be undone." [79]

The municipal reform movement in New York was primarily a conservative reaction to boss rule. Most of the reformers were merely interested in clean, efficient, and economical government. Perhaps Lawrence Veiller's words were too strong when, speaking about the reformers, he remarked, "while well-intentioned, [they] never got anything done." [80] Yet, aside from a few notable exceptions, their chief contribution was educational; in general, their activities were more verbal than practical.

To an extent, Folks fit the mold of the municipal reformer type. He had faith in American capitalism; his basic economic creed was individualism, and he was sufficiently patrician and conservative to attract support from the "better classes." But he was different in that his desire to do good was not abstract; his social consciousness went beyond theirs; his interests far transcended the mugwumpish fetish for "good government." He was interested in social welfare. Unlike most of the other political reformers, moral-minded individuals who dabbled in politics out of a sense of noblesse oblige or a desire for "business-government," Folks was a dedicated, full-time professional reformer who gave himself unselfishly to the needy and the helpless. His was the larger crusade for an efficient utilization of the nation's human as well as physical resources.

Had he remained in politics, Folks would have made a good professional politician. Former Governor of New York, Secretary of State Charles Evans Hughes, recognized this when, speaking of Folks's influence in Albany, he told an audience in 1923 that Homer Folks "is the most successful politician I know." [81] Folks had the energy and industry needed for political life. Also, his temperament was well suited for political advancement. He made few enemies; as a result of his tact and mastery of facts even those he disagreed with respected him. He could do the proper thing well without offending anyone. Moreover, he learned that all politicians are open to and must accept criticism: it was part of the political game. As a result, he could engage in hard-fought campaigns. Finally, he was an excellent political strategist. He rigidly defended principles but was flexible and opportunistic when it came to details.

Although Folks was considered as a fusion candidate for mayor in 1905, when he relinquished the Commissionership he never again held public office.[82] Yet his short political career was important and personally valuable. In two years he transformed New York's Department of Public Charities from a neglected, backward, and politically corrupt Tammany tool into the nation's leading and most progressive charities department. From beginning to end, that transformation was a tribute to his inexhaustible talent for organization and administration, tireless dedication, and political shrewdness. Folks was not only a legislative draftsman, organizer, and strategist of pressure groups, he was a talented administrator as well.

Folks's strong and earnest appeal that the Department of Public Charities be removed from political influence was not, in the future, always heeded. Nevertheless, it comforted him to know that the department never again sank to its previous depths.[83] At present, the department's Bureau of Dependent Children and use of the boarding-out plan are just two among many lasting tributes to Folks's administration. Furthermore, his tenure in office provided a valuable case study that was often pointed to by those calling for the trained expert in public administration. In the long run, this may have been Folks's greatest contribution.

Personally, Folks's activities in municipal reform further taught him the fundamentals of the political game. This strengthened the political adroitness that typified his work. His excellent grasp of machine politics, mastery of the processes of government, and a political shrewdness and sagacity were invaluable complements to his idealism.[84]

Above all else, Folks's political career reinforced his later work with the State Charities Aid Association. For from his experience he learned firsthand that a bureaucracy like the Department of Public Charities, unless continually prodded, would become rigid; routine would replace initiative and imagination. In other words, Folks's experience as a public servant confirmed the wisdom of the State Charities Aid Association's founder and the faith of its secretary in the value of a permanent voluntary association to look after the interests of public reform: such an organized, well-informed body of private citizens was needed. "I believe in our public institutions of charity," said Folks in 1904, but, he continued, "I [also] believe we [the SCAA] can [help] make them better." [85] However, as his work in the fields of probation and child labor legislation indicates, improving municipal charities was not the only way Folks helped those in need.

5

JUVENILE COURTS
AND CHILD LABOR

AT the beginning of the nineteenth century there was not a single institution in the United States for the reformation of juvenile delinquents. Children convicted of offenses were committed, along with adult offenders, to jails and prisons. The history of improvement in juvenile reformation during the last century may be summarized in a single sentence—youthful offenders were removed from association with adults convicted of crimes and were placed in special institutions or private homes, where they were treated from an educational and reformative rather than a punitive point of view.[1]

With the growth of special institutions for juvenile delinquents (New York's House of Refuge, established in 1824, was the nation's first juvenile reformatory) and the breaking down of the prison atmosphere, juvenile delinquency came to be recognized as a social problem requiring more delicate machinery than mere criminal law. Progressive penologists and charity workers demanded that children be tried in courts apart from those for adults. Massachusetts was the pioneer state in the establishment of special court procedures for juvenile offenders; in the 1870s it required separate hearings for children's cases. However, the first full-fledged juvenile court in the world, the Cook County Juvenile Court, was established in Chicago in 1899. A year later the Juvenile Court of Denver, Colo., presided over by the famous Judge Benjamin S. Lindsey, was founded. Since the main trend in child care from 1890 to 1905 was emphasis on home rather than institutional care for needy children, and since Folks and other child welfare workers demonstrated the advantages and possibility of placing- and boarding-out youthful offenders, judges of these courts increasingly permitted offenders to remain in their own homes under a suspended sentence. The juvenile court movement and use of the suspended sentence were rapidly advancing at the turn of the century.[2]

Important steps in securing better treatment for juvenile delinquents in New York State began in 1900 when the boroughs of Manhattan and the Bronx established a system of separate hearings for youthful offenders. At first no separate courts were created to deal with children's cases. Rather, all children arrested for any offense were taken to a police station and arraigned in a Magistrate's Court under the same procedure applied to adult criminals. However, New York City's revised charter, which took effect January 1, 1902, conferred upon the Court of Special Sessions the power to try all except capital cases affecting children under sixteen years of age. Thus, in 1902, with the removal of children from the jurisdiction of the city's seven Magistrate's Courts, New York began a modified children's court system.[3]

In 1903 the State's Penal Law was amended to provide for the extension of such "juvenile courts" to the rest of the state. But elsewhere, like in New York City, no separate children's courts were yet established. A part of the (criminal) Court of Special Sessions was set aside for the hearing and treatment of cases involving children. The judges of the Courts of Special Sessions were assigned by rotation to hear children's cases.[4] The noted and popular Franklin Chase Hoyt was one judge of the Court of Special Sessions who often presided over the children's part of that court. But administration of the cases suffered by recurring changes of authority and the lack of opportunity for judges to study intensively the special needs of each defendent. Furthermore, children were still arrested and taken to police stations before court proceedings began. Many New Yorkers interested in child welfare sought to bring the state's backward system up to date by separating entirely juvenile cases from the criminal courts. Thanks to the agitation of the Committee on Criminal Courts of the Charity Organization Society of New York, led by Lawrence Veiller and Homer Folks, the situation was improved when separate buildings for the trial of juvenile offenders were established and special justices designated to hear only children's cases.[5] This latter step was taken in 1912, when four justices of the Court of Special Sessions were relieved of all duty in the criminal court and assigned for exclusive service to the children's division. An act of 1915 made the juvenile court system of the city a separate division of the Court of Special Sessions. The connection between the two was in name only; the new children's court was in fact an entirely separate one.[6]

Finally, in 1921 a constitutional amendment was adopted authorizing the state legislature to set up a system of children's courts as independent entities with full power to handle and adjudicate their own cases. In accordance with this amendment, in 1922 the legislature passed an act providing for the establishment of a statewide system of juvenile courts.[7]

The object of the juvenile court movement was to avoid the stigma of crime by conducting proceedings separately from those for adult offenders. In fact, criminal procedure was dispensed with, and the hearings were held in an informal atmosphere. The role of the judge was, on the whole, that of a parental guide; treatment was individualized as much as possible. Re-education rather than retribution was the aim of the juvenile court; it was not to punish offenders, but to save them.[8] Along with the aim of treatment instead of punishment of the juvenile offender, the principle of prevention was implicit in the movement. One of the major objectives was to check adult crime by giving a constructive direction to the life of the potential criminal while he was still in the formative stage. Proponents of juvenile courts realized that measures for the protection of individual children were also measures for the protection of society as a whole.

Since at the base of the juvenile court was the theory that the individual child and his needs should be considered, rather than the offense and its legal penalty, the establishment of such courts was obviously a part of and gave added emphasis to the movement for the noninstitutional care of delinquent children. As Folks clearly pointed out, juvenile courts had two main functions. One was based on a determination of fact: does this boy or girl come under the legal definition of a child in need of the community's protection? The other function was to provide such protection. The first was a judicial function; the second was an administrative one. Wherever possible the administrative function (re-education) was to be carried out in the delinquent child's own home.[9]

A necessary adjunct of the juvenile court, therefore, was an effective system of probation, the instrument through which the juvenile court applied most of its treatment. The nation's first juvenile court was authorized to appoint "one or more discreet persons of good character" to serve as probation officers. Other juvenile courts followed suit. In almost all cases, however, probation officers received no, or very little, compensation because those promoting the early laws feared the cost involved might defeat the bills and also, because if paid adequately from public funds, officers might be selected on a political basis.

New York's first probation law, passed in 1901, was a permissive one which stated merely that every city in the state could, if it chose to, appoint probation officers to help adult offenders paroled from prison adjust to their new environment. In 1903, however, a statute was passed extending the probation system to all offenders, regardless of age. In New York, though, as elsewhere, most courts were not supplied with enough funds to employ an adequate number of probation officers and, as Folks pointed out, it was impossible for presiding judges to properly oversee probation. Moreover, such oversight and direction was an administrative, not a judicial, function.[10]

For Folks, probation—"the most striking fact in the history of child-saving work in the United States"—was not an act of clemency by the judge; it was a positive measure for individual and community welfare.[11] Although neither a rigid personal moralist nor an absolute environmentalist, Folks was convinced of the relevance of social and economic conditions to ethical conduct; he understood that individuals were largely products of their environment rather than simply independent moral agents who diverged from or adhered to fixed moral norms. When someone was brought into court for committing a "wrong act," therefore, it was not just a personal but a community matter, for it probably was brought on by a long train of influences and factors, personal and social, which had exercised an unfavorable influence upon the offender: crime, like poverty, to which it was often related, was "a joint product of the individual and his environment." [12] The delinquent was someone who needed assistance in finding his proper place in society. To provide this, Folks maintained, it was best not to remove the child offender from his home; in fact, inquiry into home conditions and changing environmental factors were necessary to help the child. Unfortunately the institutional method of dealing with offenders recognized only the individual element in wrongdoing. The probation system, on the other hand, which involved a suspended sentence and permission for the child to return to his home under the oversight of a probation officer, Folks pointed out, "takes into account both the individual and his surroundings, regards his offense as the joint product of his individuality and his environment, and seeks to influence both factors so that they will work together for good." [13] Folks's belief that, along with individual adjustment to prevailing conditions, favorable changes in the social environments of youngsters could prevent delinquency and presumably promote social progress, richly illustrates that he was already committed to social meliorism, the hallmark of the larger progressive reform movement sweeping the nation during the early years of the twentieth century.[14] Folks, however, was quick to point out the possible dangers of the system and he warned that it was no panacea for the reformation of all offenders. He felt that probation, like all placing-out, should not be implemented haphazardly or superficially, and its operation and effectiveness needed careful study.[15]

Unfortunately, where probation was used to help delinquent children there was widespread diversity in its practice. Sometimes it was properly implemented, more often it was not. Sometimes it was a political plumb; friends of the judge or political hacks were appointed officers. On the whole, however, it was a volunteer effort; officers were untrained private citizens, court clerks, or police officers. Frequently, individual cases were referred by magistrates to the "Gerry" and other anti-cruelty societies for investigation and supervision. As a result, there was a compelling need to work out a satisfactory plan for administering probation work; for outlining the duties of probation officers, securing special training for them, holding probation officers to the faithful and efficient performance of their duties, discovering the limitations of the system, and in general making it a vital factor in the conduct of those placed under its care.[16] Given his penchant for order, his regard for child welfare and home care, and his larger social concern for humanity, it is no surprise that Homer Folks turned to this important need.

In 1905 Folks suggested to the Governor of New York that he appoint a committee to study all phases of the subject and examine the operations of the system in the different courts in various localities throughout the state. The idea met Governor Frank W. Higgins' approval. Accordingly, a bill was passed providing for appointment by the governor of a special commission "to investigate and report upon the operations of the probation system" throughout New York State.[17]

Folks was appointed to and elected chairman of the fourteen-member commission, which included such noted reformers as Samuel J. Barrows, secretary of the New York State Prison Association, Lawrence Veiller, and Frederick Almy, executive secretary of the Buffalo Charity Organization Society.[18] The commission began hearings on November 1, 1905. After four and a half months of testimony and intensive study, its completed report was sent to the Governor.[19] The lengthy document, referred to by the New York *Post* as "an excellent specimen of the invaluable work constantly being done for the state by unsalaried and public spirited workers," condemned the probation work practiced in the state as irresponsible and inefficient.[20] The commission concluded that better results would be obtained if the power to appoint probation officers were taken from the magistrates. Specifically, it recommended the creation of an unpaid probation commission in each city of the first class (New York and Buffalo) with the power to appoint and remove officers and to establish general probation rules and regulations. New York City's probation commission should consist of seven members appointed by the mayor from suggestions submitted by charitable agencies. The mayor of each second-class city should appoint a five-man probation commission. In counties without large cities, the county judge should appoint the commission, again from a suggested list. The report ended by recommending that the State Board of Charities supervise the entire system.[21]

The probation commission was a temporary body which passed out of existence after submitting its report. Immediately, however, Folks drafted and had introduced in the legislature a bill, the Cox probation bill, which embodied the commission's recommendations. He and other representatives of the State Charities Aid Association and leading charitable societies defended the proposed measure at public hearings before the Senate Judiciary Committee.[22] But the forces of reaction were too great. Judges of Special Sessions and Magistrate's Courts, police station and politically appointed probation officers, and Gerry Society spokesmen violently opposed the measure. In favor of retaining magistrates' control over the appointment of probation officers and fearful of state supervision, they managed to have the bill defeated.[23]

At Folks's suggestion, in the fall of 1906 the State Charities Aid Association appointed a special committee on probation legislation. Felix M. Warburg, banker and SCAA Board member, served as chairman, and Folks as secretary. This committee prepared a bill, drafted by Folks, which, like the defeated Cox probation bill, put into effect the principal recommendations of the 1905 probation commission. It called for an efficient system of state supervision of probation work, which Folks considered the most important feature of the earlier report. However, instead of placing the duty upon the State Board of Charities, it provided for the creation of a new permanent state probation commission to exercise this function.[24] Bitter controversy and heated debate arose when the bill was introduced in the legislature. After it had failed twice Folks personally took the bill to Governor Hughes, who used his influence to get it through the legislature. The measure became law on June 6, 1907.[25]

The law called for the creation of a permanent seven-member Probation Commission, the first such commission in the United States, to consist of four persons appointed by the Governor, one by the State Board of Charities, one by the State Superintendent of Prisons, and the

Commissioner of Education, ex-officio.[26] All members were to serve without compensation. Folks was appointed to the commission and summoned to the executive chamber by Governor Hughes to help select the rest of the staff; later he was elected its president and served in that capacity until 1917.[27] Specifically, the commission's duties were to "collect and publish statistical and other information as to the operations of the probation system; to keep informed of the work of all probation officers; [and] to inquire from time to time into their efficiency." [28] Thus, broadly speaking, the commission's chief duty was not so much to promote the wider use of probation, but to standardize it and to secure a harmonious and effective system throughout the state.

To a large extent, the probation officer going into the child's home was, in Folks's words, "the very essence of the probation system." [29] He was not merely an investigator or a dispassionate observer, but an active influence on the delinquent child; he was a creative practitioner who therefore had to be well trained. For that reason, as Folks realized, probation work had to be made appealing. The work had to be freed from political control and the compensation made sufficiently attractive to encourage competent people to undertake probation work as a career.

Under Folks's leadership, the commission succeeded in establishing an effective system of probation manned by skillful and well-trained personnel. Thanks to these efforts, which aroused a great deal of interest in the subject, New York and other cities throughout the state increased their appropriations for probation work.[30] The establishment of a complete and adequate system of probation records was achieved for the first time. Civil service examinations were drawn up and salaried probation officers were appointed on a competitive basis from eligible lists. In 1908 Folks framed and introduced a bill, which became law, authorizing the counties to provide salaries for probation officers. As a result of this bill, considered by Folks "the most important legislation secured by the . . . State Probation Commission," the way was opened for the appointment of full-time competent probation officials in rural areas as well as urban centers.[31] In 1904 there was not a single paid probation officer in New York State; by 1908 there were 35. A year later the number was 75, and by 1921 there were 249 salaried officers.[32] Skilled and adequate probation staffs as effective tools of juvenile courts were thus achieved; probation became a well-organized, rational, and efficient system.

As a result of the commission's activities, over 16,000 persons—juvenile and adult offenders—were placed on probation in 1913.[33] By January 1919 more people were on probation than were in prison.[34] Commission studies "proved" the effectiveness of probation in more ways than one. In addition to its greatest value, improved conduct and citizenship, the probation system had important financial advantages. In 1918, for example, the entire cost of administering the system was $206,976. The average number of persons on probation during the year was 9,434, and the average per capita cost of a year's probation work was $21.94, one-tenth the cost of a year's imprisonment.[35]

At the turn of the century probation and juvenile courts were only parts of a larger concern for the problems of childhood. The growing emphasis on the preventive aspect of health and welfare services, and a more general appreciation of the need for conserving human resources, led many to give increasing attention to the exploitation of minors as one of the by-products of industrialization.

On the whole, Folks had thus far channeled his efforts in one particular stream—the protection of dependent, neglected, and delinquent children. By the early years of the twentieth century, however, he began recognizing that every effort to achieve what is comprehensively termed social and industrial justice, indeed, all movements for social betterment, were directly and immediately related to child welfare. As a result, he entered eagerly into other related activities. One of the first to engage his attention was child labor. "Effective and adequate child-caring work," he declared in 1904, must include the enforcement of proper child labor laws; "they are an essential part of the child-caring system."[36] And while Folks was not at the center of anti-child-labor activities, his efforts along those lines were important enough, both for his own development as well as for the history of the movement, to warrant mention here.

For the most part, Americans had always assumed not only that poor children had to work, but that, within reason, work was good for all youngsters; work removed young boys and girls from the unwholesome influence of the streets. In short, it was a cure for juvenile delinquency and female promiscuity. In addition, American economic conditions and the old Puritan notion that idleness was sinful and somehow related to poverty seemed to demand approval of child labor. Nevertheless, numerous legal restrictions on the employment of minors testify to the fact that by the late nineteenth century some abuses were not completely being ignored.[37]

Most early attempts at restrictive legislation, however, were sporadic and unsuccessful. As a result, at the turn of the century ten- and twelve-year-old children frequently toiled under brutalizing and unhealthy conditions twelve hours a day and seven days a week, especially in the cotton textile mills, mines, glass factories, and tenement ("home-work") shops of the garment and artificial flower industries. These conditions were either totally unregulated by law or regulated by ineffectual or unenforced statutes. Such terms as "minimum wage," "maximum hours," and "industrial disease" were unknown.[38]

The National Consumers' League was one of the earliest and most important agencies working to establish child labor legislation. Its general secretary and leading spirit was Florence Kelley, licensed attorney, former chief factory inspector of Illinois, and socialist daughter of the long-time Republican congressman from Pennsylvania. As early as the 1890s she advocated government responsibility for ending the callous exploitation of child labor.[39] She and others, including Jane Addams, Grace Abbot, and Julia Lathrop, embarked upon a campaign of public education to prepare the community, intellectually and ethically, to accept and enforce factory laws.

So widespread was the evil of child labor, and so powerful the interests profiting from its continuance, that other organizations devoted to the cause were needed. The campaign was taken up by humanitarian-minded citizens all over the nation. Edgar Gardner Murphy, an Episcopalian clergyman shocked by conditions in Alabama's textile mills, became leader of the fight in the South. Convinced of the need for a more informed public opinion, he formed in 1901 the Alabama Child Labor Committee, the first organization of its kind in the United States.[40]

In the North, reformers in New York led the way. At the suggestion of Florence Kelley and the head of New York's Nurses Settlement, Lillian D. Wald, the Association of Neighborhood Workers, which was composed of representatives of New York's thirty-one settlement houses, appointed in the spring of 1902 a temporary committee to investigate the city's child labor situation. Under the leadership of Robert Hunter, head resident at University Settlement, the committee's first study confirmed among other things what many reformers had suspected; contrary to the convenient and most widely used rationalization of proponents of child labor, the earnings of most children were not essential to the support of their families.[41] The results of the investigation convinced many of New York's reformers that they, too, needed a permanent child labor committee. Consequently, in November 1902 an independent organization known as the New York Child Labor Committee was organized.[42]

Like the Alabama committee and similar ones being established elsewhere, the New York organization, made up at first mainly of social workers, reformers, and academicians, immediately enlisted the support of prominent and wealthy men and women, as well as newspapers and religious and civic groups.[43] It waged a campaign of education and propaganda and then turned its energy to legislation. Despite violent opposition from business interests, the Gerry Society, many school authorities (who feared that child labor legislation would lead to overcrowded schools), and those who objected to child labor legislation on the grounds of interference with personal liberty and parental control, the committee was eminently successful; it harmonized the state's incongruous factory and education laws, widened existing legislation, succeeded in partially regulating some previously unregulated areas, and strengthened the penal code dealing with violators of child labor legislation. In less than a year this fledgling committee had five bills passed, which brought about more significant changes in New York's child labor laws than had occurred in the preceding century, making New York in this area the most advanced state in the nation.[44]

Folks, an early and effective spokesman against child labor, and one whose opinions, because of his prominence and public stature, carried great weight, applauded the committee's actions and became an active publicist of its work. Echoing the prevalent message, Folks frequently told audiences that child labor was "cruel, stupid, and uneconomical." Over and over again he hammered home the point that every dollar spent in preventing such labor, and in promoting the health and education of children, was not only a humanitarian, charitable, and ethical gesture, but also that it was essential for community health and welfare, social stability, and orderly progress.[45] Folks joined the battle against the employment of children in mine, factory, street, and field, as he had the tenement house crusade, because it aimed at improving youngsters' lives. He sought regulation consistent with protecting children against exploitation in their early years and guaranteeing to them immunity from such labor as would interfere with their proper physical, mental, and moral growth.[46]

He constantly pointed out the bad economic and social consequences of child labor. Long hours of highly taxing daily labor, as well as the moral dangers involved in going to and from employment at night, tended to stifle bodily and mental growth and injure the child's full development. This, in turn, often led to delinquency, dependency, and a purposeless life. Related, and equally important for Folks, was that children who labored from sun-up to sun-down were either deprived of, or else too tired to receive, an education, something to which all children, rich or poor, had an inherent right. He believed the one great job of childhood was to become fitted for life; this was accomplished through education, not labor.[47]

Folks believed the question of child labor was in part a relief problem. He was one of the few social workers who from the beginning directly accepted this challenge. Though the number of parents aided by their children's wages was greatly exaggerated, he did not deny that each advance in child labor standards decreased the income of at least some families to the point where they had to be given help from the outside. But he believed the burden should not be put on the shoulders of children; rather, it should be borne by the community. In his mind, the disadvantages of outdoor relief were far outweighed by the dangers and permanent harm caused by child labor. Thus, a year before the first such provision was enacted anywhere in America, he supported the idea of giving "scholarships" to families, in amounts either equivalent to the child's earnings or based on the family's needs, which would enable the child to attend school and allow the family in question to live in accordance with reasonable standards.[48]

Aside from humanitarian considerations, Folks's view of such relief was that "an ounce of prevention was worth a pound of cure." In comparison to the enormous costs of ill health and dependency, the expenditures entailed in giving such relief were superficial; in the long run they paid handsome dividends. The sick and the infirm received the greatest amount of relief, costing the taxpayers millions of dollars each year. But one of the greatest causes of illness and infirmity, Folks pointed out, was a childhood interrupted by hard labor that only the resources of a fully matured body could meet. The high incidence of tuberculosis, heart strain, curvature of the spine, and permanent bone and muscle injury verified his contention. It was therefore economical to abolish child labor. Folks thus enunciated the main lines of his theoretical attack; it was harmful to children, it was unnecessary, and since a rise in illness and poverty heightened the financial burden of every member of the community, to permit it was contrary to the public interest.[49]

Folks was convinced that having the support of prestigious individuals and organizations, and getting laws passed, were not enough to abolish the heinous evil. The *enforcement* of child labor laws was equally important. Consequently, he gave as much time to expounding enforcement programs as he devoted to efforts to secure new statutes and improve existing ones.[50] He felt that to expect voluntary compliance was visionary; strict supervision and control were necessary. Thus two conditions had to be met. First, adequate governmental machinery had to be provided. To accomplish this Folks called for large appropriations to create an effective public department to carry on systematic inspection of all industries employing children. To successfully resist all attempts to undermine the department by injecting spoils politics or corruption into its administration, it had to be staffed by a large corps of well-paid, full-time public officials selected for the work from a civil service list.[51] Second, an alert watchfulness on the part of all citizens was needed. This could be accomplished by educating the public. In the final analysis, then, according to Folks the outcome of the child labor movement depended upon the community, for we all "create the public opinion which, in the long run, dictates the laws . . . and manner of their enforcement." [52]

Despite the success of the New York and other child labor committees, reformers grew increasingly aware of the need for a larger organization that would spearhead a nationwide campaign and coordinate the activities of the various state and local groups. As a result, when Murphy followed up his child labor work in Alabama by presenting a powerful address on "Child Labor as a National Problem" at the 1903 National Conference, he was enthusiastically received. A year later the movement had grown to such proportions that his suggestion was accepted and a National Child Labor Committee was founded.[53] Under the leadership of Dr. Felix Adler, head of the Ethical Culture Society, professor of political and cultural ethics at Columbia University, and leading figure in the New York Child Labor Committee; Lillian Wald; Jane Addams; William H. Baldwin, Jr., president of the Long Island Railroad; Murphy; and Folks, who played a leading part in the organizational meeting and was extremely active in helping build up a strong committee, the national committee won the support of prominent men and women in all parts of the country.[54] The National Child Labor Committee represented a new phase of legislative effort for a social reform. It secured so prominent and influential a national membership that it commanded a respectful hearing in every state of the union.

A board of trustees, under the chairmanship of Adler and vice-chairmanship of Folks, and composed of members who lived near enough to New York City to attend the meetings, determined the general policy and legislative goals and directed the work of the organization in the intervals between annual meetings. For the first three years the real day-to-day work of the committee, however, was under the guidance of its general secretary, Samuel McCune Lindsay, professor of sociology at the University of Pennsylvania and then of economics at Columbia University. Ably assisting Lindsay in supervising work in the South was A. J. McKelway, Presbyterian clergyman-social worker, while Owen R. Lovejoy, an Albion classmate whom Folks talked into giving up the ministry for a career in social welfare, was at Folks's suggestion named assistant secretary in charge of the committee's work in the North. And in retrospect it seems that one of Folks's most important contributions to the cause proved to be this suggestion in 1904 that Lovejoy be appointed to the staff of the national committee. A dynamic figure and an extremely popular and effective public speaker and propagandist, Owen Lovejoy became the committee's chief executive in 1907 and remained so until 1926. While building a strong and large staff, with field investigators, legislative agents, writers, speakers, and money raisers, he lectured all over the country and his name became synonymous with the child labor reform movement.[55]

Although Folks was not one of the chief "public spokesmen" on child labor once the committee had become a strong organization with a competent staff to perform most of its functions, he nevertheless remained involved in its work. He regularly attended board meetings, actively and persuasively participated in its discussions, served on many special board committees appointed to consider numerous specific problems, was always available to the chief executive and staff for advice and counsel—which were frequently sought—influenced other distinguished people to join the board, and often recommended and always supported suggestions for an expanded program and new approaches to eliminate child labor. Finally, with Lindsay's resignation in 1935 of the chairmanship of the National Child Labor Committee, Folks accepted the position and held it until 1944. And while at this time he did not directly participate in its daily activities, because of his age and preoccupation with the more immediate affairs of the SCAA, Folks nevertheless remained the board's guiding light, greatly helping the committee remain an important organization during this trying period.

The purpose of the National Child Labor Committee was to supplement the work of local committees. In those states where such committees did not exist, it sought to promote their organization and help them to "investigate and report the facts about child labor," "assist in protecting children by suitable legislation against premature or otherwise injurious employment," and "aid in promoting the enforcement of laws relating to child labor." [56] Through research, study, publicity, and propaganda the committee aimed to educate the public on the sources and consequences of this social evil.[57]

The national committee's earliest efforts were directed at securing state minimum age and hours legislation and the prohibition of night work. By 1909 it helped secure new child labor laws, or amendments to previous statutes, in forty-three states. Although the first ten years of its existence saw the greatest advance ever achieved in this country in the adoption of child labor laws, progress in state child labor regulation was slow and uneven.[58] Although the more progressive states passed relatively satisfactory laws, many of the southern states remained backward. As a result, states with high standards suffered from the competition of the low-standard southern states and every effort to improve a state law brought objections from manufacturers who feared this "unfair" competition. Moreover, by expending its money and energy in securing the passage of laws, the national and local child labor committees were unable to successfully follow up on their enforcement; in many places factory inspection was weak and corrupt. Having discovered that state regulation thus was an inadequate solution to the problem, especially after the 1910 census and the publication in 1913 of a federal investigation by the Secretary of Commerce and Labor into the actual conditions of women and child workers clearly showed that the infamous situation in all its wretchedness still prevailed and the gap between the more progressive and more backward states was growing wider, not narrower, reformers slowly shifted to the possibility of uniform federal action.[59]

From the outset, Folks considered child labor a national problem.

With the growth of industry on a nationwide basis, the new problems created in its wake lay beyond the reach of individual states. Moreover, from his experience with dependent and delinquent children, particularly the slow removal of children from almshouses, he recognized that the progress of social reforms requiring legislative action offered peculiar difficulties in a nation in which more than forty separate states acted independently of each other. Consequently, he and a mere handful of other reformers, such as Florence Kelley, Jane Addams, and Samuel McCune Lindsay, saw long before most others that there was a need for uniform national legislation.[60]

Although the Knights of Labor focused attention on the need for federal action in this area as early as 1880, it was not until 1906 that federal child labor legislation was introduced in Congress. Sponsored by Senator Albert Beveridge of Indiana, the measure, designed to prohibit the interstate transportation of articles produced in factories or mines employing child labor, received Folks's hearty endorsement.[61] The National Child Labor Committee, however, was not yet ready to concede Beveridge's contention that the states were unable to deal with the problem. Moreover, it was thought that to support federal legislation in a field heretofore considered the domain of the states, would handicap the committee in its work in the South, where the worst child labor abuses were found. The committee, therefore, did not actively support the measure and it went down to defeat. Eight years later, despite opposition from southern members, the NCLC reversed its stand and from then on (1914) supported federal child labor legislation.

By 1912 Folks was more firmly convinced than ever that to unite local reform groups and overcome the frustration and disappointment of detached and partial effort, reform had to be carried to the national level. In that year, for the first and one of the few times in his career, except for his aldermanic race in 1897, and against the advice of more timid and conservative-minded friends and colleagues, he publicly supported a partisan political party.[62] Folks not only helped launch and support Theodore Roosevelt's Progressive Party, but he played an important role in making the new party stand for real social reform.

Along with more noted reformers such as Gifford and Amos Pinchot, Jane Addams, William Allen White, Paul Kellogg, and others, he helped write the social and industrial planks of the party platform, planks which, by the way, had their origin in a committee of social workers—the Committee on Standards of Living and Labor—appointed at the National Conference in 1909.[63] Thus many of the measures for industrial and social justice which Folks and his colleagues had for so long worked, including the abolition of child labor, were placed before the public by a national political party.

The planks that Folks helped write were, at the time, considered by Roosevelt and his followers, and since have been considered by most students of history, the most important of the entire platform, a platform that, boiled down to a phrase, called for the "use of government as an agency of human welfare."[64] The Bull Moose Party saw industrial and social problems as national, not local, issues and its platform was perhaps the most radical any major party had yet presented to the electorate.[65]

Like other third parties, the Progressive Party demonstrated that new parties ultimately write the history of future administrations. After his victory, President-elect Woodrow Wilson met informally with a group of prominent social reformers, including Folks, most of whom had supported Roosevelt. They urged him to support a number of important social measures, including federal child labor legislation. Those who attended the meeting, the *Survey* reported, "came away with the feeling that under the Wilson administration the proposals of social workers would receive 'not only an interested but a thorough consideration.'"[66] Wilson may have been influenced by the group. His first term in office was at least characterized by a series of measures, including federal child labor legislation, that induced Folks and many other Bull Moose supporters to vote for him in 1916.[67]

While the history of the National Child Labor Committee (and federal child labor legislation) is interesting, and important, this is not the place to detail it.[68] It is sufficient to say that although the national committee did not succeed in abolishing all child labor, it nevertheless achieved a great deal. The committee's national campaigns, which resulted among other things in the passage of two federal child labor laws, a proposed constitutional amendment, the child labor provisions of the National Recovery Administration's industrial codes and the Fair Labor Standards Act, as well as a great deal of state legislation, did much to rally the public to the support of the movement to protect children from the dangers of premature employment. If the impulse that led to the formation of the committee was a reflection of a demand for change, the committee in turn created new public interest in child labor. Attacking the evil on a patient trial-and-error basis, it accomplished as much as was possible.

Folks's child labor activities clearly indicate that by the early twentieth century he had come to the conclusion that the conditions making child-care work and charity necessary must themselves be eradicated. He, along with other pioneer social workers, elaborated and worked to implement reform programs that were a vital part of the progressive era; and, as his ideas about reform and his efforts on behalf of the Bull Moose Party point out, he supported that brand of progressivism which emphasized the importance of the national government in bringing about change.

Along with his work to eliminate child labor, Folks engaged in many other good causes devoted to the same end. They, too, indicate how far he was willing to go to enrich the lives of all children.

6

SAVING BABIES AND
PRESERVING THE FAMILY

BY the early years of the twentieth century a growing number of welfare workers believed that no family should be broken up simply because it was destitute. They contended that whenever possible children should be helped in their own homes, even if this had to be done through the distribution of outdoor relief. Responsibility for this form of relief, they felt, could and should be undertaken by private agencies. The "home care movement" received further stimulus and general acceptance as a result of the historic 1909 White House Conference on the Care of Dependent Children.

The idea to call a White House conference on children came from James E. West, a Washington lawyer and close friend to Theodore Roosevelt who was to become head of the Boy Scouts of America.[1] After promising to make West judge of the first juvenile court to be organized in the nation's capital, and then remembering that he had already offered the position to somebody else, President Roosevelt said apologetically to West, "You have got a draft on me anytime you want to call; anything you want come in and ask it."[2] An orphan who had grown up in an institution, West was interested in the problem of caring for destitute children. He thought that a conference on the care of dependent children might be useful and attract widespread attention, especially if held in the White House at the call of the President. Accordingly, he suggested to Roosevelt that such a conference be organized. The President, a former State Charities Aid Association member, expressed some interest in the idea. As governor of New York, Roosevelt had relied heavily upon Folks's advice; he now told

West to bring the matter to Folks's attention. Roosevelt promised to endorse the conference if Folks favored the proposal.[3]

Folks caught the spark of West's idea and from the beginning threw himself wholeheartedly behind the plan. He immediately contacted prominent child welfare workers throughout America, nine of whom joined in a letter to the President requesting that he call such a conference. The letter, written on December 22, 1908, reminded Roosevelt that, generally speaking, through juvenile courts, probation officers, and reformatories, the cause of the delinquent child had been well advanced. This was not the case, however, with regard to the class of unfortunate children who made no trouble: "Their care and protection," it was pointed out, was "left in many localities to the fidelity of voluntary agencies without requiring proper standards of method or efficiency, and without definite responsibility to the state or community." Folks and his colleagues felt the problem was acute and worthy of national consideration, and, in the end, they hoped the President would "cooperate in an effort to bring the problem before the American people."[4]

Roosevelt, a firm believer in family care, doubted the value of such a conference. Nevertheless, impressed "with the very great importance of the subject," he agreed to sponsor a meeting to discuss the matter.[5] Consequently, he invited over two hundred prominent men and women from all parts of the country to Washington on January 25 and 26, 1909, to consider the best type of care for dependent children.

Folks spent a great deal of time in Washington working on preparations for the conference. On January 10, 1909, he, West, and Thomas Mulry were called to the White House and officially appointed a Committee on Arrangements.[6] In addition, President Roosevelt made Folks first vice-chairman and presiding officer of the affair. In that connection Jane Addams related a small, but amusing and revealing, incident which occurred at one of the conference sessions. As the speakers were waiting to file onto the platform Miss Addams heard Folks mutter to himself, "Are we all here? Yes, here is my Catholic speaker, my Jewish speaker, the Protestant, the colored man, and the woman. Let's all go on."[7] While for obvious reasons

Jane Addams' agony was that women always came last, for Folks, having "all" people represented was probably more important than the order in which they ascended the platform. In any event, years of apprenticeship had given him an understanding of how vital accommodation and "politics" of this sort were to the business of social welfare; he had mastered his trade.

As presiding officer, Folks was pre-eminently adept in handling the meetings. When discussions became cloudy he cleared the atmosphere in a few sentences. He had an uncanny ability to pick out the basic problem or fundamental aspects of the subjects under discussion, making complex issues dramatic and understandable. His influence was felt and what he said had an effect. He largely shaped the conference which, for the first time, brought the entire subject of dependent children before the nation. Under his guidance and leadership the White House Conference on Dependent Children gave to social work a dignity and place in the national life that it never before had.[8]

By providing an interchange of ideas among leaders in the field and recommending a general plan for the care of dependent children, the conference served both of its purposes. Hastings H. Hart, pioneer child welfare worker, was chairman of the Committtee on Resolutions which drafted a report, unanimously adopted by the conference members, containing a fourteen-point program that served as an index to the progressive thought on child welfare at the time. Although Hart received the credit, it was in fact Folks who wrote that memorable report which proclaimed as its keynote, "Home life is the highest and finest product of civilization" and "children should not be deprived of it except for urgent and compelling reasons"; except in unusual circumstances, "the home should not be broken up for reasons of poverty." As for children who for sufficient reasons must be removed from their own homes, or who have no homes, the report stated "it is desirable that . . . they should be cared for in families whenever practicable. The carefully selected foster home is for the normal child the best substitute for the natural home." [9] Finally, the committee also recommended the plan Folks had originated fourteen years earlier, that child-caring agencies, public and private, be incorporated, with state approval, and the state be given the power to inspect their work.

It was the unanimous opinion of those familiar with conditions in 1909 that the conference had far-reaching practical effects. The strong recommendation in favor of family, instead of institutional, care solidified nationally the movement for placing-out dependent children. It not only contributed greatly to the notable development of adoption agencies, but it stimulated even more the development of the boarding-out system for children unavailable for adoption. The expansion of the cottage plan in place of the congregate institution was another outcome of the conference, which in these and other ways undoubtedly aided substantially in the development of higher standards of child care. Moreover, the 1909 conference established a precedent, still maintained, for decennial White House conferences concerned with child problems and needs, all of which have had a far-reaching effect on concepts of child care and the formulation of progressive child welfare programs.[10]

One of the most important effects of the first White House Conference, however, was the creation three years later of the United States Children's Bureau. In 1909 a children's bureau was not a new idea. Although at first the National Child Labor Committee did not support proposals for federal regulation of child labor, it did from the beginning favor the creation of a federal children's information bureau. The committee felt that much of its energies and resources were being expended in collecting information that might be better collected by a governmental agency. Therefore, at the suggestion of Florence Kelley and Lillian Wald, the National Child Labor Committee drafted a bill proposing such an information bureau. The committee took the measure as its main legislative goal and devoted two years, 1904–1906, to marshaling support for it among important individuals and child welfare agencies throughout the nation.[11]

In 1906 the National Child Labor Committee finally managed to get the bill into Congress. Folks, whose work on behalf of child labor legislation indicated he believed in the necessity of federal aid as a means of social progress, recognized that many might argue that child labor legislation was a matter for the various states; "the collection of *information* upon which such legislation can be based," however, was in his opinion, clearly "a Federal duty." [12] Many others did not agree. Opposition to the measure was violent, mainly from the same forces opposed to the regulation of child labor. Although the bill had a great deal of popular support, nearly three years elapsed and it hadn't even received a hearing.

Then in 1909 the force of the White House Conference on Dependent Children was brought to bear on the matter. Since it was impossible to secure from state authorities any uniform or comprehensive statistics on, among other things, the questions of child dependency as well as child labor, the White House Conference strongly recommended that the proposed bill for the establishment of a federal children's bureau be passed and that a special presidential message on its behalf be sent to Congress.[13] In response to the resolution, Theodore Roosevelt sent a message to Congress urging the passage of the measure: "It is not only discreditable to us as a people that there is now no recognized and authoritative source of information upon . . . subjects related to child life," the President informed the nation's legislators, "but in the absence of such information as should be supplied by the Federal Government many abuses have gone unchecked; . . . public sentiment [and, he should have added, scientific investigation] with its great corrective power, can only be aroused by full knowledge of the facts." [14]

Thanks to the White House Conference's well-publicized recommendations and President Roosevelt's support, Congress no longer could entirely ignore the bill. Congressional hearings were scheduled early in 1909. Folks and a number of other people who attended the White House Conference testified at the hearings. Recognized as a knowledgeable person and a man of extraordinary integrity, Folks commanded the respectful attention of even his opponents when he spoke. Over the years he had appeared many times before committees —public and private—and he was always ready to be challenged. He knew his facts and worked hard to prepare them for presentation, no matter whether he faced a committee that was friendly or hostile. Famous for his quick, good-humored replies, he was not only a welcome platform speaker but also an effective voice at long and tedious committee meetings. His testimony set the stage for a renewed assault upon congressional opposition to the extension of any federal action in the field of social welfare in general and hostility to this measure in particular.[15]

Giving what Frank Bruno has called "a classical outline of arguments of the opposition," Folks, in mocking fashion, stated that some opponents of the bill claimed it went too far; others, that it did not go far enough. Some maintained that the subject was covered adequately by existing laws; others declared that the objective was good but that it should be achieved under different auspices. Finally, still others felt that the public could not afford the additional expenditure, that it would destroy our form of government, and, in any event, that it was unconstitutional. As Folks's analysis of the delaying tactics employed to defeat the measure indicated, none of the objections were based on the actual merits or demerits of the proposal.[16]

In support of the proposed bureau, Folks continued with wry humor and impressive logic, stating that in his opinion children were more important than animals. He argued that the federal govenment and the public apparently disagreed. To cite an example, he pointed out that through the Bureau of Animal Husbandry, which had a staff of over 1,000 and an annual appropriation of $1,427,860, the national government engaged in animal research. At the same time, on constitutional and financial grounds, Congress had in the past refused to pass the children's bureau bill, which called for an appropriation of $50,000 and a staff of 14. Pointing out that the death rate for young animals was much lower than for babies, Folks asked why animals were suitable for federal protection but not children? Emphasizing the long history of federal aid for the "general welfare," the importance of facts, and the serious lag in child welfare knowledge, he concluded with a ringing declaration for federal aid for the conservation of childhood.

After several more years of effort on its behalf, by 1912 most public health and welfare workers, and various social and civic organizations, labor unions, and other groups actively supported the measure. Finally after more hearings, agitation, publicity, and five days of bitter floor debate, the bill passed the Senate on January 31, 1912. Two months later it passed the House and the nine-year struggle came to an end on April 9, 1912, when the measure was signed into law by President Taft.[17] In the words of the bureau's historian, Miss Dorothy E. Bradbury, "the [Children's] Bureau had two mothers—Lillian Wald and Florence Kelley. But among the men who fathered the idea . . . and gave the support so urgently needed to get presidential support . . . [was] Homer Folks." [18]

The Children's Bureau was given the modest appropriation of $25,640 and placed in the Department of Commerce and Labor, from which it was transferred the following year to the newly created Department of Labor. It had no administrative power. Rather, the bureau was directed to "investigate and report . . . upon all matters pertaining to the welfare of children and child life among all classes of our people." It was charged especially with investigating "infant mortality, the birth rate, orphanages, juvenile courts, desertion, dangerous occupations, accidents and diseases of children, employment, [and] legislation affecting children in the several States and Territories." [19] The bureau's responsibility, then, was to establish the facts and call the nation's attention to the conditions affecting the lives of all children.

Despite its limited function, the establishment of the Children's Bureau was an historic event; it marked a new departure in government policy. For the first time the federal government recognized the importance of children and the advisability of creating special machinery to study and protect them. Even more important, however, was the fact that this was the first occasion in which the federal government entered the broad field of welfare services, as distinguished from public health or education.[20]

President Taft appointed Julia Lathrop, former Hull House resident and member of the Illinois State Board of Charities, to head the new bureau. Miss Lathrop was faced with the task of laying the path the bureau would follow in the years ahead; she frequently turned to Folks for help in charting its course. Folks felt that to keep congressional support, the bureau must at the outset avoid controversy and establish a reputation for scientific disinterestedness and factual accuracy. Thus he pointed out to Julia Lathrop the advisability of avoiding for the time being child labor studies. He suggested, instead, giving the highest priority to the study of infant mortality.[21]

Actually, by about 1910 the "baby-saving" campaign in America had become fairly well organized. Real progress in the promotion of infant health began in 1908 with the establishment of the Division of Child Hygiene in New York City's Health Department. This was the first time a great municipality admitted that child hygiene was worthy of, and required special attention from, a health department.[22]

This event was followed by the historic Conference on the Prevention of Infant Mortality, held in 1909 at Yale University at the call of the American Academy of Medicine. Attended by leading social workers, educators, sociologists, and civic leaders as well as medical personnel, the conference resulted in the creation of the American Association for the Study and Prevention of Infant Mortality.[23] In large part, thanks to Folks's efforts, over the next two decades this and other associations became important educational agencies which helped to markedly reduce the infant death rate. In addition to serving as president of the American Association for the Study and Prevention of Infant Mortality (1915) and playing a major role in the formation of its branch societies throughout the nation, Folks induced the Russell Sage Foundation to finance various projects for the prevention of infant mortality.[24] Also, after the Children's Bureau accepted his advice and undertook as one of its first projects a house-to-house inquiry on what selected American cities were doing to prevent infant mortality, it too provided from that time forward an important impetus to the child hygiene movement throughout the nation.[25]

In Folks's mind, the importance and underlying purpose of the infant mortality movement was its preventive, rather than remedial, nature. He assumed that through education and a general public health program many infant deaths were preventable and moreover, that they could be prevented speedily, at moderate cost, and with relatively little effort. In fact, Folks declared, "there is no other way of

reducing the general death rate so quickly, so surely, and so cheap-
ly." [26] In addition, however, he pointed out that infant welfare work
was not simply an effort to prevent mortality. It was also aimed at preventing infantile illness and misfortune, which often caused diminished
vitality or incomplete development. In other words, the movement
aimed "at constructively raising the standards in all matters affecting
infant welfare," in the knowledge that by so doing it was dealing in a
positive way with some of the conditions that led to dependency,
neglect, and delinquency. In short, he felt that protective health
services for infants was an essential part of a community child welfare
program, that the interests of social welfare workers overlapped with
those of physicians.[27]

Early Children's Bureau investigations showed a shockingly high
maternal as well as infant death rate; the death rate from maternity
was higher than that of any other cause except tuberculosis, and it was
the highest of all civilized countries in the world. It was also found
that a large proportion of infant as well as maternal deaths resulted
from remedial conditions existing before birth. The protection of
infants and mothers, then, were inseparable. The means for protecting
both lay in instruction and supervision of the mother before the birth
of her child, and suitable care during and immediately after confinement.[28] Because Folks of course knew that saving lives of mothers
was, among other things, a most important child welfare measure, he
supported efforts to eliminate the serious social problem of women
dying unnecessarily during childbirth.

As a result of the information obtained through the bureau's infant
and maternal mortality studies, Julia Lathrop drew up and published
in her 1917 annual report a plan for the "public protection of maternity
and infancy." The program was designed to aid the states to establish
maternal and child health services, particularly in their rural districts,
by offering federal grants-in-aid to states whose provisions for such
services met specifications set up by the Children's Bureau. The federal
grants were to be administered in most instances through state health
departments. While the program was mostly educational in nature, it
also included demonstration centers, clinics for prenatal care, more

public health nurses to serve pregnant women and new mothers and their infants, and the inspection of maternity homes.[29]

In 1918 this infant and maternity bill was introduced in Congress. During the campaign for its enactment it met with intense opposition, including highly organized propaganda of misinformation; the absurd charge that the bill was "Russian in origin" was made part of the official record in Congress as well as elsewhere. A large part of the medical profession opposed the bill and invoked against it the bugaboo of "state medicine" and interference with private practice. After three years of agitation and debate, however, on November 19, 1921, the Maternity and Infancy Act, popularly known as the Sheppard-Towner Act, became law.[30] Through numerous speeches, State Charities Aid Association resolutions, and communications with various legislators, Homer Folks helped arouse support for the measure. More important, when New York State refused to accept its allotment of federal grants, Folks and Hermann Biggs, the state's great Health Commissioner, shamed the administration into appropriating its own money for the purpose; thus the Sheppard-Towner Act accomplished its goal in New York as well as elsewhere.[31] Moreover, in 1927 Folks also was instrumental in getting congressional support for extending for two more years the original five-year limit on the authorization for the bill's appropriation.[32] Although initiative for the measure lay elsewhere, Folks's support was important.

Unlike the Children's Bureau, the Sheppard-Towner Act brought the federal government to the child welfare problem through the field of health. It was also significant because it was the first time the federal government provided "direct" aid for child welfare. Equally important was the role it played in arousing the lay public's interest and activity in an area that traditionally had been considered the function and responsibility of the medical profession. Although the measure's appropriations were for various reasons not continued after 1929, its influence did not die. On the foundation laid by the Infant and Maternity Act was erected the cooperative federal-state program for maternal and child health under the Federal Social Security Act of 1935; Title V of the SSA included a provision for federal aid to be administered through the Children's Bureau to the states for infancy and maternity work.[33]

The Children's Bureau and the infant and maternal mortality movements were in large part offsprings of the 1909 White House Conference on the Care of Dependent Children. That gathering also gave added impetus to another highly significant development in child welfare-work which swept the country within a decade following the conference—the widows' pension movement.[34]

The main theme of the 1909 White House Conference had been that "home life is the highest and finest product of civilization" and the "home should not be broken up for reasons of poverty alone." The conference, however, reaffirmed the older practice of keeping families together by means of private charity, not public relief. Shortly thereafter, however, some people began to doubt the adequacy of private resources to meet the problem and threw their support behind a campaign for (public) mothers' allowances, or widows' pensions, on the grounds that public outdoor relief was not as harmful as removing children from their own homes and placing them in institutions or even foster homes. However, aside from a few notable exceptions, such as Jane Addams, Grace Abbott, Julia Lathrop, and some of their colleagues, at first most charity workers vigorously fought such suggestions for aid to dependent mothers.[35]

Although he once shared the prevalent view of public outdoor relief, Homer Folks was among the earliest social workers to favor widows' pensions. A staunch believer in the maintenance of the home, Folks's opposition to public outdoor relief waned rapidly when he realized that private resources were inadequate to cope with the problem. As a result of insufficient funds, dependent mothers were forced to seek employment. Most of these women could not earn enough money to support their children and at the same time provide adequate supervision for them. The results of forcing women to make the attempt were frequent cases of mothers breaking down under the double burden of being wage earner and homemaker, and children becoming demoralized and delinquent; both, in the end, required further assistance and/or institutional care. It was therefore cheaper as well as better to give dependent mothers adequate pensions enabling them to remain at home and properly care for their children. Going one step further, a year before the first mothers' aid law in America was enacted, Folks suggested that to avoid the stigma of pauperism that still clung to the recipient of public assistance, such payments should be "pensions" regarded as earned "for meritorious services in bearing children and rearing them through infancy." Moreover, Folks also advocated giving such aid in accordance with the actual need of individual families, further raising mothers' pensions above the status of ordinary public aid.[36]

Widows' pensions, then, as much a preventive as an ameliorative force, were viewed by Folks as a proper assumption of the public's responsibility for those who were dependent through no inherent personal fault. He was convinced that it was a new kind of public assistance which by its enactment would not only end the separation of mother and child on the grounds of poverty alone, but would help promote the kind of home surrounding needed for proper child development. Thus it represented an important step forward not only in the child welfare, but also in the larger social welfare movement, and Folks worked to secure its adoption. Obviously, by now Folks had adopted the view that outdoor relief, properly utilized, actually possessed constructive possibilities for personal and family rehabilitation.

Meanwhile, the mothers' allowance movement had been gaining ground steadily. In 1911 Missouri and Illinois enacted the first laws in America, permissive ones, allowing aid for dependent children in their own homes out of public funds. Other states quickly followed their lead. Within two years, laws authorizing financial assistance from public funds to widowed mothers had been passed in seventeen other states.[37] In 1912 a bill authorizing the New York City Department of Public Charities to dispense outdoor relief to dependent mothers was introduced in the state legislature but failed. The legislature, however, created a commission to study the question throughout the state.

Folks followed closely the activities of the Special State Commission on the Relief of Widowed Mothers. The commission's *Report* declared that the existing forms of outdoor relief and private charity in New

York State were financially inadequate. It recommended "the immediate enactment into law of the principle of state aid to the dependent
children of widowed mothers." A model bill—popularly known as the
Child Welfare Act—incorporated in the commission's *Report* failed to
pass the state legislature in 1914 but was enacted the following
year.

The Child Welfare Act of New York provided for the setting up of
local boards of child welfare which were authorized to grant allowances to widowed mothers. Two important factors influenced the
creation of separate local boards of child welfare, set up outside the
state's existing poor relief machinery: (1) the desire of widows' pension advocates to remove the stigma of "poor relief" from this form of
child welfare, and (2) the distrust felt by many toward the dispensing of public outdoor relief by officials who might be subject to political influence. The terms of the act governing allowances were quite
restrictive and eligibility was limited to widows.[38]

Folks was unhappy over many of the Child Welfare Act's provisions. In view of the fact that he had called for the removal of the
"pauper taint" from such relief, it is difficult to comprehend why he
objected to the establishment of city and county boards of child welfare
to administer the funds. He objected to the restrictive terms of the
measure, however, for an understandable reason; Folks favored the
principle of adequate relief for all needy mothers, not simply widows.
He wanted to include those mothers who had illegitimate children,
whose husbands were sick, in prison, or were for other reasons unable
to support their families. As a result, the State Charities Aid Association immediately had introduced in the legislature a substitute bill that
provided adequate relief for all mothers with dependent children, but
it failed to pass.[39] In subsequent years however sections of the law
gradually were liberalized. Restrictive clauses were removed one by one
and eligibility was extended to include additional categories of needy
mothers. For example, in 1927 Governor Alfred E. Smith signed the
Fearon-Hofstadter bill, which empowered Child Welfare Boards to
grant allowances to mothers whose husbands were suffering from
tuberculosis.[40]

The Child Welfare Act marked a definite turning point in public welfare policy. In New York, like similar acts elsewhere, it opened the way toward removing from a large section of dependent children the stigma associated with charity, it broke down long-standing traditions in New York City and other communities against public outdoor relief, and it indicated a turn to a broader policy of relieving the needy individual in his own home whenever possible.

Moreover, like the Maternity and Infancy Act, mothers' pension laws laid a firm foundation for the child welfare program under the federal Social Security Act. The recommendations presented by President Franklin D. Roosevelt to Congress as the basis for the Social Security Act represented months of study by the President's Committee on Economic Security, which included, among others, Harry Hopkins, Federal Emergency Relief Administrator, who previously had served as the first executive secretary of New York City's Child Welfare Board created in 1915 under the provisions of the Child Welfare Act. In the fall of 1934 the Committee on Economic Security called a group of interested people to Washington for a series of meetings to assemble facts and make proposals for federal legislation on a children's program. Folks, a member of the committee's Advisory Committee on Child Welfare, attended these meetings and was the opening speaker at one of the sessions. On the basis of the facts and proposals presented at these meetings, and information supplied by the Children's Bureau, the committee's report recommended the expansion of the widows' pension system through federal, state, and local cooperation. Title IV of the Social Security Act—aid to dependent children—established a federal program of cash payments to mothers deprived of their husbands' support.[41] Thus, with federal participation, the widows' pension movement was carried to its logical conclusion and the chief recommendation of the 1909 White House Conference, that needy children should be maintained in their own homes whenever possible, received its fullest recognition.

The concept of child welfare or, as he defined it, "the realization on the part of all children of all their possibilities," [42] was fundamental to Folks. He devoted his entire career to building practical programs and procedures to implement that ideal. Starting with the individual and remedial measures to provide home life for dependent and delinquent children, Folks later saw the elemental importance of the family as the basic institution of society and he moved to the larger concern for preventive health measures to conserve not only childhood, but the home in its totality. Few things point this out as clearly as his advocacy of complete medical supervision for all people.

Although several European countries had universal school medical inspection in the nineteenth century, it was not until well after the turn of the century that such a program developed to any significant extent in the United States. At first, the primary purpose of such inspection was to seek out in young children unrecognized cases of contagious diseases. Some time later, however, it was recognized that school medical inspection had far greater possibilities for doing good; the idea slowly grew that it was the community's responsibility to look after the general health of its school children. By the second decade of the twentieth century the program in the United States included extensive health education and dealt with everything connected with the child's medical well-being—mental illness, heart, eyes, teeth, nutrition, and the like.[43]

The work of school medical inspection met with a great deal of opposition, especially from Christian Scientists, who objected on religious grounds, and from practicing physicians, who objected to it on the supposed grounds of "statism." Folks defended school medical inspection and called for its extension.[44] More important, as early as 1910 he felt it was so wise to prevent and quickly treat illness in adults as well as youngsters that he called for an adequate system of medical oversight and care for all persons through a system of medical socialism. He no doubt shocked many when he declared, "I am distinctly in favor of socializing the medical profession, just as we have socialization of education."[45] In Folks's mind needless illness and death were not only inhumane, but in the long run a far greater burden to the community than an adequate system of medical oversight and care. He was filled, then, with both moral passion and a cool pragmatic realism: this was no paternalism, but an act of self-protection for the greatest good.

As a crusader, Folks continued to go forward with the years, traveling an ever-widening but straight path. By the early twentieth century he obviously was convinced that child dependency, neglect, and delinquency were largely products of the breakdown of family life. The assurance of security and the prevention of conditions inimical to life and health, then, were of major importance to child welfare. Welfare workers therefore needed to concern themselves not only with the protection of children, but also with their parents and the whole community. As he put it years later in an address before the Child Welfare League of America, "While our immediate problem may be to secure the best type of care for dependent children, our work will only be half done if we do not concern ourselves with preventing children from becoming dependent because their fathers and mothers die too soon." [46] Just as Folks saw the interrelationship of social and medical protection in the field of child labor regulation, he now recognized that the social well-being of children depends upon the foundation which is built for the preservation of the family and the community by eliminating all preventable hazards to life and health. Complete medical inspection and protection for all, public health, was a necessary basis for child welfare. No more striking example exists of the change, both in program and in method, which occurred in Folks and child welfare work than this concern for public health.

Even before Folks recognized that sickness and all other fundamental maladjustments were causes of dependency with which child welfare workers had to deal, he had turned to an area in need of dynamic action—improving the condition and the care of the mentally ill. With a waning emphasis on amelioration, he quickly became a leader in the movement to prevent mental illness and the modest program he implemented for the aftercare of the insane won national acceptance.

7

MENTAL HEALTH

LOUISA LEE SCHUYLER'S successful attempt to secure the State Care Act of 1890 did not end the State Charities Aid Association's concern for New York's mentally ill. On the contrary, it began a long and lively interest in the subject which, under Homer Folks's leadership, was transformed into a constructive effort of immense importance.

Thanks to Miss Schuyler and Homer Folks, by 1896 the three counties that chose to remain outside the State Care Act, New York, Kings, and Monroe, were brought under its provisions.[1] In the same year the SCAA drafted and played a vital part in the enactment of a bill that created the Craig Colony for Epileptics at Sonyea, N.Y., the second separate institution for epileptics in the United States.[2]

In 1902 complete control and management of state hospitals was placed in the hands of the State Commission in Lunacy. Two years later when Governor Higgins was elected on a platform that included the promise to re-establish local boards of managers for mental institutions, he called upon Folks for help. Believing that local boards had some advantages—they could be more alert to causes of abuse or neglect and would provide a personal warmth and sense of hope not only for the inmates but for the staff as well—Folks drafted and had introduced in the legislature a successful compromise bill that provided for the restoration of local boards with broad powers of management; financial matters, however, continued to be supervised by the State Commission in Lunacy.[3]

Finally, ably assisted by Dr. Thomas W. Salmon, prominent physician, onetime medical examiner of immigrants and subsequent director of the National Committee for Mental Hygiene, Folks was also instrumental in having the provisions of the Immigration Act pertaining to the alien insane amended. Wishing to correct many of the measure's abuses and revamp the entire system of reception and examination of aliens, on several occasions they visited the United States Surgeon General, the Commissioner of Immigration, the Secretary of Commerce and Labor, the clerk of the Senate Committee on Immigration, and several of the most active members of the House Committee on Immigration and Naturalization and suggested to them ways to improve the care and examination of insane and alleged insane aliens. The 1906–1907 revisions of the federal statutes regulating immigration resulted largely from their efforts.[4] Thus, by 1906 Folks and the Association had set the pattern for their later fight to prevent insanity and aid the mentally defective.

In a paper on "The Assistance of Destitute Convalescent and Recovered Patients, Discharged from Hospitals for Insane," presented in 1905 at the National Conference, Dr. Richard Dewey of Wisconsin expressed an idea new to most members of the Conference—aftercare of the insane.[5] Actually, the idea of "aftercare," or providing temporary assistance for needy persons discharged from hospitals for the insane, was an old one widely used in Europe, particularly London and Paris.[6] Moreover, in 1896 the State Charities Aid Association had authorized its Committee on the Insane "to inaugurate and maintain for convalescents leaving hospitals, who may be friendless, a system of 'after-care,' whereby they may be strengthened in health, protected and cared for until able to support themselves." [7] The plan, however, had never been implemented in this country. Now, a decade later, Folks caught the idea expressed once again by Dewey and succeeded in making it a most important feature of the Association's work.

First, however, working in conjunction with Alexander Johnson of what at that time was the New York School of Philanthropy, Folks hired two students to make a thorough investigation of the condition of all the discharged patients (ninety) from the Manhattan State Hospital during the period October 1, 1905, to January 15, 1906. Of these, thirty-one could not be found, although at most only three months had elapsed since their discharge. Of the remaining ones, it

was discovered that some were doing well, some were in danger of re-
lapse, and a few were once again seriously disturbed. It appeared certain that some of the former patients would have benefited by proper
aftercare at the time they were discharged.[8]

On the basis of this study and his belief that the social environment
of patients could contribute to the prevention or effective cure of mental illness, in January 1906 Folks called a conference attended by members of the State Commission in Lunacy, the superintendents of all but
one of the state hospitals for the insane, and officers of the State Charities Aid Association. Conference members adopted several resolutions
in favor of Folks's plan to have the State Charities Aid Association
launch a statewide aftercare system. A month later the Association organized a Sub-Committee on the After-Care of the Insane under the
chairmanship of Louisa Lee Schuyler. This subcommittee immediately
began plans to establish volunteer aftercare committees for each state
mental hospital, to work under the general direction and control of
Miss Schuyler's statewide committee. On February 15, 1906, the Manhattan After-Care Committee of the State Charities Aid Association
was formed—the first functioning committee of its kind in this country—with duties defined as follows:

1. To devise and inaugurate preventive measures for the benefit of
nervous persons in the districts of the Manhattan and Central Islip State
Hospitals, who, without such assistance, might become insane.

2. To provide temporary assistance, employment, friendly aid and counsel
for needy person discharged recovered from the Manhattan and Central
Islip State Hospitals.[9]

Aftercare work was a manifestation of the larger progressive reform
movement that emphasized the individual and his social control. As
Folks indicated, its essence was the recognition of a patient as a human
being, not simply as a case, and it was based on the conviction that an
individual's behavior was determined, to a large extent, by his environment. "The process of cure is not completed when the hospital door
opens and the patient leaves," Folks declared. "The opportunity and
the need for treatment, advice, aid, and counsel," he continued, "are
only little less in the period immediately following release from the

hospital than they were in the period preceding such release." [10] In large part, then, aftercare work was a formal recognition of the medical value of a constructive intellectual and emotional environment in the treatment of what is now called neurotic diseases. It was no accident that it paralleled the rise of psychotherapy and behaviorism in psychiatry and psychology and the "progressive movement" in education, which attempted to socialize the school by expanding its work and relating it to surrounding family and neighborhood life.[11]

By the end of the first year aftercare committees had been appointed for four state hospitals. In June 1907 Folks presented a paper to the National Conference on "A Year's Work in the After-Care of the Insane," in which he called upon other states to quickly adopt similar programs.[12] By the end of 1907 not only every state hospital for the insane in New York had an aftercare committee, but interest in the subject was widespread and organizations in other states began to take up the work. Within five years the State Charities Aid Association's Manhattan After-Care Committee alone had helped over five hundred people. On September 27, 1911, the committee was disbanded when its work was taken over by the state and made part of the New York State hospital system.[13] If Folks cannot be considered the father of aftercare, he must at least be recognized as the one who brought it to life in the United States.

The State Charities Aid Association's aftercare work had much broader consequences. In New Haven on May 6, 1908, Clifford Beers, the "catalytic agent" who provided so many others with the impulse to work for mental hygiene, organized the Connecticut Society for Mental Hygiene, the first state society of its kind, thus beginning the organized mental health movement in America. The following year Beers invited a group of interested nationally known people to come together in a New York hotel to create the famous National Committee for Mental Hygiene (now the National Association for Mental Health). According to its founder, "Work previously done . . . in behalf of the insane in New York by the State Charities Aid Association . . . made it easier to formulate part of the plans of the National Committee, namely," Beers continued, "those features relating to State care and to after-care of the insane, in both of which fields the New York State Charities Aid Association had done the pioneer work [in] . . . this country." [14] Aftercare work has become, in theory at least, if not always in practice, an integral part of the services in all mental hospitals throughout the United States.

Aside from a few prominent physicians such as William A. White, Thomas W. Salmon, Adolph Meyer, William H. Welch, and a handful of others who recognized insanity as an illness, during the early years of the twentieth century few people in the United States knew, or for that matter cared, much about mental illness. It was only about the time the National Committee for Mental Hygiene started its active work in 1912 that many citizens woke up to the enormous problem. Despite the courageous and energetic work of Dorothea Dix more than a half-century earlier, there still were shocking abuses in the treatment of the insane. The inhuman punishments inflicted upon mental patients by ignorant attendants resulted largely from the belief that the insane were wicked and "possessed"; the demonological as opposed to the medical point of view still prevailed. Needless to say, the movement in the direction of preventive medicine had almost entirely neglected the discussion of mental hygiene. [15]

Unlike many physicians and most laymen, Folks recognized that insanity was not altogether a personal matter; rather, it was the joint product of the individual and his environment. Insanity was a disease, and like other diseases some of it was subject to prevention and cure; it needed quick attention by kind, intelligent, and well-trained physicians. [16] As early as 1901, a full year before the first psychiatric hospital in America was established, Folks had laid special emphasis upon the need for them. [17] Such hospitals would, in large part, meet the special need for improved care and treatment of early and curable, as well as borderline, cases of mental derangement that could be prevented from passing into permanent insanity. Psychiatric hospitals also would fulfill the need for better instruction in psychiatry.

Folks recognized that there was some agreement among medical men on the causes of certain forms of insanity. He prepared a statement on those causes, "so far as they [were] . . . known," which was endorsed by eminent leaders in the field. Long before the public openly discussed social hygiene and the venereal diseases, Folks pointed out that general paralysis, or paresis, resulting in most cases from syphilis, was a leading cause of insanity. Although he realized the "presentation of these subjects to the public involve[d] unusual difficulties," they had to be overcome, for paresis was a late-stage syphilitic infection of the brain, which might be prevented by early treatment. Far more concerned about the possibility of immense human waste than the moral aspects of the problem, Folks therefore believed it was necessary to break down the barriers of ignorance, prudery, and false modesty; he declared, "It must be made plain to the average man, by some means, that to indulge in vice is to invite irreparable physical disaster." [18]

Folks also called attention to alcoholism as a cause of insanity. Another leading cause of insanity, he maintained, was physical illness. He pointed out that such diseases as typhoid, diphtheria, and influenza sometimes so weakened the body that interference with the nervous system occurred and mental breakdown followed. Finally, he called attention to "bad mental habits"—day-dreaming, brooding, anxieties, fears— as causes of insanity.[19] Thus Folks not only elaborated the widely believed somatic causes of mental illness, but he also mentioned some of the psychic causes that were just being popularized at the time.

Although heredity was thought to be one of the main causes of insanity until well into the twentieth century, for Folks it played only a secondary role; in his opinion, one did not inherit insanity. He felt mental instability could be inherited, but this was no reason for alarm. The individual whose family had mental trouble might often escape the disease by proper surroundings, healthful and temperate activities, and proper mental and physical habits. The most important fact in regard to heredity and insanity, Folks asserted, was that the vast majority of ancestors of every individual were normal. Therefore, he pointed out, "Heredity tends rather more strongly toward health than toward disease." [20]

In the course of two years aftercare work led naturally and inevitably to the work of prevention. Significantly, in 1908 the State Charities Aid Association Sub-Committee on the After-Care of the Insane changed its name to the Sub-Committee on Prevention and After-Care. The newly named subcommittee hired trained agents to work with cases of "threatened mental disorders." Although not called that, these agents were the first paid psychiatric social workers in this country, antedating by many years psychiatric social work as a profession.[21] Two years later the subcommittee desired to further increase both its scope and emphasis; it became a Special Committee on the Prevention, Relief and After-Care of Nervous and Mental Diseases. Finally, it became the Committee on Mental Hygiene of the State Charities Aid Association.[22]

There was a real need for a popular, scientific, educational campaign dealing with the causes, prevention, and adequate treatment of abnormal mental conditions. In the belief that man tends to be rational, and is educable, Folks's statement on the causes of insanity formed the basis of a movement to fulfill that need. The Committee on Mental Hygiene, which Folks served as secretary, now spearheaded a statewide movement aiming at the early diagnosis, prevention, and treatment of mental disturbances.

While the humanitarian considerations of the movement were uppermost in Folks's mind, as usual, he also pointed out that the "economic aspect . . . is one sufficiently serious to engage the attention of any to whom other considerations might not make a conclusive appeal." Pointing to the high incidence of insanity and the fact that about one-sixth of the state's total income was expended for care of the insane, Folks repeatedly asked, "Can anyone question the wisdom of expenditure of a modest sum in an effort to secure the effective application of our present knowledge as to the causes of insanity?"[23] The prevention of insanity, then, courted two natural instincts—self-interest and altruism; by helping prevent insanity, one served both one's pocket and humanity.

After securing through voluntary contributions a fund of $10,000 per year for a period of three years, in 1910 the Committee on Mental Hygiene enlisted the active support of prominent laymen, physicians and specialists in nervous and mental diseases, and state authorities to help in its campaign to prevent insanity and promote mental health. The dignity and prestige of the state effectively complemented the initiative and interest of private benevolence. Hundreds of thousands of leaflets endorsed by eminent physicians were widely distributed. The committee supplied news releases to papers and periodicals, sponsored lectures in the large cities throughout the state, and prepared exhibits for conventions, conferences, and other meetings; all these vividly testified to Folks's originality and understanding of the strategic importance of molding a sympathetic public opinion.[24]

Sympathy, however, was not enough. Folks saw the vital importance of having resources in the community for detecting and treating the illness: it was of little help to understand the needs of the mentally ill if treatment was impossible because those who needed the care were not provided it in the community. For this reason, the committee's chief goal was the establishment throughout the state of free child guidance clinics and dispensaries or outpatient departments for the early detection, diagnosis, and treatment of mental disorders.[25] Folks challenged state mental hospital officials to interpret their duties broadly and establish closer relations between their hospitals and the communities they served through the creation of such outpatient services. He also issued a call to social workers "to use every effort, both as individuals and in their official capacities, to uphold, strengthen, dignify and develop [mental] health administration": [26] efficient social services, he reminded them, were a necessary corollary to successful clinical work. Moreover, a reduction in mental illness would not only lessen suffering but also release a vast sum of money which might be expended on more constructive measures for social betterment.

In the meantime, Clifford Beers inaugurated his national crusade for the proper care and prevention of mental illness. His National Committee for Mental Hygiene was instrumental in promoting the improvement of mental hospitals and in arousing public concern throughout the nation for the proper treatment of all mental cases.[27] But it was Folks and the State Charities Aid Association's militant, well-organized campaign, which anticipated the work of the National Committee, that created in New York State a more intelligent and sympathetic understanding of those suffering from mental illness. By bringing the preventable causes of insanity into public and official consciousness, this campaign helped prepare a climate of opinion and lay the groundwork for acceptance of the larger mental health movement. By 1923 forty free clinics for mental patients had been established at all the important centers of population throughout New York State. At these clinics anyone could receive expert medical consultation and treatment as well as assistance and social service from field agents, trained nurses, and social workers attached to the staffs of state hospitals.[28]

In its broadest terms, the mental health crusade, through its efforts to create a wholesome physical and social environment as a key to mental hygiene, can be interpreted as part of the more general struggle after 1900 to preserve the nation's human resources. Like other reforms that sought to improve the social conditions of men, women, and children, the drive to prevent mental illness simply represented an effort to liberate the human personality from another kind of repressive burden.

In addition to playing a leading part in the movement to prevent insanity, Folks joined in the campaign for the identification, custodial care, special education, and social supervision of higher-grade defectives, the feeble-minded.[29] The ugly aspects of neglected feeble-mindedness had been revealed many times to Folks through his child welfare work. In response to appeals for help in behalf of dependent children the Association's county children's agents often discovered whole families and even groups of feeble-minded families.

Most early studies of the feeble-minded, such as Robert Dugdale's *The Jukes* and Rev. O. C. McCulloch's *The Tribe of Ishmael,* supposedly supplied data in support of the thesis that the feeble-minded tended almost invariably to reproduce and multiply their kind in increasing numbers. In addition, it was popularly believed that the feeble-minded were habitual inebriates and criminals, immoral, and carriers of venereal diseases. The first large-scale systematic survey of the care and control of the feeble-minded was undertaken by the British Royal Commission in 1904, In 1908 the commission published an eight-volume report that reaffirmed most of the stereotypes, including the hereditary nature of feeble-mindedness. As a result, the mentally deficient, like the insane, were tucked away in custodial institutions and forgotten.

Concern about the problem of mental deficiency was aroused in this country as a result of the British study. A series of further studies, investigations, and reports on the subject followed. One of the earliest of these, *The Feeble-Minded in New York,* was made for the State Charities Aid Association by Dr. Anne Moore. Published in June 1911 by the State Charities Aid Association's Special Committee on Provision for the Feebleminded, which Folks served as secretary, the introduction to the study stated that "the horrors attendant upon feeblemindedness have in no way been exaggerated" and "there is a crying need for concerted action looking toward control of the situation." [30]

Folks agreed with Dr. Moore's findings. In his opinion, although the insane and the feeble-minded were both mentally defective, they differed in many ways. On the whole, feeble-mindedness occurred earlier in life than insanity. Insanity was due largely to external factors while feeble-mindedness seemed to be congenital. Most important, a large degree of insanity was preventable by hygienic measures whereas feeble-mindedness appeared to be controllable only by sterilization or segregation during the reproductive years.[31] To a few alarmists, euthanasia became a popular solution to the problem of the feebleminded.

Wiser counsel concentrated on eugenics, the science of the improvement of the human race by better breeding through the use of sterilization or segregation. Despite the conservative implication of hereditarian thought, eugenics was in large measure a reflection of the rise of the preventive ideal among reformers. By preventing the birth of a child condemned by defective heredity to a life of squalor, ignorance, evil, and idiocy, eugenicists thought of themselves as humanitarians seeking to reform society.[32] Sterilization ultimately became accepted as public policy; its enactment into law in sixteen states from 1907 to 1917 indicates that many reformers were convinced of its efficacy as a remedy for certain social problems.

New York passed a sterilization law in 1912, but there, as in most other states, the net results of the statute as a measure of social control were practically nil.[33] Although Folks expressed agreement in principle with the advocates of eugenics, he remained a calm voice in the babble of the day and opposed sterilization on the grounds that the hereditary transmission of mental and moral qualities according to well-known (Mendelian) laws, although apparently true, was not yet conclusively proven. He did believe, however, that the feeble-minded were a real menace to the community, that the problem was the state's responsibility, that the state had "hesitated, faltered and fumbled" in this responsibility, and that the most practical and acceptable means to control the reproduction of the feeble-minded was not with a scalpel, but through increased institutional provision for their segregation during child-bearing age.[34]

The State Charities Aid Association publication in 1911 stimulated the first extensive interest in New York State for the control of the feeble-minded. Folks and the Committee on Provision for the Feeble-minded carried on an educational campaign to secure more adequate institutional care for these mental defectives. They made further studies of the problem and, reporting concrete evidence, from year to year brought the situation to the attention of the state legislature. Several editions of the Association's newspaper, the S. C. A. A. News, were devoted entirely to the problem of feeble-mindedness, stressing the overcrowding in institutions, the evils that resulted from allowing the feeble-minded to be at large, and the way in which feeble-mindedness complicated problems of child care, family rehabilitation, public health, and the like.[35]

In response to these efforts, the state legislature appointed a Committee to Investigate Provision for the Mentally Deficient. In 1915, after holding numerous hearings and making extensive studies, the legislative committee strongly urged more institutional care and segregation to cope with what they found to be a large problem. Despite this, segregation in New York State failed to meet the demand. In 1923 it was estimated that only 8 per cent of the state's feeble-minded were in proper institutions for their care.

The impossibility of securing complete segregation and the belief, from further study, that all the mentally deficient did not need institutional care for their own protection or for the best interests of the community led to the development of a different program. Folks was aware of the more recent research that revealed a much larger proportion of nonhereditary types of feeble-mindedness than formerly had been realized. In addition, critical examination of the belief that the feeble-minded were extremely prolific and were outnumbering the normal population indicated that this, too, had not been well founded. Folks was among a group of broad-visioned workers who on the basis of these new findings, as well as European examples, faced up to the problem and helped to develop "extra-institutional measures" to meet the need. He helped evolve in this country a newer conception of the institution, one not for permanent custodial care (although certain patients would need such care) but rather for training and restoring to society all of the mentally deficient capable of adjusting socially; in short, a constructive rather than merely a repressive program.[36]

Along this line, the parole and colony plans for the feeble-minded, long used in Scotland, Belgium, and Germany, were developed in America.[37] Under the parole plan, persons deemed suitable for normal life were permitted to return on a trial basis to the community while they remained under the continuing supervision of the institution's field agent or social worker. Dr. Walter E. Fernald of Massachusetts was the first one in this country to successfully train his mentally deficient charges for life in the community.

The colony idea rested on the principle that it was both inhumane and uneconomical to confine in the wards of an institution at considerable public expense many strong, able-bodied persons simply because of a mental deficiency. To Dr. Charles Bernstein, superintendent of the Rome State School for Mental Defectives at Rome, N.Y., goes the credit for having first established in an extensive and practical way a colony for the feeble-minded in America.[38]

Folks, who as a result of his child-care work had considerable experience with and faith in both the parole and placing-out plans, became a leading spokesman in the movement for their use with the mentally deficient. He believed it was possible and desirable to remove some inmates from the institution proper and place them in a more normal living and working environment where they could be practically self-supporting and still be maintained with the necessary degree of supervision to protect them and the community. Moreover, he realized that both of these plans offered the further advantage of releasing institutional beds for more serious cases. The "wisdom and usefulness" of these plans, wrote Stanley P. Davies, an historian of the control of the mentally deficient, "have been amply demonstrated." To the patients they provided an outlet for energies, contentment, practical vocational training, and "real" development as well as an opportunity to prove their ability to return to community life. To the general public, the parole and colony systems offered a means of segregating and training large numbers of feeble-minded without any heavy tax burdens.[39]

For obvious reasons, not all of the mentally deficient were brought under state or medical supervision. Large numbers remained "free" and attended public schools. As a result, a large and important part of the entire mental hygiene program theoretically fell upon the public schools. Consequently, Folks and the State Charities Aid Association Committee on Mental Hygiene turned their attention to this problem by helping to organize special classes for these handicapped pupils. Although in America the first special class for mentally deficient children in public schools was established in Providence, R. I., in 1896, thanks to a law which Folks helped secure in 1917 New York was one of the earliest states making the establishment of such classes in its public schools mandatory. Moreover, state aid for these classes, which the Association also helped to secure, was effective in increasing the number of new classes. In addition, it raised the work standards of these special classes by requiring teachers to fulfill certain qualifications in order to receive the aid.[40]

Despite the movement to prevent insanity and the measures to restore to the community all patients who could be returned safely, the number of mental defectives in need of institutional treatment in New York State continued to soar. The number of mental patients totaled all other dependents of the state put together. Overcrowding in hospitals for the insane was extremely serious, interfering with proper care of the patients. Moreover, most of the institutions were fire traps and in dangerous disrepair. On February 18, 1923, a fire in the fifty-three-year-old Manhattan State Hospital killed twenty-three patients and three attendants.[41] Three days later, in a special message, Governor Alfred E. Smith appealed to the state legislature to submit to the people of New York a referendum on a bond issue of at least $50,000,000 for the construction of new institutions for the safe and adequate care of the state's wards.

In response to the Governor's message, a bill for a $50,000,000 bond issue was introduced in the legislature. The measure, actively supported by the State Charities Aid Association Committee on Mental Hygiene, passed both houses and was approved by the Governor on May 22, 1923.[42] Actually, the State Charities Aid Association had long advocated such a plan. As early as 1909 Homer Folks called for a state bond issue to provide money for needed improvements in state institutions. And in 1915 a special Association committee submitted to the 1915 constitutional convention a recommendation in favor of a bond issue for the construction of additional state institutions.[43]

However, because New York's residents never before had been asked to vote on such a question, many friends of the needy feared the outcome. In response to a request from Governor Smith, the State Charities Aid Association organized a statewide committee to conduct an educational campaign to acquaint the people of the state with the desperate need for the bond issue. Folks served as secretary to this Citizens' Committee on Protection of the State's Unfortunates, which had a membership of 275 and included such leading New Yorkers as George W. Wickersham, President Taft's Attorney General. With branches in every county of New York, the committee widely publicized the facts about the state's mental institutions.[44]

In addition, Folks served as secretary of the Association's Committee on Mental Hygiene, which along with the central association for months devoted almost all of its time to the intensive statewide campaign. As he related to Miss Schuyler, "We are all, metaphorically speaking, standing on our heads and working day and night on the Bond Issue Campaign."[45] The September and October issues of the

S. C. A. A. News were special "Bond Issue Numbers." In articles and pamphlets, on the platform, and in letters to friends and influential people Folks contended that financing state institutions from current expenditures had failed in the past; a bond issue was a necessity. It was a just, wise, and statesmanlike plan. Suitable buildings would last for generations and there was no reason why one group of taxpayers should bear the entire financial burden when, through a bond issue, it could be distributed over a period of years.[46]

The carefully thought-out and well-managed campaign, which was financed in large part by contributions from the Russell Sage Foundation, ended on November 6, 1923, when by a three-to-one vote the people of New York State repudiated the pay-as-you-go plan for maintaining the state's unfortunates. With a majority of over 707,000, the referendum was approved by a larger number of citizens than ever before had voted for any person, policy, or appropriation in the history of New York State.[47]

This interest that New Yorkers showed in their mental institutions did not spring up suddenly from barren soil. For a long time Folks and his colleagues had been tilling the field and planting the seeds. While many individuals had worked hard to popularize the need for adequately caring for the mentally defective, no one had been a more consistent or effective exponent of the idea than Homer Folks, who looked upon this success as one of his most highly prized achievements.[48] In commenting on that achievement, a lengthy editorial in the November 1923 issue of *Mental Hygiene Bulletin,* the official publication of the National Mental Hygiene Committee, said:

The campaign has demonstrated again two things: the effectiveness of a popular campaign of education, well directed; and the value of a local organization composed largely of laymen, well informed, well advised, and having talents and abilities, skill in organization, and resources. . . . Once more the State Charities Aid Association has demonstrated the effectiveness of such an organization. In doing this it has . . . helped to preserve the self-respect of the citizens of New York [and] brought much needed relief to 45,000 incapacitated . . . [souls].[49]

In a letter to Homer Folks, Governor Smith expressed his personal thanks and the appreciation of many others when he wrote, "Permit me to take this opportunity to thank you . . . for the earnest hard work you did to help bring about a better condition for the unfortunate wards of the state. Nothing that I could say would adequately express the State's thanks for . . . [your] generous grant of time and effort." [50]

By May 1927, however, it became apparent that additional aid for state hospitals was needed. The number of mental defectives had increased so rapidly that the institutions were actually more congested than ever before. It was estimated that even after completion of all the construction provided for by the bond issue, in two years the state would have 5,000 more patients than it could care for. [51] Governor Smith invited the State Charities Aid Association Citizens' Committee to a conference to discuss further steps to relieve the situation. Shortly after Smith left office, Folks discussed with his successor, Franklin D. Roosevelt, a proposal for a second $50,000,000 bond issue. After Roosevelt received Folks's assurance that the State Charities Aid Association once again would conduct an active campaign for the referendum, the Governor supported the idea. [52] Subsequently, Roosevelt sent a special message to the legislature urging the enactment of a bill to submit the issue to the voters. In 1930 New York's voters once again approved a $50,000,000 bond issue for the construction and improvement of the state's mental institutions—this time by an even greater margin than before. [53]

Despite the enormous building program that resulted from the two bond issues, because of an approximate annual increase of 2,500 patients New York's mental institutions remained overcrowded. Consequently, throughout the 1930s Folks and the State Charities Aid Association continued to urge wider use of family care and parole work among the mentally ill. In addition, two years after insulin shock treatment as a potential cure for some forms of mental illness was first introduced to this country, the Association conducted a study and sent a report of it to Governor Herbert H. Lehman; the study concluded that through increased use of the new method of treatment as well as "extra institutional" care of suitable patients, the state could speed up the recovery of some of its wards, conserve public funds, and free institutional beds for those patients most in need of them. [54] The chief executive appointed Folks chairman of a semiofficial commission created to consider the advisability of acting upon the SCAA findings. This Temporary Commission on State Hospital Problems, headed by Folks and charged with the specific task of surveying the possibilities of diminishing the population of the state hospitals by such measures as increased and earlier use of parole, outside care (boarding-out), and insulin shock treatment, included such famous experts in the field of mental health as Doctors Clarence Cheyney, William L. Russell, Frederick W. Parsons, William J. Tiffany, and George S. Stevenson.[55]

The commission held its first meeting on December 6, 1940; three and a half years later it submitted its final report to Governor Thomas E. Dewey. Based on an intensive study of 1,128 insulin-treated mental patients over a period of five and a half years, the commission concluded (1) that in many cases insulin shock treatment had reduced hospital stay, (2) that the use of such treatment should be extended, (3) that it was possible and desirable to increase the number of mental patients on parole, and (4) that it was desirable and practical to board-out carefully chosen mental patients.[56] Although the commission's findings were later questioned and, due to a shortage of trained personnel and the appearance of two cheaper and more easily executed forms of shock therapy (Metrazol and electric), interest was turned in other directions, the immediate impact of the report was great. It resulted in the extended use of both insulin shock therapy and "outside care" for mental patients and, as a result of the increased use of these medical and social services, the rate of growth of the state's mental institutions was reversed for the first time in the fifty years of state care of the insane.[57]

Folks had a special genius, an innate ability, to quickly grasp the meaning of trends in human affairs. This insight enabled him to sometimes initiate trail-blazing measures and, at other times, to develop schemes conceived but untried by others to enhance the physical and mental well-being of the afflicted. He was always ready and willing to accept and try new ideas. An outstanding example of this was the program during World War II for aiding in the psychiatric examination of men called for military service.

During the early stages of World War II, as during the previous world war, because of the large number of men drafted, the speed with which they had to be examined, and the limited number of psychiatrists, eliminating the mentally unfit from the draft was an enormous and largely impossible task. In the hasty procedures at draft boards and induction centers draftees were given five-minute psychiatric examinations to determine their "mental fitness" to serve in the armed forces. Mistakes were costly to the military, the taxpayers, and the individuals involved.

In March 1941 it became evident to Miss Katharine Ecob, secretary of the State Committee on Mental Hygiene of the State Charities Aid Association, that voluntary mental hygiene agencies could assist the Selective Service boards in dealing with such problems. It appeared to her that the screening of drafted men would be vastly more effective if, among other things, social histories of the registrants were available to the medical and psychiatric examiners at induction centers.[58] She prepared a program designed to take advantage of the resources in New York State that could be of assistance in this connection and then related her idea to Folks, who, after listening to her plan, said, "It is almost impossible but by all means go to Washington. It is worth a try." [59] Folks assured her that he and the Association would fully support the plan. At the end of Miss Ecob's hurried trip to the nation's capital, the plan was approved and accepted on a trial basis by Dr. L. G. Rowntree, Chief of the Medical Division, National Headquarters, Selective Service System.[60]

Specifically, the plan implemented a six-point program whereby the State Charities Aid Association's Committee on Mental Hygiene would act as an intermediary between those in need of psychiatric service and those willing to provide it, ranging from offering psychiatric review courses to a follow-up program for men declared unfit for military service. Of most immediate importance, however, was the social service for securing and providing to the examining psychiatrists at induction centers social histories of all men called up for the draft.[61]

All available information about registrants was secured by volunteer, trained social workers attached to local boards as field agents. They canvassed the communities in which the selectees lived, including employers, welfare agencies, school reports, court and hospital records, and the like; any history indicating undesirability for military service was summarized and presented to the local draft boards and induction centers. By the close of 1942 the State Charities Aid Association had enlisted the volunteer services of over 700 social workers, attached to every draft board in New York State. At the peak of the work some 19,000 names were investigated monthly by these workers. Originally planned for the Army, Selective Service officials found the program so helpful that it was extended to all the armed forces.[62] In the spring of 1943 Folks was asked to help prepare a Medical Bulletin issued by the New York State Selective Service System that made it mandatory for all local boards in the state to use social workers to secure social histories of selectees as an aid to their psychiatric classification. Finally, in October 1943 the War Manpower Commission announced the adoption of the plan on a comprehensive, nationwide scale. Before the end of the war the services of several thousand social workers were utilized in obtaining histories of more than a million men.[63]

Near the end of his long career Folks still held forth the same four "bright hopes" for future progress in mental health that he had, in different words, elaborated many years earlier: more fully trained psychiatrists in the hospitals; new methods of treatment; a better understanding of the relation between environment and mental disorder; and, most important, creative imagination and greater efforts applied to the prevention of mental illness.[64] With the passage of the National Mental Health Act and the establishment of the Mental Hygiene Division of the United States Public Health Service in July 1946, Congress took steps toward making Folks's hopes a reality. The primary purpose of the act was to develop preventive health measures. It provided for an extensive mental health program by enabling the states and private institutions to secure federal funds for research, training of personnel, and the extension of clinics for the prevention of mental disorders.[65] Thus the campaign to correct abuses in the institutional care of the mentally ill had developed into a broad movement for public health—a plan Folks had called for almost a half-century before.

Folks's historical contribution to the mental hygiene movement was educational, not medical. He was a layman, not a physician, and he acquired from others most of his scientific knowledge in regard to insanity. However, despite the fact that for the most part he followed the medical trail marked out by others, Folks added a new element that was an important contribution to the struggle for mental health and promoting human welfare. Going straight to the core of the problem from the start, he was one of the first to popularize the idea that patients suffering from mental deviation were not blameworthy and should not be dealt with by force or punishment. Mental disease, he pointed out, should be regarded as any other disease and, when so approached, it was in large measure susceptible to treatment, cure, prevention, and research. By so doing, he helped merge the mental hygiene crusade with the general field of social work, thus extending the scope of both.[66]

Not only was the program against mental disease brought into the general movement for public hygiene and preventive medicine, but, with its new concern for mental health, social work finally moved to extend its boundaries beyond those of the economically disadvantaged.

8

SOCIAL THOUGHT

FOLKS'S personality and appearance contributed largely to his success. To many people he was the image of the "old world gentleman-public servant," the epitome of the ideal English aristocrat.[1] To some who did not know him, his tall and imposing frame, which commanded respect, may have projected an air of superiority and aloofness, but behind this façade was an extremely good-natured and even merry man with a sharp wit and lively sense of humor.[2]

Folks displayed a rare combination of intelligence, breadth of vision, idealism, and practicality. He also had a logical mind and wrote and spoke well and succinctly. His unruffled personality and equable disposition were widely acknowledged; he was calm, reasonable, and deliberate, yet firm in the prosecution of activities he felt to be in the public interest.[3] Because he was engaged in a great many activities and was widely sought after as a counselor and speaker, one complaint heard of him was his occasional unavailability.[4]

However, he never allowed himself to be absorbed entirely by official business. Throughout his busiest years Folks made sure not to neglect his private life. There was hardly a time when he was not planning some event or gift to make someone happy, a pastime which gave him as much pleasure as it did the recipient of his kindness. His primary concerns, however, were his wife and family. In fact, his reputation of being a loving and thoughtful husband and father is still vividly recalled.[5] In a taxing career that forced him on occasion to be away from his wife and rapidly growing children, he frequently looked for relaxation in the simple pleasures and calm repose of his home; he made sure that the family spent as many hours together as possible. Speaking of a yearly vacation he and Mrs. Folks took when his apparently inexhaustible reserve of energy finally began to run low, at age seventy-two, he related that "our friends . . . poke much fun at us for always being with each other, in fact it's kind of an annual honeymoon, though in all seriousness, I am inclined to think the whole nearly forty-eight years [of our marriage] has been pretty much of a continuous honeymoon." [6]

After more than twenty years of uninterrupted hard work, except for brief outings and summer holidays, in 1911 Folks took his family on a six-month European vacation. He found the Continent enchanting and restful. Besides visiting churches and other sights, he went rowing and sailing, took steamship rides, and often walked for hours at a time enjoying Europe's idyllic scenery. He also enjoyed Continental cooking: "The family say I am getting 'fat,'" he related to a colleague. "I don't think so," he went on, "but I certainly feel that I am laying in stores of nervous energy for future use." [7] Nevertheless, however relaxing his vacations, he found himself always talking shop: "I am anxious for some S.C.A.A. news," he wrote from Italy.[8]

The trip abroad made 1911 an especially eventful year for Homer Folks; two other incidents made it a memorable one. In recognition of "his distinguished labors for the public weal" Ohio Wesleyan University conferred upon him the honorary degree of Doctor of Laws.[9] More noteworthy, however, was another distinction, perhaps the highest he could have achieved in that or any other year—the presidency of the National Conference of Charities and Correction.

At the closing session of the 1910 conference president Jane Addams passed the traditional gavel to her newly elected successor and remarked that although she had received it "with some doubt and many misgivings," she now handed "it over with every confidence for an able and brilliant administration under . . . Mr. Homer Folks of New York." [10] All those present agreed. To Edward T. Devine, the news "could not have been more gratifying . . . or better evidence of sound judgment [on the part] on the Conference." [11] Robert W. deForest felt the same way but lamented that the honor "should have come earlier." [12] The Rochester (N.Y.) *Democrat Chronicle* summed up the favorable press reaction to Folks's election in the following manner: "The work which he has done for neglected and dependent children alone will cause the next generation to rise and call him blessed. Indeed, to catalogue the philanthropies in which he has taken a leading part during the past two decades would be to write a history of systematic benevolent effort . . . during the period." [13]

In 1913 Folks and his family traveled to northern New York State, where they purchased a tract of land and a year later built a modest summer retreat—Camp Deer Trail. Beginning in 1914 they went there each year to escape the hot weather and enjoy a rewarding vacation together. The Adirondacks were admirably suited to Folks's needs. Blue waters and heavily wooded banks and hills provided a summer refuge where he could enjoy nature's beauty, remain active, and be with his family, dropping from his shoulders the responsibilities that weighed so heavily upon him the rest of the year. Situated at Big Simonds Pond, Tupper Lake, N.Y., inaccessible by road and without plumbing or electricity, Folks's cottage each summer gave him what he had found in Europe, inexpressible rest and refreshment.[14] He loved the outdoors and, with the exception of a few hours each morning in his study, he spent his summer days with his family and occasional guests boating, fishing, doing carpentry work and various chores, walking over the area's many trails, and watching the sun set over the lake.[15]

Over the years, the long rail trip to Tupper Lake gave way to an automobile ride, but, as a letter from Folks to Miss Schuyler indicates, it apparently was an equally long one for the cautious beginner: "I have mastered the rudiments of driving my car, and Mrs. Folks and I are leaving for the Adirondacks tomorrow," he wrote, "starting very early in the morning so as to get through Yonkers before the traffic begins. I fear we shall have to keep on the rural route." [16] Although he went to the Adirondacks to escape from New York City and rest his mind, body, and spirit for the rigors of the coming year, he could, of course, never forget entirely the SCAA and the tasks that lay ahead. And because, despite more than twenty years of active service, those tasks were in some ways just beginning, it may be appropriate to look back over the road he had traveled thus far.

Folks's varied activities were not as unrelated as they appear. His intellect developed in an orderly fashion. From an early interest in the amelioration of child dependency he moved to a concern for maintaining the family. He did not look upon the needy as inferior or condemn them for their imperfections; he realized that in most cases the causes of dependency were rooted not in personal failure but in social conditions, especially ill health. It could be argued that an emphasis on health was a reaffirmation of the simple faith that if one removed oppressive physical evils, the social evils would disappear as well, and that this approach therefore still dealt with symptoms rather than with basic economic and political causes. But experience and studies indicated to Homer Folks and others at the turn of the century that ill health was a leading cause of death, poverty, and dependency. Certainly the premature death of one or both parents was a chief cause of child dependency. Without question, then, promoting good health was one of the most basic and soundest ways to conserve life and prevent distress. It also represented a giant step forward in the adoption of the preventive ideal, for it involved looking outside the individual for the solution to his problems.

With emphasis on prevention well entrenched in Folks's thinking, all of his seemingly independent interests and projects were aimed at a single goal—the conservation of the nation's human resources, the enrichment of all lives.[17] And one of Folks's unique attributes was his broad approach to that goal. Unlike many, in helping others he never staked out as his own a particular field or domain of interest. Thus, when conditions, and therefore needs, changed, he could and did make the necessary accommodations. Folks never hesitated to repudiate outgrown beliefs or, by blazing new trails of service, to broaden the scope and usefulness of the State Charities Aid Association. In fact, in his 1911 presidential address before the National Conference Folks took social workers to task not only for their "slow rate of progress" but for their narrow approach to the social problem. Recognizing the relationship of poverty to modern industrialism, Folks, in the words of Edward T. Devine, was among the first to issue a "clarion call" for "more attention to the standard of living and less to the relief of actual destitution." [18] Realizing that people constantly in danger of becoming dependent cannot really be free, Folks called for a broad attack upon the causes of dependency—sickness, accident, invalidity, old age, unemployment, and especially the premature death of the family breadwinner.

Folks was a Methodist by heritage and his humanitarianism sprang in part from a religious fervor.[19] His religion had always been a "practical" Christianity; he had scant use for religion divorced from social action. The early religious influence on his life remained strong despite his later rejection of supernaturalism or formal religion.

More central in his philosophy, however, was his deep ethical concern for social justice, his strong feeling for mankind. Folks was a secular reformer who staunchly believed that the attainment of individual moral integrity and the fulfillment of one's social responsibilities was the duty of all. His concern for the condition of the needy arose, then, from both a disciplined moral individualism, as well as from a conception of Christian love. On both accounts society owed every man the opportunity to realize his full potentialities. In Folks's opinion, professional social work opened to the practitioner a field in which to serve himself, his Maker, and his fellow man.[20]

Folks placed some faith in the inherent virtue of man. He did not, however, share the idealists' belief in the perfectibility of the human race. He often spoke of the weakness of human nature and of man as a reasoning animal who, although not wholly rational, "tends to be rational." [21] While he believed the power of reason and good will could win some converts to the side of righteousness, he also realized that, for others, power rather than the ideal of Christian brotherhood regulated human affairs. Thus he appealed to man's altruism and spirit of self-sacrifice, while at the same time he favored restrictive legislation and the application of the state's power to enforce justice.

Folks believed in progress, but a piecemeal progress that traveled a slow and rocky path. History provided him with confidence that "although progress is not continuous" and "there is such a thing as flipping backward, it is unmistakable that the general trend is toward a wiser, saner, better balance, a more nearly civilized life." [22]

Folks could not accept the complete optimism and too-easy schemes of the reconstructer of society, nor the professed extreme individuality of the older agrarian ideology; if opposed to laissez faire, he didn't embrace what he considered to be the opposite extreme—socialism. "Neither the theory of individualism nor that of socialism," he declared, "offers us any practical relief from our troubles. The one says do nothing, the other the impossible." [23] He would not commit himself to dogmas or any rigid creed; rather, he maintained that he had "no clear convictions as to the ultimate forms of social organization." Frankly, he said, "[I] am an opportunist in governmental development. . . . My only guide as to the future of government activity is such study as I am able to make of its present and past." [24] Actually, he advocated a program of government-sponsored social reform in accordance with the philosophy of what later was called the welfare state.

Folks had a deep-seated conviction that the family lay at the basis of civilized life and, although society was fragmented, he believed social antipathy was unnatural. He was committed to the ideal of a society based on the morality of social cooperation, which he felt he saw emerging all around him: "The most marked characteristic of the present decade," he wrote in 1894, "is undoubtedly an extraordinary development of *social consciousness.*" There is coming upon the community as a whole, he continued, "a sense of its corporate existence, the consciousness of a vital unity. And it is the dawning of social consciousness, this realization that humanity is something more than an aggregation of isolated units, that is now bringing before our minds a multitude of social problems." [25] In short, another basic strain in Folks's philosophy was an organic view of society. Society was not an aggregation of individuals, but a living, growing organism; he had a concept of social unity.

The road to social unity could be shortened in at least three ways—via the routes of charity, education, and government. For Folks, charity was the essence and heart of Christianity.[26] But it was not an end in itself. It was not a means of individual regeneration; if properly dispensed, it was a tool to alleviate suffering, build the responsible, self-maintaining family unit, and create a more healthy social environment.[27] In Folks's mind, charity was traveling an upward course from spasmodic, indiscriminate relief to organized, systematic, persistent efforts to raise the whole level of life among the poor. He called upon the church and the faithful to share their means, time, and strength with those in need, and as a proponent of social Christianity he reminded them that the "church that engaged in practical work will prosper. . . . Many stumble at the creed," he argued convincingly, "but all mankind understands and applauds an unselfish deed. Christian is, as Christian does."[28] In true social gospel fashion, then, Folks made society itself the subject of redemption and sought not so much to convert individuals but to provide them with a Christian society in which to live.

Charity, however, was not merely a religious obligation. It was also a secular imperative. As an inherent part of our sociopolitical system all individuals had a clear duty, he explained, "to let no occasion pass, to leave no word unspoken, no duty undone, which might contribute directly or remotely to a better fulfillment, by our democracy, of the obligation which it has voluntarily assumed, the burdens it has voluntarily taken up in behalf of its most helpless members."[29]

Folks stood committed to the proposition that prolonged the lives of the needy, sick, and enfeebled through outside assistance was socially desirable. He defended the charitable impulse from the pseudo-scientific attacks of social Darwinists who claimed that charity and the reduction of infant mortality merely rescued from distress and preserved the unfit and therefore retarded the advance of civilization. While accepting the evolutionary theory he reinterpreted it in a way that made it serviceable: social workers and public health officials, he emphasized, were not simply allowing the unfit to subsist; they were reviving them and restoring their fitness to serve, thus introducing "rational selection" and actually raising the level of the evolutionary process.[30] Moreover, he pointed out that true civilization actually aimed to diminish the struggle for existence through hospitals, medical research, and sanitary laws. In other words, the charitable impulse survived because of its usefulness; every step since earliest days "has been a step away from unrestricted individualism, and toward establishing . . . a greater degree of cooperation, mutual consideration, and organized action of larger and larger groups. It was not a matter of choice," he contended. "Civilization would not have progressed in any other way. Extreme individualism [is impossible, it] defeats itself." [31]

Folks maintained that social unity also could be furthered through education.[32] He felt that knowledge was not only a vital instrument for enriching personal life; it was also a tool for creating a more just and tolerable social order. He believed in the social responsibility of scholarship. A more generally diffused intelligence would help make a more healthful and desirable home and neighborhood as well as teach people to exploit their humanitarian impulses. He applauded the rapid growth of the social sciences in the nation's colleges and universities, especially the science of society, sociology.

By unearthing and gathering the "scientific knowledge of society," sociology sought to place man in some specific, purposeful relationship with his fellow man so that there could be more effective action for the promotion of general welfare. This, of course, implied a rejection of laissez faire individualism (with its belief in the establishment of social harmony through the beneficent working of natural laws). So, while Christianity and democracy provided the purposes, the ends of life, the function of sociology was to discover and suggest methods and ways by which they could be attained. In 1892 Professor Albion W. Small, the noted educator, reformer, and founder of the *American Journal of Sociology,* sought Folks's advice and accepted several of his suggestions in regard to establishing a sociology department and curriculum at the new University of Chicago.[33]

Although he did not contend that all men were inherently good, Folks believed that most people were malleable and educable. Moreover, like most progressive propagandists, especially the muckrakers, he assumed that once people knew the truth many of them would want to act upon it. Hence he and the Association engaged in various popular educational campaigns. For example, Folks maintained the whole question of public health was "fundamentally a question of public education, a question of changing the mind of the average

individual, a question of making the scientific attitude universal, . . .
of getting people really to believe that we can be healthy, if we are willing to be." [34]

Keeping in balance the individual and society, Folks firmly believed
that to a considerable degree man could make and remake his own
world; he was deeply convinced that organized social intelligence
could shape society and improve social conditions. In addition, a reader
of William James and John Dewey, whom he knew personally, Folks
held that the ultimate test of knowledge was its accomplishments—not
theory, but results.[35] He emphasized facts, experiences, change, and
flexibility, and never adhered to a belief in absolute truth and morality.
His was the scientific approach and he contended that social workers
must correct one by one the evils at hand, continually studying the
results of their efforts, comparing, analyzing, classifying, and testing
them until gradually they developed an empirical science of social
progress. Philanthropy must learn by doing, he affirmed; that is its
method.[36] Like Jane Addams, Folks was "something of a pragmatist
determined to test ideas and values about life in the actual laboratory
of life." [37]

Committed, then, to education and the scientific method, Folks
found reform somewhat limited; it could not create quickly a new
society in which all inequity disappeared. Like his old Harvard
mentor, Professor Peabody, Folks counseled his fellow workers to
"give up the notion of reforming the world *en masse*." [38] Reform was
a slow developmental process that would take time to achieve its
goals. "Great is the power of patience," he was fond of repeating.[39]
Ever the champion of law and order, he incorporated a certain conservatism in his social philosophy.

Although there was no express track to progress, men should act,
Folks believed; they were not helpless creatures in a vast maelstrom of
forces. On the contrary, evils were cured by intelligent and well-
directed efforts on the part of human beings. Moreover, men of intelligence and training could and indeed should direct these efforts, as they
were best suited to keep them going in the proper direction.[40] Thus
Folks was among the first, if not the first, to call for the professional-

ization of benevolent work and encourage college men to enter the field that has since come to be called social work.[41] Also, he insisted upon the use of experts in the revision of New York City's tenement house law, he used medical experts in the campaign to prevent insanity, and he constantly advocated civil service reform. Professional experts, with their supply of detailed and specialized knowledge, were to lead the crusade for social change and betterment.

There was no reason why government (like charity and education) could not also be used as a force for reform. Folks had no hesitation about an increasing role for government, especially since he recognized that it was in large part "an inevitable result of the nature of urban life. The closer people live together, the more government they must have," he observed.[42] And when questioned about his feelings toward the expansion of government services, he replied, "It is a very long journey, . . . we can stop whenever we like, [but] . . . so far as we have gone [I] . . . like the trip." [43]

To him, government in a democracy was society manifest, and as such it had a great responsibility to each individual not only to provide certain political rights, but also the basic economic and social necessities for satisfactory living.[44] In fact, if democracy did not do this, it was a failure. In return, each individual must contribute toward the advancing welfare of the whole social organism. Since all individuals controlled the government through a democratic political structure, there was no conflict between individualism and public welfare. Unlike those who still viewed individualism as sacrosanct, Folks thought security was basic to freedom; one grew out of the other and both were needed. Welfare, then, was a social matter.[45]

Because Folks had an uncanny insight into the dangers of bureaucracy, he stressed repeatedly the duty of all private citizens to help maintain sound standards of health and welfare. For the same reason he frequently argued for the primacy of local control. But for needs not met at the lower level, or for those that transcended the limits of a particular locality, he did not hesitate to call for state or federal action. To mention only a few, he called for state regulation of child welfare agencies and federal legislation in regard to such matters as child labor and the Children's Bureau. In 1916, thirty years before its actual creation, Folks favored the idea of a Division of Mental Hygiene within the United States Public Health Service.[46]

Folks realized that the United States Constitution, especially when interpreted by nineteenth-century-minded jurists, frequently hampered progressive government. In a lecture significantly titled the "Failure of Government in America," delivered in 1910 before more famous progressives—Theodore Roosevelt and Charles Beard—attacked the sanctity of the courts and the Constitution, Folks denounced the "fragmentary and unsatisfactory nature of legislation here as compared with foreign countries," placing the root of the trouble in the too diffused responsibility between local, state, and national authorities: "Our Constitution," he said, "places artificial obstacles in the way of [the] . . . natural and desirable increase in governmental functions." [47] To remedy the situation and ensure the endurance of a free society, we had to adjust our legal and judicial institutions to current conditions by gradually devising "some new means of securing effective control nation-wide." [48] Hence, when the Supreme Court invalidated the federal child labor laws, Folks supported a federal child labor amendment to the U.S. Constitution.

In summary, then, with his moral fervor, optimism, environmentalism, and emphasis on leadership by a benevolent intellectual elite within the framework of a democratic society, Folks was in step with the progressive era. In his ideas about the role of the state and hence law in promoting social welfare, he definitely was at the front of the movement, especially within his own field. In a period when many social workers feared state action and ignored the many welfare activities in which the state was engaged, Folks's beliefs approximated those known later as the "welfare state." For him, the state was an effective and necessary instrument for the promotion of human welfare; through positive action it should address itself directly to the health, safety, and economic security of its inhabitants. Motivated by conscience and a passion to create a more humane society in which all citizens were protected against injustice, Folks's social philosophy indicates that if the need had arisen he would not have hesitated to demand a state in which the individualistic ethic would be completely discarded in favor of the social one.

Yet Folks was not a radical, in part, because he was a practicing humanitarian preoccupied with good works rather than ideology. Also he remained, on the whole, within the right wing of the reform movement due to the nature and success of the American welfare system—public and private—which, by "relieving class and group tensions and . . . facilitating the growth of social well-being . . . has in a sense been the American equivalent for socialism."[49] Moreover, Folks's pragmatism and commitment to the scientific method, as well as his realistic assessment of the gradualness of change, prevented him from suggesting any bold new social experiments. Finally, although he dedicated his entire life to the abolition and prevention of distress, Folks was intelligent enough to realize that no social scheme could underwrite all the hazards and misfortunes that created need. Since many recipients of relief were defectives unable for one reason or another to support themselves under any system, he never expected the complete eradication of suffering. "We need [and will always need] justice *and* charity," he declared in 1899 and again thirty-five years later.[50] As a result, Folks remained within the American reform tradition. In fact, his life testifies to the validity of the assertion that the "line of descent from the social justice movement of the early 1900's to the New Deal is clear and straight."[51] By rejecting emotional do-goodism and embracing the application of a form of scientific experimentalism, Folks was helping lay the necessary groundwork for the social justice movement that came to fruition in the 1930s.

9

PUBLIC HEALTH—TUBERCULOSIS

FOLKS was a pioneer in seeing that advances in the field of public health were intimately related to overcoming other social and economic problems. He was one of the first social workers to realize and point out that sickness, which increases expenses and interrupts income to worker and family alike, was a primary cause of destitution and that no success could be made in eliminating distress unless both problems were attacked simultaneously.[1] "Poverty and disease are reciprocally and mutually cause and effect," he carefully explained, "and no one, of whatever profession, can deal effectively with one without taking the other into account at every stage."[2] Focusing upon the medical rather than the moral roots of poverty and dependency, Folks above all else devoted himself after 1906 to the problems of ill health and to eliminating, as much as possible, the need that was caused by the contagion of disease. His eminently successful efforts on the local and national level to eliminate tuberculosis and other preventable diseases helped to make the fruits of scientific medicine the common possession of all, to bring preventive medicine into the organized social welfare crusade of the era, and, most importantly, to save countless lives.

Public health activities began early in the history of civilization. Whenever and wherever people gathered in communities they felt a need for some kind of regulation to protect the public health. However, a fully developed, enlightened, and successful public health program in the United States did not really start until after the 1870s, when Louis Pasteur and Robert Koch established the true etiology of disease—germs. Prior to that time the few scattered laws on health matters either dealt with quarantine or were local ordinances concern-

ing smallpox, or, because of medical ignorance concerning the true nature of disease, were largely ineffective. Sanitarians believed that disease was caused by environmental factors, namely filth, and that
therefore the elimination of dirt would solve most problems of public
health. And while a sanitary program based on this belief won considerable popular support and scored several notable victories upon which
later developments rested—as, for example, the establishment of municipal boards of health—because it was based upon a faulty understanding of the etiology of disease it did not produce significant results.
Only when Pasteur and Koch proved that bacteria were not the end
products of diseases, as had long been believed, but rather that they
were the causative agents, that, in other words, specific micro-organ-
isms were responsible for specific diseases, were major advances in the
field made. Discovery of the bacteriological origins of man's most
ancient scourges occurred rapidly in the last two decades of the nineteenth century.[3]

Although the new knowledge allowed health officers to quickly
identify disorders, the germ theory and preventive medicine remained
in a relatively primitive stage until the importance of the personal
factor in contagion was realized. Only after the role of the infected
individual in spreading disease was understood did sanitary control
operate efficiently. This came near the end of the nineteenth century
with recognition of the "human carrier": disease germs are parasites,
adapted to life in the human body, their primary host; in view of their
parasitic nature, disease germs must be transferred rather promptly
from one human being to another if new infection is to occur; the
major mode of transmission is direct or indirect contact.[4] As a
consequence, personal cleanliness and segregation superseded environmental sanitation as the central life-saving steps and bases of preventive
health action, resulting in what has been described as "the golden age
of public health."[5] During this period, approximately 1890–1910,
municipal and state boards of health began to apply the recent discoveries in bacteriology to the prevention and care of disease, medical
education was vastly improved, and medical research was highly
organized.

Two other important developments in the new era of public health were the establishment of diagnostic laboratories by city and state boards of health and the organization of campaigns to educate the public in the fundamentals of modern hygiene.[6] New York City's early drive against tuberculosis, the city's most prevalent and fatal disease, illustrates the progress of these developments. In November 1893 the New York City Board of Health requested Dr. Hermann M. Biggs, head of its year-old Bacteriological Division, to prepare a report on tuberculosis. On the grounds that the disease was both communicable and preventable, Biggs recommended several remedial measures. The most important of these included a campaign of public education and the free examination of sputum by the Board's Bacteriological Division. The Board approved Biggs's suggestions and agreed to attract attention to the infectious nature of tuberculosis. It pointed out the measures necessary to guard against infection and its spread, distributing throughout the city circulars on the subject printed in several languages. Thanks to Biggs's far-sighted vision the first and one of the most successful attempts in the United States to control tuberculosis as a communicable disease was made by the New York City Department of Health.[7]

As a result, preventive medicine began to give increased attention not only to pathological research and laboratory diagnosis, but also to well-organized programs of public health education. Up to about 1900, however, war against disease was solely a business for professional sanitarians, health officials, and medical men. After the turn of the century a new line of attack on disease was opened that had a far-reaching and incalculable significance for the entire public health program—mobilization of the lay force of the community for the control of disease. Few people worked as long, as hard, as persistently, and most importantly, as successfully, to help bring this about as Homer Folks.

Social workers had a large stake in the new medical progress, for, as Folks pointed out, there was a direct connection between poverty and ill health: "The moment any individual or society turns its attention to the causes of poverty," he declared, "that moment it finds itself in the thick of the public health movement." [8] Social work and public health, then, had much in common. They were concerned with essentially the same problems—relieving distress in the home, which often resulted from death due to preventable disease. In fact, as Folks observed, "Social workers and health officers . . . met because their work . . . brought them to the same place, namely, the home in which there is both communicable disease and poverty." [9] Broadly speaking, then, social work embraced health work. Social workers almost had to be interested in building up health activities, for to them fell the somber task of trying to correct the damage caused by unchecked disease. By calling this to social workers' attention Folks helped give rise to medical social service.

Tuberculosis was the first communicable disease attacked on a large scale. This is understandable, for at the turn of the century it was the chief cause of death throughout the world, responsible for 10 per cent of all fatalities. While the tuberculosis mortality rate was higher for males than females (and among men most deaths occurred between the ages of twenty-five and thirty-four), it took the greatest toll of both sexes between the ages of fifteen and forty-four. In that age span about one-third of all deaths were caused by this one disease; the greatest loss was therefore among those who were in their most productive years. Since this illness often struck the breadwinner of a family, it robbed both victims and dependents of their livelihood, just at the time when money was needed for medical care. It caused more sorrow, suffering, and greater economic loss than any other human affliction. In 1903 it was estimated that the annual cost of tuberculosis to the nation, direct and indirect, totaled $330,000,000. It truly was, as one concerned American pointed out, the "Real Race Suicide." [10] Efforts to prevent tuberculosis would reduce both distress and economic losses.

Social workers provided the first comprehensive analysis of tuberculosis as it existed in the United States. This was undertaken in 1903 by the Committee on the Prevention of Tuberculosis of the Charity Organization Society of New York. Under the leadership of Edward T. Devine, this committee was organized in January 1902 at the suggestion of several physicians. Lay as well as medical members were included, a rather novel achievement for that period.[11] The committee undertook investigations of the social and other nontechnical aspects of tuberculosis. Its principal task, however, was to educate the community to the seriousness of the disease, its symptoms, incidence, and the means by which it could be prevented or arrested. It sought merely to arouse the public. Its aim was not the enactment of legislation.[12]

Physicians knew the pathology and etiology of tuberculosis, but they could not induce either active or passive immunization and they commanded no specific therapy other than a healthy diet, fresh air, and rest, helpful only in incipient cases. These limitations, in addition to the growing costs of medical care and the lack of financial support for the patients' dependents, highlighted the need for avoiding exposure to infection. Besides, only a few hospitals were available to care for the tubercular, so the prospect of removing most carriers of the infection was dim.[13]

Although the Committee on the Prevention of Tuberculosis emphasized most of all the dangers of infection, the public was more concerned with therapy than preventive measures. Treatment appealed to those most immediately concerned; preventive measures seemed vague, impractical, or of uncertain value. While New York City, thanks to the efforts of Dr. Biggs and the Charity Organization Society's Committee, made some headway in the drive against tuberculosis, inertia and indifference best characterized the response to the challenge elsewhere. Even when in 1904 a few state and local anti-tuberculosis groups appeared, to Lilian Brandt of the Charity Organization Society it seemed incredible that so little had been done to eliminate the "white plague." "This situation is a reproach to our intelligence and our public spirit," she declared.[14]

The National Association for the Study and Prevention of Tuberculosis was organized in 1904 to intensify and coordinate popular knowledge of the disease in the belief that education would lead to ultimate control. Like the COS committee, the association's functions were chiefly educational, promotional, and advisory; it did not locate cases, provide relief, or found hospitals. Instead it encouraged the formation of other volunteer bodies, which in turn performed those functions. Its goal was not to initiate a public health program from above by government; it was to begin one with the population at large and work up through the official agencies under the guidance and co-ordination of the national association.[15]

From the start, Homer Folks took part in the anti-tuberculosis movement. As Commissioner of Public Charities he had established the first municipal tuberculosis hopsital in the United States. He served on the Committee on the Prevention of Tuberculosis of the Charity Organization Society of New York, and he played a prominent part in the National Association for the Study and Prevention of Tuberculosis, serving for many years on its Board of Directors. When the Executive Committee of the national association planned its first annual meeting it included a sociological as well as a pathological and bacteriological section. The sociological section, created to consider such matters as the construction of tenements, hospitals, health board regulations, the incidence of tuberculosis in the various races, and the employment of discharged patients, was largely in the hands of Devine, Brandt, and Folks. He served as its first chairman and from the outset helped to guide the national organization's destiny from purely medical aspects into areas of social action as well.[16]

At the national association's first annual meeting, held in Washington in May 1905, Folks presented a notable paper that received national attention. Speaking from experience, he appealed to common sense, self-interest, and compassion in emphasizing the costs of tuberculosis and the need for convincing municipalities that large expenditures to fight the disease were both feasible and, in the long run, economical. Deploring the prevalence of the preventable disease, he went on to express the opinion that the many reasons for this "may be resolved into one, namely, that we do not realize the value of public health as an investment; that we are not yet ready to devote sufficient means to the saving of human life, even when the opportunity is placed squarely before us."[17] To implement his plea for recognition of the money value to the community and the country in checking this disease, Folks made the then unusual suggestion of issuing city and state bonds to raise large and immediately available funds for sanitary measures against consumption; it would be a wise and prudent investment of public money.

Meanwhile, the anti-tuberculosis movement grew steadily. The activities of the national association expanded, affiliated bodies were formed, and state and local societies and institutional facilities multiplied. Nevertheless, a much greater effort was needed. Even in New York City, for example, despite the valiant efforts of Biggs and the Charity Organization Society, which resulted in a reduced death rate, twenty-six years after the discovery of the tubercle bacillus there were 8,000 annual deaths from tuberculosis. The number was even greater outside of New York City where no organized anti-tuberculosis movement existed. Accordingly, at two successive board meetings near the end of 1906, Folks suggested that through its county committees the State Charities Aid Association make a special effort to reduce tuberculosis throughout New York State. Although the suggestion was turned down largely because of a lack of funds, the board unanimously adopted a resolution introduced by Folks, which read:

Whereas, Pulmonary tuberculosis is one of the leading causes of illness and death and therefore, suffering, destitution and pauperism in New York State

Whereas, it is now possible to take practical and effective measures for the restriction thereof

Whereas, the Charity Organization Society has worked effectively in New York City and nothing has been done elsewhere in New York State

RESOLVED, that it is desirable, if sufficient funds therefor should become available without impairing the income of the Association for work to which it is already committed, that the Association should take up actively, through its county committees, with the aid of a paid secretary, the promotion of measures for the restriction of tuberculosis in the State outside of New York City.[18]

In search of funds, Folks turned to the newly created Russell Sage Foundation, established in 1907 "for the improvement of social and living conditions in the United States of America." Folks had an excellent relationship with the new foundation since Mrs. William B. Rice and Louisa Lee Schuyler were among its first trustees. Moreover, he had a long acquaintance with John Glenn, the foundation's first director, a social worker who was associated with the anti-tuberculosis movement in Baltimore before coming to New York. As a result, his request to the Russell Sage Foundation for funds to enable the State Charities Aid Association to launch an anti-tuberculosis campaign in "upstate" New York was granted. With the promise of $5,000 from the foundation, Folks again brought the matter before the Association's board; this time it was approved.[19]

Actually, Folks had already begun an active campaign for the prevention of tuberculosis ten days before the board's final approval when he enticed a bright young Columbia University graduate student, John A. Kingsbury, to join the Association's staff as a full-time "field agent" in charge of the tuberculosis work. Kingsbury, like Owen Lovejoy before him, was among the earliest of an enormous legion of men and women recruited, guided, and directed by Folks to a successful career in social work or public health. Folks's unusual quality of insight in the selection of subordinates was again typified in the choice of Kingsbury, who contributed imagination, resourcefulness, enthusiasm, great energy, and valuable showmanship to the undertaking.[20] When Kingsbury in turn hired people to help him, New York became the first state in America to have a field staff organizing local tuberculosis associations.

The Association created a Committee on the Prevention of Tuberculosis, composed of laymen, including Kingsbury and Folks, and physicians noted for their public health work. The national association appointed the committee its affiliated state organization for New York, exclusive of New York City. As in the past, the Association sought to cooperate with public officials and in November 1907 invited the State Department of Health to join the State Charities Aid Association in a joint statewide educational program emphasizing the prevention of tuberculosis.[21]

Complete and accurate information on existing conditions was the foundation for any campaign of public enlightenment. Accordingly, the Committee on the Prevention of Tuberculosis sent its field agent to one city after another to conduct systematic and scientific investigations of the disease's prevalence and the measures in force, if any, for relief of consumptives and the protection of the uninfected. The compiled facts served as the basis for the committee's educational efforts, directed at securing in each locality the largest possible number of practical measures to prevent the disease.[22]

The campaign began in Utica, New York. With the help of John Kingsbury, who conducted the sanitary survey, the Oneida County Committee of the State Charities Aid Association appointed a sub-committee on the Prevention of Tuberculosis for the city of Utica. This subcommittee cooperated with the central association and the State Department of Health in organizing the popular educational campaign. The exhibit, a method of mass communication used success-fully by the Charity Organization Society and the national association, was employed. A display that could be moved from one city to another, the exhibit consisted of models, photographs, tables, and charts indicating comparative death rates, lantern slides showing unsanitary surroundings, desirable dwellings, sanatoria, and so on. The committee also distributed thousands of free leaflets and pamphlets and sponsored lectures and held meetings on the subject which were attended by local doctors, nurses, teachers, students, and local and state officials.

Thus, information concerning the communicability, preventability, and curability of tuberculosis was widely disseminated in the campaign endorsed and supported by the most active and influential people in the community, and elsewhere, including Governor Charles Evans Hughes. As a result, Utica immediately initiated a comprehensive anti-tuberculosis program, including a free tuberculosis dispensary and a public nursing service. The local board of health also passed a resolu-tion favoring compulsory registration of the disease.

The exhibit was taken from Utica to Rome, where a similar campaign was conducted. From there it was carried to Troy, Cohoes, Albany, Schenectady, Geneva, Auburn, Cortland, Kingston, New-burgh, Yonkers, White Plains, and ultimately to most of the cities throughout the state.[23] In Albany the campaign ended on January 27, 1908, with a public meeting which, "for the quality and size of its attendance, for the eminence of its speakers and for its extraordinary effectiveness, set a standard that in . . . a period of fifty-five years has not been surpassed anywhere in this country." [24] Joseph H. Choate, Governor Hughes, Dr. William H. Welch, "dean" of the nation's medical profession, Homer Folks, and leaders of the state legislature were the principal speakers. Five mayors of nearby cities, state officials, and other dignitaries occupied one hundred seats of honor on the stage. All 2,800 seats were filled and, for lack of space, hundreds were turned away from this meeting, reputed to be the largest nonpolitical gathering ever held in the capital city.[25] President Theodore Roosevelt sent Folks a telegram, which he read at the meeting and which, in part, said: "Permit me as an old friend and member of the Association, a former Governor of the State, and a very earnest sympathizer with your practical work for social betterment, to tender to the State Charities Aid Association, through you, the assurance of my interest, sympathy and approval in the work they [sic] are undertaking to organize local effort for the prevention of tuberculosis. . . . Such effort is peculiarly necessary, and I earnestly hope for its success." [26] The meeting gave a tremendous impetus to the tuberculosis movement throughout the state.

The Association's campaign was not based upon the assumption that it could defeat death; Folks did not expect to bring about a society in which no one died except of old age. But just as he worked to restrict illness that destroyed the young, Folks also utilized the new knowledge and the growing armament of defensive and preventive medicine to battle communicable disease, especially tuberculosis, which destroyed, hampered, or devitalized those in the prime of life. He knew, however, that this could not be accomplished without the sympathy and intelligent support of the community at large. As a first step, then, Folks and the Association made New York's residents aware of the communicable nature of tuberculosis in the hope that they would at least begin to take necessary preliminary steps to avoid spreading the infection. Folks and the Association thus became medical "muckrakers" attempting to overcome the public ignorance or apathy that stood in the way of improved public health.[27]

Within a year six dispensaries were opened, a visiting nurse service for tuberculosis patients was provided in six cities, two large hospitals were being built, and many other similarly important steps were taken. It was no wonder that in 1908 the International Tuberculosis Congress awarded the State Charities Aid Association a cherished gold medal for conducting the best state anti-tuberculosis campaign in America.[28]

Despite the progress, Folks felt the campaign was not going fast enough. Moreover, to Folks, a realist who never believed that statistics and information alone would solve social problems, it became increasingly evident that however rapidly disseminated, knowledge alone certainly would not prevent the spread of tuberculosis. Contacts within the family were so intimate and prolonged that, despite awareness of communicability, infection spread to an alarming degree. As a result, he now centered his attack on one of the fundamental weaknesses in the situation—the lack of basic tuberculosis laws. His political experience, learned not from textbooks but firsthand, once again served him well.

A factor that greatly retarded control of tuberculosis was the unwillingness of the public and the medical profession to report cases. In many communities tuberculosis was regarded as a disgrace (or public menace); to avoid that stigma, victims frequently went unattended. To protect the sensibilities of their patients who did seek medical help, physicians often reported cases of consumption as bronchitis or pneumonia. In fact, so untrustworthy were physicians' death reports for tuberculosis and other actively contagious diseases that Chicago's Board of Health felt obliged to organize the city's undertakers and obtain from them information on the causes of death; and it was on the undertakers', not the physicians', reports that the authorities relied. Many doctors also believed that the knowledge that tuberculosis was contagious would disrupt families and drive large numbers of patients to suicide. Thus they felt that to report cases was a violation of professional confidence.[29] But efficient public health control depended, above all else, upon prompt discovery, registration, and segregation of all carriers of disease. Accordingly, Folks, with the assistance of medical experts, framed a bill that defined the powers and duties of local health officials and boards of health, in connection with tuberculosis. It provided for the mandatory reporting of cases by physicians, home supervision of reported cases, free sputum analysis, disinfection and renovation of apartments occupied by consumptives or vacated by death or removal, and the prosecution of willfully careless cases. The State Board of Health, which favored the bill but thought it would not pass the legislature, refused to support it.[30] A vigorous campaign on behalf of the measure, in which Folks sent thousands of letters asking constituents of legislators who did not actively support it to join in the united effort against the disease, bore fruit; the Governor signed the measure into law on May 19, 1908.[31] In the opinion of one well-versed in such matters, the "enactment of . . . [this] bill into law, and the execution of the law, . . . place[d] the State of New York in the front rank among the governments which . . . [were] most active and successful in the control of tuberculosis."[32]

A year later an equally important measure was passed—the County Tuberculosis Hospital Law. Drafted by Folks, this measure resulted from the International Congress on Tuberculosis, which met in Washington, D.C., in 1908. Attended by leading figures in this country as well as distinguished foreign delegates, the congress produced several significant papers that emphasized the futility of home treatment. Most important was a paper read by Dr. Arthur H. Newsholme, Chief Medical Officer of the Local Government Board of England, possibly the foremost English-speaking authority on vital statistics. Newsholme demonstrated that the tuberculosis death rate declined directly in proportion to the adequacy of hospital accommodations. Since the carrier necessarily was a radiating center of infection, treatment and prevention were related; the proper care of the sick in hospitals secured the best protection from contagion for those who were well.[33] Folks left the congress convinced that, both on humanitarian grounds and in the interest of public safety, no substitute could be found for adequate institutional care.[34]

New York, like the other states, had an appalling lack of proper accommodations for its "white plague" victims. The vast majority of consumptives were still in contagious wards of general hospitals, almshouses, or in their dark tenements or wretched dwellings. As Dr. S. A. Knopf, a world-wide authority, put it: the majority of America's tuberculous are going to die, "not because they are incurable, but because there is no place to cure them." [35]

Folks carefully considered how best to remedy the situation. He concluded that private charity was unable to erect and maintain the needed hospitals. Moreover, since such institutions would be as much a preventive as an ameliorative force, they were viewed by Folks as a public responsibility. Consequently Folks, Dr. Biggs, Dr. Livingston Farrand, and other members of the State Charities Aid Association's Committee on the Prevention of Tuberculosis met with a group of legislators in Albany to discuss New York State's hospital needs. The lawmakers, however, opposed complete state hospital provision for all tuberculosis cases. The impossibility of securing appropriations from state funds for complete care led Folks and the others to consider some form of local provision. They finally agreed on a permissive law that gave to the counties the power to establish tuberculosis hospitals. Framed by Folks and Kingsbury, the bill became law on May 13, 1909. This measure not only began New York State's campaign for tuberculosis hospitals, but also marked the start of sustained tuberculosis legislation throughout the United States. [36]

The law authorized each county to establish and maintain a tuberculosis hospital. The costs of the sites and the construction of the buildings could be met by the sale of bonds, while maintenance charges had to be met by taxation. All patients had to be received in the order of application. After admission their financial circumstances were to be ascertained, and, if able, they were expected to pay in whole or part. But the poor and well-to-do were to have an equal right to admission and treatment. [37]

The County Tuberculosis Hospital Law had two shortcomings. It was permissive rather than mandatory, allowing ample opportunity for the opponents of such hospitals to postpone and defeat practical acceptance of the measure in many counties. An equally serious fault was its "means test." Because the superintendent of the hospital could inquire into the ability of a patient, or his relative, to pay for treatment, the onerous investigation and the stigma of charity associated with it often kept patients from seeking medical care early when serious complications could still be prevented. Thus, in part, it defeated the purpose of the law and the effectiveness of the campaign against tuberculosis. For these deficiencies, however, Folks cannot be blamed. The state legislature simply would pass no other kind of law. Folks knew, too, that practical politics and public hygiene were hard to combine. As a result, he knew and worked for what was obtainable, accepting advances piecemeal; and in this case, half a loaf was better than none.

Folks and the Association's Committee on the Prevention of Tuberculosis concentrated next on educating County Boards of Supervisors to the need and advisability of establishing local hospitals. By 1910 the building of eight county hospitals was assured.[38] But a serious difference of opinion arose within the movement over the merits of hospitalization and segregation as the most effective means of large-scale prevention. Many people felt that, at best, hospitals could accommodate only a small percentage of those in need. Besides, most hospitals, they argued, received patients with advanced cases who had spread infection long before they were hospitalized. Resistance to infection, not hospitalization, they argued, was the only answer. The development by Dr. C. Von Pirquet in 1907 of the tuberculin tests seemed to fortify their claim. These tests indicated that early infection was so widespread that it was almost a constant. Von Pirquet found that large numbers of people were infected without ever becoming ill, which implied that resistance (immunity) might be the most important variable.[39] If this were the case, the best way to prevent tuberculosis would be simply to promote good health. In a word, shift the emphasis from a campaign against specific infection and segregation to one in favor of general health.

Unfortunately, just as the resistance factor was ignored in the early years of the campaign, many people now went to the other extreme and virtually ignored segregation. Folks and the State Charities Aid Association, however, did not forget the importance of either. When in

1912 Folks was elected President of the National Association for the Study and Prevention of Tuberculosis, the first, and for many years the only, layman to hold that position, he delivered an address in which he correctly emphasized the need for both general good health and segregation of the infected in a well-rounded preventive program.[40]

To help carry out that program in New York State and overcome the delaying tactics of various County Boards of Supervisors, Folks drafted another bill, which became law in the spring of 1914. The measure's most important provision stated that a County Board of Supervisors might submit the question of establishing a tuberculosis hospital to the voters of the county at a general election. In the next two years twelve new county tuberculosis hospitals were established by public referenda; in every case in which the proposition to establish a hospital was submitted to the voters it was adopted.[41]

Three years later, when still another bill framed by the Association's Committee on the Prevention of Tuberculosis was enacted into law, the movement to provide institutional facilities for New York's tuberculosis victims reached a high point. The latest measure made the establishment of a tuberculosis hospital *mandatory* for all counties of the state with a population of more than 35,000, thus overcoming one of the major shortcomings of the earlier, permissive law.[42]

A quick glance at tuberculosis statistics testifies to the wisdom and effectiveness of the State Charities Aid Association's campaign against the disease. In 1907 there was no tuberculosis legislation in New York State outside of New York City. Ten years later the state had the most advanced tuberculosis laws in the nation. In 1907 the disease was the greatest single cause of death in the state; the mortaliy rate per 100,000 was 152.18 Twenty-five years later it ranked seventh in the causes of death; the mortality rate was 59.2, a decrease of 61 per cent. The tuberculosis campaign annually saved thousands of lives in New York State.[43]

As James H. Cassedy has indicated, historians of the so-called progressive era have either ignored altogether or underestimated the contributions of pioneer public health crusaders to the larger reform movement during the early twentieth century.[44] Whether working to conserve human resources by making provisions for the isolation of infectious carriers of disease, or by extending compulsory medical inspection for school children, or in any number of other ways, these reformers made some of the most outspoken statements on behalf of public control; they should not be relegated to the "underworld" of progressivism. Certainly, Folks's career bears witness to the fact that it was no mere coincidence that the public health movement in America emerged during the progressive era. No better illustration of this exists than Folks's attempts to improve and make more efficient the administration of public health measures by divorcing it from "politics," a problem with which more "traditional" progressives also dealt.

This was necessary for, in general, public health officials were incompetent; almost none had special training. Most were political appointees with as little concern for as knowledge of their tasks. As a result, the administration of public health was bad. In most cases, therefore, it was necessary for the public-spirited citizen, rather than the public-supported health officer, to assume leadership in the reform movement. Relations between various anti-tuberculosis organizations, composed largely of "private" citizens, and public health officers varied widely. Sometimes there was harmony and cooperation. Quite often, however, there was mutual irritation, as reformers criticized the inertia of health officers, who in turn resented the proddings from nonofficial groups. Throughout his career Folks was careful to cultivate the best possible relations with New York State's public health officials. In the spirit with which the Association was founded, Folks placed increasing emphasis upon cooperation with official organizations. Public health, he held, is primarily a function of government; health officials must undertake the actual operation of programs. Voluntary agencies should support, supplement, and strengthen public agencies.[45]

It was important, though, that public health be administered properly; despite the activities of public-spirited citizens, ultimately the success of the movement depended upon public-supported health officials. In New York, as elsewhere, the situation needed improvement. Not only were public health officials political appointees, but the state, outside of New York City, was burdened with an array of uncoordinated and thus inefficient state and local authorities. Health legislation was administered by approximately fourteen hundred health officers attached to five or six hundred unconnected health boards in various towns, villages, and cities.[46] In 1912 Folks took advantage of an opportunity to bring order to this chaotic system.

In the fall of 1912 William Sulzer, a strange, controversial figure, was elected governor of New York.[47] Although a demagogue and a cog in the Tammany machine, once in the governor's chair he broke with the Hall and lined up with the state's progressive forces. Ignoring the machine in his appointments, he instituted a graft investigation, vetoed an election bill passed by the Tammany-dominated legislature, and, to the chagrin of Boss Murphy, even demanded a direct primary law. On orders from Murphy, instead of passing a primary law, for which they were called into special session, members of the legislature appointed a committee to investigate the Governor's campaign expenditures. The committee found that, in violation of the law, Sulzer had concealed campaign contributions and used portions of the funds for speculating in stocks. Later he attempted to tamper with witnesses and influence the course of the legislative investigation. As a result, on August 13, 1913, he was impeached and removed from office.[48] Thanks to Folks and some of his associates, however, Sulzer's brief and politically disastrous nine months of gubernatorial service were marked by one of the most notable social advances in the state's history—the progressive reorganization of its health services.

Shortly after Sulzer's election, Homer Folks and John Kingsbury asked Henry Morganthau, State Charities Aid Association Board member, chairman of the Finance Committee of the Democratic National Committee, and friend and large contributor to Sulzer's campaign, to arrange a meeting for them and a number of other reformers and executives of various health and welfare agencies with the Governor-elect. At Folks's suggestion, Morganthau invited Sulzer and the reformers to a dinner at his home in order to allow them to meet and briefly lay before the chief executive the needs in their respective fields of interest. In addition to Folks and Kingsbury, the guests included such well-known figures as Lillian D. Wald, Owen Lovejoy, and Edward T. Devine.

After dinner each of the guests spoke for about ten minutes on the needs in his or her special field. Representing the State Charities Aid Association, Folks presented to Sulzer a picture of the vast opportunity for protecting the health and lives of the people of New York State through a more vigorous public health program, especially by an attack on tuberculosis. When Kingsbury, Wald, and others strongly supported the suggestion, Sulzer showed interest in the matter.[49]

Shortly thereafter Folks and Kingsbury again discussed the idea with Sulzer, also inquiring about his plans for the Health Commissionership. When the Governor replied that he wanted "the best health man in the United States" for the job, Folks pointed out that it might be impossible for, according to statute, appointment of a state resident was required. "Well, let's change the law," was Sulzer's response. In return, Folks immediately suggested that a commission be created to revise the state's entire system, including the Department of Health. To his surprise, Sulzer consented. Accordingly, on January 10, 1913, only ten days after he was inaugurated, Sulzer appointed a special commission for the purpose of "receiving suggestions and making such recommendations as may seem fitting with regard to what changes, if any, are advisable in the laws of this state relating to and affecting public health, and in public health administration." [50]

Folks was offered chairmanship of the commission. Because he was a "layman," he wisely refused it in favor of Dr. Hermann Biggs, a renowned physician who undoubtedly would give more weight and prestige to the commission's suggestions, especially with the medical profession.[51] Instead, Folks was appointed secretary (and vice-chairman) of the special commission, which also included Kingsbury, Professor M. A. Nutting, head of the Department of Nursing and Health at Teachers College, Dr. J. C. Otis of Poughkeepsie, Mr. Ansley Wilcox of Buffalo, Dr. E. R. Baldwin of Saranac, and Dr. W. E. Milbank of Albany.[52]

The group worked at record speed. In a period of about one month it held ten public hearings in Albany, New York City, and Buffalo. Seeking advice from local health officers and investigating in detail the health administration of several counties, the committee received over 1,000 pieces of mail and personally questioned 60 people, filling the record with 836 typewritten pages of testimony.[53] Thanks to such strenuous efforts, a 40-page report was presented to the Governor on February 15, 1913. Four days later Sulzer transmitted it to the law-makers, informing them that in the near future a bill embodying the commission's recommendations would be introduced in the legislature. He strongly urged its early and favorable consideration.[54]

In addition to many minor reforms, the commission's recommendations consisted of three major changes. In estimating their significance it should be remembered that at the time state boards of health held only advisory power over local communities within their jurisdiction, most of which were poorly and inefficiently administered.

The first and most important reform was the provision for a Public Health Council, to be composed of the Commissioner of Health and six other members appointed by the Governor. The council would have two main, and unique, powers—to enact and amend a sanitary code for the entire state, excluding New York City, and to establish eligibility rules or qualifications for various public health positions, such as sanitary supervisors and public health nurses.[55] Since the subjects of sanitary legislation were so complex and technical that they could not possibly be dealt with properly in a legislative session, delegating quasi-legislative ordinance-making power to a small expert administrative body would be an enormous advance in public health administration. According to Dr. Granville Larimore, the state's current Deputy Commissioner of Health, more than anything else, when it became law this novel provision enabled New York to raise and maintain its health standards above those of every other state in the nation.[56]

Second, besides recommending the establishment of a high minimum wage for all health officers, including the State Commissioner, in order for public health work to be able to attract and hold men with special training, the commission urged that in addition to the six exist-

ing divisions within the Health Department, three new ones be-
created—Child Hygiene, Public Health Nursing, and Tuberculosis.[57]
In the words of the noted authority, Dr. C. E. A. Winslow, the "broad-
ening scope which these new divisions involved mark[ed] all the
difference between the public health program of the nineteenth and
that of the twentieth century." [58]

Finally, the commission recommended that the State Department of
Health supervise directly certain aspects of local health work. It hoped
the State Commissioner would be given the power to enforce both the
public health law and the sanitary code, and exercise general supervision over localities. In its estimation, the state, outside of New York
City, should be divided into twenty sanitary districts. For each of these
an expert Sanitary Supervisor would be appointed by the Health
Commissioner to supervise the local health officers of his district,
enforce all public health laws, carry on a health education program,
and secure full registration of communicable diseases, births, and
deaths.[59]

On March 12 the commission submitted to the Governor a bill
embodying its recommendations. The measure was transmitted to the
legislature without change.[60] It immediately won wide press and
popular support throughout the state. Commenting editorially on the
bill the New York *Evening Post,* wrote in words characteristic of most
other newspapers that "the manifold benefit that may be expected from
infusing into the making and administration of health regulations a
higher degree of intelligence and vigor is so manifest that there should
be no doubt of the adoption . . . of the Commission's recommendations." [61] Such statewide lay and professional organizations as the
Grange, the Federation of Women's Clubs, the State Sanitary Officers
Association, and others endorsed the measure.

Folks took nothing for granted. He remained in Albany whipping
his forces into line. Patient, friendly, and remarkably persuasive, he
testified before legislative committees, dined out in political society,
guided conversation into the proper channel, stimulated dozens of
organizations to pass appropriate resolutions, asked influential people
to write personal notes to their representatives, and went from legisla-

tor to legislator seeking support. He enlisted the interest and support of
Speaker of the Assembly Alfred E. Smith and Senate majority leader
Robert F. Wagner; they played important parts in pushing the bill
through their respective chambers. The measure became law on May
17, 1913.[62]

The 1913 Public Health Law "unquestionably marked the most
important landmark in the history of state health administration in the
United States since the creation of the first state health department by
Massachusetts in 1869." [63] Although amended in details several times,
the law still remains the basis of public health administration in New
York State. More important, however, it served as a model for many
other states, at least thirty of which have reorganized their health
departments according to the provisions of New York's law.[64]

Homer Folks was the chief draftsman of both the Special Health
Commission Report and the model Public Health Law.[65] Ten years
after its enactment, Dr. Hermann Biggs, the commission's chairman
and subsequent State Commissioner of Health, informed an audience
that the "public health law of New York State is the result of Mr.
Folk's [sic] skill as a bill drafter." Furthermore, Biggs added, "Ever
since that law ['a great contribution to public health not only in New
York but throughout the United States'] was passed in 1913 . . . practically every important modification or amendment has been drafted
by Mr. Folks. And not only was it drafted by him," continued Biggs,
"but to a large extent through his tact and ability have these amendments been passed by the legislature." [66]

Along with such eminent doctors as Hermann Biggs and Simon
Flexner, director of the Rockefeller Institute, on June 27, 1913, Governor Sulzer appointed Folks to the state's first Public Health Council.
Serving as vice-chairman, a position he held continuously from its
establishment until his resignation in 1955, having been reappointed by
Republican and Democratic governors alike as each of his five-year
terms expired, Folks was an active, vigorous, and influential member
of the council. He added a great deal to its deliberations, often keeping
the meetings moving, sharpening discussions, and through his tact
mediating between members, especially doctors who frequently became

too involved in medical details. Also, Folks's knowledge and skill in framing legislation was very helpful to the council, particularly in forcing precise wording in regard to the provisions of the sanitary code and other statutory decrees.[67]

Although enactment of a sanitary code was the first matter of business, the Public Health Council devoted a great deal of time at its early meetings to establishing procedural policy, defining its powers, limitations, and jurisdiction. It had to transform a legal provision into an operating reality. Council members differed in opinion over their powers and duties. While he believed the council had the widest possible jurisdiction under the law, and technically could act on any matters affecting "life and health," Folks wisely insisted that in the early stages of its work the council refrain from legislating on anything which might be construed as outside its authority. To do otherwise, he pointed out, might impair its status:

Unless these are matters which are serious and important, why should we undertake to deal with them? Isn't there so much that is immediate and important to be done affecting practically the reduction of sickness and the death rate that it would be a mistake to devote any of our powers or the time of local health authorities . . . to doing things that are on the border-line, and risk a decision perhaps by the Attorney General or a court or somebody else, an adverse decision, because we ventured beyond the line of our law which was clear.[68]

Folks played an especially large part in establishing standards and qualifications for all public health officials and health personnel throughout the state; he was instrumental in eliminating residency requirements.[69] And it was in this area that the council made one of its most important contributions to public health. For by providing for the appointment and tenure of public health personnel to be determined solely on the basis of merit—experience and education—the possibility of appointing incompetent and unqualified health personnel was reduced and public health work was taken out of politics.[70]

Actually, the Public Health Council was only a quasi-legislative body. Its decrees and resolutions were not necessarily or immediately acts of law. To achieve legal status they had to be promulgated by the

State Commissioner of Health and filed by the Secretary of State, neither of whom was obligated to do this. Furthermore, the statutory acts of the council were subject to review by the courts. In this connection, however, it is interesting to note that since its creation no State Commissioner of Health has ever failed or refused to carry into effect the council's wishes, nor has a Secretary of State ever refused to file any of its recommendations. Also, no court has ever overruled any of the council's acts.[71]

That is not to say, however, that the new public health program did not run into dangers. Its greatest threat came in 1915 when the Republican Party regained control of the state's executive and legislative branches and tried to nullify the law that had been enacted two years earlier by a Democratic legislature, on recommendation of a Democratic governor, and then implemented by a health commissioner, Dr. Biggs, who came from traditionally Democratic New York City. Folks's special abilities—his dauntless courage, his amazing qualities as a fighter for the things in which he believed, his capacity to sense approaching danger, prepare for it, hit hard at vulnerable spots, and marshal and use his forces appropriately—were shown many times, but perhaps never more dramatically than in this incident.

Early in the 1915 session Senate majority leader Elon R. Brown announced that appropriations for the State Department of Health would be cut in half. In addition, Republican Assemblyman H. J. Hinman of Albany introduced five bills in the legislature that would have set back by many years the state's health work. The first of these intended to reduce the sanitary districts of the state from twenty to ten and the supervisor's salary from $4,000 to $2,550. The second would have made permissive instead of mandatory the nine administrative divisions of the Health Department. The third took from the Public Health Council the power to fix the qualifications of health officials. The fourth proposed requiring the provisions of the sanitary code to be re-enacted by the state legislature. The fifth made the Health Commissionership and the Divisional Directorships full-time positions which, while good in theory, was designed to force the resignation of Biggs and many of his most able assistants.[72]

Argued in the name of "economy" and local rule, and with the party leaders and the overwhelming majority in both houses of the legislature pledged to support them, it appeared as though the Hinman bills would be carried without any difficulty. The first three bills were sent to the Senate after passing the House with unprecedented speed. At this point Folks responded to the challenge with all his political skill. He noted that six of Biggs's highest eight staff appointees and eleven of the twenty Sanitary Supervisors were Republicans, indicating the nonpartisan attitude of the Health Department. He pointed out that in the one year since enactment of the law the number of deaths in New York State, outside of New York City, had been lowered by two thousand. Under the caption "Dollars or Lives, Which?" he made an impassioned plea for support of the Health Department.[73]

Words, however, were not enough. After receiving a special donation to cover the expenses of an active campaign to oppose the Hinman bills, Folks and three assistants devoted full time to the task of pressuring the legislature. They visited thirty-three cities, suggesting to the people they met that they write letters of protest to their legislative representatives and local health officials. They prepared and distributed to newspapers numerous articles and special bulletins, as well as paid advertisements. In addition to distributing thirty-five thousand leaflets on the subject, they circulated widely a special memorandum in opposition to the bills. A special health issue of the S.C.A.A. News was sent to thousands. They sent a signed letter of protest to all the members of various anti-tuberculosis organizations. Folks and his aides secured the cooperation of the Federal Council of Churches and similar organizations, which in turn sent letters on the subject to thousands of their members. Nearly six thousand officers of the Grange were informed of the situation. In these and still other ways, including the sending of hundreds of telegrams to prominent citizens throughout the state, Folks gained support for his cause to keep the government committed to the concept of public health.[74]

The press almost unanimously opposed the Hinman bills; it wanted the legislature to preserve the public health law intact and appropriate adequate funds to the State Department of Health. The New York

Tribune declared editorially, "This is a question of lives against dollars. The state must not put the dollar above human life." The New York *Evening Post* argued that to "take such a step would be simply barbarous," while the New York *Globe* asked, "Is the state, because of a few selfish interests that object to reasonable regulations, to be thrust back into the dark ages?" [75]

People and organizations from all parts of the state responded similarly. Heeding Folks's advice, they sent letters and telegrams, resolutions and personal representatives to Albany to protest against the measures and the proposed cuts in the Health Department's appropriations. It was, as Folks wrote, "altogether a most impressive and convincing demonstration that the people of New York want public health and are willing to pay for it." [76] He might have added that it also was a tribute to the State Charities Aid Association and its secretary, who eight years earlier decided to cultivate an enlightened public opinion in matters of public health; their seeds had not fallen on stony soil.

The result of such unprecedented public support was a foregone conclusion. The first three Hinman bills were not reported out of Senate committee; the other two were never even sent to the House. This was probably one of the most important victories of Folks's career. It not only settled the particular issue and demonstrated the wide support for public health in New York, but it also set a pattern of fighting that would not be forgotten. Never again would a given measure be considered secure simply because it went through the legislature. More than ever, Folks realized the necessity for social workers to remain interested in and identify themselves with the measures they advocated, regardless of who was charged with their administration.

Most important, however, the unsuccessful attack on the state's progressive Health Department made politicians wary of attacking that organization. As Folks related in recalling the episode years later, from the day the Hinman bills were defeated "the subject of public health has been a non-partisan one in the state of New York." [77]

Advances in public health were an accurate index to advances in civilization, for its growth as a social force was in reality the growth of an appreciation by the people that each individual had a responsibility to the community; each person, each family, had to contribute to the welfare of the whole, and in so doing furthered his own personal and family welfare. As Dr. Hermann Biggs indicated, few people worked harder for acceptance of that ideal than Homer Folks. Pointing to his accomplishments, the famed physician said, "I don't think there is any man in this country—certainly no layman—who has contributed more to the promotion of health than . . . [Homer Folks] has." [78]

Without doubt, by the early 1920s New York State stood in the forefront of the public health movement, especially in the fight against tuberculosis. With great resources and such enlightened leaders as Biggs and Folks, public health was placed there far ahead of other states. Yet, despite the many notable achievements, even in New York where appropriations for health work were relatively high and health officials, in general, were by then of a good caliber, much remained to be done.

Obviously, anti-tuberculosis work was increasingly concerned with the question of public health in general; the broadened scope of the work grew out of the necessity to consider other community health needs and facilities in order to prevent illness and provide efficient care for those already sick. In short, there was a need to unite all health activities. Actually, ever since the appointment of the Public Health Commission in 1913 the State Charities Aid Association recognized that need. In February 1920 however, the Committee on the Prevention of Tuberculosis changed its name to the Committee on Tuberculosis and Public Health. The change in name did not imply a change in object or method, but in part a recognition of what had been fact for several years and, in part, a premonition of what was to come. Under Folks's guidance the State Charities Aid Association already had provided vivid testimony for Dr. C. E. A. Winslow's contention that "the discovery of the possibilities of widespread social organization as a means of controlling disease was one which may almost be placed alongside the discovery of the germ theory of disease itself as a factor in the evolution of the modern public health campaign." [79] However, with a broadened view of the scope of its work, as its new name implied, the State Charities Aid Association would further increase its usefulness. Moreover, not only did New York State and the United States benefit from that work, but when America entered World War I Folks's efforts were extended abroad.

10

AMERICAN RED CROSS

DURING the early years of the twentieth century a new chapter was written in the story of human welfare. Along with unprecedented political, economic, and social reforms, sickness and death, man's two worst enemies, were increasingly subjected to human control. In short, life was made richer, happier, and longer. As a result, Folks, like so many of his contemporaries, looked forward with confidence to the future.[1]

Then came the shouts from Europe that war was imminent. Folks's initial reaction was complete skepticism. War denied the validity of all he and his associates stood for. It diverted attention and funds from saving life to destroying it. War declared that darkness, cold, hunger, poverty, disease, crippling, killing, hate, orphanage, and widowhood were the accepted conditions of life. Folks therefore felt that war was impossible: the world had outgrown war; it "had become too wise, too humane, too sensitive to suffering, too high-minded, too rational, too moral."[2] When the storm broke out with startling suddenness in mid-summer of 1914, he observed it in horror, thanked Providence for the Atlantic Ocean, and continued steadfastly to labor for the uplift of American society.

With America's entrance into the war in April 1917, Folks could no longer ignore the calamity; we were in it, and the only way out was forward. He thought of war as though it were an infectious disease. Once the patient had the disease the best that could be done was to relieve some of the worst symptoms. He would not let the welfare of women and children be forgotten while men were fighting. Leaving the ideology of the affair to others, Folks turned his energies to the practical problems involved in the holocaust. In other words, the situation was neither good nor desirable, but the best must be made of it. Folks was accustomed to facing undesirable situations. The SCAA's Board of Managers, having adopted a resolution offering the organization's services to the nation "in such form as may be considered advisable and most efficient," now suggested that its local committees assist in every way possible "with national, state, county and city authorities and with the American Red Cross and other agencies, in work in behalf of soldiers, sailors and their families, and to meet such other exceptional conditions as may be incidental to the war."[3] Folks was authorized to carry out the resolution.

He immediately urged the Association's local committees to make a more strenuous effort in the field of public health. Mobilization of the nation's manpower, and its effectiveness, he pointed out, depended upon the health of its citizens.[4] Events abroad verified Folks's contention. Misery, disease, starvation, and death stalked Europe. As important as military assistance abroad was the need for civilian relief.

In the thirty-one months before the United States entered the war three major American relief organizations crossed the ocean to help war victims—the Hoover Commission, the Rockefeller Foundation, and the American Red Cross. By spring 1917 an even greater relief effort was needed. Deaths caused by communicable diseases, especially tuberculosis, were increasing in prevalence in every country on the Continent. Especially alarming reports about the high incidence of tuberculosis came from France. Consequently, the Rockefeller Foundation sent Dr. Hermann M. Biggs to France to investigate the situation. Biggs found that the great prevalence of tuberculosis among both the military and civilian populations in France constituted one of the most serious problems confronting the allied nations. A previously high morbidity and mortality rate had increased sharply because of war conditions. Moreover, the facilities for the care of tuberculosis were inadequate and most French people were uninformed about the nature of the disease. Biggs recommended that the foundation attempt to remedy the situation by introducing the type of controls used in the United States, including public health education, development of laboratory services, dispensaries, and tuberculosis hospitals. In response, the Rockefeller Foundation created through the International Health Board a Special Commission for the Prevention of Tuberculosis in France. This commission was headed by Livingston Farrand and included Dr. James A. Miller, one of America's most prominent tuberculosis specialists, Professor Selskar M. Gunn, executive secretary of the American Public Health Association, and Homer Folks.[5]

In the meantime, after the United States entered the war the American Red Cross modified its overseas program. On May 10, 1917, President Wilson appointed a War Council to carry on its war work, under the chairmanship of Henry P. Davison, a partner in the house of J. P. Morgan and Company. Eleven days later the council met officially for the first time and decided to end indiscriminate Red Cross relief to all combatants; instead, it would send a commission to Europe to help the allied countries in greatest need.[6]

In response to the appeal from France to help save her war-scarred population, especially from the ravages of tuberculosis, the War Council decided to set up in that country a Department of Civil Affairs, including a tuberculosis bureau. The next day Grayson M. P. Murphy, vice-president of the Guaranty Trust Company of New York and newly appointed head of the American Red Cross Commission to Europe, asked Folks to go to Europe in charge of its work for the prevention of tuberculosis.[7] Guided by his belief in the worth of all individuals and the importance of saving human lives, as well as a generosity that made it impossible for him to refuse to respond to the appeals of suffering Frenchmen, Folks accepted Murphy's offer. When the Executive Committee of the American Red Cross approved the War Council's decision to aid France and the other needy allied nations, through Homer Folks the American Red Cross and the Rockefeller Foundation joined hands in an "Alliance Against Tuberculosis."[8]

Despite his convictions, the decision to go abroad and leave his wife and family behind, at least for the time being, wasn't an easy one for Folks. Not just a social worker, but a man with warm husbandly and fatherly instincts, he would miss his wife and family—and they would miss him. However, the fifty-year-old reformer felt better about sailing for Europe when his daughter Gertrude secured permission to use a Vassar College fellowship (Borden Fund for study abroad) to meet living expenses while doing civilian relief work in France, and thus accompanied him when he left the country on July 9, 1917.[9]

Two weeks later, only a few minutes after he arrived in Paris to supervise the anti-tuberculosis work, Murphy asked him to take charge of all relief efforts for French civilians. "I found that everybody was waiting for *me,* think of it, poor little *me,*" Folks wrote in his first letter home. "They wanted me to take general charge of . . . the [whole] Department of Civil Affairs." [10]

Folks considered carefully whether to accept this position, one of great importance and enormous responsibility. While he looked upon the war with great horror, he also realized that it, like earlier national crises, offered extraordinary opportunities for constructive advances in the social field.[11] This was particularly true in the field of public health, where according to Folks there was never "a time in any country where the possibilities of accomplishment have been as great as they . . . [were] in France" in 1917. While not glossing over any of the tragic spiritual and material consequences of the war, he pointed out that for "the first time in history two great nations are combining their mental, moral and financial resources to deal with the problem of preventive disease in a single country. It has become possible," Folks continued, through this "international adventure" to "take in a few years forward steps which in other times would require decades." [12] To an extent, then, Folks viewed World War I with the same exuberant spirit he had viewed the progressive era: earlier he had crusaded for the reconstruction of society at home; now he would do the same abroad. In anticipation of all that could be accomplished as head of the entire Department of Civil Affairs, Folks accepted the position and with it the rank of major.

When the Department of Civil Affairs, located in a large building at No. 4 Place de La Concorde, was placed in Folks's hands it had a staff of thirteen which already had begun working in Paris on the acute refugee problem. However, large areas of France had just been liberated and under Folks's leadership the department assumed the gigantic task of returning the refugees to their homes and rehabilitating the devastated areas. The chief task was to give French civilians the help that would enable them to become self-supporting. Working with and through the French Red Cross and other relief agencies, the department's activities included organized efforts to rehabilitate refugees (dispense relief, help build homes), re-educate "mutiles" (a word not in the dictionary but one Folks constantly used when referring to people deprived of a limb or any other important part or parts of the body), establish a comprehensive plan for the treatment and prevention of tuberculosis and other communicable diseases, and, above all else, see to it that every child was given the best possible chance for normal development.[13]

Folks wasted no time getting to work. In three days he prepared a budget which, to his surprise, was accepted without a single change and was used by Murphy as the model for all other department heads to follow in order to have their financial requests approved.[14] For administrative purposes Folks established nine bureaus, later consolidated into six—Reconstruction and Relief, Children and Infant Mortality, Repatriates, Tuberculosis, Refugees, and Re-Education of Mutiles. A three-hundred-member American Friends Unit, a Business, and an Editorial and Historical Division were added to the department later. Folks successfully secured "persons of special experience and professional attainments" as chiefs of his bureaus. By September first the staff totaled sixty-one full-time employees and the work extended to hundreds of cities, villages, and hamlets throughout France.[15]

Tons of supplies were pouring across the Atlantic. Shipload after shipload of medicine, hospital equipment, foodstuffs, clothing, agricultural implements, furniture, household utensils, and countless other articles arrived in France for Folks to distribute. In favor with Murphy who, Folks related, "seems to swear by me and thus far has stood by me beautifully," he played a key part in Red Cross affairs. As chief of the Department of Civil Affairs he was responsible for about 60 per cent of the Red Cross's work abroad. He was also a member of several committees, including the six-man Finance Committee, the real on-the-scene power behind the organization's European activities.[16] In fact, according to Folks, it was "whispered about that everyone else in the Red Cross . . . [was] getting afraid that there . . . [would] soon be nothing but my department," but this, he continued, was a mere exaggeration.[17] On a later occasion, however, he reported that he heard "from the highest sources the wish expressed that military affairs were going as well as civil affairs." [18]

Folks found his work absorbing. "I have no time to think whether I am lonesome or homesick or happy or glad I came, or anything except how to get things done, and that quickly," he wrote home. "I have been neither depressed nor elated but just busy and satisfied that things seem to be moving," he went on to say.[19] At times, however, things slowed down, as a letter to his wife indicates: "I have had what all Americans, or nearly all get, usually soon after arriving, a [case of] diarrhea. I neglected it for three or four days thinking it would disappear, but it did not, so I took a large dose of caster [sic] oil and went to bed . . . staying home for three days and resting up." [20]

Folks operated under the assumption that the task of complete reconstruction was really a matter for the period following the war. In fact, it even opened "new vistas in international relations" and started "new hopes for the world that will be after the war." [21] It was evident, however, that for France's survival and in order to have postwar reconstruction proceed on sound lines, every opportunity to correct bad sanitary and living conditions had to be taken immediately. Folks therefore decided to send members of his Bureaus of Refugees and Relief throughout France to aid in the reception of returning war victims. The work of these delegates, mostly Americans experienced in social work, recruited by Folks, varied greatly according to circumstances. For example, some aided in evacuation, while others drove ambulances. Most, however, dispensed relief. In a four-month period members of these two bureaus alone gave direct medical relief to more than 17,500 people, material relief (food, blankets, clothing) to more than 515,000, lodgings to more than 55,000, and found employment for nearly 50,000, thus aiding at least 620,000 people in that short time.[22]

Folks's Bureau of Tuberculosis worked in close cooperation with the Rockefeller Foundation and with French authorities in an admirable program of community public health. He and Farrand decided not to hurry and produce one plan to fight tuberculosis. Rather, at first, they gave advice and won the confidence of the French officials. When the French showed interest in seeing how Americans dealt with the disease, special districts—the nineteenth arrondissement of Paris and a rural area—were singled out for model educational campaigns and intensive anti-tuberculosis efforts. The program included health education, the typical dispensary, public health nursing, social service, hospitalization, and sanatoria. The Department of Civil Affairs also took over the varied activities of the Tuberculeux de la Guerre, established earlier by Mrs. Edith Wharton. These American efforts gave new life and vigor to the nationwide effort to combat tuberculosis. Only three months after he arrived in France Folks cabled home that if "the present rate of progress can be maintained it is possible that France will have in four years . . . an equipment of agencies for the prevention of tuberculosis . . . second to no state in America." [23]

Serbians who sought shelter in France were in great need of medical help, especially in the care and prevention of tuberculosis. As a result, Folks established a special Division of Serbian Relief in the Bureau of Tuberculosis.[24] Before the war ended the Red Cross and the Rockefeller Foundation established dispensaries throughout France, trained French personnel in the techniques of anti-tuberculosis work and public health education, and organized throughout the country permanent local anti-tuberculosis committees; the tuberculosis death rate declined considerably as American methods became standard practice in France.[25]

Folks's work for repatriates was very taxing. For example, at Evian, "a gateway to freedom," in 1917 alone 50,000 sick, infirm, and helpless refugees were released by the Germans. Immediate medical attention was not sufficient. These rehabilitees had no place to go in already overcrowded France, so Folks had to build hospitals and convalescent homes on the spot for them. Likewise, the Bureau of Re-Education of Mutiles had a great deal to do. It established agricultural training stations in connection with a center for physical therapeutics, where mutiles were trained in scientific farming. It engaged in occupational therapy and vast educational campaigns to arouse and invite mutiles to its re-education program. It also provided financial assistance to French schools for this work and did such things as make artificial limbs and portrait masks for soldiers whose faces had been disfigured by the war.[26]

Folks's efforts on behalf of France's suffering children were perhaps the most widely applauded. As a Marseilles newspaper indicated, for France the saving of children meant its future: "There can be no real victory unless we can successfully combat child mortality. If we consider the enormous adult death rate for the war period, we can only conclude that after the war nothing will be left of France but a glorious skeleton—glorious in name but depleted in substance." [27] The health of French children who had homes was nearly as bad as that of the repatriated ones. Most were dirty and half-clothed, many were dying from tuberculosis. Malnutrition was rife and epidemics multiplied while the supply of local doctors and nurses dwindled. Peril to child life loomed high.

Folks's Children's Bureau undertook a comprehensive child health program that included the operation of twenty-five hospitals and convalescent homes, which cared for thousands of children. With the arrival of additional American doctors and nurses the child welfare program rapidly grew into one of the most extensive branches of Folks's work. Nurseries, baby clinics, and health centers were established throughout France for the medical care of children. A traveling dispensary, an automobile hospital with drugs and supplies of all sorts, left Paris and went through the countryside administering medical assistance to children afflicted with various ailments. The Children's Bureau also gave financial assistance to dependent mothers, making it possible for them to stay at home and care for their babies.[28]

Far-reaching campaigns of public health education accompanied the relief work. Bureau workers in automobiles toured French towns and villages and distributed pamphlets and placards on child care. The bureau held mass meetings in large cities, showed slides, and displayed traveling exhibits. In addition, at Folks's suggestion, model health centers were established at chosen localities to demonstrate public health activities. For this, the American Red Cross made a special appropriation of a million dollars.[29]

Lyon was selected as the scene of the first model child health center. Since it was held at the time the Germans were staging an offensive, and only two hundred miles to the north men were dying under enemy guns, most people felt it wouldn't be well attended. But in one week more than 100,000 people crowded in to see demonstrations of milk sterilization, the washing of babies, the use of toothbrushes, to hear talks on the value of playgrounds and exercise, and to receive instruction in the essentials of hygiene and sanitation. Speaking passionately, Folks told the large crowd assembled at the opening session, including doctors, lawyers, government officials, and the city's leading citizens, that the "soldiers at the front and your workers here are engaged in two sides of the same task," for "liberty and democracy . . . [are] meaningless in desert or wilderness. Of all the sinister by-products of the war, none threaten more seriously the future than the falling birthrate and the rising infantile deathrate." Therefore, he continued, "there is no more pressing and important task than the one in which you are here engaged."[30] This and other demonstrations, as well as direct American relief, had important symbolic, in addition to material, value. Through these baby-saving measures the French were given a striking demonstration of American sympathy and support. It was the effort of the Red Cross "to still the cries of the children that went straight to the heart of France," declared the head of the War Council. In his opinion, "If all the rest had been beyond our power, this one thing would have won for us undying gratitude."[31]

Folks's staff grew quickly. From 13 when he arrived in July, it had grown to 364 by December; it would eventually total nearly 1,400. Folks stood up well under the terrific strain; although lonely for his wife and daughter Evelyn, who joined him in January 1918, he enjoyed the work, ate well, and remained in good health. By mid-November he "arrived at the impression . . . that things are really going well. We are doing more institutional work [than expected] . . . and the educational work has to get under way more slowly," he reported, but, "we do find . . . everywhere a most receptive attitude and a very widespread interest in the subjects we are dealing with." In fact, Major Folks went on, this is "by all odds, the most interesting experience I have ever had, not excepting, I think, even the Commissionership of Public Charities. We have had sufficient funds, substantial freedom to use them, absence of the countless limitations and traditions attached to governmental work and a complete absence on the part of all those concerned of all personal considerations." [32]

Although Folks tried to keep out of the limelight and purposely "boosted" Murphy's work, his efforts were appreciated by all who knew of them. Murphy felt it was impossible "to make clear . . . the absolute necessity of Homer Folks in connection with our enormous program of civilian relief work. . . . If he were to leave," he declared in December 1917, "I do not know where we could possibly turn for his successor." [33] A year later when Dr. R. R. Reeder, a leading American child welfare worker, returned to the United States after supervising institutions for war orphans in France, he made the same comments.[34] One of the highest tributes paid Folks, however, came from George W. Simmons, a Red Cross official who told the National Conference of Folks's tact, wisdom, and statesmanship. In France, Simmons said, "We are doing magnificent work, which I had the privilege of inspecting in the company of the chief of our department of civil affairs, a man who has done more perhaps than any other to make the American people thoroughly beloved by the French people. I refer to Homer Folks." [35]

The full story of the civilian work of the American Red Cross in France can never be correctly or fully told. The vast program resulted in the expenditure of $2,400,000 in the anti-tuberculosis campaign, $3,000,000 for assistance of needy children, $3,800,000 for the help of families of French combatants, and $9,800,000 for the relief of refugees. But these figures are only part of the story. It was, as Folks saw from the beginning, "an international adventure," a chapter in the history of war different from any other chapter in the history of any previous war. Never before in wartime had battalions of doctors and nurses and social workers, professional and business men and women, crossed the sea to aid in fighting tuberculosis and infant mortality, to reconstruct shattered villages, shattered hearts, and shattered hopes. The civilian work of the American Red Cross in France was a unique effort of one nation to stand beside another nation and to work with her to build a common future. That effort was handled admirably. Although the American Red Cross, like the military and other civilian organizations authorized to operate abroad, had its share of misjudgment, bumbling, and ineptitude, the results were what counted. Those results, according to one historian of the organization, "were such that the Red Cross emerged from the ordeal with apparently more honors, and fewer scars of criticism, than any other official or non-governmental organization" engaged in the vast enterprise.[36] General Pershing later wrote that the value of the Red Cross work was "beyond computation." [37]

For this Folks deserved a large measure of the credit. When he turned the department over to his successor, Ernest Bicknell, Folks humbly expressed his gratitude to the members of the War Council for the opportunity they gave him to serve his country during the war. "I am well aware of the many imperfections in my civilian relief work," he said, but, he concluded, "I have the lasting satisfaction that we did make some . . . contribution toward the war problem as a whole." [38] The French and Serbian people agreed. In recognition of his services for Serbian refugees in France he was decorated by the Serbian government through a royal decree creating him Commander in the Order of the White Eagle. The French Government also conferred upon Folks a most deserved honor—the Cross of Chevalier of the Legion of Honor.[39]

As the war in eastern Europe degenerated under revolutionary movements, or came to a halt with the Armistice in November 1918, some members of the American Red Cross saw the need to turn to postwar problems of civilian relief. First, however, data had to be gathered so that those needs could be examined scientifically and a reconstruction program be determined. For this the Red Cross turned to Homer Folks.

The war had strengthened and enlarged Folks's perception of the real social unity of not only Americans, but all mankind. His experiences abroad convinced him that no one person or no nation was safe as long as any other nation was at war or in need; a world made safe for democracy must be made safe from physical misery and distress.[40] As a result, he accepted the chairmanship of a special Red Cross commission ordered to make a survey of the needs existing in several countries where the Red Cross was asked to help. In addition to studying the property losses, in each country he was to determine the effect of the war upon the civilian population and the changes it had wrought in social and family life. As Folks confided to a colleague, in view of the crumbling international situation,

this special mission of mine may prove to be timely. I shall try to present a picture of the net results of the war . . . and outline the job which must rest upon the shoulders, if not of the American Red Cross, then of the American government or the allies generally, or the league of free nations, if some of the main damages of the war are to be made good. These damages were not the ruined buildings which are so much in evidence . . . but the ruined social structure and resources of the allied countries.[41]

Folks, now promoted to Lieutenant Colonel, left Paris on November 12 with a staff that included food and health experts, photographers, and interpreters. He traveled through Italy, Greece, Serbia, Belgium, and France, often not knowing if he would survive the trip. At one point a small steamer carrying the commission nearly foundered in the Aegean Sea. They reached the island of Sciathos after being perilously storm-tossed and close to disaster for days, only to find they were prohibited from going ashore because of an influenza epidemic on the island; Folks and the others subsisted on bread and cabbage for the next four days.[42]

Rail travel was also unpleasant, as an inscription in Folks's diary indicates: "November 17, 1918—Left Salonikie at 11:45 for Uskab, (Skopalie), by special train. . . . No light nor heat. Slept on narrow board seats. Weather became very cold toward morning. Dressed with all the clothes I could keep on, and with blanket and blanket-roll covering, was just warm enough."[43] Later, Folks developed a temperature of 104 degrees and was sent to a Serbian military hospital. "When I get back from this jaunt and we get home," he cabled to his wife, "we will settle down for about five years without going anywhere." [44] He continued the trip, however, and wherever he went he painted a vivid picture of the horrible human destruction, devastation, and degradation that the war had brought. "The situation in the Balkans and Asia Minor," he reported, "is enough to make your head swim. It seems that of two million Armenians some 400,000 only survive and that they will die before spring unless more help gets to them soon, and this is just a sample of the mess things are in." [45] Along with the battle casualties and devastated lands, he observed that the war had decreased the birth rate, increased the infant mortality rate, and greatly lowered the standard of living. In many places it had destroyed the whole structure of organized community life.

The paralysis of trade and commerce and the almost complete breakdown of transportation resulting from the war created unbelievably distressing conditions. Hundreds of thousands of ragged refugees, verminous, inadequately clothed, and suffering from hunger, streamed back to what had been home only to find that nothing remained. Consequently they were forced to live like cavemen in huts, shelters, and basements without light or ventilation. The prevalence of tuberculosis and the sweeping epidemics of typhus fever and other diseases became even more threatening because of the tragic lack of hospitals and medical facilities to protect the public health. Folks concluded

that the magnitude of the disaster . . . far exceeds any estimates or descriptions hitherto made; that though the relief work . . . has been on an unparalleled scale, nevertheless, it has been able to deal with only a fraction of the need; and that, besides the remedial distresses of the war, there are far deeper, more far-reaching, and fundamental human losses, from which recovery can take place only after decades, if, in fact, they can ever be made good. [46]

Although most people knew the Red Cross only as a wartime agency that came into being to meet certain needs, one which was expected to disappear when the war was over, Folks, sensitive to the vast needs and complex problems of the world, appreciated its potential for peacetime work. He saw the Armistice not as an end of Red Cross usefulness but as the beginning of a new and wonderful opportunity for the service of mankind. He recommended to the Red Cross that it send people experienced in public health work to the devastated countries. Money, good will, or democracy, he said, will not help them; trained public health personnel will.[47]

Originally, when the American Red Cross sent foreign commissions abroad in 1917 and 1918 it did not expect to become engaged in expansive peacetime activities. However, partly as a result of Folks's trip and reports to the Chairman of the Red Cross Commission to Europe, new commissions were created and two years after the war ended there were still over two thousand American Red Cross workers overseas fighting epidemics, helping feed children, running relief stations and dispensaries, and doing countless other things for hundreds of thousands of Europeans. Between 1919 and 1922 the Red Cross poured over ninety million more dollars into the cause of Continental rehabilitation.[48]

Folks did not confine his pleas for continued overseas relief to Red Cross reports. He addressed a considerable number of audiences on the subject and declared that peace was no less demanding of aid than war. He also wrote a series of twenty-four articles for the press and periodicals on various phases of European needs. All expressed his fervent internationalism and reiterated in different ways his first statement after returning from Europe when he declared that the nations of Europe "need our help most urgently now. We must continue to aid Europe. . . . We cannot fail to see the job through, and it is far from being done. Our allies still need food, clothing, doctors, nurses, medicines, shelters, and perhaps above all need to continue to feel sure that rich America . . . still cares for them and will continue to bind up the wounds caused by the war. Hunger and disease are not yet demobilized." It would be inhuman, shortsighted, and un-Christian to say "good-bye" to Europe, he said on a great many occasions, and he urged Americans to "recognize the gravity of the danger and the greatness of the opportunity" not only by continuing to support the Red Cross, emergency relief, and sending trained personnel abroad to battle disease, but by joining the League of Nations and canceling the war debts.[49] Thus Homer Folks added a social-humanitarian consideration to the administration's more political and diplomatic pleas for

America's acceptance of its postwar responsibilities to the rest of the world.

Finally, in a book entitled *The Human Costs of the War* (1920), Folks magnificently summed up the appalling toll the tragedy had taken in life and suffering. Written to provide the facts so that Americans could "think and act with the . . . realization of . . . [their] responsibilities in the world," Folks's scientific evaluation of the human costs of the conflict, drawn from his overseas work, was a cold and convincing indictment of war; he humanized the statistics to make them yield their hidden story of misery. One reviewer predicted that his study "will certainly take a place among the widely read and permanently useful books of the epoch." [50] Another reviewer, David Starr Jordan, prominent peace advocate and chancellor of Stanford University, said of the book, "No more terrible exhibit of the nature of war has been written." [51] The New York *Times* recommended the work to all those who opposed the League of Nations: "No one who has even the first faint beginnings of a social conscience . . . can read the book without being urged to effort that will help any movement endeavoring to prevent the recurrence of any such ghastly racial tragedy as was the World War. For that reason it ought to be read by everybody opposed to the League of Nations." [52] While *The Human Costs of the War,* of course, did not prevent another great disaster, it at least stirred some people to benevolent endeavors overseas.[53]

In spite of its continued overseas relief work, the American Red Cross faced a period of transition and readjustment in the years following the war. On February 28, 1919, the War Council relinquished control of the organization and responsibility reverted to the Executive and Central Committees. Despite the unprecedented growth in every phase of Red Cross operations during the war, after the Armistice an internal struggle developed over the organization's future. On one side stood such people as Folks, Davison, and Eliot Wadsworth, Davison's successor as head of the War Council, enthusiasts who foresaw for the American Red Cross a future in which it would build itself into a dominant force in all fields of social service. On the other side stood the old guard—William Howard Taft, Mabel Boardman, and Robert deForest—who favored retrenchment and contended that it was time to forget the emergency. They preferred an American Red Cross that, in the main, stood quietly and waited to cope with domestic disasters as they arose. This immediate postwar struggle ended with the progressive forces emerging victorious. The ambitious overseas rehabilitation program stood as testimony to their willingness to expand the organization's usefulness.[54]

In spite of their victory, however, the "progressives" realized that extensive American Red Cross overseas projects, which rested entirely upon voluntary financial contributions, could not be maintained much longer; they were at variance with popular feeling at home. Increasingly, the American people were becoming absorbed in their own individual concerns once more. With former associates quarreling about the spoils of war abroad, and industry and labor battling at home, appeals for further large-scale sacrifices in behalf of overseas humanitarianism carried little weight. Postwar reaction and apathy toward further foreign commitment replaced the wartime idealism.[55]

As a transitional step toward ultimate Red Cross withdrawal, plans were made to substitute for the general emergency relief program a more limited effort of "constructive work," which could be carried on by Europeans when the American personnel left. These plans took final form in the spring of 1921 as a child welfare project. The program called for a cooperative venture with other American relief agencies to provide some relief, but mostly medical care and preventive health services for sick and destitute children in central and eastern Europe. The Red Cross projected the establishment of approximately one hundred child health centers, to be turned over as promptly as possible to public or private agencies in the nations concerned. To implement the program the Red Cross once again turned to Homer Folks. "In laying out this plan which will involve on the part of the Red Cross a probable expenditure of $10,000,000," said Livingston Farrand, chairman of the organization's Central Committee, "we feel the one man to initiate the program is Mr. Folks." His "experience makes him the outstanding man for this service, and with him we feel that success is assured," Farrand continued.[56]

At Farrand's request, the Board of Managers of the State Charities Aid Association gave Folks a four-month leave of absence so that he could go abroad to advise and assist the American Red Cross in the reorganization of its work in Europe. Without defining in detail Folks's specific job, or authority, Farrand asked him to proceed to Paris at the earliest possible time. "I know that you will be of invaluable aid and assistance in assuring a feasible and constructive program," he hopefully added.[57]

When Folks sailed for Europe on February 3, 1921, sixteen child health stations already had been established and thirty-five more were being organized under the leadership of Robert E. Olds and Dr. Kendall Emerson, Red Cross Commissioner and Deputy Commissioner to Europe. Folks traveled through Poland, Serbia, Czechoslovakia, Lithuania, Latvia, and Esthonia visiting the health stations and inquiring into proposed child welfare activities. Unhappy with the work he found being done in Europe, wherever he went Folks sent back scathing reports. He accused those abroad of subverting the Red Cross program, condemning the projects for their emphasis on "welfare" and relief rather than medical and preventive health activities. Moreover, the work had progressed too slowly and he felt there was too much reliance upon local medical and nursing personnel, who in his opinion were not well suited for the work. For the speedy development of the program he called for the employment of more American doctors, nurses, and experienced social workers.[58]

Although motivated by a worthy ideal and good intentions, Folks was too harsh in his criticisms of European child welfare work. He had no intimate knowledge of the conditions Olds and Emerson faced; postwar Europe had many contrasts with America as a field for social service. Red Cross plans for child health work were based on the assumption that the need for food and clothing among European children would be fulfilled by 1921. However, that need was not yet fully met, and such immediate problems as feeding and dressing children had to take priority.[59] In addition, Folks may have been too critical of the slow rate of progress and the extensive use of local health personnel. With the view in mind of establishing a permanent program to be carried on by local effort after the American Red Cross left, it was absolutely necessary to use and train local citizens in the work, and this was time-consuming.

Moreover, he failed to take fully into consideration the question of economy. Working abroad in peacetime on a limited budget that had to be stretched to the utmost was far different from working as he had in France with virtually a bottomless treasury to meet the war emergency. Recruiting large numbers of American workers for overseas work was financially impossible for the American Red Cross in 1921.[60] In addition, it was not possible to build permanent health agencies based on American models for another reason. Suggestions to do things as they were done in America often irritated Europeans who, bursting with national pride, did not want anything completely imposed upon them from elsewhere. As a result, American Red Cross workers abroad merely adapted to necessary circumstances. Folks, so entirely devoted to high ideals of technical social service, failed to grasp the true nature of this situation.[61]

Ironically, through his criticisms of the overseas child welfare program Folks served the cause of those in favor of retrenchment and helped keep the Red Cross from becoming the great social agency he and others favored. His reports further increased the internal strife and bitterness in the organization. Directly, they led to Emerson's resignation as Deputy Commissioner to Europe. A month later Livingston Farrand followed suit.[62] By the end of 1921, with internal bickering, reduced revenue, and the public's distaste for foreign involvement, the decision was reached to wind up the overseas program as soon as possible. In some instances when the Red Cross withdrew, the work that it had developed was taken over by other relief agencies or by the local government. The short duration of the program, however, prevented it from having a long-lasting effect.[63]

After the war Folks not only remained active in Red Cross overseas activities, but, more successfully, he also helped chart a new course for the organization at home. The postwar question of whether the American Red Cross was to revert to its prewar skeletal status with functions limited to relief in national emergencies, or attempt to maintain the large-scale organization created during the war, also had domestic implications. Farrand's appointment in 1919 as Chairman of the Central Committee symbolized the victory of the progressive forces, whose ideals now found concrete expression at home as well as abroad.

Farrand felt that the Red Cross must not once again become "a drowsy giant to be aroused only by fire, sword, storm and flood—acts of God, war and pestilence." [64] Long associated with public health work and preventive medicine, he wanted the organization to turn to a great national effort in the prevention of disease through the establishment of health centers. Believing also that health work would be appealing to the public and thus attract and keep membership and contributions high and at the same time give volunteers rewarding work, he announced the new Red Cross policy: "The mobilization of Red Cross interest and influence for the establishment of Health Centers in every community where conditions are desirable and possible." [65] Folks, Farrand's close friend, was instrumental in leading the Red Cross into this line of interest. It was he who drafted the organization's important health center statement.[66]

Folks was asked to accept a full-time position with the Red Cross to help implement the new health program. Unwilling to leave the State Charities Aid Association, he suggested dividing his time between the two organizations. To help facilitate the coordination of Red Cross health center work with existing social agencies, including the State Charities Aid Association, the national headquarters accepted the offer.[67] Folks was appointed chief executive officer of the New York County Chapter of the Atlantic Division of the American Red Cross. Confident that Folks's appointment "will give to the chapter the executive management it has long needed," national headquarters instructed Folks to begin his duties at once.[68] Folks exercised general supervision and direction over the civilian relief and public health work of the New York County Chapter, and, in addition, several weeks later he accepted similar responsibility for the entire Atlantic Division of the Red Cross, which included all of New York State, New Jersey, and Connecticut.[69]

In formulating a new public health program, the Central Committee laid down certain basic principles to govern its operation. The Red Cross would not try to supplant other agencies, public or private, in the public health field. Its purpose was to "supplement, reinforce and support" what they were already doing. Like the State Charities Aid Association, its function was primarily educational, experimental, and promotional. When other agencies or organizations were able to take over where it pioneered and demonstrated what could be done, the Red Cross would withdraw and turn to new activities. Although subject to over-all control from national headquarters, the individual chapters were to retain a large measure of autonomy in developing their own local health projects.[70]

Homer Folks organized the Health Service of the American Red Cross, Atlantic Division, on January 5, 1920. This service, under his supervision, was responsible for the development and maintenance of the health services of all chapters, branches, and auxiliaries within the division. The Atlantic Division, operating under the program formulated by Folks for the Central Committee, urged and assisted in the establishment of health centers that focused attention on the importance of the coordination and cooperation of health agencies. At the end of one year thirty-eight health centers were established in twenty-eight counties within the division, most of which were in New York State. Varying degrees of health services were also established in sixty-one other places.[71]

The most striking and successful example of American Red Cross encouragement and financial support to health centers during the postwar years was New York City's East Harlem Health Center.[72] Late in 1920, at Folks's suggestion, the New York County Chapter appointed a Committee on Health Service composed of distinguished professional and lay health authorities. Dr. James Alexander Miller, president of the National Tuberculosis Association, was chairman, and Folks served as secretary of this committee, which in Folks's opinion was "the ablest, most high-minded, practical and effective committee I . . . ever served." [73]

The committee realized that inconviently located and poorly publicized facilities often led to neglected health. It therefore considered and adopted a health center plan submitted by Dr. Miller that proposed to bring together in one centrally located headquarters all the public and private health and welfare agencies scattered throughout a selected district. The plan did not call for amplifying any of their services; it simply sought to coordinate them so that they might work in a closer and thus more effective relationship. The center was to be, in Folks's words, "a department store of health." [74]

Folks personally went to Washington to present the idea to the association's Central Committee. He received its approval and the project, known as the East Harlem Health Center, became a reality in the autumn of 1921. This center, the first general health center in New York City, was a pioneer experiment designed to "demonstrate the methods and the value of coordination of all health and kindred activities in a defined local area." [75] The Red Cross contributed the funds for a suitably equipped building and for its operation and maintenance for three years.

The East Harlem Health Center brought together in one building twenty-one voluntary agencies (all of which retained complete autonomy) and an office of the New York City Department of Health. Because the services were unified and conveniently located, more people used them and, according to reliable sources, apart from the cost of the building, approximately twice the number of services were rendered annually for the same amount of money as previously.[76] More important, after three years the district's death and illness rates were lowered considerably. Starting at a mortality rate 3 per cent below the rest of Manhattan, after ten years East Harlem's Death rate was 29 per cent below the average, thus saving thousands of lives—a good return for the investment, for in ten years the center spent only $300,000.[77] The East Harlem Health Center was an outstanding demonstration of how health agencies, official and voluntary, could work together under one roof in a prescribed district to accomplish better results. It proved the effectiveness of bringing health services directly to the people to reduce the incidence of disease and death.

In March 1928, after pointing to the effectiveness of the East Harlem Health Center, Folks called upon the New York City Health Department to spend $15,000,000 for the establishment of public health centers throughout the city.[78] In July 1929 New York City Health Commissioner, Dr. Shirley W. Wynne, chairman of the East Harlem Health Center, appointed a Committee on Neighborhood Health Development to in effect study the advisability of Folks's suggestion.[79] Chairman of the committee was Bailey B. Burritt, head of the Association for Improving the Condition of the Poor and a member of the executive staff of the East Harlem Health Center. The committee conducted a study and, "having in mind the experience of the early health centers," recommended the establishment of thirty health districts with local health centers and full-time health officials throughout New York City. The Health Department accepted the committee's recommendations and fully committed itself to the development of health centers. The first such center opened in December 1930 in central Harlem; the city took over the East Harlem center in 1935. By 1944 fourteen city health centers existed and eleven more were in the planning stage. Since then the work has been completed.[80] Thus, under Folks's leadership the American Red Cross with its pioneer undertaking, the East Harlem Health Center, was largely responsible for extending the value of neighborhood health organizations throughout New York City.

In the meantime, despite the evident success of its public health work, especially the health center idea, enrollment in American Red Cross fund drives to finance that work dropped drastically. The lesson was clear: "The American people had not shown any overwhelming enthusiasm for a great, nationwide public health program financed by popular subscription." Criticism from within and from without the organization continued. Critics of the decision to undertake the promotion of public health pointed to the dwindling resources as evidence of slight popular support for such a departure from established tradition. As a result, during the next decade the American Red Cross went through organizational and structural changes that, on the whole, returned it to a disaster-meeting organization. The major purpose behind these changes was economy, which, of course, crippled ambitious and costly public health programs.

Although the Red Cross was compelled to give up most of its public health work, in large part it fulfilled the avowed aim and underlying purpose of its domestic postwar program—stimulating other agencies to take over where it had shown the way. In the words of one official historian, Foster Rhea Dulles, the American Red Cross "made a recognized contribution to public awareness of health problems and the elevation of prevailing standards of welfare work." [81] Moreover, the organization's decision to drop out of the movement to unify health activities and bring health services closer to the people through community organizations stimulated Folks to intensify State Charities Aid Association efforts along that line.

11

MORE PUBLIC HEALTH

WHEN the war came to an end social workers were convinced that the time was ripe to complete unfinished reform business and launch new programs to reconstruct the social life of the nation. If America had succeeded in mobilizing for war against militarism, reformers felt the nation could now be mobilized for war against sickness and poverty.

To help alleviate distress caused by these powerful enemies, more social workers than ever before favored and whole-heartedly endorsed compulsory health insurance programs. Actually, the movement for compulsory health insurance in America had been launched in 1912 by the American Association for Labor Legislation. In the years preceding and during America's participation in World War I, though, little was done. After the war, however, because of the unstable social and economic conditions and because the rejection of so many young men from military service for reasons of poor health dramatized the need for more positive health measures and the more equal redistribution of the financial burden of sickness, many reformers placed health insurance at the top of the priority list.[1] Edward T. Devine echoed an often repeated theme in 1919 when he called the National Conference's attention to the possibility of eliminating illness as a factor in distress by insuring against its economic and financial results: "A system of universal compulsory health insurance," he declared, "is nothing else than a practical, already amply demonstrated remedy, for that particular poverty which is caused by disease. Those who want to take the disease factor out of poverty," he advised, "should get behind the growing movement for health insurance."[2]

Health insurance bills were introduced in New York and other state

legislatures across the country. In his annual message to the legislature
in 1919, and again in 1920, Governor Alfred E. Smith of New York
made eloquent pleas for passage of health insurance legislation. All
efforts to obtain appropriate legislation, however, were defeated in
New York and elsewhere by a strange but nevertheless well-organized
fellowship of manufacturers and merchants associations, commercial insurance companies, Christian Scientists, the medical profession, and the
American Federation of Labor, which, despite endorsement from
many members, feared the effect of health insurance upon its growth
and activities. Emotions aroused during and immediately after the war
against the "insured Hun" and the equally wicked Bolshevik were
used to defeat health insurance, pictured by its opponents as a symbol
of both German regimentation and militarism and Soviet commu-
nism.[3]

Although these forces were responsible for the actual defeat of health
insurance measures, others also were unenthusiastic about such legislation. At Folks's suggestion, late in 1919 the State Charities Aid Association formed a Committee on Health Insurance "for the purpose of
making a thorough investigation of the subject . . . including a study
of its operations in European countries."[4] After intensive study, Folks
presented the committee's report to the Association's Board of Managers on February 18, 1920. "The committee is clear," said Folks, "from
such data as are available . . . that, so far as the prevention and more
adequate treatment of disease are concerned, health insurance is by no
means the only, nor is it the most desired and effective way to accomplish . . . desirable results, if, in fact, it makes any large contribution
toward health betterment."[5]

The committee recognized the serious and persistent problem of economic loss due to sickness—a social rather than an individual matter.
Moreover, it realized that without some provision for security of person and income against the hazards of illness, human freedom was
placed in jeopardy. Therefore, it was not unalterably against all
medical insurance plans. But, as Folks pointed out on a great many
occasions, health insurance was not aimed at the prevention of illness
or providing good medical service at the time of confinement; it

merely helped to defray the costs of treatment. And not only were most health insurance schemes primarily palliatives, but they were bad ones at that, for they were financed by contributions from the prospective beneficiaries, thus placing a tax on those usually least able to bear it, lowering the standard of living where it already was lowest. In addition, it was costly to collect payments for such schemes and in most cases they did not provide security for many in need, such as the families of the contributors.

Charitable relief and health insurance were not the only alternatives. In the belief that there was no better insurance company than the government, Folks advocated universal government provision for health services that reached all in need, rather than an inequitable system that reached only a contributing group after it became ill. He favored a system of public health facilities to *prevent illness* and *provide care* and services for all those who could not provide it for themselves, maintained on the same basis as public education—open to all, free to all, paid for out of the total community resources through a system of graduated taxes, "a contributory scheme, but the most equitable kind." [6] He preferred the preventive to the ameliorative ideal. Folks's program was not only more equitable and just than any health insurance plan, but it would have gone a long way toward eliminating one of the worst blights of American society and raising the standard of living for everyone.

Folks expressed his views most clearly in a widely heralded report on "The Distribution of the Costs of Illness in the United States," presented in 1928 to the International Congress of Social Work in Paris.[7] Over six thousand copies of this laborious and painstaking work were distributed on request.[8] In it, Folks conclusively demonstrated that under existing conditions almost the entire burden of sickness was borne by those in the most unfortunate circumstances. As a result, many people went without medical care, a situation that brought on chronic illness and loss of future earning power. The price paid for this wasn't confined to individual sufferers; it had social consequences as well. Folks calculated that in terms of money expended on cure and sacrificed earnings, sickness cost the American people over fifteen billion dollars a year, and as much as 93.8 per cent of the total was borne by the patients themselves or their families; only 6.2 per cent was met by taxation, contributions, and insurance schemes.[9] More important, only 0.5 per cent of that amount was spent annually for its prevention. And again, while Folks did not deprecate various insurance plans for anticipating and distributing the losses from illness, he urged first the establishment of an effective program for prevention:

> It would not occur to anyone to doubt that it is far better from an individual and a social point of view to prevent a preventable illness or death than it is to distribute the losses arising from such illness or death. While this is axiomatic, a word of caution may be needed lest the subject of distribution be confused with that of prevention and we may devote time and energy to plans in the impression that we are promoting health, when, in fact, we are simply promoting a distribution of the losses arising from illness. Prevention and distribution are both necessary and are both important, but as to illness and deaths known to be preventable, no more serious mistake could be made than to allow any program of distribution to delay in the slightest degree an effective program for prevention.[10]

Perhaps it is worth noting that Folks served on the famous Committee on the Costs of Medical Care, which, under the chairmanship of Secretary of the Interior Dr. Ray Lyman Wilbur, collected a large body of data and presented its report after five years (1927–1932) of concentrated work. The majority report, which Folks signed, and the twenty-eight monographs presenting the findings, corroborated Folks's earlier study, which showed that the poorest segment of the population, which needs most medical care, received the least; sickness was an expensive luxury which only the well-to-do could afford. The committee concluded, among other things, that some form of insurance or prepayment of medical costs was necessary, but also that local and state preventive health services and public health work should be developed and correlated closely with curative work.[11]

Folks, unlike many others, especially most physicians, subscribed to the opinion that medical care was within the province of public health. He continually stressed the combination and integration of preventive and therapeutic services. Therefore, in 1920 when New York State Commissioner of Health Hermann M. Biggs proposed a statewide system of health centers for the prevention and cure of disease, Folks heartily supported the measure: "It is broadly humanitarian and fundamentally democratic," he declared. The health center plan "recognizes that it is in the public interest that every citizen receive intelligent medical attention; that it is a public calamity when preventable disease is not prevented or curable disease not cured." [12]

The Sage-Machold bill, an epoch-making public health measure embodying Biggs's proposal, was introduced in the state legislature on March 25, 1920. Worked out by Folks and such enlightened physicians as Biggs, T. M. Prudden, and Simon Flexner, the bill called for what amounted to a system of state medicine. Designed to meet the great need to prevent disease and furnish medical care in rural communities as well as industrial centers, it provided for a comprehensive, statewide extension of public health work through the establishment of complete health centers, including hospitals staffed with medical, surgical, and diagnostic facilities and specialists. The measure called for state aid to supplement expenditures by counties and cities to construct, equip, and operate the health centers, whose services were to be provided free to the needy or near-needy, and at a moderate cost to those who could afford them. Such centers were to be established by a county, city, or a consolidated health district.[13]

Like the County Tuberculosis Hospital Law, the Sage-Machold bill was faulty in that it was permissive and retained what amounted to a means test. However, unlike some other measures that merely provided "outside" aid to build hospitals, the health center bill was particularly strong in its provision for state aid to maintain, as well as construct, the center. The bill recognized that the poorest rural areas with the greatest need for medical and hospital facilities were unable to guarantee funds to maintain them.

The New York *Times* endorsed the Sage-Machold health center bill, as did the State Department of Health. The State Charities Aid Association felt that its enactment "would be one of the most important steps ever taken in this state toward the better prevention of diseases and the better care of the sick." [14] Folks took steps to organize public support for the bill throughout the state. Recognizing that the mea-

sure's success depended upon winning approval from physicians, Folks
wrote to noted medical and public health authorities throughout the
world seeking their support, pointing out that "if such a bill can be
enacted in New York, it would . . . mark the beginning of a new
epoch in public health as, undoubtedly, the example in New York
would soon be followed by other states." [15]

The bill received impressive endorsement from national and international leaders in the public health field, including such eminent authorities as Dr. Charles V. Chapin, Dr. Theobald Smith, and Surgeon
General H. S. Cumming. Dr. C. E. A. Winslow felt the bill "was the
most important contribution yet made in the United States toward the
sound organization of medical service." [16] Members of the State Federation of Labor, the State Federation of Women's Clubs, the Grange,
and a notable list of public health and welfare organizations backed
the measure at a public hearing, which in Folks's opinion "was most
encouraging as to the variety and scope of the support of the bill." But,
he added in a letter to Miss Schuyler, "we shall not . . . get the bill
this year. It went in too late and the idea is too new. The Legislature,
however, is most friendly to it," he continued, "and I feel most encouraged about the outlook for next year." [17]

In part, Folks was correct. The bill was far ahead of public, particularly medical, opinion. While Dr. J. F. Rooney, chairman of the Legislative Committee of the New York State Medical Society endorsed
the measure, it became clear that the state's doctors did not ap-
prove of his action.[18] Physicians rallied against the bill, on various
grounds, most notably on those of "statism" and "paternalism." They
really opposed it, however, because they feared a loss of practice would
result from the establishment of public clinics and health centers. Biggs
and Folks reviewed the evidence of a serious shortage of physicians,
nurses, and hospital facilities in rural areas, a gap the bill was designed
to overcome. The plan, they also pointed out, would in no way super-
sede local medical practitioners, who no less than the patient were
often penalized by the existing haphazard system of medical care; it
would furnish many of them with the facilities they did not have and
could not afford to buy. Moveover, in part, state aid would be used to

better compensate physicians and health officers who, because of inadequate compensation, did not wish to serve in rural areas or sometimes worked night and day for a bare living while many people went without adequate medical care. In addition, because of low and uncertain income in rural communities, a growing number of doctors specialized and flocked to urban centers, leading to increased medical costs to the patient and decreased income for the average doctor. These and other arguments were to no avail. Physicians and county medical societies joined hands with the State Christian Science Society in violent opposition to the measure. As a result, the Sage-Machold bill never even reached the House floor.[19]

When the health center idea was revised in 1921 and reintroduced in the legislature as the Robinson-Moore bill, it too died in committee. However, that year the legislature did pass an important piece of legislation supported by Biggs and the State Charities Aid Association—the General District Health Law. This law authorized the Board of Supervisors of any county, with the approval of the State Commissioner of Health, to establish a county or any part of it as a general health district with its own board of health headed by a full-time health officer. This step, the first toward utilizing the county as a unit for health control, resulted logically from (1) the realization that effective health administration called for full-time specially trained officers, and (2) the realization that the financing of effective health programs required a government unit with greater resources than were available in most small cities, towns, and villages.[20]

In 1923 two other bills designed to fill the gap in medical and hospital facilities in rural areas became law. Prepared and enacted with the help of Folks and the State Charities Aid Association, these measures were permissive laws authorizing the establishment of community medical services with state aid.[21] Specifically, one law provided that whenever a County Board of Supervisors appropriated and spent funds for public health programs, the state was to reimburse up to 50 per cent of the money to the county if the State Commissioner of Health endorsed the program. The other law made specific provision for state aid to counties for laboratory services. "You will be interested in seeing the bill[s] which passed the legislature as the net outcome of the lack of medical and health facilities in rural districts," Folks informed Miss Schuyler, adding, they "could have been improved, if there had been more time," but they "at least established a principle." [22]

More than a principle was established. Although there was no mention of the word "health center," these acts, together with the 1921 Health District Law, made possible practically every one of the objectives of the defeated Sage-Machold bill. The principle of state aid to rural areas for the establishment, construction, and maintenance of public hospitals, clinics, dispensaries, and any other public enterprise or activity for the improvement of health became a reality. Speaking of the health center bill a decade after it was introduced in the legislature, Dr. Winslow properly remarked to Folks, "The idea that the bill failed to pass is a mistaken one. The name was abandoned," he pointed out, "but the essential elements in the original program were all enacted law." [23] As evidenced in these laws, by 1923 New York State recognized the two fundamental principles that have dominated the development of public health policy throughout the nation ever since: (1) the principle that the provision of adequate facilities for the prevention and treatment of illness is of public importance, and (2) the principle that rural communities cannot secure such facilities without financial assistance from some other source, usually the state or federal government.

As acceptance of these principles indicates, although World War I required the inculcation of many principles contradictory to the philosophic underpinnings of progressivism and humanitarianism, and adversely affected society in many ways during the postwar years, participation in the war obviously did not put an end to the progressive movement. Nor did the election of 1920 liquidate the progressive spirit, as has been assumed too often in the past.[24] These events may have led to the temporary submergence of the prewar social climate, but many reformers continued throughout the 1920s to work for humanitarian reform and the establishment of a better world. Certainly Folks and many of his colleagues never surrendered to the forces of reaction, a theme that will reappear in the next chapter.

Since the new statutes were permissive, not mandatory, there was a need to convince New Yorkers of the extraordinary benefits to be secured by implementing the legislation. Folks and others moved to fill that need. With financial assistance from the Milbank Memorial Fund they developed three unique model health demonstrations, which put into operation more intensive health programs than had ever before existed in any city or county in the state. These demonstrations proved the value of modern public health work and their influence permeated public health thinking and planning throughout the United States and the world.

Elizabeth Milbank Anderson, long-time State Charities Aid Association Board member, born in New York City in 1850, lived a benevolent life, giving a great deal of money to various good causes. In 1905 she established the Milbank Memorial Fund "to improve the physical, mental, and moral condition of humanity." In its early years the fund was primarily a vehicle for the personal contributions of its founder. In 1921, however, following her death, administrators of the fund sought to extend its activities and adopt a new policy. Rather than continue making small grants to many independent charitable agencies, they decided to concentrate on a few major projects in the field of public health.[25]

In the meantime Folks, a close friend to the late Miss Anderson and John A. Kingsbury, now chief executive officer of the Milbank Fund, filed with that organization a request for a $235,000 appropriation to finance a model county health demonstration. In outlining this project he drew upon his experience from working on what probably was the first of the now common community public health surveys—the Community Health and Tuberculosis Demonstration in Framingham, Mass.—which, financed by the Metropolitan Life Insurance Company and directed by the National Tuberculosis Association, developed widely applied yardsticks for tuberculosis control.[26] He proposed that such a demonstration be carried on for five years in some county in the state to determine whether it was possible to reduce further, and materially, the mortality and morbidity from preventable diseases, particularly tuberculosis.[27]

In the spring of 1922 the Board of Directors of the Milbank Fund appointed a Technical Board to recommend, keep in touch with, and supervise public health activities sponsored by the foundation. Dr. William A. Welch was chairman of the Technical Board, which also included Dr. Biggs, Dr. Livingston Farrand, Dr. James A. Miller, Dr. Linsly R. Williams, Biggs's associate in the New York State Health Department, and Kingsbury, Bailey Burrit, and Folks. The Board of Directors, on the recommendation of Welch's board, decided to finance the health demonstration as suggested by Folks. Rather than one, however, it decided to finance three such projects, each in different types of communities—a rural county (50,000–70,000 population), a medium-size city (100,000 population), and a section of a large metropolitan area (200,000 population). The object of the program was to increase the volume and efficiency of public health services in each of the areas in an effort to determine if sickness and mortality could be further reduced within a reasonable period of time at a reasonable per capita cost.[28]

With a five-year annual appropriation of $325,000, these demonstrations differed from all previous ones in that they were more intensive and more comprehensively carried out; they represented the first varied and large-scale effort to adequately use all existing knowledge about the problems of public health. Needless to say, Folks was the chief directive mind planning these demonstrations.[29]

It was decided not to create new operating agencies and facilities to carry out the demonstrations. Instead, the Technical Board chose to utilize existing organizations in the field and designated the State Committee on Tuberculosis and Public Health of the State Charities Aid Association as the "principal operating agency" for the upstate demonstrations. Its functions were many, but in general it exercised primary responsibility for seeing that the recommendations of the Technical Board were carried into effect. The actual responsibility for carrying out the activities, however, lay with the local public health authorities and agencies.[30]

The three areas chosen for the demonstrations were Cattaraugus County, the city of Syracuse, and the Belleville-Yorkville section of

New York City. Cattaraugus County organized the state's first full-time county health department. In Syracuse, where health services were already organized, they were developed further and reorganized into an effective health bureau. The Belleville-Yorkville demonstration, like East Harlem, provided for a general health center, but with vastly greater resources; it became the most important testing ground for improved metropolitan district public health procedures.

Eyes of health authorities throughout the world turned toward these demonstrations. In an address on "Impressions of the Cattaraugus County Health Demonstration," Sir Arthur Newsholme, the world renowned public health expert, declared that

the chief features of this Demonstration . . . are first of all that it is an admirable combination of official . . . with voluntary work, such a combination . . . as I have never seen in any other locality. . . . I have devoted more than forty years of public service to public health work and during the whole of that period I cannot say that I have met any other example of work which is so complete in its organization as this.[31]

Dr. Ernst Lowenstein, professor of experimental pathology at the University of Vienna, Austria, felt that the "Syracuse Health Demonstration . . . [was] the most complete city program for the control of tuberculosis . . . in the world."[32] Dr. G. B. Roatta, Director of Dispensaries, Florence, Italy, said the same for Cattaraugus County: "In Cattaraugus County you have an intensive case-finding of tuberculosis far in advance of anything I have seen anywhere else in the world, and you are certainly setting new standards in the discovery and control of tuberculosis in rural areas and small cities."[33] United States Surgeon General Hugh S. Cumming felt the "Health Demonstrations represent a phase of public health which is probably doing more good for this country as a whole than any other thing." He announced that the experiments had attracted such favorable attention in Europe that the League of Nations cabled him to come to Geneva to present their methods and results before its members.[34]

Permanent record of these three demonstrations and their results can be found in three published volumes.[35] Briefly, however, they showed, in Dr. Biggs's words, that "public health is purchasable." Through intensive application of known health measures the extent of sickness was greatly reduced within a reasonable period of time at a reasonable per capita cost.[36] More specifically, in all three demonstrations a considerable number of lives were saved, as shown by decreased infant and communicable disease mortality rates. Translating saved lives into economic terms, the value to the communities equaled from two to six times the cost of the entire health program in each instance. It was also demonstrated that the general program of a full-time county health unit in a rural area was practical, effective, and, with state aid, financially possible. In addition, as evidenced by increased annual public appropriations for the health boards involved, the demonstrations pointed out the capacity of the public to comprehend, evaluate, and support such a program. In other words, it was proved that people will pay for health.[37]

These demonstrations had far-reaching influence. The Belleville-Yorkville demonstration, along with the East Harlem Health Center, led to the establishment of the health center idea as the fundamental basis of New York City's health program. As a result of Cattaraugus County's experience, the Rockefeller Foundation and the United States Public Health Service began their notable work in the development of full-time county health departments with grants-in-aid to rural health enterprises, especially in the South. Finally, thanks to the success of the Syracuse experiment in the use of a full-time qualified city health commissioner, in 1931 the New York State Legislature enacted a law requiring each city with a population of more than 50,000 to appoint a full-time health commissioner.[38]

The health demonstrations also pointed out the inevitable trend toward uniting all health activities. Originally planned as campaigns primarily against communicable diseases, especially tuberculosis, the demonstrations soon expanded to include all phases of health work. This, of course, met Folks's hearty approval. Nevertheless, he clearly argued that diseases were of varying social significance; declining rates of mortality from various diseases were of unequal value—the harm to the community caused by different diseases was not indicated simply by their mortality rate. The victims' ages, number of dependents, loss of earning power, and so forth were more important than mere numbers. He felt these factors should be considered by health workers when they attacked the preventable causes of illness.[39]

For example, by 1925 the battle against tuberculosis was half won. Since 1900 it had declined more than 50 per cent. It ranked sixth in the number of annual deaths. Yet, with regard to persons between the ages of twenty and fifty, the "productive period of life," tuberculosis still led in fatalities. Taking these social consequences into consideration, in 1925 Folks felt tuberculosis still was the number-one objective against which major public health efforts should be directed.[40]

Along with completing the fight against tuberculosis, the control of diphtheria and the venereal diseases ranked high. They both had relatively high "social-mortality" rates. Moreover, in view of the knowledge of effective methods of controlling these diseases, there were good prospects of achieving favorable results, another factor Folks felt should be considered. As a result, the State Charities Aid Association broadened its scope to include aggressive and successful campaigns against diphtheria and syphilis, once again demonstrating the effectiveness of modern administrative and educational methods of combating disease.[41]

In 1925 physicians possessed a more complete knowledge of and power over diphtheria than any other communicable disease. Through the use of antitoxin and toxin-antitoxin, they had every weapon needed to prevent and treat the disease, yet it still occupied third place among the communicable diseases and killed thousands of people each year.[42] Accordingly, the State Charities Aid Association adopted a resolution authorizing the State Committee on Tuberculosis and Public Health to formulate a program to eliminate diphtheria in New York State. The committee developed publicity material, rendered assistance in community organization, and planted in the public mind the importance of immunization. Folks and others carried the message of diphtheria protection through immunization, especially for all children under ten years of age, to every community, town, and city in New York State. In five years the campaign, which evoked national interest, resulted in a drop from 4,370 to 1,600 annual cases. The death rate went from 6.4 per 100,000 in 1925 to 2.5 in 1930, a fall of 60.9 per cent.[43] The committee carried on the campaign and a decade later diphtheria almost reached the vanishing point. In 1940 there were only four deaths from the disease in upstate New York, a death rate of 0.06 per 100,000. United States Surgeon General Thomas Parran summed up the State Charities Aid Association's successful fifteen-year effort succinctly but well when he addressed the Association's members and said, "You have pioneered in the most effective mass demonstration of diphtheria control ever made in this or any other nation." [44]

Like tuberculosis and diphtheria, syphilis was a communicable disease that could be both prevented and cured. Similar to tuberculosis in many respects, its early recognition and adequate treatment were major factors in prevention as well as cure; its cure was slow and expensive, while prevention was fast and cheap. Syphilis was, in Folks's words, "the next to go." [45]

Actually, Folks had begun to fight syphilis in 1906 when he spoke before the New York Society for Sanitary and Moral Prophylaxis and urged that an effort be made to enlist the cooperation of the press to center public attention on the damage caused by venereal disease. As early as 1913 he proclaimed that "by laying aside a little of our prudery, by requiring reports of this [syphilis] as of other contagious diseases, . . . by requiring a medical examination . . . as a condition for issuing of a marriage license, by providing dispensaries and hospitals for the diseased, and by making the fullest use of efficient forms of treatment, the ravages of syphilis can be reduced to but a small fraction of its present proportion." [46]

However, over the years, despite the creation all over America of many social hygiene organizations, little was done about the disease until January 1932, when the State Charities Aid Association became the first organization in the nation to undertake a comprehensive state-wide campaign against it; the Association's Board of Managers resolved "to participate in all suitable ways . . . in the promotion of measures looking to the more effective control of the venereal diseases." [47]

Once again, through newspaper publicity, movies, radio broadcasts, and exhibits, the Association undertook a statewide educational campaign, this time on the prevention and treatment of syphilis. It mobilized health officials and voluntary health organizations as well as the general public in the campaign, which led to the establishment of statewide clinical facilities for the diagnosis and treatment of venereal diseases.[48] Folks played a leading part in the campaign and along with Surgeon General Parran, State Health Commissioner Dr. Edward S. Godfrey, Jr., and Dr. John L. Rice, New York City Commissioner of Health, was instrumental in drafting and having enacted in 1938 what was regarded as the most effective legislation possible for the control of syphilis—statutes requiring blood tests of all expectant mothers and applicants for marriage licenses.[49] These two state laws, the first of their kind, were extremely helpful in uncovering syphilitics in need of treatment. They also served to reduce materially the number of stillbirths and cases of congenital syphilis.

As it turned out, New York State was a proving ground for what became a national effort for syphilis control when, several months later, the federal government joined the effort against the disease. Congress passed the LaFollette-Bulwinkle bill, authorizing a large appropriation to the United States Public Health Service for research and allocation to the states to improve programs for syphilis control. Thus, as the Surgeon General and the American Social Hygiene Association noted, with the extension of the State Charities Aid Association's work to other states through federal grants-in-aid, the Association proved the value of voluntary citizen organization and service in this, as in other, fields.[50]

In the meantime, the progress of the anti-tuberculosis campaign had subsided. Despite the health demonstrations, county units were not being organized. In 1927, representatives of the Board of Supervisors of twenty-one counties, the State Department of Health, the State Medical Society, the State Charities Aid Association, and other agencies attended a conference called by governor Alfred E. Smith to urge that for reasons of efficiency and economy the county be made the basis of public health administration. Smith argued that "the results obtained in furnishing health protection to the people of Cattaraugus County

. . . should point the way to other counties doing likewise." [51] Although the proposal was widely endorsed, it was not implemented.

At Folks's suggestion, three years later Governor Franklin D. Roosevelt called another conference to discuss the state's health program.[52] Out of this conference emerged a Special Health Commission, appointed by Roosevelt on May 1, 1930, to study the Public Health Law and the activities of state and local authorities dealing with the promotion of health. This marked the first time in seventeen years that the state's health machinery was placed under official scrutiny. Several members of the State Charities Aid Association's Committee on Tuberculosis and Health served on the Health Commission, which included Farrand as chairman, Folks as vice-chairman, Parran, and Linsly Williams.[53]

On February 16, 1931, the commission submitted its findings and recommendations to the governor. The report urged the adoption of another state health program aimed at further and better application of accepted health measures. The commission felt the need for a more intensive effort for the early detection of tuberculosis, increased support for public health nursing, a better organized and more intensified health education program, more facilities for the treatment of syphilis, mental illness, and cancer, and increased state and local laboratory services. To round out the program and ensure its effectiveness, the commission recommended two chief provisions: first, to fulfill the state's sanatorium needs and provide for every resident of New York easy access to a public tuberculosis hospital, the establishment of three State District Tuberculosis Hospitals; second, mandatory establishment of county health units. Instead of hundreds of town, village, and city Boards of Health and health officers, fifty-seven County Health Departments would be created, each under the direction of a well-qualified, specially trained, full-time health officer.[54]

Three days after Governor Roosevelt received the report he transmitted it to the legislature with a special message urging the early enactment of its recommendations into law. The historic fifteen-page message began with the declaration that "the success or failure of any government in the final analysis must be measured by the well-being of its citizens. Nothing can be more important to a State than its public health: the State's paramount concern should be the health of its people." Roosevelt concluded, "I know that you will cooperate with the members of the commission who have so clearly pointed the way. These public health experts have sent to me their prescription for their patient—the State of New York. You and I can, and should, join hands in filling this prescription in the form of legislation." [55] Roosevelt, like Folks and other public health enthusiasts, without stepping outside the framework of a capitalistic society probed clear to its foundations. The state had to do things for its people if it was to survive. Roosevelt accepted the public health reformers' disturbing challenge, not revolutionary in any doctrinal sense, not tilting at established institutions, but rather demanding that those institutions be made to serve the good of humanity.

Folks, however, was not as optimistic as the Governor. As he pointed out, there would be opposition "from health officers of towns and villages, who [with the establishment of county health units] can hardly be expected to view the possible abolition of their position . . . with approval; and perhaps from some physicians who . . . have a vague fear that in some unforeseen way the improvement and extension of public health activities may adversely affect them." [56] Therefore, when the Wicks-Hutchinson bill, embodying the Health Commission's recommendations, was introduced in the legislature, the State Charities Aid Association again initiated a statewide effort to arouse support for the measure.

Folks secured nonpartisan legislative approval of the bill. Several former presidents of the State Medical Society even backed the proposed law, as did numerous public health experts. Many people agreed with Dr. C. E. A. Winslow that the "viewpoint presented by the commission . . . [was] a thoroughly sound one and the document as a whole . . . [was] a contribution of the first importance to the cause of public health [which] will prove of scarcely less significance" than the 1913 Public Health Commission Report.[57]

By April 1931 the legislature enacted into law nearly all of the Special Health Commission's recommendations, including the provision for three state tuberculosis hospitals to meet the needs of the counties that were too small to build and suitably operate their own sanatoria. Such prompt acceptance of the recommendations, when most states were drastically reducing public health appropriations because of the depression, was conclusive evidence of the state's active interest in tuberculosis control. Only the provision for the establishment of county health departments did not receive legislative approval. Although the county is now recognized as the logical governmental unit to provide necessary health (and welfare) services, especially in rural areas, local health officials, still clinging to their outmoded positions, were preventing the state legislature from acting upon this measure even in the 1960s.[58]

The first of the three state tuberculosis hospitals, located at Ithaca, N. Y., was named in honor of Dr. Hermann M. Biggs, who died in 1923. Former New York State Commissioner of Health, Surgeon General Parran, felt the second hospital should be named after "the one man who," in his opinion, did "more than any other to promote the control of tuberculosis" in New York State—Homer Folks. Thanks to Folks's efforts, Parran informed Governor Herbert Lehman, the tuberculosis control movement demonstrated for the first time that a disease for which there is no specific cure can be brought under control by arousing the forces of public opinion. He recommended that the Oneonta Tuberculosis Hospital be named in Folks's honor.[59] Governor Lehman agreed and endorsed Parran's suggestion. A bill to that effect was introduced in the legislature and "in recognition of Folks' long and devoted services in the cause of tuberculosis control, public health and social welfare," the measure was unanimously passed and signed into law on May 28, 1936.[60]

The recognition Folks thus received was as unique as it was deserved. As others pointed out, to have been placed on the role of distinguished humanitarians alongside Dr. Biggs was honor enough; to have been placed there during one's lifetime was an honor few, if any, others had achieved. It was a true indication of the esteem in which he was held by the people of New York State.[61]

High on a hillside overlooking the beautiful Susquehanna Valley and the city of Oneonta, before a gathering of more than one thousand outstanding public officials, prominent leaders in public health and social welfare, and citziens from throughout the state and nation, on July 9, 1936, Governor Lehman stood up to dedicate the Homer Folks Tuberculosis Hospital "to the high purposes for which it has been established." Lehman turned to Folks and said, "Mr. Folks . . . I hail and salute you as an eminent humanitarian, social engineer extraordinary, and statesman in public health and welfare. Long may the State of New York and its people . . . continue to have the benefit of your genius and leadership in the organization, interpretation, and advancement of public health and social reform." [62]

Profoundly appreciative and grateful, the genial Folks, who radiated warmth and enthusiasm (and such affection that all his subordinates, whether top assistants or lowly typists, drove from New York City for hours on that sweltering day to attend the ceremonies), responded: "To be associated in this way with any one of the state's institutions would be a great honor; but of all of them this would be my first choice—the highest type of life-saving agency, expressing the concern of all the people of the state for each of its constituents in this district who has felt the menace of tuberculosis." He did not suggest that the state should rush headlong into all things but, he concluded, "this hospital is a final proof that, when all the indications point to the state as the unit best fitted to serve some purpose, we need not, and must not, be restrained by an unfounded fear" from seeking its aid. [63]

By the same token, when circumstances pointed to the federal government as the unit best fitted to serve the anti-tuberculosis movement, Folks did not hesitate to call upon it for aid. By 1938 the anti-tuberculosis campaign needed a new impulse. Thousands were still needlessly dying from the disease that, Folks felt, could be eliminated simply through devoting greater financial resources to the task; only the federal government could provide those resources.

The desire for federal participation in the anti-tuberculosis movement was not entirely new. In 1916 so much concern had been aroused over migratory consumptives that the National Tuberculosis Association supported the ill-fated Kent bill, a measure designed to provide federal subsidies to the states for the care of such nonresident indigent patients. Folks was a member of the National Association's Executive Committee, which debated the subject and adopted a resolution declaring that "the participation of the Federal Government in the study and control of tuberculosis is desirable and necessary." [64]

At the same time, in an address before the National Tuberculosis Association, Folks made an urgent plea for the establishment of a strong Division of Tuberculosis in the nation's Public Health Service. The time has come, he argued, in 1916, "when the Federal authorities should assume that degree of efficient leadership which they are exercising in the problems of agriculture and other economic interests. Only through the United States Public Health Service," he maintained, "can any degree of uniformity of method and efficiency . . . in forty-eight states be secured." [65] Not until the great depression, however, did the suggestion of federal support for the anti-tuberculosis program again crop up.

Beginning in 1936, Folks worked silently for two years on a program designed to secure federal participation in the movement to eliminate tuberculosis. When it was completed, he sent copies of the draft to such leading authorities in the field as Dr. Reginald Atwater, executive secretary of the American Public Health Association, Surgeon General Parran, Dr. Robert E. Plunkett, general superintendent of Tuberculosis Hospitals in New York State, and Dr. Kendall Emerson, managing director of the National Tuberculosis Association, all of whom agreed that the plan was "masterly," "statesmanlike and realistic," "a blueprint for national action," and "the only possible way by which [to] . . . obtain a significant reduction in tuberculosis over a five or ten year period." [66]

Folks's "Nation-Wide Federal, State, Local Program to Prevent Tuberculosis" proposed to eradicate the disease through an intensive case-finding and an extensive hospital-building and maintenance plan. The six-year program was designed to intensify the use of X-ray techniques and add forty thousand tuberculosis beds throughout the nation. Folks estimated its total cost at $269,000,000. The federal government would contribute 80 per cent of the cost of hospital construction

and 50 per cent of the maintenance and case-finding expenses—
$176,522,000, or approximately two-thirds of the total amount.[67]

In February 1938 Folks presented the plan to the Board of Directors
of the National Tuberculosis Association, which after further study
approved it. Then he was appointed chairman of a Special Committee
on Federal Provision for Tuberculosis, which drafted a bill "to propose
additional duties upon the United States Public Health Service in
connection with the investigation, treatment and control of tuberculosis." [68] The New York *Times* hailed Folks and the program and
happily informed its readers that a "national tuberculosis campaign on
the magnitude proposed might set the precedent for an even broader
campaign to put all medical knowledge at the disposal of all our people." [69] The measure was brought to the United States Senate floor on
June 5, 1939, by Senator James E. Murray of Montana. Opponents of
the bill, especially the American Medical Association, labeled as "statism"
increased federal participation in public health and, as a result, it went
down to defeat. Introduced in a later session by New York's Senator
Robert F. Wagner as part of his general national health bill, the act
again failed to pass although it commanded wide popular support.[70]

World War II, however, intervened and highlighted as nothing else
could the need for good health. The nation's defense and war effort
depended to a large extent upon the elimination of sickness and disability. When the tuberculosis death rate rose during the war Congress
finally recognized tuberculosis as a major health problem. In July 1944
the National Health Tuberculosis Bill became law.[71] This measure
provided for the establishment of a Tuberculosis Division in the Public
Health Service "in order to develop more effective measures for the
prevention, treatment and control of tuberculosis." Given a $10,000,000
appropriation for the first fiscal year, the law was patterned on the 1938
LaFollette-Bulwinkle Act. In accordance with its provisions, a system
of federal grants-in-aid to the states, and through them to the localities,
was established for the control of tuberculosis. As a result, every state
in the nation could implement programs to control the disease. Fourteen years earlier Folks had written a few words to his friend and
colleague John Kingsbury which he may have recalled at this occasion:

"I learn anew from year to year that things which look very difficult can be done, and done with good success, if you have sufficient faith in them and in yourself." [72]

The remarkable reduction in the morbidity and mortality rates of tuberculosis and other communicable diseases cannot be attributed solely to the movement for improved sanitary laws, health education, clinics, dispensaries, hospitals, public health nursing, and the like. New scientific discoveries, better service by private medical practitioners, improved social and economic conditions, adoption of health and safety laws governing industry, free school lunches, and improved diet, as well as numerous other things have all contributed to the saving of lives. Nevertheless, viewed in historical perspective, a large share of the extraordinary progress that was accomplished resulted from the organized public health movement. Few people, certainly no layman, gave as much assistance, direction, counsel, and inspiration to that movement as did Homer Folks.

In the short period of his career he helped the public health movement grow from an idea in the minds of a few people to a well-organized, widely recognized effort dispensing millions of dollars and saving thousands of lives annually. At the time of his retirement in 1947 the State Committee on Tuberculosis and Public Health of the State Charities Aid Association, organized at his suggestion forty years earlier, was the parent body of fifty-seven county and five city Tuberculosis and Public Health Associations with a total membership of approximately four thousand citizens interested in the prevention of tuberculosis, the venereal diseases, diphtheria, and in helping to promote the establishment of effective public health departments, sanatoria, clinics, and other tax-supported lifesaving facilities.[73] These health agencies, always ready to adapt their programs to the rapidly changing needs of their communities and never neglecting to unite their efforts with those of the official agencies, stood as a monument to the foresight, intelligence, and perseverance of Homer Folks.[74]

Folks occupied himself less with speculation and prophecy than with deeds. By helping to integrate the many fields of medicine with the many fields of social work in the desire to create a working team,

Folks gave the public health movement new roots and helped social work translate faith into action. He was, in the opinion of many, the most notable example of a statesman in the field of public health, one whose wisdom was combined with high purpose, energy, and enthusiasm to accomplish fantastic results.[75]

12

SOCIAL SECURITY

THE general disillusionment and dissatisfaction following World War I were accompanied on many fronts by conservatism and reaction. In addition, the prevailing philosophy of the Harding, Coolidge, and Hoover administrations was, on the whole, not conducive to social reform; those who profited from postwar prosperity were largely indifferent to the needs of the less fortunate. To a degree, even reformers reflected this general attitude.

Social work was in a transitional period in the 1920s. Concerned more than ever before with perfecting casework, defining standards, winning professional status, and focusing on new methods and techniques, especially psychoanalysis, many social workers lost their enthusiasm for social reform. This infatuation with technique and procedure on the one hand, and with Freudianism and psychotherapy on the other, with its emphasis on the mental process and the adjustment of the individual to his environment, tended to shift many social workers' orientation away from social reconstruction. Historians are correct in their belief that this concern for individual adjustment, together with the growing specialization within social work, and the increasing bureaucratization of its functions and its passion for professional status, contributed greatly to the dampening of enthusiasm for broad social action. This, however, is only part of the picture.

During the "prosperity decade" not all social workers lost concern for reform; social action and legislation continued to occupy the attention of many. As Clarke Chambers has demonstrated, although at times apathetic and/or rebuffed, during the 1920s many social workers "kept alive and vital the crusade for social action, and thus formed a viable link between prewar progressivism and the New Deal."[1] Merely to list the activities and many successes of Folks and the State Charities Aid Association during the 1920s in the fields of child welfare, mental hygiene, and public health is to suggest that discouragement and frustration were not the sole, or perhaps even the dominant, tones of the decade; Folks and others sparked many social crusades that anticipated the reform programs of the following decade.

Folks continued to be an effective crusader for good causes during this period, in part, because he remained zealous. Although he bemoaned the dampening enthusiasm for broad social action, he saw that the need for social reform had not lessened and he always remained optimistic about the future. "To my individual thinking," he wrote in 1921, "there has not been a time . . . when there seemed so little genuine widespread interest in social welfare . . . as just now; but cannot we read a lesson from the events that followed the Civil War? This apathy is bound to be followed by the emergence of a great new wave of interest in human welfare. . . . [Soon] the world will want to devote itself to great measures of human betterment as never in the past." [2]

While Folks recognized that in certain instances "psychiatric relief" was necessary and good, he felt caseworkers and psychiatric social workers had gone overboard in their concern with personal inadequacy and individual maladjustment. They had become status-seekers overly absorbed in method and, as a result, professionally parochial; they had alienated themselves from the broad purpose of social work, which was not individual treatment but the prevention of social dependency. Moreover, Folks deplored as a by-product of the professionalization of social work the adoption of a new vocabulary; he remained an amateur in that sense. He had an unusual power to communicate with others. When he wrote or spoke he was understood by all because of his effective command and use of simple words. He saw no reason why other social workers could not do the same. On one occasion he told a large audience of his colleagues, "Good, simple, plain old-fashioned English should meet all our needs." [3]

Folks saw the growing division between social reform and social work as a false dichotomy. Both were essential. However, since for him social action to promote community betterment was always more desirable than the amelioration of individual distress, he continued to stress public health as the best way to help many people avoid dependence, live fuller, richer lives, and thus prevent the need for personal readjustment and rehabilitation. Elected president of the fiftieth anniversary meeting of the National Conference of Social Work in 1923, the only person in the history of the Conference to hold that position twice, Folks in his presidential address urged his colleagues to get back on the right track. Pointing out that casework could not redeem society, he said that prevention is a legitimate concern of social work; it must not be regarded as a distinct and separate field of human action. As the incidence of tuberculosis goes down, he declared, living standards go up: "Every untimely death prevented means less waste, more income, better standards of living, more happiness, and more general well-being. Improvements in health and in welfare are not separable, nor even different—they are the same thing." [4]

For Folks, social work always remained a community profession, not a private humanitarian crusade. Despite his concern for training, skill, and raising the standards of service, he felt the tendency to rely solely on trained social workers "is a tendency which should be resisted." As head of a voluntary organization, he never abandoned his allegiance to the principle of widespread lay participation; rather, he sought to strike a balance between paid and volunteer service. The mobilization of community forces (with their power, influence, and financial support) for the constructive promotion of social progress was, in his opinion, required for success. The wise social worker, Folks often asserted, "has no more serious responsibility than that of increasing the number of public-spirited citizens [and public officials] who feel themselves vitally identified with, and an essential part of social welfare agencies and movements." [5]

Folks never was devoted to prevention for its own sake; he saw it as a step on the path to something more important. He was chiefly concerned with and emphatically devoted to social construction—the positive creation of a freer, fuller, more secure, and more abundant life. In a speech significantly entitled "Social Engineering," Folks emphasized this theme. Social policy, he said, should be aimed at releasing an individual's best energies. It should not tell a man what to do; rather, it should allow him to do what he pleases. "The community should seek not only to restrict unsocial behavior," he maintained, "but to open up new avenues of opportunity." Human happiness was the ultimate concern of the social worker whose function was to guarantee that "no single person . . . be thwarted in the normal development of his personal life." [6] In short, the goal of social work was not simply to provide assistance to individuals or society when something was wrong, but to provide assurance of security and opportunity for everyone at all times.

In Folks's mind, social engineering, or "the conscious effort to correct . . . conditions which thwart . . . human lives," was not simply a phrase. It was "a present, concrete, actual possibility." [7] Believing that human affairs were manageable and that man, through the application of known facts, particularly of medical science, could improve social and thus individual well-being, Folks led the State Charities Aid Association always toward that end. The fundamental merit of the Association was that despite its flexibility and adaptability, over the years its chief executive kept it from departing from its original purpose—the releasing of human resources.[8]

Thus Folks, and other reformers, employed the concept of social engineering long before the great depression. The image of themselves as social engineers caused some social workers to replace human sympathy and interest with a cold and growing scientism. Folks sensed this danger, however, and did not have to be reminded to remain compassionate. He was not just a crusader. He had a rare genius of combining his reform zeal with a simple humaneness. A tenderness of heart and subjective human considerations complemented his concern for efficiency.[9]

The New York State Public Welfare Law of 1929, which he helped frame, was an outstanding example of Folks's creative activities in the 1920s that anticipated in broad concepts some of the ideas that supposedly distinguished the New Deal. New York's Poor Law, which the 1929 law replaced, consisted of a nineteenth-century statute and over 140 conflicting amendments, exemptions, and special applications to it, many of which were as old as the law itself. This patchwork of confusing and chaotic provisions was made even worse by the division of responsibility for its implementation. Commissioners of Charity, County Superintendents of the Poor, Town Overseers, City Councils, Boards of Supervisors, and Town Boards were all responsible for distribution of poor relief.

In 1924 and 1925 the New York State legislature appropriated money to study the revision and codification of the law. Folks welcomed the action and at his suggestion the State Charities Aid Association appointed a special committee to suggest revisions to the legislative appointee in charge of the work.[10] Judge Peter Cantline of Newburgh, N.Y., served as chairman and Folks as secretary of this committee.

Financed by a grant from the Russell Sage Foundation, the committee worked in conjunction with the State Board of Charities and the Association of City Superintendents of the Poor and Poor Law Officers. After two years of study Folks, Cantline, and Miss Elsie Bond, Association staff member, drafted a progressive, modern statute to replace the old law. The bill dealt clearly and comprehensively with the problem of public care for needy people and outlined explicitly the duties and responsibilities of town, city, and county officials. It provided adequate relief for the poor as well as careful study of the causes of dependency. It also encouraged the administration of public relief by competent, full-time officials with facilities, personnel, and funds to do the job properly. Finally, the bill called for the administration of public relief by a system of counties and cities; it eliminated Town Overseers of the Poor. All relief functions except for emergency home relief, at that time relatively unimportant, were removed from the town. County and city welfare districts were created (unless a city voted to become part of the county district in which it was situated) with a full-time commissioner of public welfare in each.[11]

The draft was submitted to the legislative committee in charge of revising the Poor Law. Accepted with only slight modification, it was introduced in the legislature for the first time in 1927, when, despite widespread public support, the measure was defeated. Folks and the

State Charities Aid Association, however, kept the bill alive and after enlisting further interest and backing got it through the legislature two years later. The climax of the prolonged struggle against the obsolete law with its archaic social implications came when Governor Franklin Roosevelt signed the Fearon-Shonk bill into law on April 12, 1929. Hailed with enthusiasm as an enlightened piece of legislation herald- ing the dawn of a new day in the development of New York State's public welfare system, Governor Roosevelt declared, "The enactment of this law marks an epoch in public care of the poor . . . and will place New York State in a position of leadership in this field." [12]

Roosevelt was correct. With the passage of this law advanced con- cepts in social welfare were written into the state's statute books. Ac- cording to one authoritative account, the "law constituted in essence the declaration of a new state policy toward the needy, superseding the harsh, repressive principles underlying the [old] poor law." [13] Far more important than the administrative changes was the new law's progressive spirit, which deserves careful consideration.

The old law was characterized by a negative approach and oppres- sive provisions. As indicated by the change in nomenclature from Poor Law and Overseer of the Poor to Public Welfare Law and Public Welfare Officer, the new law avoided harsh and humiliating terms. More important, unlike the old law, which discouraged home relief, emphasized institutional care, and in general was concerned with keeping relief to a minimum, the new law recognized in principle a far wider scope of public responsibility and contained the principle that as "far as possible families shall be kept together, and they shall not be separated for reasons of poverty alone. Whenever practicable, relief shall be given a poor person in his own home." The old law concerned itself only with material relief for the destitute. The new law empha- sized "services" and "prevention"; public welfare officials were charged with the duties of administering "such services to those liable to become destitute as may prevent the necessity of their becoming public charges." Finally, the new law made the provision of medical care at public expense mandatory not only for the destitute, but also for those unable to secure such care but who otherwise were self-supporting.

Medical care thus was recognized as a necessity of life and made available as a public provision for those who could not afford it.[14]

Translating the law from principle to practice was a long and difficult process. Nevertheless, based on the recognition that poverty and need were often related to illness and other factors beyond the individual's control, the Public Welfare Law of 1929 did much to raise the standards of social service throughout New York State and condition its residents for what followed. Although under the new act public welfare officers still dispensed relief, for the first time "adequate" relief in the home was written into law. More important, by stressing prevention and services, including medical care to the near-needy as well as the destitute, the new law completely reversed the trend of the old Poor Law. The 1929 Public Welfare Law may be looked upon as an attempt not only to rescue, care for, and rehabilitate "victims," but to conserve and constructively utilize the inherent values of individual and family life.[15]

Folks, like many others throughout the 1920s, was also concerned with the problem of dependency among the aged. Old age dependency was chiefly an outgrowth of modern social and industrial development, forces altogether beyond the individual's control. Technological unemployment hit the nation's oldest citizens first. They were being eliminated from major industrial occupations while advances in medical science and public health were at the same time increasing their life span. The problem grew more serious each year as the percentage of aged in the population increased.

Actually, the movement for old age pensions dated back to 1907, when Massachusetts appointed a commission to study the question of old age dependency. It was not until 1915, however, that the first old age pension law in America was passed (in Arizona), but it was soon declared unconstitutional. Largely through the efforts of the American Association for Labor Legislation, which after the collapse of the health insurance movement worked for the advancement of old age security, in 1923 three states—Montana, Nevada, and Pennsylvania— placed old age pension laws on their statute books. These laws, however, were weak in that they were permissive, or optional, laws with the county designated as the unit to provide the funds. Two years later Wisconsin also passed a county option law, but one that contained a new provision—the state was to reimburse the counties for one-third the cost of the paid pensions. As late as 1928 only six states had old age pension laws, and of these only two—Montana and Wisconsin—were actually paying pensions, and then only in a few counties. The year 1929, however, marked a turning point in the history of old age pensions. Several new states added such legislation while similar bills were introduced in many more legislatures, indicating widespread interest in the subject. Most important, three states—California, Utah, and Wyoming—passed old age pension laws of a new type, mandatory for all counties in the state, with the California statute providing for a state contribution to the cost of the pensions.[16]

Such were the conditions when, in his first annual message to the legislature in 1929, Governor Franklin Roosevelt, who favored a contributory scheme, recommended immediate study of the problem in New York State.[17] The legislature approved the recommendation and created a commission to investigate and report on the "most practical and efficient method" of providing security for the state's senior citizens.

At the same time Folks suggested that the State Charities Aid Association form a Special Committee on Care for the Aged. Folks and William Chadbourne, prominent lawyer and Association board member, headed the newly created committee. After a year's study the State Charities Aid Association committee reported that New York's "aged [were] . . . not receiving enough aid" and "that a new public agency and method of relieving the aged in their *homes* must be established."[18] According to the committee, the decision to grant old age relief should be based primarily on the applicant's ability to care for himself outside an institution.

Just as the Association earlier pushed for the idea of foster home care for dependent children, it now recognized that old people didn't want to and shouldn't be institutionalized; it was cruel and inhumane to do so. And, at a time when not a single state had a system financed entirely by state funds, Folks mentioned to an audience that included

Governor Roosevelt, that "reasonably adequate, dependable and suitable relief for the aged . . . will not and cannot be secured unless that relief is given directly by the State itself, and from the State treasury. . . . The State itself," Folks emphasized, "is the only agency through which a modern, effective, sufficient relief system for the needy aged can be secured." [19]

Chadbourne and Folks presented their recommendations to the official New York State Commission on Old Age Security. While this Commission agreed with the State Charities Aid Association on the need for a mandatory old age security law, to be financed by general revenues, not personal contributions, it favored adopting the more popular plan of sharing the cost equally between the state, cities, and counties. In 1930 the legislature enacted into law the official commission's plan.[20]

The provisions of this measure were aimed at removing the state's needy aged from the category of general poor relief. Like the earlier old age pension laws, assistance was granted to needy people over seventy years of age who fulfilled a long residency requirement. The law was unique, however, in that no fixed allowance was specified.[21] Rather, public welfare officers were instructed to provide "adequately" for those eligible for assistance. A Division of Old Age Security was created within the Department of Social Welfare to have general supervision over the new form of public assistance.

Folks felt the system of relief administered by counties and cities with partial reimbursement by the state was "at best a somewhat clumsy system," which in the end might "be rather expensive for the results which it will accomplish." But although he fought publicly for a measure more fully in accord with the principle of complete state aid, here again he recognized the need, at times, for compromise; the measure was at least a step in the right direction. As a result, he lent it his support.[22]

Actually, old age assistance, usually allowances based on need, were not "pensions" as they were popularly called. Unlike widows' pensions, the New York law, for example, in reality created a new form of poor relief, since age plus indigence (a means test), not mere age, was the qualifying test for receiving aid. Nevertheless, despite its limitations, the old age security law was a momentous measure, for even partial outright state aid in New York to the destitute, other than indigent transients and dependent mothers, was noteworthy. Moreover, it substituted adequate assistance in the home for institutional care and thus helped further to remove the stigma and loss of respect that characterized relief-giving under the old poor law system.[23]

Obviously, then, although in the 1920s the social reform urge may have become weakened, it did not completely die. Even in a decade of prevailing social complacency, Folks and others did not default from the task of helping to provide means for individual and community betterment through social action. Convinced that personal security was necessary for individual liberty, not antagonistic to it, Folks remained firm in his "progressive faith" and through political action helped develop new lines of theory and practice, particularly with regard to providing insurance against the hazards of dependency and old age, which anticipated in concept, and often in detail, the predominant welfare consensus that marked the New Deal. He also stood ready to face the future with a factual, undogmatic approach to economic and social issues. A social worker "belongs to no one school of sociology, economics or government," Folks told members of the National Conference in 1923. And, in words similar to those heard more frequently several years later, he continued: "He looks only to results; he is not made afraid by any labels or precedents, or any device or plan which, to the satisfaction of all reasonable tests, contributes to human well-being." [24]

The events following the stock market panic of October 1929 caught most statesmen and financial experts as well as the general public completely unaware. Mass suffering to an extent unknown in the country's history followed the economic calamity. Folks, however, anticipated the results. From the outset, he predicted to a disbelieving State Charities Aid Association staff that widespread unemployment and hardship would follow; immediately he saw that private charity would be unable to combat the depression's effects.[25]

Folks was correct. As the largest manufacturing state in the nation,

New York experienced a major share of the hardship caused by the depression. There, as elsewhere, the task of relieving the jobless and their families was at first undertaken mainly by private agencies, which, like relief authorities, were unprepared and unable to meet the enormous rise in human needs.

Numerous schemes were tried in an effort to combat the growing unemployment and relief emergency. Municipalities and the state generally attempted to initiate or expand their public works programs as the principal method of relieving unemployment. In New York City, where the charter prohibited the use of public funds for outdoor relief, private agencies such as the Association for Improving the Condition of the Poor started work projects. In September 1930 the AICP and the Charity Organization Society organized a citizens' emergency employment committee under the chairmanship of Seward J. Prosser, a leading banker. The Prosser Committee raised money to finance a work project administered by a newly created Emergency Work Bureau.

At Folks's suggestion, the New York City Welfare Council, which he helped create and served as Executive Committee chairman, formed a hundred-member Coordinating Committee on Unemployment headed by former Governor Alfred E. Smith and staffed by Folks and Smith. In making public the plans for this committee, composed of the city's social and business leaders, Folks stated that "in an unemployment crisis the first and most important public duty is to organize all the public and private relief authorities of the city so as to provide food, shelter and clothing for those in need." [26] In other words, as Folks pointed out, for the time being social workers had to put aside their concern for preventing and eliminating the causes of dependency and once again return to the basic job of ameliorating suffering. In any event, the Coordinating Committee itself raised no funds but worked in close cooperation with the Prosser Committee in an attempt to unify and thereby strengthen the relief program in New York City. At the Welfare Council's urging, New York City also established its own work relief program in April 1931, when it became obvious that the Prosser Committee's funds would soon be exhausted.

In the meantime, noting that the situation was grave and that the time had come to face the problem constructively, Governor Roosevelt outlined in March 1930 a five-point program for relieving unemployment. In connection with this program, which emphasized the immediate creation of more local public works projects, Roosevelt appointed a Committee on Stabilization of Industry. Several months later this committee issued an ineffective report which contained a series of proposals similar to the ones outlined earlier by the Governor.

Through the Association's county committees, Folks kept up with activities of public welfare departments throughout the state. He watched with concern the unemployment trends and increasing requests for relief, interpreted and analyzed the disheartening results, and placed them before Governor Roosevelt. Consequently, in October 1930 Roosevelt changed the name and extended the scope of his Committee on Stabilization of Industry to make it serve as a general statewide coordinating committee on the unemployment relief emergency. The committee's membership was increased from five to twelve and it included Folks, who was made chairman of a subcommittee on Coordination of Relief Activities.[27]

Immediately Folks suggested that the Committee on Unemployment Problems send a group of experienced field workers to visit all the cities in the state to make an on-the-spot study of their relief and unemployment problems, and the measures undertaken to meet them. He volunteered the State Charities Aid Association's services for the job, and the State Department of Social Welfare offered its help as well. Those two agencies then undertook a joint investigation not only to obtain the essential facts in the state's fifty-nine cities, but also to make available to the mayors, other city officials, and welfare leaders, information on the successful ways in which some communities were meeting the emergency.[28]

After the survey was complete, the Joint Committee on Unemployment Relief of the State Board of Social Welfare and the State Charities Aid Association submitted to the Governor in January 1931 a twenty-two page report signed by Victor Ridder, president of the State Board of Social Welfare, Charles H. Johnson, State Commissioner of

Social Welfare, and Folks. This report, which indicated a "serious unemployment problem," concluded that relief was, on the whole, inadequate in amount and poorly administered. Better coordination was
needed between public and private relief-giving agencies. The report
also stated that there was a substantial amount of concealed suffering
among needy families who refused to apply for aid. As a result, the
physical and mental health of many of the state's residents was beginning to deteriorate. The Joint Committee recommended the institution
of state public works projects, not direct relief, as a major instrument
for relieving distress. It also called for larger appropriations to departments of public welfare and a $40,000 emergency grant to the State
Department of Social Welfare to enable it to operate an advisory
service for local welfare authorities and agencies. A pamphlet, *Work
Relief; A Memorandum on Work as a Means of Providing Unemployment Relief,* issued by the Joint Committee in June 1931 was influential in securing state work relief legislation.[29]

Folks kept constant vigil on the situation throughout the state. "All
reports and information from upstate cities," he notified the Governor
in mid-February 1931, "indicate that [the] emergency relief situation is
even more serious than when [the] State Welfare Department and
ourselves visited each city in December."[30] He predicted that the need
for unemployment relief would continue indefinitely and suggested
that the time had come to turn to a permanent, rather than an
emergency, relief program. He also advised that the Joint Committee
make a second upstate survey, designed particularly to study the effects
of the work relief projects carried out under private and public auspices during the previous winter.[31]

The suggestion was accepted and the survey began in July. A month
later the Joint Committee issued its second report, which on the whole
was similar to the first. The outstanding fact shown in this report was
that practically every city in the state had spent nearly as much, or
more, for home relief in the first half of 1931 as for the entire year of
1930. Equally large expenditures were expected in the second half of
the year. All the evidence pointed to the inadequacy of the relief that
had been provided thus far. As in the earlier recommendations, the

Joint Committee again suggested the expansion of public and private work relief and provision for a State Advisory Service to assist the cities to improve their public relief administration and coordinate the work of public and private relief agencies. However, this time the committee concluded the "the major part of the necessary work relief and *direct relief* must be provided from public funds." [32]

The findings of the two Joint Committee surveys placed New York State in the unique position of having accurate information on the unemployment relief situation in all parts of the state. It was quite apparent that private and local agencies could no longer play the leading part in meeting the growing emergency. With this evidence indicating the gravity of the situation before him, Governor Roosevelt call the state legislature into special session at the end of August 1931 to consider the findings and recommendations of the two Joint Committee reports. He delivered a message in person to the legislature emphasizing that "modern society acting through its government owes the definite obligation to prevent the starvation or dire waste of any of its fellow men and women who try to maintain themselves but cannot." Significantly, Roosevelt declared that aid to jobless citizens "must be extended by Government, not as a matter of charity, but as a matter of social duty." [33]

The State Unemployment Relief Act, better known as the Wicks Act, which Folks and the State Charities Aid Association helped draft and have enacted, emerged from this special legislative session. Through the Wicks Act, New York became the first state to put into operation the principle of state aid for emergency unemployment relief.[34] Folks, whose forethought during 1930 in many ways paved the way for the State Unemployment Relief Act, which became a model for other states, hailed the measure as "timely and courageous."

Briefly, the Wicks Act, signed into law September 23, 1931, established an eight-month emergency period (November 1, 1931, through June 1, 1932) during which time $20,000,000 in state aid was extended to localities throughout the state for work and home relief. The money was expended under the direction of a separate agency, the Temporary Emergency Relief Administration, headed by three people appointed by the Governor. Harry Hopkins, administrative director of the New York Tuberculosis and Public Health Association and long-time friend of Folks, who introduced him to welfare work shortly after he came east from Iowa in 1912, was made executive director of TERA. Half the appropriation was allocated to reimburse 40 per cent of local expenditures by public welfare officials for home relief, and $8,300,000 for assisting municipalities with work relief programs. With respect to work relief, the act required the establishment in each welfare district of an emergency work bureau as a prerequisite for state aid. The bureau was to plan and administer work relief projects under TERA's general supervision. The balance of the appropriation was used for various purposes, including administrative expenses, such as the salaries of additional trained personnel hired to dispense home relief.[35]

Like the 1929 Public Welfare Law, TERA helped establish the constructive social value of adequate relief as a substitute for the backward notion that adequate grants tend to demoralize and "pauperize" recipients. Furthermore, the Wicks Act, with TERA, a prototype and a forerunner of later New Deal alphabetical agencies, provided experience, key personnel, and a general model for later national policies for the administration of federal unemployment relief.

Folks worked closely with TERA. He was often called upon to assist in the development of its policies and methods. In addition, five State Charities Aid Association staff members were loaned on a full-time basis to TERA; they comprised one-fourth of its staff.[36] The state system of unemployment relief proved remarkably effective. "The TERA," Folks reported to the Governor, "has been doing a perfectly corking job."[37] State aid strengthened local welfare departments and stimulated local efforts to meet the emergency through work relief projects. It also proved advantageous in securing trained workers to assist in the administration of public relief.

However, on the basis of close observations of local conditions and relief funds throughout the state, it became obvious to Folks that relief needs were even greater than anticipated. He informed Roosevelt that in his opinion TERA and state aid would be needed far beyond their expiration date of June 1, 1932. In the belief that unemployment relief had to be met in larger proportion by state funds, Folks urged the extension of the Wicks Act only two and a half months after it became effective.[38]

Roosevelt agreed and suggested that Folks draft a bill to extend the life of the Temporary Emergency Relief Administration. Several times during February 1932 Folks met with Cornelius Bliss, chairman of the New York City Emergency Work Bureau, Jesse I. Straus, chairman of TERA, Harry Hopkins, its executive-director, and Frank A. Taylor, New York City Commissioner of Welfare, to confer on amendments to the Wicks Act. Finally, Folks drew up a bill that ultimately became law and extended the life of TERA.[39] The chief new provision of this law was that after June 1, 1932, state aid for work relief was granted to the localities as a 40 per cent reimbursement of work wages paid, thus putting it on a basis comparable to home relief. An additional $5,000,-000 was appropriated to continue state aid until November 15, 1932. At the same time the legislature authorized a popular referendum on a $30,000,000 bond issue to finance the state aid program in 1933.[40]

The State Charities Aid Association, which had successfully conducted state bond issue campaigns in 1923 and 1930, was the natural agency to organize and carry out another statewide campaign of public education about the proposal. In July 1932 Folks informed Governor Roosevelt that the Association would gladly devote itself to the task. When Roosevelt favored the idea, Folks initiated the campaign under the theme, "Shall We as a State Help to Feed the Hungry, or Will We Let Them Starve?" The Association carried on a wide range of activities throughout the state in support of the bond issue. As earlier, it formed a Citizens' Committee, this time on the Unemployment Emergency Relief Bond Issue, to mobilize popular interest in its favor. The campaign included widespread press coverage, distribution of leaflets and pamphlets in various languages, billboard and placard advertising, and radio talks. A special edition of the *S.C.A.A. News* was issued, and Folks persuaded both major political parties to include planks in their platforms favoring the referendum. These and other measures proved successful. In November the bond issue referendum was carried by a vote of approximately 1,780,500 to 473,400, or a 3.8 to 1 margin.[41]

After 1933 most of the funds for state participation in unemployment relief were also obtained through bond issues approved by popular referenda. They were proposed and passed in 1933 ($60,000,000), 1934 ($40,000,000), 1935 ($35,000,000), and 1936 ($30,000,000); in each instance the State Charities Aid Association led the successful campaign.[42]

As has been indicated, Folks contributed in many ways to New York City and New York State's response to the depression. He also helped in many other ways that have not been discussed. Equally important as his contributions to specific welfare measures were his efforts toward the formation of a new relief policy and making permanent the advances achieved under the stress of the emergency. Long impressed with the fact that in an industrial system as complex as America's, unemployment was as much an industrial hazard as accidents and should therefore be ensured against in advance, he was deeply concerned with removing the stigma and the damage to self-esteem that was still attached to the acceptance of relief.

To him, unemployment assistance was not a form of charity. It was a public obligation to which the jobless were entitled as a matter of right. Unfortunately, community misconceptions about public relief, frequently referred to as the "dole," added enormously to the distress, humiliation, and deterioration of vast numbers of people. In his opinion, one "of the most harmful prevalent misconceptions is that the person getting relief is receiving something for nothing." Relief funds, he pointed out, come from taxation, the cost of which was passed on to all the people of the community; everybody paid for relief. Those who received relief had contributed to its cost during their days of self-support and thus did not receive something for nothing. Since relief was paid for by everybody in porportion to their ability to pay, and since contributions to public welfare were on the same basis as those for other public services, it "ought not to be more disgraceful to seek aid than to send your child to the public school," Folks maintained.[43]

Going one step further, Folks explained that relief, intelligently, honestly, and skillfully administered, was "a binding, cohesive force, in the life of the community." It was "a fine expression of the intent of the community that no one of its members shall suffer." [44] Therefore he urged that public relief be made a social policy, rather than the "yellow dog of the administration of public affairs."

Folks's plea for a radical reconstruction of relief policy stemmed from his desire to establish a system to protect all individuals against losses from major and minor catastrophes arising from social and economic institutions and practices. Specifically to that end he waged a successful battle in favor of cash relief. While the payment of work relief wages in cash was mandatory under the Wicks Act, cash grants were prohibited to recipients of emergency home relief; they were limited to allowances in kind and consisted mainly of inadequate food supplies.

Folks persistently called for more adequate food allowances, relief in the form of rent, and, more important, cash relief. The ability of relief recipients to re-establish themselves depended largely upon the degree to which their morale was protected while they received relief. "Perhaps no factor could count more strongly on the side of the maintenance of a good morale . . . than to provide some or all of the relief in cash," he declared. [45] Cash payments, Folks argued, would help eliminate the stigma attached to relief and at the same time assure relief recipients of a chance to manage their own affairs. It would provide the freedom of action the needy desired. It would, as he called for in his earnest predepression plea for "social construction," provide for the positive creation of a freer, more abundant life. In March 1934 the state legislature finally amended the Wicks Act, permitting TERA to authorize municipalities to grant home relief in cash. Folks helped draft the amendment. [46] While some social workers still remained suspicious and fearful of public outdoor cash relief, and thus resisted the advance of such welfare measures, nothing could better point out Folks's repudiation of this inadequate, but nevertheless once dearly held, principle.

Although the amounts of money appropriated and expended to meet the emergency seemed to be staggering, relief in New York, as else-where, still fell far short of actual need. TERA cited statistics gathered by emergency work bureaus which showed that only a fraction of the steadily growing volume of applications for work relief could be ac-cepted, owing to a lack of funds. As a result, in January 1933 the State Charities Aid Association's Board of Managers resolved that "the necessity of the continuance of state aid to localities for unemployment relief, and the inaccessibility of state credit for that purpose . . . make recourse to Federal funds for unemployment unavoidable." [47] That same month New York's Governor Lehman also concluded that the state was "forced to look to Washington for assistance." [48]

With signs of deepening despair and social unrest as a result of prolonged unemployment and unrelieved and increasing poverty, the need for federal intervention in public relief became so overwhelming that it could no longer be postponed. In May 1933 after much delibera-tion, President Franklin Roosevelt broke with tradition and launched the national government upon an era of federal aid that had tremen-dous consequences for social welfare. He signed the Federal Emer-gency Relief Act into law, which made available $50,000,000 to be dis-tributed as grants-in-aid to states for relief purposes. It represented the first instance of direct federal participation in unemployment relief through the medium of outright grants.[49]

The law was closely patterned on New York State's Wicks Act. Under the federal act, the first national relief agency, the Federal Emergency Relief Administration, was established to carry out the provisions of the law. Significantly, Harry Hopkins, executive director of New York's TERA, became head of the FERA. Authority for determining the extent of grants-in-aid to states was vested in the head of FERA, but like the Wicks Act the actual responsibility for adminis-tering relief remained in the states and localities. In each state a relief administrator or commission acted as a FERA agent (like New York's Emergency Work Bureaus), exercising varying degrees of supervision over the local authorities. Like its prototype, FERA granted aid on the basis of matching expenditures whenever the state was able to provide funds. Although from the outset the main emphasis was placed on

emergency work problems, federal aid finally covered all forms of unemployment relief, which was to be "adequate" and paid in cash.[50]

The "emergency" attitude (as signified in the titles of the previous
relief acts) soon gave way to the view that the problems of social welfare needed lasting attention and that measures of a permanent character had to be taken. A system of security was not only humane, but it
was needed for social and economic stability. In this atmosphere President Roosevelt sent a special message to Congress on June 8, 1934, in
which he urged the establishment of a system of social security.

Three weeks later Roosevelt created a Committee on Economic
Security to formulate a policy upon which he could construct appropriate recommendations for congressional action. The committee employed a group of experts, including Folks, to study the situation and
draft a program. The findings, which emphasized the particular need
for making social services available in rural areas, where they were
practically nonexistent in many states (something Folks had for years
been trying to remedy in New York), were included in a comprehensive report submitted to the President on January 17, 1935. It was on the
basis of this report that President Roosevelt made his recommendations
to Congress for the enactment of a social security program. These
recommendations were embodied in a federal social security bill sponsored by Senator Robert F. Wagner of New York. The measure passed
into law in August 1935.[51]

The Social Security Act included four main points: (1) unemployment compensation; (2) old age benefits; (3) federal aid to dependent children through grants to states for the support of existing
mothers' allowances systems and for the protection and care of homeless, neglected, dependent, and crippled children, especially in rural and
"other areas of special need"; and (4) additional federal aid through
the United States Public Health Service to state and local public health
agencies. Obviously, despite many new terms, the principal provisions
of the act (which was influenced by earlier, successful experiments in
federal-state cooperation in a social welfare program, like the Sheppard-
Towner Act) were not novel; nearly all of them rested upon a firm
foundation laid in many of the states long before 1935.

The Social Security Act was, at best, a compromise measure and became a target of criticism for both conservative and liberal forces. While it was attacked by some for being subversive to the American tradition, Frank J. Bruno, for example, referred to it as "a series of miscellaneous provisions in the field of public welfare which altogether do not furnish a logical plan for social security." It can "only be called a measure to furnish such means as do not arouse serious opposition," he declared.[52] Financed in part through personal contributions, the act was in some ways a deflationary measure siphoning millions of dollars in taxes from the purchasing power of workers. Most important, however, were the act's glaring omissions, especially health insurance, considered by many to be the chief business of social security.[53]

Despite its defects and inadequacies, however, the Social Security Act marked a tremendous advance in the development of social welfare in the United States. It brought expansion and improved standards of public welfare activities all over the nation. More important, destitution was no longer regarded as a question of individual weakness. It was recognized instead as a fundamental problem that had to be attacked by society as a whole. For the first time the American people accepted what Folks had helped achieve in New York, the assumption of the relief applicant's right to public assistance and the belief that security of family life is a matter of concern to the whole community.

Perhaps the most notable aspect of the Social Security Act, however, was that by the terms of the law the federal government embarked upon a permanent policy of public welfare. As a result of the depression and the pitifully inadequate attempt of private relief to meet the needs of the growing number of destitute citizens, the public finally recognized that voluntary charity was insufficient to establish justice or alleviate suffering. Deeply rooted political, economic, and humanitarian individualism and voluntarism finally gave way to what Folks and others connected to the State Charities Aid Association subscribed to from the start—the acceptance of government as a necessary tool in furthering the nation's social welfare.

The New Deal, then, obviously drew heavily upon the knowledge and actions of social workers. Without minimizing the importance of the reforms of the 1930s, the measures adopted were in many instances mere implementations and amplifications of the program of ameliorative, preventive, and constructive social work Folks and many others helped formulate years earlier. As one of the New Deal's leading architects, Robert F. Wagner, observed, "one could not overestimate the central part played by social workers," in laying the legislative ground work as well as in "bringing before their representatives in Congress and state legislatures the present and insistent problems of modern-day life." [54]

In New York State, however, relief still was not organized on a completely permanent basis. It was administered and supervised by two separate state bodies. The Department of Social Welfare was responsible for the functioning of "permanent" programs, while TERA handled "emergency needs." The State Charities Aid Association took the lead in advocating the study and evaluation of the unemployment relief system in the hopes of having it reorganized on a permanent basis.

In August 1934 Governor Herbert H. Lehman appointed a commission to "make a detached and impartial study and evaluation of the administration of unemployment relief." Composed of thirty representative laymen, welfare executives, and legislators from all over the state, this Commission on Unemployment Relief was headed by Allen Wardwell, vice-president of New York City's Bar Association. Folks served as a member of the commission's Executive Committee and chairman of the subcommittee on Local Welfare Organization.

In the course of two years the Wardwell Commission submitted several reports on employment services, home relief in New York City, work relief in the state, relief for transients, and an analysis of state and local welfare organization. Its chief recommendations, which Folks played a large part in formulating, called for a drastic reorganization of the state's relief system, placing it on a permanent basis, including the gradual liquidation of TERA and the transfer of its home relief functions to a reorganized State Department of Social Welfare.

The commission recommended a permanent system of state aid to the localities for home relief, a small State Board of Social Welfare with the State Commissioner of Social Welfare appointed by the Governor instead of the state board, and, finally, reorganization of the local welfare system to make the county the sole unit of administration.[55]

Governor Lehman, who considered the Wardwell Commission's proposals "extraordinarily thorough and well-reasoned both in analysis and in its conclusions," submitted the final report to the legislature.[56] The commission's findings strengthened sentiment throughout the state for a thorough reorganization of its welfare services. After much debate, in 1936 the legislature enacted a compromise bill that, based upon the commission's recommendations, reorganized the state's welfare apparatus.

The plea for a small nonadministrative State Board of Welfare with a governor-appointed commissioner was not heeded, nor was the request for establishment of the county as the unit of welfare administration. Despite these disappointments, however, termination of TERA and the establishment of state aid and supervision for local relief administration in a permanent state department was a landmark in the history of public welfare administration.[57]

One problem still remained. New York State's constitution, which had not been revised since 1894, recognized only local responsibility for public relief. It lacked specific mention of the powers and responsibilities of the state with regard to public welfare, health, or mental hygiene. The vast increase in state activities in these areas in the twentieth century was justified solely under the implied but unstated "police" and "public welfare" powers. Moreover, a phrase in the constitution declared that state aid should not be given to assist individuals or private undertakings. Thus some doubt was cast on the constitutionality of the use of state funds for relief purposes.

Folks saw the need to remedy the situation. Accordingly, months before the 1938 constitutional convention began, the State Charities Aid Association appointed a Special Committee on the Constitutional Convention. This committee, with Folks's aid, formulated recommenda-

tions for changes in the state constitution and then offered them to
Edward Corsi, chairman of the Social Welfare Committee of the Convention.

The recommendations called for a new article to the constitution
that, in addition to specific provisions, outlined in broad scope the
state's powers and responsibilities with regard to public welfare,
public health, mental hygiene, and correctional services. Corsi incorporated the State Charities Aid Association's recommendations into
bills which were introduced to the convention. At the convention and
elsewhere the Association helped stimulate study of the proposals,
which won widespread support and were included in the constitution
placed before the people of the state in November 1938. With the
acceptance of the new constitution public health and welfare were
clearly recognized as state functions; all doubt in regard to the constitutionality of the state's new relief policies was removed.[58]

Even without public expressions of recognition, Folks's friends and
associates knew how much and how well he had contributed to the
best interest of the community. Yet, as Dr. Stephen Smith, the renowned social reformer and a founder of the State Charities Aid Association, once said, "The wise and prudent man regards the anniver-
saries which occur in his business as beacon lights which illumine his
future pathway and enable him to avoid the pitfalls of failure and seize
the fleeting moments of success."[59] Folks's friends felt that February
18, 1937, his seventieth birthday and fourty-fourth year as head of the
State Charities Aid Association, was such an occasion.

Four hundred people attended a dinner in Folks's honor arranged by
New York's leaders in social welfare, public health, and business
affairs. Mayor Fiorello LaGuardia began the jovial occasion with a
witty but revealing statement; with the controversy over Roosevelt's
"court-packing" scheme obviously in mind, he observed, "What a remarkable man Homer Folks is, seventy years of age and both President
Roosevelt and Chief Justice Hughes [who had sent congratulatory
messages] like him."[60]

Charles C. Burlingham, president of New York City's Welfare
Council, presided and the speakers included Allen Wardwell, Professor

C. E. A. Winslow, and Solomon Lowenstein, executive vice-president of the Federation for the Support of Jewish Philanthropic Societies of New York City. The event was another moving example of the tremendous personal influence Folks exerted on the lives of so many people, professionals and volunteers in public health, mental health, and social welfare. Reviewing various phases of Folks's career, the speakers, along with hundreds of others, as their sentiments in letters and messages expressed, attested to Folks's outstanding quality of "perspicacity in envisaging events and trends years ahead of their actual occurrence." [61]

Folks was called upon to make a speech and to discuss the highlights of his career. Standing tall and slender even now, with his white head glistening, his face tanned, and eyes sparkling, he began in his typically humorous fashion: "I have listened to what the speakers had to say with interest. I thought they did very well considering the limitation of their subject." By 1937 it was clear to Folks that America had changed greatly since he began his ministry in New York forty-four years earlier. Social workers were being listened to in Washington as never before, the suffering of the destitute was admitted to be a national, not a local, problem, and ideas long repressed were suddenly coming to fruition. Folks therefore looked back not regretfully, but with pleasure and a great sense of accomplishment. Nevertheless, rather than reminisce he took advantage of the occasion to counsel his fellow workers on the task that lay ahead.

Speaking with the authority of age and experience, he said that in the past forty-odd years social workers had come to understand better the nature of poverty, to see in better perspective its social and economic causes, and to better care for those afflicted by it. But, he continued, they must not stop here. While he had spent a good part of his life preventing disease and illness, two of the major causes of poverty and dependency, he and other reformers now had to attack poverty in other ways. Poverty, Folks re-emphasized, "must be prevented." And he stated almost thirty years before the "Great Society's" federal anti-poverty program that the government may be the only agency capable of doing the job. As if to emphasize something he had believed for so long but which many social workers, and most others, had just recently and often reluctantly begun to accept—the federal government's role in creating a more stable, humane, just, and equitable society—he added, if "we turn to government with confidence, and act with vigor we will not be disappointed." [62] In effect, Folks was merely repeating what he had said early in the century when he initiated the anti-tuberculosis movement in upstate New York: social services designed to help man enjoy his human potential and lead a full life cannot operate without basic economic security, without a floor that will assure Americans in all contingencies of life a minimum income sufficient for an existence in accordance with prevailing concepts of decency.

Folks concluded by saying that to him the past had been an adventure—a grand continuous adventure. "Adventure is the real spice of life. There is no turning back or any stopping in an adventure. So to all my friends," declared the seventy-year-old reformer, "I say, not 'Au Revoir,' but 'come on!'"

Although he glanced ahead and bid his friends to "come on," Folks knew that the time for retirement was approaching. He had been in social work for nearly half a century and his strength was not as inexhaustible as before. Despite the fact that he had not lost any of his intellectual vigor or his youthful radiance, and he was not physically impaired, he frequently felt weak and tired; his vitality began to ebb. Years of enormous activity had started to take their toll as occasional illnesses came more frequently. Having a loyal and efficient staff upon whom he could and was willing to rely, Folks went on few out-of-town "business" trips, attended fewer committee meetings, started taking mid-winter Florida vacations, and began freeing himself from bothersome administrative details that earlier had occupied much of his time. He intended to shed even more of his duties in the near future "in order to have time to think, reflect, and write." [63] Actually, Folks revealed to those present, he had thought of claiming his leisure some years earlier but the depression had intervened; when the emergency ended he planned to choose a successor.

13

STATESMAN EMERITUS

THE depression led to increased governmental action in fields that previously were occupied in varying degrees by voluntary agencies. As a result, private charitable agencies had to reconsider their functions. In some cases this required a redefinition, and in others a diminution or discontinuance of certain activities. However, since the State Charities Aid Association was different from most private welfare organizations in that its main function was to aid the development of public agencies and services, the changed conditions necessitated extending its activities, not cutting them back. Homer Folks welcomed the challenge, but he was growing old.

When the economic crisis hit the nation, Folks had put aside thoughts of retirement in order to help meet the threat. When the emergency neared its end, the aging but still square-shouldered State Charities Aid Association secretary again spoke of resigning. He looked forward to May 1942, when after fifty years of service to the Association he would retire at the age of seventy-five.[1]

Honors continued to come his way. In October 1940 Folks was awarded the (Theodore) Roosevelt Memorial Association's Medal of Honor for "distinguished service in the advancement of social justice." When James R. Garfield, President of the Roosevelt Memorial Association, made the presentation he stated that Folks illustrated the working of the democratic process at its best. "Theodore Roosevelt used to say," Garfield remarked, "that defense of the nation depended not only on military preparedness but social and economic, moral and spiritual preparedness as well, all harmoniously developed." Folks, he concluded, had as a private citizen, "without the prestige or power of public office . . . contributed notably to the strength of the American people and served to prepare the nation for whatever ordeal the coming years may bring." [2]

Suddenly, that ordeal arrived. As war clouds began to drift over America Folks issued a call to which he himself was the first to respond. Should an emergency arise, he wrote, the State Charities Aid Association members and staff "must be ready . . . to double their duties, stretch out their hours and days, . . . and generally do the impossible." [3] There would be no time for personal considerations. Six months after the United States entered World War II Winthrop Aldrich, president of the Association, told an audience of six hundred people that the seventy-five-year-old Folks "has become progressively more active as the days have gone by. I believe," Aldrich added, "that at this moment he is working harder than he ever has in his life." [4]

It was true. Acting twenty years younger than he was, Folks became totally absorbed in the struggle, taking remarkably few holidays considering his age and health. His record of selfless absorption in official duties would be difficult to match. With many State Charities Aid Association staff members in uniform, he doubled his efforts and poured all his energy into the task of winning the war for security at home, which he properly realized was vitally related to the fighting abroad.

To Folks, who this time viewed the conflict as an ideological one, the war was a "world-wide struggle for democracy." The rise of totalitarianism offended his deepest instincts. He believed in the brotherhood of man and this meant, among other things, the preservation of human dignity, something lacking in the Fascist states. He never doubted the ability of democracy to withstand the danger. However, he felt that "the ultimate fate of democracy [did] . . . not depend on the soundness of its theory or philosophy, but on what democracy [did] . . . to serve the interests of the people of the state." [5] Democracy and welfare, then, were inseparable—they had to "stand or fall together." Every act impeding governmental efficiency and service was an injury to democracy and every step taken by a citizen to aid the operation of public service reinforced the structure of democracy, strengthened its vitality, and helped to ensure its permanence. The State Charities Aid Association's duty was clear; it had to "buttress democracy" by vigilantly protecting and improving the public services, by helping to frame wise laws, and by securing their sound administration. If well done, this would conserve and increase the efficiency of the state's population and thus help mobilize the nation's manpower for the military struggle. It would also demonstrate democracy's ability to work in war as well as in peace, encourage the citizenry to adhere to most of their democratic and capitalistic traditions, and arouse the loyalty needed to carry the nation through the long struggle.[6]

But, as Folks pointed out, this was exactly what the Association had always done: "The State Charities Aid Association all its sixty-nine years," he declared, "has actually been, in fact, an aid, supporter, interpreter, and developer of Democracy."[7] In effect, the Association's entire program was one of preparedness—preparedness for whatever the future brought. Thus, even months before Pearl Harbor, Folks affirmed that the State Charities Aid Association's work of promoting public health, public welfare, mental hygiene, and the security of family life was, and would continue to be, an important contribution to the national defense. Throughout the struggle Folks and the Association continued without stint to further democracy and the war effort by adhering to their central and unchanging purpose—conserving and constructively releasing all possible human resources.

Folks, however, also recognized and pointed out that the tremendous changes taking place throughout the world might seriously affect the nation's social and economic structure. He urged public and private authorities and agencies to look ahead and gear their work to meet the postwar problems, at home and abroad. A recurring note in his writing was the recognition that the totality of child welfare rested upon the stability of the family in which he was nurtured, and that family health in turn depended upon the security that society afforded. For the State Charities Aid Association, then, Folks outlined two future objectives: first, to help develop facilities and services to protect all individuals from the hazards of unemployment, sickness, and old age; second, to help develop the public welfare structure so that it would provide the skilled services necessary to care effectively for those whose distress was caused or complicated by physical or mental disability. In short, after the war the Association would continue the work it started many years earlier—to provide freedom from want, and health and security for all people.[8]

The Association, however, would have to proceed without Folks. He carried it through the war, but the terrific strain, and the calendar, finally caught up with him. In November 1946 he suffered a slight stroke and was unable to return to work. On February 1, 1947, fifty-four years after he joined the organization, Folks asked to be relieved of his duties. Two weeks later the State Charities Aid Association's Board of Managers accepted Folks's resignation "with profound regret" but "with . . . gratitude for his long and distinguished leadership and . . . pride in the far-reaching achievements of his unique career."[9]

Folks's retirement was sober news to all his friends and colleagues, indeed, to all who cherished the public welfare. There was not a single person prominent in social service who recalled a time when Folks was not at the center of affairs. Those who knew him, or of him, lamented the end of his active service, but they all agreed that at the age of eighty this wise, compassionate man seasoned in good deeds deserved a rest.[10]

The New York State Department of Health saluted Folks "as a humanitarian whose discernment and leadership [had] . . . been progressive forces in the advancement of public health and welfare."[11] The New York County Medical Society, which in the past had its disagreements with Folks, hailed him as "a proponent of sound progressivism in medical affairs, and as such, . . . a true friend of the best traditions of the medical profession."[12] The New York *Sun* felt "it was the great good fortune . . . of all Americans that he was able to serve so long," while the New York *Times* stated that Folks "preached and practiced the charity that [was] . . . an expression of benevolence, affection and brotherhood. He had the courage to support good causes before they were popular, the persistence to hammer away year in and year out at the aims he knew were right, [and] the intelligence to discern what was right."[13] And the New York *PM* declared that Folks's "remarkable achievements over a half century . . . in behalf of health and improved social services for children, the sick and the aged [were] . . . unmatched in the annals of American humanitarianism." [14] But the *American Journal of Public Health* best summarized the sentiments expressed by many when its editors exclaimed that Folks provided a "notable example of the fact that powerful pressure groups can function in the public interest as well as in the service of some private cabal seeking special interest. He was much more than a politician, however," they continued, he "was a statesman of the public good, a wise and judicious adviser, a tireless and inspiring leader." Folks's retirement, the journal's editors concluded, "marks the end of an epoch." [15] His resignation did in fact close an era of social work for, as was widely recognized, there was literally no one left who could represent his type or perpetuate his tradition.[16]

Living with his wife at their Yonkers, New York, home, where they had resided for nearly fifty years, Folks maintained his characteristic gaiety and whimsical humor; it was not in his temperament to indulge in selfish sorrow. Although the world grew more lonesome each day as friends passed away, his memories of them were happy ones. Moreover, the devotion of his two happily married daughters and their husbands and families kept his spirits up.

In August 1955, however, his wife Maud died. Her death, of course, was a severe blow for Folks. It was both a deep personal loss and a reminder of his own advancing age, and he was deeply saddened. Another of the few remaining links with the bright days of his youth was gone. Folks now moved into the home of one of his daughters (Mrs. Lawrence Orton) in Riverdale, New York, where he quietly spent his remaining years. On February 13, 1963, several days before his ninety-sixth birthday, he died.

Telegrams, telephone calls, and letters began to pour in. The family had known that he was loved and admired during his honor-filled lifetime, but the show of such esteem from a younger generation of public servants and private citizens after Folks's almost twenty years of inactivity indicated that his work and influence on present and future generations had been and will continue to be appreciated and carried on.[17]

Folks's contributions, while difficult to measure, cannot be denied, for he left his imprint upon every area of American life in which he labored. Today, the things he worked for—child care and welfare programs, child labor legislation, probation, infant and maternity protection, mental hygiene, and public health—are all taken for granted. The pioneering advances have tended to be forgotten. They did not spring full blown; their roots lie deep in the past six or seven decades when Folks and other reformers acted to curb and remedy some of the existing social abuses. Unknown to many today, Folks's name nevertheless will remain a symbol of the long fight for these achievements. Few other men worked so long, so hard, or so persistently for the public's health and welfare.

Folks played an important role in helping to establish and keep charity and social work on the road to social reform. Progress toward recognition of the idea of social action as a functional area in social work was gradual and intermittent. It triumphed only when social workers were motivated not simply by a moral-minded conscience or paternalism (or, rather, maternalism), but by a concern for furthering the democratic philosophy on which America was founded. Only then did large numbers of social workers look beyond individuals to the conditions under which they lived. When they did this, they realized that basic problems were, for the most part, social in nature; a commitment to reform resulted. Homer Folks played a vital role in that development. When, later, professional social workers concentrated on individuals again and forgot that they had a responsibility to society and the public welfare, Folks, always aware of the direct influence of the health of society upon the health of individual clients, continued to demand social justice through social reform. Today, many social workers once again claim as one of their distinctive functions (along with therapy) the stimulation of social legislation and institutional change.

Social work now also recognizes something else that Folks and only a few other representatives of private charitable societies maintained a long time ago—that the mandate in which it has its origin and its continuing growth comes from the community. "Social work," Karl deSchweinitz has written, "lives in, through, and for the community. . . . Social work gains in effectiveness the closer it is identified with the public from which it sprung up and which it serves." Man does not exist apart from his social relationships; in an increasingly interdependent society he has not only rights but also responsibilities to other men. Recognizing this, social workers now preach, as Folks did six decades ago, "team work, citizens and social worker moving together in the exercise of a civic statesmanship." [18] Long before group work and community organization and planning emerged as self-conscious specialties in professional social work, a recent phenomenon, Folks not only recognized and emphasized its importance, but became expert in it.

Along this line, Folks added another element, which perhaps was his greatest contribution to the struggle for health and welfare—bringing the public health movement into the organized social welfare crusade of the era. Despite its present limitations,[19] public health has made enormous achievements, achievements that in large part were spearheaded by social workers. The movement for good public health, a story of the improved treatment of disease on the one hand and its prevention on the other, has annually saved thousands of lives and prevented multitudes of families from being broken. Actually, health progress has affected virtually every American. Many diseases have been brought under control, death rates have dropped, and the chances for longer life have greatly increased. Few people did more than Homer Folks to help bring this about. Convinced that the solution to social problems, especially poverty and dependency, involved the abandonment of the false dichotomy between health and welfare in favor of a vigorous and whole-hearted cooperation among all citizens interested in the public welfare, Folks was one of the first to recognize the vital importance of mobilizing the entire community—public officials and private citizens, health officers and social workers, physicians and laymen—in the war against illness and insecurity.[20] And while this concept may not have been his alone, few, if any, succeeded as Folks did in carrying it out. In short, as a result of his ability to successfully fuse all these elements into a working team, Folks helped extend the scope of social work, thereby making it a valuable and welcome addition to the economic and political machinery organized for the improvement of the community.[21]

Folks demonstrated an amazing capacity to get things done. His qualities of mind, character, and personality help account for his achievements. He was extremely vigorous and seemed to possess a limitless amount of energy. He had a ready wit and a keen sense of humor which enlivened many a dull conference or board meeting. He made his decisions after carefully weighing the available information. He was a good listener, welcoming and even seeking the advice of others, especially of respected authorities. When his judgment was formed he went ahead courageously and fearlessly to take his position, regardless of its nature. No amount of opposition by those less informed could influence him to change his mind. He was willing, however, to learn and to modify that position when given reason to do so. Moveover, he was never in a hurry to force public opinion; he was content to wait for the truth to permeate the public. Understanding the slow and often painful progress of social reform, he refused to subscribe to panaceas or easy solutions to social ills. He accepted impediments in the way of achieving his social aims as necessary stones in the path of progress which must be removed by patient effort.[22]

Folks was kind, gentle, and compassionate. He was not easy-going, though, for his interest in his fellow man and social justice was too strong for that. He possessed a steady, deep, unchanging sympathy for those in need and a single-minded dedication to their service. His manner was quiet and reserved. He was extremely even-tempered and rarely showed irritation. Folks had no interest in personal recognition or advancement; the public interest was his only concern.[23]

His remarkable aptitude for gaining the confidence of important people was matched by his extraordinary ability to organize groups and mobilize public opinion. His persuasiveness and skill in the presentation of arguments was a great asset. His talent for quickly mastering the essential factors in any public movement and his unfailing tact and patience, along with great competence and control of his subject, made him highly respected in New York, Albany, Washington, and elsewhere. He won the confidence not only of his colleagues, but of legislators and executives of both political parties, and was instrumental in preventing political considerations from having a large influence in the selection and retention of public health and welfare officials.[24]

Folks also possessed the proper blend of idealism and realism. Although far-sighted, his political sagacity enabled him to keep his vision clear. Facts and experiences were more important to him than abstract and untested ideas. He had a keen insight into the administration and the broad principles necessary for successful public work. Many have said that he was a legislative genius. He certainly was an expert legal draftsman and was equally adept at steering bills through the legislature. Staunch in his integrity, he never compromised ideals, but being practical he worked for what was attainable, accepting advances bit by bit. Administrative work involves a kind of subtle strategy and a quick and unerring ability to distinguish between important questions of principle and minor questions of policy, a quick sense of the difference between very important and relatively less important questions. He had this rare gift, so important in successful public welfare administration work.

Folks also never failed to grasp the significance of the widening scope of government in the twentieth century. He and the State Charities Aid Association played an important part in initiating social measures and creating agencies whose activities subsequently were transferred to municipalities, the state, and in some cases to the national government. As such, they played an important part in increasing the role of government through enactment and operation of laws and services that have affected the welfare of millions.[25]

Folks had opponents, but he made few enemies. Some feared him, others disagreed with him. Everyone, even his critics, however, respected him. Folks was a man of stature, whose radiant personal charm and earnestness of purpose were magnetic. He inspired a great following. His staff, and others, were affectionately loyal to him. He was an excellent executive, and he expected and received a great deal from those who worked under him. Commanding such confidence and respect, he had an unusual ability to inspire prodigious effort from those who worked with him. Along with inspiration, he never failed to supply counsel and direction to those who sought it. John A. Kingsbury, one of his "pupils," said that although Folks was "a leader perhaps in a greater variety of special fields of social work than any one else, . . . in no field . . . has he rendered greater service than as a teacher." [26] In every single phase of social welfare there were leaders who came under his influence, many of whom he personally trained and encouraged to take added responsibility. Indeed, the State Charities Aid Association has been called a "training school" for social work.[27]

On the whole, Folks pursued moderate solutions to social problems. He was a crusader, but no radical. He was therefore trusted by businessmen, civic and service groups, and other interests that traditionally are slower to accept change. This was another factor that played a part in his successful career. Moreover, unlike some, Folks was able to operate successfully in many lines of effort. Although he frequently did more than what most individuals are capable of doing, his work did not suffer as a result; no one project was ever less effective due to his responsibilities to others.

This is a highly flattering picture of Homer Folks. He was, however, a remarkable man. And like most people who bring about important changes, Folks had his critics—although few in number. Most were legislators or members of the State Board of Charities (later Social Welfare) or similar official bodies. Jealous of the position Folks attained as a private citizen without ever having been elected or appointed to state office, they privately voiced the opinion that he commanded too much influence and power. While this may have been dangerous in the hands of some, Folks did not exercise it unduly or in any but the public interest. At times they remarked that Folks was vain. He was not. Folks was merely human, and like most he had a healthy ego. He sought the approval of others and enjoyed being praised occasionally. Finally, some of Folks's opponents said he was devious and untrustworthy.[28] Unfortunately, his patience, his ability to discern the essential from the nonessential and thus on occasion his willingness to compromise, and his charm, finesse, and knowledge of psychology were misunderstood for deviousness by his critics. Folks was an excellent politician, a successful diplomat. Although he could be blunt and direct when occasion demanded it, rather than attack openly those who disagreed with him, he preferred to work behind the scenes, "pull strings" where they counted, or win over his adversaries through the force of facts and an aroused public opinion. Folks was astute enough to realize that victory was not enough, for reaction often followed success. By working slowly and through others, carrying as many as possible along the path, few of Folk's achievements were reversed.

Folks's one basic weakness was an inability to step down from his job at the right time.[29] Only when he reached eighty years of age and became physically unable to continue did he relinquish his position. Despite the fact that he delegated a great deal of responsibility and power to others, he always felt that large projects were so dependent upon him that he found it virtually impossible to leave them entirely to others. Consequently, during the last few years of command, when he lost some of his earlier dynamism and vigor, the State Charities Aid Association waned considerably. Blinded by his own success and never able to face up to the end of his career, Folks did not choose and train a successor. As a result, when he was forced to step down there was no one to fill his place; the powerful organization he had so painstakingly built floundered even more and sank into a relative ineffectiveness from which it took nearly a decade to recover. It is ironic that a man of such good judgment and common sense, noted for training others for leadership, at the end did not leave a pupil in charge.

Folks's weakness, however, should in no way detract from his success and significance. He was not a social philosopher. His theories consisted of faith in human ability to master its destiny, in peace, democracy, equality, justice, and freedom. Evils in need of reform appealed to him. Action was his instinct. He believed that good citizenship meant more than preaching; it also meant serving. He insisted that private citizens had a duty to help maintain sound standards of health and welfare; he preached what he practiced. He enlisted private citizens to assist government bring about better public health and welfare services. The State Charities Aid Association was a striking example of public services rendered by private organizations, privately directed, in the public interest.

Folks was not only a highly competent and exceptionally influential social worker, he was a true social statesman. His breadth of vision, his ability to understand the unexpressed and often unfelt needs of the people and formulate plans to meet those fundamental needs, enabled him at times to pioneer in the social field. At other times he developed, promoted, and executed ideas originated by others. Moreover, while he took into account the problems of individuals, he never lost sight of his larger subject. He looked for the social shortcomings against which the individual was helpless. He realized that larger and larger segments of the community had to be involved in successful social welfare work, and he marshaled these forces for the improvement of social conditions. It is true that his life coincided in time with a significant epoch in American history, and it is also true that social advancement is achieved through the activities of numberless undistinguished, but in the aggregate very important, people. However, in striding forward and making the most of the pioneering opportunities that handicapped lesser men and women, in anticipating challenges, in meeting them, and in providing the leadership for others to do likewise, Folks, like a few individuals in each generation, stands out as a major instrument in the promotion of a better America; his social statesmanship, in other words, contributed substantially to the making of that epoch.

The secret of Folks's life consisted in combining continuity with change. That life of selfless service, which left as its monument not only institutions, but better lives, is eloquently summed up in the citation—more apt than most citations usually are—that accompanied his Roosevelt Memorial Association award:

For the medal for distinguished service in the field of social justice, I present the name of one of the ablest of those good Samaritans who are the bright particular splendor of our American civilization. For fifty years his merciful hand has been on those who have fallen by the wayside,—the neglected, the homeless, the sick, the criminal, the insane, and the impoverished. He has labored for the cure and the prevention of disease, has fought the most dreaded of man's physical enemies and, in his home state, all but overcome it. A dreamer, he has dreamed not of power, but of mercy; a crusader, he has glorified not the sword but the flaming heart; a statesman and a man of action, he has brought to his own and other lands not destruction and heartbreak but healing and new horizons, the echo of a beloved footfall, and a word that rings through time—"Arise and walk"— Homer Folks.[30]

NOTES

I

EDUCATION

1. Alfred Folks to Harriet Folks Norfolk, April 18, and May 21, 1856. Also see undated letter from Harriet Norfolk Weir to Emma Norfolk sent to Homer Folks on Dec. 29, 1938. All these may be found in the Homer Folks Collection, Homer Folks Room, Columbia University School of Social Work, New York City (hereafter cited as HFC). Also see the Detroit *News*, Feb. 20, 1957.

2. *History of Jackson County, Michigan; Together with Sketches of Its Cities, Villages and Townships, Educational, Religious, Civil, Military and Political History; Portraits of Prominent Persons, and Biographies of Representative Citizens* (Chicago: Inter-State Publishing Co., 1881), Preface, pp. 275, 878–80; Colonel Charles V. DeLand, *DeLand's History of Jackson County, Michigan, Embracing a Concise View of Its Early Settlement, Industrial Development, Together with Interesting Reminiscences to Which Is Appended a Comprehensive Compendium of Local Biography, Embracing Life Sketches of Many Well-Known Citizens of the County* (B. F. Brown, 1903 [no city of publication given]), pp. 26, 138, 425.

3. *History of Jackson County*, pp. 878–79; Harriet Norfolk Weir to Homer Folks, n.d., HFC.

4. *History of Jackson County*, p. 881.

5. DeLand, *DeLand's History*, p. 425.

6. Detroit *News*, Feb. 20, 1957. In reference to Homer Folks the reporter for the Michigan newspaper wrote: "The commentator admits astonishment to learn that such a man came out of Hanover, Michigan, a place which until yesterday he never knew existed."

7. Obituary of James Folks, Michigan *Hanover-Horton Local*, n.d., HFC. James Folks died on June 7, 1896.

8. James Folks's and Esther Woodliff's marriage certificate is in the HFC. Also see Savel Zimand, "Homer Folks: A Biographical Sketch," in Homer Folks, *Public Health and Welfare: The Citizens' Responsibility*—

Selected Papers of Homer Folks, ed. Savel Zimand (New York: Macmillan, 1958), p. xvi.

9. Homer Folks, "Response to the Presentation of a Silver Tea Service," in *Thirty Years of Service: A Tribute to Homer Folks* (New York: Klebold, 1923), p. 40, HFC.

10. DeLand, *DeLand's History,* p. 293; *History of Jackson County,* pp. 318ff. Many people claim that the Republican Party was organized and founded in Jackson County, Mich., on July 6, 1854.

11. There are a number of "model scholar" certificates from Public School No. 9, Township of Hanover, Jackson, Mich., in the HFC.

12. Homer Folks, "A. F. Burr—A Modern Michigan Saint," Michigan *Hanover-Horton Local,* May 9, 1929.

13. Homer Folks, "Liberty," May 22, 1882; "Evils of the Age," n.d., HFC. Along with his high school essays, copies of most of Folks's school certificates containing the grades he received in his various subjects can be found in the HFC.

14. Homer Folks, "Sources of Happiness," May 8, 1882, HFC. Forty-eight years later in a radio address entitled "The Giver's Dilemma," over station WEAF in New York City (Jan. 10, 1930), Folks said: "A man is blessed if he can give rather than receive; giving is a man's way of reaching out and continuing to reach others," and "the man who withholds remains cold and isolated." HFC.

15. Interview with Mr. and Mrs. Lawrence Orton (Folks's daughter and son-in-law), Nov. 29, 1962, New York City.

16. See, for example, Ray Ginger, *Age of Excess* (New York: Macmillan, 1965), especially pp. 3–153.

17. *History of Jackson County,* p. 882; DeLand, *DeLand's History,* p. 293.

18. *History of Jackson County,* p. 302. The inhabitants of most poorhouses were inhumanely treated at that time. Poorhouses were correctly described by a frequent visitor to them, one-time secretary of the Ohio State Board of Charities, Alexander Johnson, when he called them "social cemeteries." See his *Adventures in Social Welfare, Being Reminiscences of Things, Thoughts and Folks during Forty Years of Social Work* (Fort Wayne, Ind.: Fort Wayne Printing Co., 1923), p. 137.

19. Homer Folks, "The Reminiscences of Homer Folks," Oral History Project (Columbia University, 1949), p. 3 (hereafter cited as OHP).

20. "History of Albion College, in the Biographies of the Principals and Presidents, 1843–1898," *National Cyclopedia of American Biography* (New York: White, 1907), V, 473.

21. Folks, OHP, p. 3. 22. "History of Albion," pp. 475–76.

23. *Ibid.,* p. 473. 24. *Ibid.,* p. 474.

25. Many of Folks's college essays are also in the HFC; see "Education: Prerequisite for Thorough Statesmanship," "Bible Classes—Organization and Study," and "General Religious Work at Albion."

26. Homer Folks, "The Betrayal," HFC.

27. Homer Folks, "Was Napoleon's Life a Success?," HFC.

28. Homer Folks, Diaries, 1885–1889, *passim,* HFC. Folks's numerous yearly calendar books or diaries, kept faithfully during the years he attended college, are in the HFC. Hereafter cited as Diary. In his later years he kept a Journal.

29. Diary, Jan. 8, 9, 10, 12, 1888; Feb. 29, 1888; April 2, 1888; Nov. 6, 1888, HFC. It might be mentioned that Homer Folks was a licensed lay Methodist preacher. See his "Application for Renewal of Local Preacher's License," Aug. 9, 1889, HFC.

30. Homer Folks, untitled high school essay, Dec. 31, 1879, HFC.

31. Diary, June 9, 1889, HFC. Also see entries for Feb. 10, 17, 1888; Oct. 12, 1888; Feb. 14, 1889.

32. Diary, June 25–30, 1887, HFC.

33. Folks, OHP, p. 4; *Thirty Years of Service,* p. 40; Diary, Dec. 31, 1888; Jan. 2, 1889, HFC.

34. Interview with Mr. and Mrs. Savel Zimand (Folks's daughter and son-in-law), Oct. 25, 1962, New York City.

35. Diary, Sept. 14, 1889; Ralph Folks to Homer Folks, March 7, 1898, HFC; Michigan *Hanover-Horton Local,* May 23, 1929.

36. Diary, Sept. 19, 1889, HFC; also Sept. 16, 17, 18, 1889.

37. Diary, Sept. 24, 25, 1889, HFC.

38. Francis Russell Stoddard, "The Reminiscences of Francis Russell Stoddard," OHP, 1949, p. 6; Roger N. Baldwin, "The Reminiscences of Roger N. Baldwin," OHP, 1954, p. 17.

39. See any of the standard histories of higher education in America for Harvard's pre-eminence in the field at that time. For a good description of Harvard in the late 1880's and early 1890s by one of Folks's contemporaries, see Oswald Garrison Villard, *Fighting Years: Memoirs of a Liberal Editor* (New York: Harcourt, Brace, 1939), p. 80.

40. Raymond Calkins to Mrs. Gertrude Folks Zimand, March 31, 1963. The author is indebted to Mrs. Zimand for allowing him to see this letter.

41. Villard, *Fighting Years,* p. 84. 42. Diary, Sept. 30, 1889, HFC.

43. *Ibid.,* Sept. 27, 1889, and *passim.*

44. Folks received three A's (in German 2, Philosophy 4, and Philosophy

11) and a B (in French 1) while at Harvard. See his Harvard College grade sheet in the HFC.

45. Folks, OHP, p. 4; *Thirty Years of Service,* p. 40.

46. Jurgen Herbst, "Francis Greenwood Peabody: Harvard's Theologian of the Social Gospel," *Harvard Theological Review,* LIV (Jan. 1961), 45–69.

47. Francis G. Peabody, " 'Going Slow' in Social Reform," *The Cambridge Magazine* (Feb. 1896), pp. 23–25; "The Approach to Social Work," in *Social Problems and Social Policy,* ed. James Ford (New York: Ginn, 1923). In this essay Peabody made it clear that he believed, above all else, that social change comes about through individual regeneration of the spirit. He presented a Carlylean gospel of individual work and duty.

48. Herbst, "Theologian of the Social Gospel," p. 64; David B. Potts, "The Prospect Union: A Conservative Quest for Social Justice," *New England Quarterly,* XXXV, No. 3 (Sept. 1962), 351.

49. Folks, OHP, p. 4.

50. Frank J. Bruno, *Trends in Social Work, as Reflected in the Proceedings of the National Conference of Social Work, 1874–1956* (New York: Columbia University, 1957), p. 133; Potts, "The Prospect Union," p. 351.

51. Francis L. Broderick, *W. E. B. DuBois: Negro Leader in a Time of Crisis* (Stanford: Stanford University, 1959), p. 15; Baldwin, OHP, p. 10.

52 Potts, "The Prospect Union," p. 351.

53. Diary, Oct. 21, 1889, HFC; Homer Folks, "Homes of the Poor," HFC; Folks, OHP, p. 5; *Thirty Years of Service,* p. 41.

54. George Herbert Palmer, *The Autobiography of a Philosopher* (Boston: Houghton Mifflin, 1930), p. 46.

55. *Ibid.,* pp. 46, 58; Homer Folks, "Notes on Constructive Ethics, 1889–1890," Harvard College Notebook, HFC; Charles M. Bakewell, "The Philosophy of George Herbert Palmer," in *Memorial Addresses, George Herbert Palmer, 1842–1933* (Cambridge: Harvard University, 1935), p. 19.

56. William Ernest Hocking, "Personal Traits of George Herbert Palmer," in *Memorial Addresses,* p. 43.

57. Diary, Jan. 1, 1890, HFC.   58. *Ibid.,* Jan.–April 1890, *passim.*

59. *Ibid.,* June 14, 18, 1890; Mrs. James C. Biddle to Homer Folks, June 16, 1890, HFC.

60. Francis G. Peabody to Mrs. James C. Biddle, June 18, 1890, HFC.

61. Harvard "Faculty Minute," in *Memorial Addresses,* p. 74. The "Faculty Minute" included the following statement: "It was in part owing to this relentless objectivity [in judging people] that he was so widely sought as a counsellor in the placing of men."

62. George Herbert Palmer to Mrs. James C. Biddle, June 16, 1890, HFC.

63. Mrs. James C. Biddle to Homer Folks, June 23, 1890; July 9, 1890; Folks to Biddle, July 21, 1890; Biddle to Folks, July 23, 1890; July 24, 1890; July 29, 1890; Diary, July 27, 1890, HFC.

64. Reinhold Niebuhr, *The Contribution of Religion to Social Work* (New York: Columbia University, 1932), p. 61; Donald Fleming, "Social Darwinism," in *Paths of American Thought,* ed. Arthur M. Schlesinger, Jr., and Morton White (Boston: Houghton Mifflin, 1963), pp. 123–46.

65. Folks, OHP, p. 6; Folks, "The Millennium—Why Not?," p. 1, outline of an address delivered at Albion College, June 15, 1912, HFC; Folks, "The Place of Philanthropy in Social Progress," pp. 18–19, an address delivered before the Alumni Association of Albion College, June 26, 1894, HFC.

66. Alice Felt Tyler, *Freedom's Ferment* (New York: Harper Torchbook, 1962), p. 225.

67. Mrs. Lawrence M. Orton (Folks's daughter Evelyn) to the author, Feb. 19, 1963.

2

CHILD WELFARE—THE APPRENTICESHIP

1. Captain Willard Glazier, *Peculiarities of American Cities* (Philadelphia: Hubbard, 1884), pp. 375–77; Arthur M. Schlesinger, *The Rise of the City* (New York: Macmillan, 1933), p. 340; James Bryce, *The American Commonwealth* (2 vols., New York: Macmillan, 1889), II, 367, 387.

2. Glazier, *Peculiarities,* pp. 375, 398; Bryce, *American Commonwealth,* II, 595; Schlesinger, *The Rise of the City,* p. 350.

3. Homer Folks, *Child-Saving Work in Pennsylvania* (Boston: Ellis, 1893), p. 17, HFC.

4. For a good discussion of the British Poor Law and the ideas embodied in it see "Poor Law," *Encyclopaedia Britannica* (London: Benton, 1962), XVIII, 215–23. Also see Robert Bremner, *American Philanthropy* (Chicago: University of Chicago, 1960), pp. 60–62; David M. Schneider and Albert Deutsch, *The History of Public Welfare in New York State, 1867–1940* (Chicago: University of Chicago, 1941), pp. 6–7.

5. Bremner, *American Philanthropy,* p. 62; Schneider and Deutsch, *History of Public Welfare,* p. 17; Alexander Johnson, *Adventures in Social Welfare, Being Reminiscences of Things, Thoughts and Folks during Forty Years of Social Work* (Fort Wayne, Ind.: Fort Wayne Printing Co., 1923), pp. 137–38.

6. Massachusetts created the first State Board of Charities in 1863. See

Frank J. Bruno, *Trends in Social Work, 1874–1956* (New York: Columbia University, 1957), pp. 31ff.; Robert Bremner, *From the Depths: The Discovery of Poverty in the United States* (New York: New York University, 1956), pp. 48–50; Schneider and Deutsch, *History of Public Welfare,* p. 7.

7. Homer Folks, *The Care of Destitute, Neglected and Delinquent Children* (New York: Macmillan, 1902), pp. 72–89; Schneider and Deutsch, *History of Public Welfare,* p. 60.

8. Naturally, there was great variation in the facilities and management of these institutions, which, under one roof, often brought together anywhere from 50 to 2,000 children. In the main, however, the wards commonly slept in great dormitories or barracks and ate together in immense dining rooms. Their lives were governed by rather rigid schedules; individuality was suppressed and the whole atmosphere usually tended to be one of monotonous routine.

9. Miriam Z. Langsam, "Children West: A History of the Placing-Out System of the New York Children's Aid Society, 1853–1890" (Master's essay, University of Wisconsin, 1961); Schneider and Deutsch, *History of Public Welfare,* p. 74; Bremner, *From the Depths,* pp. 39–41; *American Philanthropy,* pp. 63–64; Emma O. Lundberg, *Unto the Least of These* (New York: Appleton-Century, 1947), pp. 76–89.

10. Lundberg, *Unto the Least of These,* pp. 85–89; Bruno, *Trends in Social Work,* pp. 65–66.

11. Folks, *Child-Saving in Pennsylvania,* pp. 6–9; Mrs. James C. Biddle to Homer Folks, Dec. 22, 1890, HFC.

12. Homer Folks, "The Reminiscences of Homer Folks," Oral History Project (Columbia University, 1949), pp. 6–7 (hereafter cited as OHP). Also, Homer Folks, "Response to the Presentation of a Silver Tea Service," in *Thirty Years of Service: A Tribute to Homer Folks* (New York: Klebold, 1923), p. 41, HFC.

13. Diary, Aug. 16, Dec. 25, 1890; Jan. 1, 1891, HFC; Folks, OHP, p. 9.

14. Diary, April 16, 1891, HFC; Folks, *Child-Saving in Pennsylvania,* p. 12.

15. Mrs. James C. Biddle to Homer Folks, Oct. 23, 1890, HFC.

16. Diary, Aug. 25, 1890–Jan. 1, 1891, *passim,* HFC; Savel Zimand, "Homer Folks: A Biographical Sketch," in Homer Folks, *Public Health and Welfare: The Citizens' Responsibility—Selected Papers of Homer Folks,* ed. Savel Zimand (New York: Macmillan, 1958), p. xxi.

17. Folks, OHP, pp. 9–10. For a good brief historical account of the National Conference see Bruno, *Trends in Social Work,* Ch. 36, "The National Conference of Social Work," pp. 353–64. Also see Johnson, *Adven-*

tures in Social Welfare, p. 269; Charles Bernheimer, *Half a Century in Community Service* (New York: Association, 1948), p. 69.

18. Homer Folks, "Home Care for Delinquent Children" (1891), in Folks, *Public Health and Welfare,* pp. 3, 5–7.

19. Charles D. Kellogg, "The Economic View of Preventive Work among Children," in *Proceedings of the National Conference of Charities and Correction* (Minneapolis: NCCC, 1891), p. 153 (hereafter cited as *Proc. of NCCC*).

20. Homer Folks, "The Child and the Family," *Proc. of NCCC* (Denver, 1892), pp. 419, 423.

21. Homer Folks, "Family Life for Dependent Children," *Proc. of NCCC* (Chicago, 1893), reprinted in Folks, *Public Health and Welfare,* pp. 9–10; Charles W. Birtwell to Homer Folks, May 24, 1893, HFC.

22. *Ibid.,* pp. 19, 22. Folks also constantly stressed the idea that from his experience it was evident that boarding-out frequently led to legal adoption. Often, families accepted children under the boarding-out plan and then became so attached to those children that they asked to adopt them.

23. Homer Folks, "College Graduates in Benevolent Work" (1893), in Folks, *Public Health and Welfare,* pp. 23–33.

24. When Dr. Amos Warner published his famous *American Charities* (1894), one of the few classics in the area of social service and the only text in the field for more than a quarter century, Folks was quoted several times. See Warner's *American Charities: A Study in Philanthropy and Economics* (New York: Crowell, 1894), pp. 232–33, 403.

25. Folks, *Child-Saving in Pennsylvania, passim.* This is a good summary of Folks's work and convictions at the time he left Pennsylvania for his new job in New York.

26. Zimand, "Homer Folks," p. xix.

27. Homer Folks to Charles W. Birtwell, May 13, 1892, HFC.

28. Diary, *passim,* but especially see Aug. 22, 1890, and Jan. 10, 1891, HFC. Also, Mrs. James C. Biddle to Homer Folks, Dec. 23, 1890, and Jan. 23, 1891; Mrs. James C. Biddle to Homer Folks, May 17, 1891; Homer Folks to Mrs. James C. Biddle, Dec. 17, 1892, HFC. Mrs. Biddle, among other things, accused Folks of being "unduly desirous of authority" and unwilling to accept the limitations of his position.

29. Mrs. James C. Biddle to Homer Folks, Feb. 18, 1892, HFC.

30. Homer Folks to the "Office Committee of the Children's Aid Society," July 23, 1892, HFC.

31. Homer Folks to Charles W. Birtwell, n.d., HFC; Folks, OHP, p. 10; Zimand, "Homer Folks," p. xxii; Homer Folks to Mr. Lawrence[?], Feb. 19, 1893, HFC. Actually, Mrs. Biddle and the society's "Office Committee"

had recommended and passed a resolution in favor of Folk's dismissal in July 1892. Due to various technical and legal difficulties, the action was not carried out. In Dec. 1892, Folks officially resigned from the CAS, at which time he was asked to reconsider the matter and was even offered a substantial raise in salary if he would change his mind. Folks declined the offer. See Homer Folks to Miss Mary Ingham, Dec. 12, 1892, HFC.

32. Homer Folks to Mr. Lawrence[?], Feb. 19, 1893, HFC.

33. Homer Folks to Charles F. Chandler, June 1, 1892, HFC. In this letter Folks discussed the financial plight of the CAS during the time he was affiliated with the organization.

34. *Minutes* of the Meetings of the Board of Directors of the New York State Charities Aid Association, New York City, Dec. 30, 1892 (hereafter cited as SCAA *Minutes*). Also see Homer Folks to Charles W. Birtwell, May 13, 1892; Homer Folks to John H. Finley, May 13, 1892; Homer Folks to Charles F. Chandler, May 13, 1892, HFC.

35. SCAA *Minutes,* Dec. 30, 1892; Mrs. William B. Rice to Homer Folks, Dec. 5, 1892, HFC.

36. Lundberg, *Unto the Least of These,* p. 276.

37. Dr. Wilson Smillie to Homer Folks, Feb. 15, 1957. The author is indebted to Mrs. Lawrence M. Orton for letting him see this letter.

38. Interviews with Mr. Gordon E. Brown, executive director of the New York State Charities Aid Association, New York City, July 11, 1962; Mr. George J. Nelbach, former executive director of the New York State Committee on Tuberculosis and Public Health, New York City, Oct. 1, 1962; Mr. Hugh R. Jackson, president, Better Business Bureau, New York, and former administrative assistant to Mr. Folks, New York, Oct. 3, 1962.

39. Walter I. Trattner, "Louisa Lee Schuyler and the Founding of the State Charities Aid Association," *New York Historical Society Quarterly,* LI, No. 3 (July, 1967), 233–48; Homer Folks, *Louisa Lee Schuyler, 1837–1926* (n.p., n.d.), p. 7; Louisa Lee Schuyler, *Forty Three Years Ago, or the Early Days of the State Charities Aid Association, 1872–1915* (New York: SCAA, 1915), pp. 4–6; George Worthington Adams, *Doctors in Blue* (New York: Schuman, 1952), pp. 3–9; Marjorie B. Greenbie, *Lincoln's Daughters of Mercy* (New York: Putnam, 1944), p. 65.

40. William Q. Maxwell, *Lincoln's Fifth Wheel: The Political History of the United States Sanitary Commission* (New York: Longmans, Green, 1956), *passim;* Bremner, *American Philanthropy,* p. 80; Richard H. Shryock, "The Origins and Significance of the Public Health Movement in the United States," *Annals of Medical History,* I, No. 6 (Nov. 1929), 648–49; Dr. Wilson Smillie, *Public Health: Its Promise for the Future* (New York: Macmillan, 1955), pp. 280–83.

41. Schuyler, *Forty Three Years Ago*, p. 6; Folks, *Schuyler*, p. 9.

42. Schuyler, *Forty Three Years Ago*, pp. 6, 8.   43. *Ibid.*, pp. 7–9.

44. *Ibid.*, p. 10; Elizabeth Christophers Hobson, "Founding of the Bellevue Training School for Nurses," in Abby Woolsey, *A Century of Nursing, With Hints Toward the Organization of a Training School and Florence Nightingale's Historic Letter on the Bellevue School, September 18, 1882* (New York: Putnam, 1916), pp. 144ff.

45. For the text of Florence Nightingale's letter see Woolsey, *A Century of Nursing*, pp. 175ff.

46. Hobson, "Founding Bellevue Training School," p. 158; Schuyler, *Forty Three Years Ago*, p. 11.

47. Quoted from James H. Cassedy, *Charles V. Chapin and the Public Health Movement* (Cambridge: Harvard University, 1962), p. 19. By 1893 thirty more such schools had been established and in 1911 there were more than 1,100 training schools for nurses in the United States. See Hobson, "Founding Bellevue Training School," p. 171.

48. *Annual Report* of the New York State Charities Aid Association (New York: SCAA, 1873), p. 30 (hereafter cited as SCAA *Annual Report*). The name chosen for the organization was suggested by Mrs. Frederick Law Olmsted, a member of the organizing committee. Although the Association was founded in 1872, it was not incorporated until 1881. The *Certificate of Incorporation* listed the objects of the SCAA as the following:

(1) To aid and promote the improvement of the mental, moral, and physical condition of the inmates of all the public charitable institutions in the State. . . .

(2) To aid directly, or through its local committees, in the care of destitute adults and destitute, neglected, and other children needing care. . . .

(3) To induce the adoption by the community at large of such measures in the organization and administration of both public and private charity as may develop the self-respect and increase the power of self-support of the lower classes in society. See SCAA *Special Act of Incorporation, 1880*; Sec. 3, Ch. 323, New York State *Laws of 1881*.

49. Schuyler, *Forty Three Years Ago*, p. 12. Brace was the founder of New York's Children's Aid Society, a minister and pioneer in the placing-out of children. Dwight, active in social welfare, was vice-president of New York's first State Board of Charities (known as Board of State Commissioners of Public Charities). Osborn, zoologist, author, dean of the faculty at Columbia University, was connected with many of New York's good causes. Roosevelt and James were well-known businessmen-philanthropists. Chandler, professor of chemistry at Columbia, was a public servant as well as an inspiring teacher. Smith, a surgeon, was a pioneer sanitarian who

drafted the bill that created the Metropolitan Board of Health for New York City. He also served on that board as well as on the State Commission in Lunacy and he was the founder and first president of the American Public Health Association. Jacobi was a prominent clinician and well-known medical figure. Wyllie, surgeon at Bellevue, was the SCAA committee member who went to London to see Florence Nightingale. Lowell was the founder of New York's Charity Organization Society. Woolsey and Hobson, both members of old and respected New York families, played the leading roles in founding the Bellevue Nurses Training School. Dodge, daughter of millionaire-businessman William E. Dodge, was an educator and pioneer in worker's education. Choate was the undisputed leader of New York's legal profession and later Ambassador to the Court of St. James. Rice, girlhood friend of Miss Schuyler's, served on the Sanitary Commission and the Board of Directors of the New York Charity Organization Society.

50. Schneider and Deutsch, *History of Public Welfare,* pp. 16, 21, 31. The title of the Association's first report was the *First Annual Report to the State Commissioners of Public Charities* (March 1, 1873).

51. Schneider and Deutsch, *History of Public Welfare,* pp. 60–61; SCAA *Annual Report* (1873), pp. 16–17, 23–24.

52. Margaret E. Rich, *Josephine Shaw Lowell* (New York: Community Service Society, 1954), p. 10.

53. Ch. 323, New York State *Laws of 1881.* The New York State Legislature amended the law on May 6, 1893, "by extending the visitorial powers of the Association, heretofore limited to town, city and county almshouses and poorhouses, to all public charitable institutions owned by the State, including State hospitals for the insane." Another amendment required the Association to make an annual report to the State Commission in Lunacy, in addition to the annual report to the State Board of Charities (SCAA *Annual Report* (1893), p. 1).

54. Folks, *Schuyler,* p. 13; Rich, *Lowell,* p. 8. For a vivid description of the condition of the insane in most poorhouses see, Johnson, *Adventures in Social Welfare,* pp. 112ff.

55. Folks, *Schuyler,* p. 13; Albert Deutsch, *The Mentally Ill in America* (New York: Columbia University, 1962), p. 2; Ch. 126, New York State *Laws of 1890;* Folks, *Schuyler,* pp. 16–17.

56. Deutsch, *The Mentally Ill,* p. 2.

57. Bremner, *American Philanthropy,* p. 89.

58. Karl deSchweinitz, "The Past as a Guide to the Function and Pattern of Social work," in *Frontiers for Social Work,* ed. William Wallace Weaver (Philadelphia: University of Pennsylvania, 1960), p. 73. For a good discus-

sion of the intellectual assumptions of three of New York's leading, and typical, charitable agencies see the following: Roy Lubove, "The New York Association for Improving the Condition of the Poor: The Formative Years," *New York Historical Society Quarterly*, XLIII (July 1959), 307–27; for the St. Vincent De Paul Society see Bremner, *From the Depths*, p. 35; and for the Charity Organization Society see Rich, *Lowell*, pp. 10ff.

59. Schuyler, *Forty Three Years Ago*, pp. 15–16. For a chronological list of the SCAA's achievements through 1929 see *Milestones in Health and Welfare, 1872–1929* (New York: SCAA Pub. No. 193, 1930).

3
CHILD WELFARE—MATURITY

1. For accounts of New York in the nineties and at the turn of the century see Wirt Howe, *New York at the Turn of the Century, 1899–1916* (Toronto: Ryerson, 1946); Allan Nevins and John A. Krout, eds., *The Greater City, New York, 1898–1948* (New York: Columbia University, 1948); William Dean Howells, *Letters of an Altrurian Traveller, 1893–94* (Gainesville, Fla.: Scholar's Facsimiles and Reprints, 1961), p. 19.

2. Charles O. Burgess, "The Newspaper as Charity Worker: Poor Relief in New York, 1893–1894," *New York History*, XLIII, No. 3 (July 1962), 249.

3. New York State Charities Aid Association *Annual Report* (1892) (hereafter cited as SCAA *Annual Report*).

4. Folks, "The Reminiscences of Homer Folks," Oral History Project (Columbia University, 1949), pp. 12, 16 (hereafter cited as OHP). Folks's feelings toward these women are well expressed in two essays written in 1926, "Mrs. William B. Rice" and "Our Founder" (Louisa Lee Schuyler), in Homer Folks, *Public Health and Welfare: The Citizens' Responsibility—Selected Papers of Homer Folks,* ed. Savel Zimand (New York: Macmillan, 1958), pp. 258–67; *Who's Who in New York* (1904), pp. 119, 216.

5. David M. Schneider and Albert Deutsch, *The History of Public Welfare in New York State, 1867–1940* (Chicago: University of Chicago, 1941), pp. 16off.; Homer Folks, "The New York System of Caring for Dependent Children," *Proceedings* of the New York State Conference of Charities and Correction (New York: NYSCCC, 1900), pp. 129–38 (hereafter cited as *Proc. of NYSCCC*).

6. Homer Folks, *The Care of Destitute Children in New York City* (New York: SCAA Pub. No. 72, 1899); Folks, OHP, pp. 28–29. The primary work of these societies was to investigate cases of alleged cruelty or neglect and present the facts to the courts authorized to consider such cases.

However, over the years the custom arose of magistrates referring depen-dent and neglected children to the societies for determination of their future. See Homer Folks, *The Care of Destitute, Neglected and Delinquent Children* (New York: Macmillan, 1902), pp. 173–75. There was a great deal of opposition to the Gerry Society, which sometimes was expressed in the following parody on a Mother Goose rhyme:

> Little Miss Muffet
> She went out to rough it,
> All up and down Broadway;
> But a Gerry man spied her
> And sat down beside her
> And frightened Miss Muffet away.

See Howe, *New York at the Turn of the Century,* p. 40.

7. Folks, *Destitute, Neglected and Delinquent Children,* p. 176; Folks, *Care of Destitute Children in New York City,* p. 5.

8. Homer Folks, "Why Dependent Children Should Be Reared in Families Rather Than in Institutions," paper delivered before the Confer-ence of Charities of New York City, June 1896, p. 3, HFC; Folks, *Destitute, Neglected and Delinquent Children,* pp. 96–97.

9. Folks, *Destitute, Neglected and Delinquent Children,* pp. 189–90; *Minutes* of the Board of Managers of the New York State Charities Aid Association, New York City, Jan. 26, 1894 (hereafter cited as SCAA *Min-utes*); Schneider and Deutsch, *History of Public Welfare,* p. 181.

10. Emma O. Lundberg, *Unto the Least of These* (New York: Appleton-Century, 1947), p. 138; Folks, OHP, pp. 11, 36–37.

11. Folks, OHP, pp. 36–37; John M. Glenn, Lilian Brandt, and F. Emerson Andrews, *Russell Sage Foundation* (2 vols., New York: Russell Sage Foundation, 1947), I, 233–34.

12. Homer Folks, "Cooperation With Local Officials," p. 5, undated manuscript in HFC; Lundberg, *Unto the Least of These,* p. 140; *S.C.A.A. News,* June 1938, p. 5. The *S.C.A.A. News* was a monthly news bulletin published by the Association beginning in Nov. 1912. Bound copies of the *News* can be found in the Association's library in New York City.

13. Folks, "Cooperation With Local Officials," pp. 2–3; SCAA *Annual Report* (1946), pp. 3, 37; *Milestones in Health and Welfare 1872–1929* (New York: SCAA Pub. No. 193, 1930), p. 5.

14. Lundberg, *Unto the Least of These,* p. 140; *S.C.A.A. News,* June 1938, p. 5.

15. Homer Folks, "State Supervision of Child Caring Agencies" (1895), in Folks, *Public Health and Welfare,* pp. 34–38.

16. Frank J. Bruno, *Trends in Social Work as Reflected in the Proceedings of the National Conference of Social Work, 1874–1956* (New York: Columbia University, 1957), p. 47.

17. SCAA *Annual Report* (1894), pp. 2–3; Folks, OHP, p. 30.

18. Schneider and Deutsch, *History of Public Welfare,* pp. 126–27; *Proceedings of the National Conference of Charities and Correction* (New Haven: NCCC, 1895), pp. 373–75 (hereafter cited as *Proc. of NCCC*).

19. A section of the Charities Article stated that the "visitation and inspection herein provided shall not be exclusive of other visitation and inspection now authorized by law," a provision specifically intended to continue the powers of the SCAA and the New York Prison Association (SCAA *Minutes,* Oct. 26, 1894).

20. *Proc. of NCCC,* pp. 373–75.

21. Charles S. Fowler, Chief Examiner, New York State Civil Service Commission, to Homer Folks, Feb. 2, 1898, HFC. Ch. 264, New York State *Laws of 1898;* Schneider and Deutsch, *History of Public Welfare,* p. 141.

22. Folks, "State Supervision of Child Caring Agencies," p. 36.

23. Schneider and Deutsch, *History of Public Welfare,* pp. 166ff.; Robert W. Hebberd to Homer Folks, Jan. 4, 1898, HFC.

24. Louisa Lee Schuyler to Homer Folks, March 12, 1898; Charles Loring Brace to Homer Folks, March 17, 1898, HFC.

25. Schneider and Deutsch, *History of Public Welfare,* pp. 132ff; New York State Board of Charities *Annual Report* (1900), I, 219.

26. Homer Folks, "Reform and Public Charities," *Outlook,* LV (March 6, 1897), 679. Under these appalling conditions the tax rate was kept down and, paradoxically, Tammany Hall claimed to be the friend of the poor.

27. *Proc. of NCCC,* p. 372; Folks, "Reform and Public Charities," p. 680; SCAA *Annual Report* (1895), p. 4; (1897), p. 5; *Proc. of NCCC* (Toronto, 1897), p. 280.

28. SCAA *Annual Report* (1897), p. 79; Edward T. Devine, *When Social Work Was Young* (New York: Macmillan, 1939), pp. 55–56.

29. Homer Folks to Mayor Strong, April 21, 1897, Mayor's Papers, New York City Municipal Archives (hereafter cited as NYCMA); Devine, *When Social Work Was Young,* pp. 55–56.

30. SCAA *Annual Report* (1898), p. 82; *Public Appropriations to Private Charities in New York City* (New York: SCAA Pub. No. 73, 1899), p. 19; SCAA *Annual Report* (1898), pp. 76–81.

31. In 1910 Folks publicly confessed that his earlier views on public out-

door relief were wrong. He still preferred outdoor relief to be administered by private charities, but he was convinced that private funds could not sufficiently take care of all of New York City's relief problem. Therefore, he felt public outdoor assistance should be provided. See *Proc. of NCCC* (St. Louis, 1910), p. 241.

32. Homer Folks to Mayor Strong, April 10, 1897, NYCMA; SCAA *Annual Report* (1897), p. 80.

33. SCAA *Minutes,* April 20, 1897; Homer Folks to Mayor Strong, April 21, 1897, NYCMA.

34. Bruno, *Trends in Social Work,* pp. 40–41.

35. Homer Folks to Professor Henry M. Leipziger, sup't. of lectures, New York City Board of Education, May 3, 1897, HFC; New York *Times,* May 20, 1898; *Proc. of NCCC* (New York, 1898), p. 443, (Washington, 1901), p. 432.

36. SCAA *Minutes,* Nov. 24, 1893; Homer Folks, *Annual Reports of Child Caring Agencies* (Boston: Children's Aid Society, 1895); Robert W. Hebberd to Homer Folks, Sept. 24, 1898, HFC.

37. Theodore Roosevelt to Douglas Robinson, April 8, 1899, in Theodore Roosevelt, *The Letters of Theodore Roosevelt,* ed. Elting E. Morison (8 vols., Cambridge: Harvard University, 1951), II, 982–83; William Dwight Porter Bliss, *The Encyclopedia of Social Reform* (New York: Funk and Wagnalls, 1908), p. iii; Lee K. Frankel, *In the Early Days of Charities* (New York: National Conference of Jewish Social Service, 1930), p. 10.

38. Mrs. Savel Zimand to the author, Feb. 24, 1965.

39. Julia Lathrop to Homer Folks, June 10, 1895; Mrs. Glen Wood to Homer Folks, Oct. 22, 1895; Mr. Stanley Griffin to Homer Folks, July 15, 1898; Dr. Stephen Smith to Homer Folks, May 9, 1896; Mr. Lispenard Stewart to Homer Folks, Sept. 20, 1895, HFC.

40. Homer Folks to Mrs. J. M. Flower, Sept. 24, 1895, HFC. Folks came to the SCAA at a salary of $1,600 per year, which was raised to $2,000 the second year. In 1895 he was earning $2,500; 1896, $3,000; 1901, $3,500; and in 1903 his salary was raised to $5,000.

41. Mr. W. B. Buck to Homer Folks, Feb. 6, 1900, HFC.

42. Miss L. D. Gill to Homer Folks, Feb. 9, 1900, HFC.

43. Hermann Hagedorn, *Leonard Wood: A Biography* (2 vols., New York: Harper, 1931), I, 269; Francis R. Stoddard, "The Reminiscences of Francis R. Stoddard," OHP, 1949, p. 14; "Charity Administration in Cuba," undated manuscript in HFC.

44. Homer Folks to Mrs. William B. Rice, April 26, May 14, 1900, HFC.

45. "Order No. 271," Headquarters, Division of Cuba, July 7, 1900,

HFC; "Cuba," manuscript dated July 25, 1900, HFC. General Wood promulgated the decree without changing a single word from Folks's draft. Interview with Mr. and Mrs. Lawrence M. Orton, New York City, Nov. 29, 1962.

46. "Order No. 271." Also see "Personal Note—Homer Folks," *Annals of the American Academy of Political and Social Science,* XVIII (Nov. 1901), 499–500. The "personal note" related that the children's bureau "was organized under his [Folks's] personal direction, and . . . succeeded in reducing the number of children in orphan asylums. . . . Some twenty five orphan asylums were closed altogether; the plan of granting subsidies to private institutions . . . practically discontinued; and the practice of caring for destitute children in Cuba now approximates that of the most progressive American states" (p. 499).

47. There are numerous copies of the Cuban Charities Law in the HFC; also see *Proc. of NCCC* (Detroit, 1902), p. 126.

48. Major E. St. John Greble to Homer Folks, May 30, 1900, HFC.

49. Major J. R. Kean, "The Charities of Cuba," *Charities,* VIII, No. 18 (May 3, 1902), 409; General Leonard Wood, "The Condition of Affairs in Cuba," *Collier's Weekly* (Nov. 3, 1900), p. 5; Lillian H. French, "Four Great Cuban Institutions for Cuban Children," *Collier's Weekly* (n.d.), p. 19, in HFC; Mr. Jerome Clark to Homer Folks, March 13, 1901, HFC.

50. "Report of the Committee on the Care of Destitute and Neglected Children," *Proc. of NCCC* (Cincinnati, 1899), p. 169; Schneider and Deutsch, *History of Public Welfare,* pp. 169, 172.

51. Frankel, *In the Early Days of Charities,* p. 5.

52. Quoted in Jane Addams, *My Friend, Julia Lathrop* (New York: Macmillan, 1935), p. 85.

53. Hastings Hart, "Improving Child Care," in *Thirty Years of Service: A Tribute to Homer Folks* (New York: Klebold, 1923), p. 21; Glenn, Brandt, and Andrews, *Russell Sage Foundation,* II, 455; Katharine Lenroot to Homer Folks, Nov. 22, 1950, Children's Bureau, Washington, D.C.

54. Folks, however, still had not yet taken enough time to examine the validity of his interest in children, to question whether the damage was not already done when a child became the subject of a society's concern. When in 1901 he wrote his first book, *The Care of Destitute, Neglected and Delinquent Children,* long a classic in the field and considered by at least one authority as "the best work on . . . [the] subject in this country," he did not inquire into the causes that had thrown 150,000 of the nation's children into the hands of public and private charities. Unfortunately, he confessed, there was no reason to think that charities for needy children would soon become unnecessary, for, he concluded (p. 246), "the forces which

produce poverty, neglect, and crime seem to be beyond our reach." Also see William B. Bailey to Homer Folks, May 28, 1903, HFC.

4
PUBLIC OFFICE

1. James Bryce, *The American Commonwealth* (2 vols., New York: Macmillan, 1889), I, 608.

2. Andrew White, "The Government of American Cities," *Forum,* X (1890), 357.

3. See, for example, Frank Mann Stewart, *A Half Century of Municipal Reform: The History of the National Municipal League* (Berkeley: University of California, 1950), *passim.*

4. Roger N. Baldwin, "The Reminiscences of Roger N. Baldwin," Oral History Project (Columbia University, 1954), p. 12 (hereafter cited as OHP); Josephine Goldmark, *Impatient Crusader: Florence Kelley's Life Story* (Urbana: University of Illinois, 1953), p. 69.

5. The historiography of the progressive movement currently is being hotly debated among historians. For a fairly good general synthesis of the movement, however, see Arthur Link and William Catton, *American Epoch* (New York: Knopf, 1963), Chs. 2–6.

6. Francis G. Peabody, *The Christian Life in the Modern World* (New York: Macmillan, 1914), p. 184; Homer Folks, "The Reminiscences of Homer Folks," OHP, 1949, p. 18.

7. Homer Folks, "Municipal Charities," *Municipal Affairs,* III (Sept. 1899), 516–27; Homer Folks, "Reform and Public Charities," *Outlook,* LV (March 6, 1897), 679–86; Wirt Howe, *New York at the Turn of the Century, 1899–1916* (Toronto: Ryerson, 1946), p. 68; Raymond B. Fosdick, *Chronicle of a Generation* (New York: Harper, 1958), p. 74.

8. Stewart, *Half Century of Municipal Reform,* p. 12; William J. Schieffelin, "The Reminiscences of William J. Schieffelin," OHP, 1949, p. 23; Lawrence Veiller, "The Reminiscences of Lawrence Veiller," OHP, 1949, p. 140; Julius Henry Cohen, *They Builded Better Than They Knew* (New York: Messner, 1946), p. 42. The City Club, founded in 1892, was an outgrowth of the City Reform Club, organized in 1889 as an anti-Tammany association. See Schieffelin, OHP, p. 23. The Republican bosses were such men as Abe Gruber, Edward Lauterbach, Job Hedges, Herbert Parsons, and Samuel Koenig.

9. Lincoln Steffens, *The Autobiography of Lincoln Steffens* (New York: Harcourt, Brace, 1931), p. 432.

10. Cohen, *They Builded,* p. 42; Steffens, *Autobiography,* p. 430.

11. William H. Tolman, *Municipal Reform Movements in the United States* (New York: Revell, 1895), p. 95; Everett P. Wheeler, *Sixty Years of American Life: Taylor to Roosevelt, 1850–1910* (New York: Dutton, 1917), p. 337; Stewart, *Half Century,* pp. 13–14.

12. Roy V. Peel, *The Political Clubs of New York City* (New York: Putnam, 1935), p. 316; Laurence A. Tanzer, "The Reminiscences of Laurence A. Tanzer," OHP, 1949, p. 19; Wheeler, *Sixty Years,* pp. 358–60.

13. Albert Shaw to William H. Tolman, March 12, 1897, HFC. For a good discussion of New York politics at the turn of the century see, Albert Fein, "New York City Politics From 1897–1903: A Study in Political Party Leadership" (Master's essay, Columbia University, 1954).

14. C. H. Strong to Homer Folks, Sept. 30, 1897, HFC.

15. See telegrams from Mrs. William B. Rice to Homer Folks, Oct. 1, 2, 1897, HFC; Folks, OHP, p. 19.

16. Robert Hebberd to Homer Folks, Nov. 4, 1897, HFC.

17. Quoted in Frederick Shaw, *The History of the New York City Legislature* (New York: Columbia University, 1954), p. 4.

18. Quoted in Raymond B. Fosdick, "Public Health and the Future," *American Journal of Public Health,* XXXVIII (Jan. 1948), 185.

19. Beatrice Webb, *Beatrice Webb's American Diary, 1898,* ed. David Shannon (Madison: University of Wisconsin, 1963), p. 63; New York *Daily Tribune,* April 8, 1890; Theodore Roosevelt, *An Autobiography* (New York: Scribner, 1920), p. 82.

20. Henry H. Curran, *Pillar to Post* (New York: Scribner, 1941), p. 130.

21. P. Tecumseh Sherman, *Inside the Machine: Two Years in the Board of Aldermen, 1898–1899* (New York: Cook and Fry, 1901), pp. 23–24.

22. Homer Folks to Henry M. Leipziger, April 20, 1898; Homer Folks to Dr. A. B. Cossaart, April 15, 1898, HFC.

23. New York *Times,* June 3, 1899.

24. Sherman, *Inside the Machine,* p. 46.

25. Roland Holt, President of Good Government Club "A," to Homer Folks, March 24, 1898, HFC.

26. Citizens' Union Circular, dated April 11, 1898, HFC.

27. Sherman, *Inside the Machine,* p. 47; Edward T. Devine, *When Social Work Was Young* (New York: Macmillan, 1939), pp. 54–55. Section 647 of the charter stated that the municipal Assembly shall have the power to establish a code of ordinances providing for all matters concerning the con-

struction, alteration, or removal of buildings or structures erected or to be erected in the city of New York and for the purpose of preparing such a code to appoint and employ a commission of experts.

28. Veiller, OHP, pp. 5, 21.

29. Homer Folks to George Waring, Sept. 19, 1898, HFC; undated, untitled manuscript in the HFC dealing with the Municipal Assembly's action in regard to Section 647 of the charter (hereafter cited as "Section 647"); Sherman, *Inside the Machine,* p. 48.

30. "Section 647," HFC; Homer Folks to George Waring, Sept. 28, 1898, HFC.

31. Homer Folks to John B. Pine, Sept. 29, 1898, HFC (italics mine).

32. John W. Pryor to Homer Folks, Oct. 3, 1898; Isaac E. Ditmars to Homer Folks, Oct. 19, 1898; Homer Folks to Foster Crowell, Oct. 19, 1898; Homer Folks to Louis de Coppett Berg, Oct. 17, 1898; Homer Folks to George Waring, Sept. 19, 28, 1898; Homer Folks to John M. Carrere, Sept. 30, 1898, HFC.

33. Homer Folks to Richard Watson Gilder, Oct. 17, 1898; Homer Folks to Louis de Coppett Berg, Oct. 17, 1898, HFC. For the work of Gilder's Tenement House Committee see Roy Lubove, *The Progressives and the Slums* (Pittsburgh: University of Pittsburgh, 1962), pp. 81–116.

34. Homer Folks to Rollins Morgan, Oct. 29, 1898; Homer Folks to Mayor Van Wyck, Nov. 17, 1898, HFC.

35. Homer Folks to Roland Holt, Oct. 26, 1898; Homer Folks to Rollins Morgan, Oct. 29, 1898, HFC.

36. Sherman, *Inside the Machine,* p. 55.

37. New York *Times,* New York *World,* New York *Herald,* Nov. 23, 1898.

38. E. R. L. Gould to Homer Folks, Nov. 20, 1898, HFC.

39. Homer Folks to John M. Carrere, Nov. 30, 1898, HFC.

40. Edward T. Devine to Homer Folks, Dec. 16, 1898; Lawrence Veiller to Homer Folks, Feb. 1, 1899, HFC. Also see Lubove, *The Progressives and the Slums,* pp. 119ff.

41. New York *Times,* Jan 3, 11, 1899; New York *World,* Jan. 11, 1899.

42. Quoted in Lubove, *The Progressives and the Slums,* p. 121; New York *World* Sept. 13, 1899. The principal changes in the new code were to give the Building Commissioners and Board of Examiners, traditionally of doubtful repute and often charged with laxity and favoritism, even greater discretionary power to vary the building laws and thus multiply their opportunities for discrimination and graft. The new code also defined apartment houses in such a way as to distinguish them from tenements and thereby take them out of the more stringent provisions of the tenement

laws, and also allowed greater laxity in regard to fireproofing and ventilation.

43. Sherman, *Inside the Machine*, pp. 49–50.

44. New York *Times*, Sept. 13, 1899, Oct. 26, 1899.

45. Roy Lubove, "Lawrence Veiller and the New York State Tenement House Commission of 1900," *Mississippi Valley Historical Review*, XLVII (March 1961), 677; Lubove, *The Progressives and the Slums*, pp. 122ff.; Veiller, OHP, pp. 10ff. Lubove, who has written the only full account of the subject, never mentions Folks in regard to tenement house reform and completely ignores this entire incident. His article on the same topic begins after the appointment of the Building Code Commission members.

46. Robert Bremner, *From the Depths: The Discovery of Poverty in the United States* (New York: New York University, 1956), p. 149; Devine, *When Social Work Was Young*, p. 80.

47. New York *Mail and Express*, June 28, 1899; New York *Times*, June 29, 1899; Homer Folks to Mrs. William B. Rice, June 29, 1899, HFC; New York *Press*, July 25, 1899; New York *Evening Sun*, July 24, 1899; New York *Evening Post*, July 28, 1899; New York *Tribune*, July 28, 1899; New York *Times*, July 29, 1899.

48. Mr. John Weekes to Homer Folks, July 17, 1899; Homer Folks to James B. Reynolds, Oct. 24, 1899, HFC; New York *Commercial Advertiser*, Nov. 1, 1899; New York *Evening Post*, Nov. 1, 1899; New York *Tribune*, Nov. 5, 1899.

49. New York *Evening Post*, Nov. 9, 1899; New York *World*, Nov. 9, 1899; New York *Tribune*, Sept. 25, 1899.

50. New York *Tribune*, Nov. 7, 1899. On the Mazet Committee see Gustavus Myers, *History of Tammany Hall* (New York: Boni and Liveright, 1917), p. 285; Harold F. Gosnell, *Boss Platt and His New York Machine* (Chicago: University of Chicago, 1924), pp. 168–69.

51. Theodore Roosevelt to John Carter Rose, Nov. 10, 1899, in Theodore Roosevelt, *The Letters of Theodore Roosevelt*, ed. Elting E. Morison (8 vols., Cambridge: Harvard University, 1951), II, 1095.

52. Quoted in Fein, "New York City Politics," p. 21.

53. Homer Folks, "The Charities Chapter of the Greater New York Charter," *American Journal of Sociology*, VII (Sept. 1901), 265.

54. John W. Keller to Josephine Shaw Lowell, Nov. 11, 1901, HFC.

55. Mrs. William B. Rice to Seth Low, Nov. 17, 1901, HFC.

56. Carl Schurz to Mrs. William B. Rice, Nov. 20, 1901; Alfred T. White to Mrs. William B. Rice, Nov. 18, 1901, HFC.

57. Seth Low to Homer Folks, Nov. 23, 1901, HFC. Thomas C. (Boss) Platt maintained in his autobiography that Folks was his appointment. Low

promised Platt a good deal of patronage in return for the Republican Party's support in the campaign. One of the appointments Low gave him, according to Platt, was the Charities Commissioner. This is highly unlikely, however, since Folks testified that he did not know Boss Platt. See Thomas C. Platt, *An Autobiography of Thomas C. Platt,* ed. Louis J. Lang (New York: Dodge, 1910), pp. 415–61; Folks, OHP, p. 23.

58. Carl Schurz to Homer Folks, Dec. 20, 1901; Alfred T. White to Homer Folks, Dec. 21, 1901; Felix M. Warburg to Homer Folks, Dec. 17, 1901, HFC; New York *Evening Post,* Dec. 17, 1901; *Charities,* VII, No. 25 (Dec. 21, 1901).

59. New York *Times,* Dec. 17, 1901; New York *Herald,* Dec. 30, 1901. For a good brief description of the connection between Tammany politics and the Department of Public Charities in New York City at the turn of the century, see Haven Emerson, "The Reminiscences of Dr. Haven Emerson," OHP, 1950, pp. 17–18.

60. New York *Evening Post,* Jan. 10, 1902; and May 25, 1903; New York *Commercial Advertiser,* May 25, 1903.

61. New York *Times,* New York *Evening Sun,* New York *Daily Tribune,* Jan. 17, 1902.

62. New York *Herald,* April 4, 1902; New York *Tribune,* New York *Times,* June 12, 1902.

63. New York *Sun,* Aug. 24, 1902, and April 3, 1903; New York *Herald,* New York *World,* Aug. 25, 1902; *Outlook,* Sept. 6, 1902, n.p., HFC; New York *Mail and Express,* New York *Times,* Aug. 25, 1902; New York *Evening Post,* Oct. 10, 1903.

64. New York *Evening Post,* Aug. 22, 1902; New York *Daily Tribune,* Oct. 2, 1902.

65. New York *Times,* March 8, 1902; New York *Tribune,* Jan. 15, 1903; New York *Brooklyn Eagle,* Jan. 19, 1903.

66. New York *Evening Post,* New York *Commercial Advertiser,* June 17, 1902; New York *Evening Post,* July 7, 1902; Devine, *When Social Work Was Young,* p. 57.

67. New York *Evening Post,* New York *Commercial Advertiser,* March 5, 1902; New York *Daily News,* Aug. 16, 1903; New York *World,* Nov. 30, 1903; New York *Evening Telegram,* Dec. 30, 1903.

68. New York *Sun,* New York *World,* New York *Times,* New York *Commercial Advertiser,* New York *Daily Tribune,* Dec. 3, 1903.

69. New York *Commercial Advertiser,* New York *Sun,* Feb. 1, 1902; New York *Daily Tribune,* March 6, 1902; New York *Herald,* March 9, 1902; New York *Commercial Advertiser,* March 11, 1902; New York

Times, July 11, 1903; New York *Times,* New York *Evening Post,* July 16, 1903; New York *Herald,* Nov. 29, 1903.

70. *The Medical Times,* June 1902, n.p., HFC; Homer Folks, "Problems in Administration of Municipal Charities," *Annals of the American Academy of Political and Social Science,* XXIII (March 1904), 275.

71. New York *Daily Tribune,* April 19, 1903.

72. New York *Commercial Advertiser,* New York *Evening Post,* Dec. 2, 1902; New York *Tribune,* Dec. 4, 1902.

73. A copy of the letter is in the HFC. Also see John C. Clark to Homer Folks, Oct. 26, 1903, HFC; New York *Evening Post,* Oct. 29, 1903.

74. *Outlook,* LXXV (Oct. 31, 1903), n.p., HFC.

75. Lincoln Steffens *Shame of the Cities* (New York: McClure, Phillips, 1904), p. 284.

76. Fein, "New York City Politics," pp. 124ff.

77. Resolution Adopted by the Medical Board of the City Hospital, Dec. 1, 1903; Resolution of the Medical Board of Randall's Island Hospitals and Schools, undated; Resolution Passed by the Medical Board of the Metropolitan Hospital, Jan. 7, 1904, HFC.

78. New York *Daily Tribune,* Nov. 24, 1903; *Minutes* of the Board of Managers of the New York State Charities Aid Association, New York City, Nov. 20, 1903; a copy of the circular letter addressed to Mayor-elect McClellan is in the HFC, dated Dec. 5, 1903; Edward T. Devine to Homer Folks, Nov. 8, 1903, HFC.

79. Josephine Shaw Lowell to Homer Folks, Jan. 1, 1904, HFC. Also see *Outlook,* LXXVI (Jan. 9, 1904), n.p., HFC; *The World Today,* Jan. 1904, n.p., HFC.

80. Veiller, OHP, p. 70; Fein "New York City Politics" *passim.* For a good discussion of the "conservative" nature of the reform movement and the "upper-class" origins of its leaders see Robert S. Binkerd, "The Reminiscences of Robert S. Binkerd," OHP, 1949, pp. 82–84.

81. *Thirty Years of Service: A Tribute to Homer Folks* (New York: Klebold, 1923), p. 13. Winslow's statement was related to the author by Folks's son-in-law, Mr. Savel Zimand, in an interview on Nov. 27, 1962, New York City; Folks, OHP, p. 25.

82. See, for example, New York *Times,* Sept. 5–15, 1905.

83. Folks, OHP, pp. 31–32.

84. Several people who worked with Folks and knew him well mentioned this to the author in personal interviews. For example, Miss Ruth Taylor, Oct. 2, 1962, Hartsdale, N.Y.; Leonard Mayo, Nov. 14, 1962, New York City; Dr. Philip Klein, Nov. 11, 1962, White Plains, N.Y.

85. Homer Folks, "Some Experiences as Commissioner of Public Charities in New York City," *Proceedings of the National Conference of Charities and Correction* (Portland, Me.: NCCC, 1904), p. 141; New York State Charities Aid *Annual Report* (1901), p. 120; New York *Times*, May 29, 1905.

5
JUVENILE COURTS AND CHILD LABOR

1. Homer Folks, *The Care of Destitute, Neglected and Delinquent Children* (New York: Macmillan, 1902), pp. 198–99. For a brief history of the development of special institutions for juvenile delinquents see pp. 198–227.

2. *Ibid.*, p. 234.

3. *Ibid.*, p. 236; Lawrence Veiller, "The Reminiscences of Lawrence Veiller," Oral History Project (Columbia University, 1949), pp. 277ff. (hereafter cited as OHP).

4. Veiller, OHP, pp. 277ff.; David M. Schneider and Albert Deutsch, *The History of Public Welfare in New York State, 1867–1940* (Chicago: University of Chicago, 1941), p. 195.

5. Veiller, OHP, p. 278.

6. *Ibid.* Justices assigned to the juvenile division were no longer justices of the Court of Special Sessions; they were judges of the Children's Court, assigned there by the Chief Justice of the Court of Special Sessions.

7. As a result of the 1922 law, the authority to commit children to institutions, traditionally vested in the justices of the peace and police magistrates, was placed exclusively in the hands of the justices of the juvenile courts. See Schneider and Deutsch, *History of Public Welfare*, p. 195; *S.C.A.A. News*, Feb. 1923, p. 2.

8. Ben B. Lindsey, *The Dangerous Life* (New York: Liveright, 1931), p. 100; Schneider and Deutsch, *History of Public Welfare*, pp. 193–94. Juvenile courts also made possible a much more satisfactory system of records, helped bring about a reasonable degree of uniformity in dealing with delinquent children, and promoted cooperation between various agencies for assisting children. See Folks, *Destitute, Neglected and Delinquent Children*, p. 236.

9. Homer Folks, "Juvenile Probation," *Proceedings of the National Conference of Charities and Correction* (Philadelphia: NCCC, 1906), pp. 117–23 (hereafter cited as *Proc. of NCCC*); Lindsey, *Dangerous Life*, p. 100.

10. Folks, "Juvenile Probation," *passim*.

11. Homer Folks, *Proceedings of the New York State Conference of Charities and Correction* (New York: NYSCCC, 1901), p. 295 (hereafter cited as *Proc. of NYSCCC*).

12. Homer Folks, "Prevention and Probation" (1908), in Homer Folks, *Public Health and Welfare: The Citizens' Responsibility—Selected Papers of Homer Folks*, ed. Savel Zimand (New York: Macmillan, 1958), p. 61.

13. Folks, "Juvenile Probation," p. 119.

14. For an interesting discussion of social meliorism and progressivism see John C. Burnham, "Psychiatry, Psychology and the Progressive Movement," *American Quarterly*, XII (Winter 1960), 457–65, esp. 461.

15. Folks, *Proc. of NYSCCC*, p. 295.

16. Homer Folks, "Juvenile Probation in New York," *Survey*, XXIII (Feb. 5, 1910), 667; Folks, "Juvenile Probation," p. 117.

17. Folks, "Juvenile Probation," p. 117.

18. New York *Commercial*, New York *Herald*, Nov. 2, 1905; New York *Times*, Oct. 18, 1905; Brooklyn (N.Y.) *Union*, March 12, 1906; Homer Folks, "The Reminiscences of Homer Folks," OHP, 1949, p. 38.

19. New York *Sun*, New York *Press*, March 12, 1906.

20. New York *Evening Post*, March 27, 1906; New York *Tribune*, March 20, 1906.

21. Brooklyn (N.Y.) *Union*, March 12, 1906; New York *Times*, March 11, 1906; Binghamton (N.Y.) *Republican*, March 12, 1906.

22. New York *Tribune*, March 20, 1906.

23. New York State Charities Aid Association *Annual Report* (1906), p. 17 (hereafter cited as SCAA *Annual Report*); Folks, OHP, pp. 38–39.

24. SCAA *Annual Report* (1907), pp. 6–8; Homer Folks, "Probation Legislation in New York," *Charities*, XVIII (June 15, 1907), 311; Homer Folks, Journal, 1906–1907, *passim*, HFC.

25. *Minutes* of the Board of Managers of the New York State Charities Aid Association, New York City, Feb. 8, 1907 (hereafter cited as SCAA *Minutes*). Also see New York *Herald*, April 19, 1907; New York *World*, April 18, 1907; Homer Folks, "A Year's Progress in Probation: An Account of the Development of Probation Work in the State of New York During the Past Year," *Charities*, XVIII (June 15, 1907), 313–18; Folks OHP, p. 39; *Proc. of NCCC* (Toronto, 1907), pp. 559–61.

26. Folks, "A Year's Progress," p. 312; Albany (N.Y.) *Press Knickerbocker Express*, July 3, 1907.

27. Folks, Journal, July 2, 1907, HFC; New York *Sun*, New York *Times*, Yonkers (N.Y.) *Statesman*, July 3, 1907; Albany (N.Y.) *Press Knickerbocker Express*, July 26, 1907.

28. Folks, "A Year's Progress," p. 311.

29. Folks, "Juvenile Probation," p. 118.

30. Folks, "A Year's Progress," *passim*.

31. *Ibid.*, p. 313; SCAA *Annual Report* (1908), p. 9; Folks, "Juvenile Probation in New York," p. 672.

32. Homer Folks, "Juvenile Probation and its Relation to Truancy," address delivered before the Hudson River Schoolmaster's Club, Oct. 23, 1908, HFC; Schneider and Deutsch, *History of Public Welfare*, p. 194.

33. Homer Folks to John A. Kingsbury, Feb. 28, 1914, John A. Kingsbury Papers, Library of Congress, Washington, D.C.

34. *S.C.A.A. News,* Jan. 1919, p. 8.

35. Homer Folks to Mayor George B. McClellan, Jr., Jan. 27, 1908, New York City Municipal Archives, New York; *S.C.A.A. News,* Jan. 1919, p. 8.

36. Homer Folks, "Effective and Adequate Child Care Work," address delivered before the Newark, N. J., Conference of Charities and Correction, Jan. 26, 1904, reprinted in Folks, *Public Health and Welfare,* p. 52; Folks, "The Charity Side of Child Labor," p. 254, abstract of address delivered at the annual meeting of the Children's Aid Society of Pennsylvania, 1904, HFC. Folks defined child labor as "any work by children that interferes with their full physical development, their opportunity for a desirable minimum education, or their related recreation. It is the employment of children in any occupation at unfit ages, or for unreasonable hours, or under unhealthful or hazardous conditions, or while the schools which they should attend are in session." See Homer Folks, *Changes and Trends in Child Labor and its Control* (New York: National Child Labor Committee Pub. No. 375, 1938), p. 1.

37. For a brief survey of the nineteenth-century literature on child labor see Robert Bremner, *From the Depths: The Discovery of Poverty in the United States* (New York: New York University, 1956), p. 76ff.; Edith Abbott, "Early History of Child Labor," *American Journal of Sociology,* XIV (July, 1908), 15–37; Elizabeth Sands Johnson, "Child Labor Legislation," in John R. Commons, *History of Labor in the United States* (4 vols., New York: Macmillan, 1918–1935), III, 403–37.

38. Josephine Goldmark, *Impatient Crusader: Florence Kelley's Life Story* (Urbana: University of Illinois, 1953), p. 2; John Spargo, *The Bitter Cry of the Children* (New York, Macmillan, 1906), pp. 140–90.

39. For a history of the National Consumer's League under Florence Kelley's leadership see Goldmark, *Impatient Crusader, passim*.

40. Maud King Murphy, *Edgar Gardner Murphy: From Records and Memories* (New York: Putnam, 1943), pp. 47–50; John Braeman, "Albert

J. Beveridge and the First National Child Labor Bill," *Indiana Magazine of History*, LX (March 1964), 10.

41. Jeremy Felt Pollard, "The Regulation of Child Labor in New York State, 1886–1942, With Emphasis Upon the New York Child Labor Committee" (Ph.D. dissertation, Syracuse University, 1959), pp. 32, 83; Goldmark, *Impatient Crusader*, p. 81.

42. The New York Child Labor Committee was the second such state organization to be founded, succeeding the Alabama committee by a year. For a good personal account of the committee's work see Fred S. Hall, *Forty Years, 1902–1942: The Work of the New York Child Labor Committee* (New York: New York Child Labor Committee, 1943).

43. The committee enlisted the support of such people as V. Everit Macy, Paul M. Warburg, and James G. Phelps Stokes. See Pollard, "Regulation of Child Labor in New York State," pp. 87ff.

44. *Ibid.*, pp. 115ff. For opposition to the committee's work see the New York *Evening Post*, March 11, 1903; Philip Van Ingen, "The History of Child Welfare," p. 295, in *A Half Century of Public Health*, ed. Mazyck P. Ravenel (New York: American Public Health Association, 1921).

45. See, for example, Homer Folks, "The Charity Side of Child Labor," *Charities*, X (March 14, 1903), 254–55; "The Charity Side of the Child Labor Problem," *Charities*, XII (March 19, 1904), 293–94.

46. New York *Globe*, New York *Commercial Advertiser*, New York *Evening Post*, May 19, 1904.

47. Homer Folks, "Child Labor and the Law," *Charities*, XIII (Oct. 1, 1904), 22.

48. Folks, "Charity Side of Child Labor," p. 255; Homer Folks, "Poverty and Parental Dependence as an Obstacle to Child Labor Reform," *Annals of the American Academy of Social and Political Science*, XXIX (Jan. 1907), 3–6; Emma O. Lundberg, *Unto the Least of These* (New York: Appleton-Century, 1947), p. 124.

49. Homer Folks, "Notes for Quaker Hill Conference Address on Child Labor," delivered Sept. 8, 1905, HFC; Folks, "The Charity Side of Child Labor," p. 255.

50. See Homer Folks, "Enforcement of Child Labor Laws," *Annals of the American Academy of Social and Political Science*, XXXV, Supplement (March 1910), 91–95; Homer Folks, "New York Laws for the Protection of Children," lecture delivered before the College of St. Angela, New York, May 11, 1905, HFC.

51. Folks, "Child Labor and the Law," p. 23.   52. *Ibid.*, p. 24.

53. New York *Times*, June 4, 1904; Bremner, *From the Depths*, p. 219; Goldmark, *Impatient Crusader*, p. 96.

54. New York *Daily News,* June 5, 1904; *Charities,* XIII (Oct. 8, 1904), 47. On the executive committee were such prominent people as Felix Adler, Gifford Pinchot, Lillian D. Wald, Graham Taylor, Paul N. and Paul M. Warburg, Robert W. deForest, and Florence Kelley. Grover Cleveland, Cardinal Gibbons, Hoke Smith, Ben Tillman, and Judge Ben Lindsey, among many others, served on the national committee. See Braeman, "Albert J. Beveridge," p. 12.

55. Interview with Mrs. Savel Zimand, former general secretary of the National Child Labor Committee, Oct. 25, 1962, New York City.

56. Folks, "Child Labor and the Law," p. 21.

57. Braeman, "Albert J. Beveridge," p. 12.

58. Folks, *Changes and Trends in Child Labor,* p. 17; Schneider and Deutsch, *History of Public Welfare,* p. 158.

59. Frank J. Bruno, *Trends in Social Work, 1874–1956* (New York: Columbia University, 1957), p. 164. Also see Grace Abbott, "Federal Regulation of Child Labor, 1906–1938," *Social Service Review,* XIII (1939), 409–30; Ned Weisberg, "The Federal Child Labor Amendment—A Study in Pressure Politics" (Ph.D. dissertation, Cornell University, 1942).

60. Folks, "Child Labor and the Law," pp. 19–22. For the views of two other reformers who preferred national child labor legislation, see Jane Addams, "National Protection for Children," *Annals of the American Academy of Social and Political Science,* XXIX (Jan. 1907), 57–60; Samuel McCune Lindsay, "Child Labor a National Problem," *ibid.,* XXVII (March 1906), 73–78.

61. New York *Evening Post,* Jan. 24, 1907; "A Bill to Prevent the Employment of Children in Factories and Mines," S. 6562 and H.R. 21404 (1906), reprinted in the *Annals of the American Academy of Social and Political Science,* Child Labor Legislation Supplement, XXIX (1907).

62. Mrs. William B. Rice to Homer Folks, July 1, 11, 24, and 26, 1912; Homer Folks to Theodore Roosevelt, July 19, 1912; Homer Folks to Mrs. William B. Rice, July 19, 1912, HFC. It must be pointed out that Folks, like many others, especially Jane Addams, was "disposed to do whatever . . . [came] to hand in the way of assisting or formulating . . . [the] right views on social and industrial questions for any platform or any presidential candidate who cares to use them" (Folks to Rice, July 19, 1912, HFC). In other words, he was more interested in making ideas and measures part of a national political campaign than he was in a particular party or candidate.

63. Homer Folks, Journal, June 7, July 18, Sept. 12, 1912, HFC; Homer Folks to Theodore Roosevelt, July 19, 1912, HFC; Paul Kellogg, "The Industrial Platform." *Survey,* XXVIII (Aug. 24, 1912), 668–70; *Proc. of*

NCCC (St. Louis, 1910), 372–91; (Boston, 1911), pp. 148–213, 574; (Cleveland, 1912), pp. 376–435. Also see Allen F. Davis, "The Social Workers and the Progressive Party," *American Historical Review,* LXIX, No. 3 (April 1964), 673–75.

64. Theodore Roosevelt to Robert S. Vessey and others, Jan. 22, 1913; Theodore Roosevelt to George W. Perkins, Aug. 23, 1913, in Theodore Roosevelt, *The Letters of Theodore Roosevelt,* ed. Elting E. Morison (8 vols., Cambridge: Harvard University, 1954), VII, 695, 742–43; William Allen White, *The Autobiography of William Allen White* (New York: Macmillan, 1946), pp. 487–88.

65. New York *Times,* Aug. 14, 1912; Chicago *Tribune,* Aug. 7, 1912; George Mowry, *Theodore Roosevelt and the Progressive Movement* (New York: Hill and Wang, 1960), p. 266.

66. Folks, Journal, Jan. 26, 1913, HFC; Goldmark, *Impatient Crusader,* p. 140; *Survey,* Feb. 8, 1913, pp. 639–40; *Survey,* April 5, 1913, p. 3.

67. Interview with Mr. and Mrs. Savel Zimand, Oct. 25, 1962, New York City. Keating-Owen bill, "An Act to Prevent Interstate Commerce in the Products of Child Labor," *U.S. Statutes,* XXXIV (1916), Part I, Ch. 432, p. 675. On Wilson, see Arthur Link, *Woodrow Wilson and the Progressive Era* (New York: Harper Torchbook, 1963), pp. 226–27; Johnson, "Child Labor Legislation," pp. 437–41.

68. The author is presently engaged in writing the first full-length history of the National Child Labor Committee. For an interesting account of the NCLC's unsuccessful attempt to amend the United States Constitution in order to give to the federal government (without impairing the states' rights) the express "power to limit, regulate, and prohibit the labor of persons under eighteen years of age," see Richard B. Sherman, "The Rejection of the Child Labor Amendment," *Mid-America,* XLV, No. 1 (Jan. 1963), 6–7.

6

SAVING BABIES AND PRESERVING THE FAMILY

1. Homer Folks, "The Reminiscences of Homer Folks," Oral History Project (Columbia University, 1949), p. 52 (hereafter cited as OHP). Apparently Theodore Dreiser, the noted novelist and editor of the *Delineator* magazine, also played an important role in calling the conference. See Harold A. Jambor, "Theodore Dreiser, The *Delineator* Magazine and Dependent Children: A Background Note on the Calling of the 1909 White House Conference," *Social Service Review,* XXX, No. 1 (March 1958), 33–40.

2. *Thirty Years of Service: Tributes to James E. West* (New York: Carey, 1941), p. 10, HFC.

3. *Ibid.;* Folks, OHP, p. 52; interview with Mr. and Mrs. Savel Zimand, Oct. 25, 1962, New York City; Ida Curry to Katharine Lenroot, Nov. 3, 1950, Children's Bureau, Washington, D.C.

4. Letter from Homer Folks, James E. West, Theodore Dreiser, and others to Theodore Roosevelt, Dec. 22, 1908, in Theodore Roosevelt, *The Letters of Theodore Roosevelt,* ed. Elting E. Morison (8 vols., Cambridge: Harvard University, 1952), VI, 1440; Homer Folks, "Four Milestones of Progress" (1940), in Homer Folks, *Public Health and Welfare: The Citizens' Responsibility—Selected Papers of Homer Folks,* ed. Savel Zimand (New York: Macmillan, 1958), pp. 392–401.

5. Theodore Roosevelt to Jacob Henry Schiff, Dec. 25, 1908, in Roosevelt, *Letters,* VI, 1440; Folks, OHP, p. 53.

6. Homer Folks, Journal, Jan. 10, 1909, HFC.

7. Jane Addams, *The Second Twenty Years at Hull House* (New York: Macmillan, 1930), p. 18.

8. *Ibid.;* Ida Curry to Katharine Lenroot, Nov. 3, 1950, Chidren's Bureau, Washington, D.C.; New York *Times,* New York *Evening Post,* Jan. 26, 1909.

9. Conference on the Care of Dependent Children, Washington, D.C., 1909, *Proceedings* (Washington: Government Printing Office, 1909), pp. 5–6 (hereafter cited as *1909 W.H. Conf. Proc.*); Hastings H. Hart, "Improving Child Care," in *Thirty Years of Service: A Tribute to Homer Folks* (New York: Klebold, 1923), p. 21; Folks, OHP, pp. 54–55, 57.

10. Folks, OHP, pp. 54–55; Addams, *Second Twenty Years,* p. 18; Folks, "Four Milestones of Progress," p. 394; Emma O. Lundberg, *Unto the Least of These* (New York: Appleton-Century, 1947), p. 20.

11. For the specific origin of the idea to create the bureau see Robert L. Duffus, *Lillian Wald: Neighbor and Crusader* (New York: Macmillan, 1938), Ch. 7, "The Children's Bureau"; Frank J. Bruno, *Trends in Social Work, 1874–1956* (New York: Columbia University, 1957), p. 152; Josephine Goldmark, *Impatient Crusader: Florence Kelley's Life Story* (Urbana: University of Illinois, 1953), p. 97; Dorothy E. Bradbury, *Five Decades of Action for Children: A History of the Children's Bureau* (Washington: Children's Bureau, 1962), pp. 1–2; Julia Lathrop, "The Children's Bureau," in *Proceedings of the National Conference of Charities and Correction* (Cleveland: NCCC, 1912), p. 30 (hereafter cited as *Proc. of NCCC*). Robert Bremner *(From the Depths: The Discovery of Poverty in the United States* [New York: New York University, 1956], p. 221) incorrectly asserts that the National Child Labor Committee was responsible for calling the White House Conference on Dependent Children, "a meeting

that appears to have been designed primarily to influence Congress to pass the children's bureau bill." While it is true that the delegates strongly favored the bill, the conference was not called for that reason. It was called because West and Folks were interested in promoting the foster home care (vs. institutional) of dependent children.

12. New York State Charities Aid Association *Annual Report* (1906), pp. 17–18 (hereafter cited as SCAA *Annual Report*).

13. *1909 W.H. Conf. Proc.,* p. 6; Bruno, *Trends in Social Work,* p. 153; Goldmark, *Impatient Crusader,* pp. 99–100; Homer Folks, "Statistics Relating to Children," *Proc. of NCCC* (Buffalo, 1909), pp. 383–87.

14. Quoted in Bradbury, *Five Decades of Action,* p. 1.

15. H. R. Resolution 24148, Establishment of the Children's Bureau in the Interior Department, Sixtieth Congress, Second Session (Washington: Government Printing Office, 1909), pp. 15–18.

16. Homer Folks, "The National Children's Bureau" (1910), in Folks, *Public Health and Welfare,* pp. 87, 88; Bruno, *Trends in Social Work,* p. 153.

17. *Congressional Record,* Sixty-Second Congress, Second Session, Vol. XLII, Part 2, p. 1571.

18. Miss Dorothy E. Bradbury to the author, Feb. 5, 1963. Miss Katharine F. Lenroot, subsequent chief of the Children's Bureau, expressed the same opinion to the author in an interview in New York City on Oct. 1, 1962.

19. "Act Establishing the Children's Bureau (42 U.S.C. Ch. 6) Approved April 9, 1912," in Bradbury, *Five Decades of Action,* p. 132.

20. Bruno, *Trends in Social Work,* p. 154; Bremner, *From the Depths,* p. 22.

21. "Informal Memorandum for Miss Julia Lathrop, Dictated by Homer Folks, May 15, 1912," Children's Bureau, Washington, D.C. Between 1912 and 1921 the Children's Bureau was largely preoccupied with getting investigations under way and reporting on the social and health problems of the nation's children, gathering and analyzing data on infant and maternal mortality and morbidity, and collecting data on the growth of infants and young children.

22. Philip Van Ingen, "The History of Child Welfare Work in the United States," in *A Half Century of Public Health,* ed. Mazyck P. Ravenel (New York: American Public Health Association, 1921), p. 292; Wilson G. Smillie, *Public Health: Its Promise for the Future* (New York: Macmillan, 1955), pp. 419–21.

23. James H. Cassedy, *Charles V. Chapin and the Public Health Movement* (Cambridge: Harvard University, 1962), pp. 140–41.

24. Julia Lathrop to Homer Folks, Sept. 24, 1915; Homer Folks to Julia

Lathrop, Sept. 25, 1915, Children's Bureau, Washington, D.C.; John M. Glenn, Lilian Brandt, and F. Emerson Andrews, *Russell Sage Foundation* (2 vols., New York: Russell Sage Foundation, 1947), I, 105–06.

25. "Informal Memorandum for Miss Julia Lathrop, Dictated by Homer Folks, May 15, 1912," Children's Bureau, Washington, D.C.; Cassedy, *Charles V. Chapin,* pp. 140–41.

26. See Homer Folks, "Are Babies Worth Saving?," address delivered at the annual meeting of the American Association for the Study and Prevention of Infant Mortality, Nov. 1915, in Folks, *Public Health and Welfare,* p. 151.

27. *Ibid.,* p. 148.   28. Bradbury, *Five Decades of Action,* p. 8, fn.

29. Goldmark, *Impatient Crusader,* p. 105; Bradbury, *Five Decades of Action,* p. 13.

30. Bradbury, *Five Decades of Action,* p. 132; Edith Abbott, "Grace Abbott—A Sister's Memories," *The Social Service Review,* XIII, No. 3 (Sept. 1939), p. 392. The Sheppard-Towner Act, as finally passed, authorized an annual appropriation of $1,252,000 for a five-year period (later extended to seven years)—$50,354 to be expended by the Children's Bureau for administration and research in problems of maternity and infant care, the balance to be divided among the states accepting the act. For an excellent short essay on the history of the ultimate general acceptance of the principle of federal aid for social welfare, see Edith Abbott, "The Long History of the Movement Toward Federal Aid for Social Welfare," in Edith Abbott, *Public Assistance: American Principles and Politics* (Chicago: University of Chicago, 1941), pp. 645–90.

31. C. E. A. Winslow, *The Life of Hermann M. Biggs* (Philadelphia: Lea and Febiger, 1929), p. 358.

32. *Minutes* of the Meetings of the Board of Managers of the New York State Charities Aid Association, New York City, Feb. 17, 1922 (hereafter cited as SCAA *Minutes*); Jane McLean (Folks's secretary) to Grace Abbott, Jan. 11, 1927, Grace Abbott Papers, University of Chicago, Chicago, Ill.; Homer Folks to Senator Royal S. Copeland, Jan. 11, 1927, HFC.

33. Bradbury, *Five Decades of Action,* pp. 21, 26; Abbott, "Sister's Memories," pp. 389ff.; Clarke A. Chambers, *Seedtime of Reform: American Social Service and Social Action, 1918–1933* (Minneapolis: University of Minnesota, 1963), p. 51.

34. Arthur P. Miles, *American Social Work Theory: A Critique and Proposal* (New York: Harper, 1954), p. 202; Folks, "Four Milestones of Progress," p. 394.

35. Abraham Epstein, *Insecurity: A Challenge to America* (New York: Smith and Haas, 1933), pp. 627ff. For an early debate between the

defenders (mainly in Chicago) and the critics (mainly Easterners) of widows' pensions, see *Proc. of NCCC* (Cleveland, 1912), *passim*.

36. Homer Folks, "Widows' Pensions," pp. 1–3, manuscript dated 1910 in HFC; Homer Folks, "The Needy Child," manuscript dated 1910 in HFC; Homer Folks, *Proc. of NCCC* (Cleveland, 1912), pp. 485–87. Also, remember that Folks realized new child labor laws reduced potential income from children and that the state had a duty to such families which could only be met by providing an adequate and reliable income to ensure the maintenance of the home.

37. Grace Abbott, "Recent Trends in Mothers' Aid," *The Social Service Review*, VIII, No. 2 (June 1934), 191–211; Chambers, *Seedtime of Reform*, pp. 49–50; Epstein, *Insecurity*, pp. 628–29.

38. Schneider and Deutsch, *The History of Public Welfare in New York State* (Chicago: University of Chicago, 1941), pp. 187–89. This attitude made it seem advisable to place the local administration of the act in the hands of individuals serving without compensation and presumably motivated by a spirit of public duty. For the terms of the act see *History of Public Welfare*, pp. 190–91; Henry Bruere, "The Reminiscences of Henry Bruere," OHP, 1949, p. 125; Lundberg, *Unto the Least of These*, pp. 128–29; Alfred E. Smith, *Up to Now* (New York: Viking, 1929), pp. 127–28.

39. SCAA *Minutes*, March 5, 1915. Some years later Folks changed his mind on this point and favored the creation of the new public authority to distribute widows' pensions. See Homer Folks, "Making Relief Respectable" (1934), in Folks, *Public Health and Welfare*, pp. 284–301; SCAA *Annual Report* (1915), p. 101; Homer Folks, "Abstract of Remarks of Homer Folks in Opening the Conference on Infant Hygiene," New York City, May 22, 1912, HFC.

40. Ch. 684, *Laws of 1927; S.C.A.A. News*, May 1927, p. 5.

41. SCAA *Minutes*, Nov. 15, 1934; *S.C.A.A. News*, Nov. 1934, p. 4. Folks's address was entitled "Child Welfare, The Spearhead of Social Security." He began by pointing out that "when we push through the phrases and titles in which the various aspects of social security are packaged and labelled, we find that the welfare of children is the very gist and essence of the underlying purpose of social security." For the difficulties associated with the advisory meetings see Edwin E. Witte, *The Development of the Social Security Act* (Madison: University of Wisconsin, 1962), *passim*. Also see Bradbury, *Five Decades of Action*, p. 43.

42. Homer Folks, "Aspects of Child Welfare," manuscript dated April 18, 1911, HFC.

43. Van Ingen, "The History of Child Welfare Work," pp. 296–97; Cassedy, *Charles V. Chapin*, p. 135.

44. Homer Folks to John H. Finley, Nov. 3, 1913, John H. Finley Papers, New York Public Library, New York.

45. Folks, "Aspects of Child Welfare," pp. 20–22. Folks felt the public schools should be infused with a sense of the physical welfare, as well as of the moral and intellectual training, of the children. In 1923 he wrote, "The public health education of the child in the school, and, through the school, the education of the parents . . . is the great hope of the future. By combining health with education—health education—we may hope finally to discover a short and really effectual way of remedying the prevalent low standards of living." See Homer Folks, "Modern Trends in the Health Care of Children," *The Nation's Health,* Feb. 1923, p. 114.

46. Homer Folks, "Outstanding Facts in Child Welfare" (1915), in Folks, *Public Health and Welfare,* pp. 239–40.

7
MENTAL HEALTH

1. *Minutes* of the Board of Managers of the New York State Charities Aid Association, New York City, 1894–1895, *passim* (hereafter cited as SCAA *Minutes*). Also see Homer Folks, "The Reminiscences of Homer Folks," Oral History Project (Columbia University, 1949), p. 97 (hereafter cited as OHP). *Proceedings of the National Conference of Charities and Correction* (New Haven: NCCC, 1895), p. 370; (Grand Rapids, 1896), p. 74 (hereafter cited as *Proc. of NCCC*).

2. For the major advantages of separate care for epileptics, on the colony plan, see Albert Deutsch, *The Mentally Ill in America* (New York: Columbia University, 1962), pp. 382–84; SCAA *Minutes,* March 30, 1894; *Proc. of NCCC* (New Haven, 1895), p. 370; David M. Schneider and Albert Deutsch, *The History of Public Welfare in New York State, 1867–1940* (Chicago: University of Chicago, 1941), p. 101.

3. Homer Folks, "New York Charity Legislation of 1905," *Charities,* XIV (May 13, 1905), 748–49.

4. SCAA *Minutes,* May 25, 1906; Homer Folks to Oscar Straus, Nov. 28, 1906, Oscar Straus Papers, Library of Congress, Washington, D.C.; SCAA *Minutes,* Jan. 11, March 8, 1907; Philadelphia *Press,* Oct. 23, 1906; New York State Charities Aid Association *Annual Report* (1909), pp. 23–38 (hereafter cited as SCAA *Annual Report*). The 1906–1907 revisions of the federal statutes regulating immigration included three specific amendments which Folks proposed: (1) doctors trained in the diagnosis of insanity and mental defects were to be employed at both the point of debarkation and entrance; (2) mentally ill aliens were to be treated at federal expense before

deportation; and (3) trained attendants, at the shipping companies' expense, were to accompany home deported mental defectives. Perhaps it should be mentioned that participation by the federal government in mental health work, which developed through these activities regarding the inspection of aliens, began in 1882 when the Congress prohibited insane persons from entering America.

5. See Richard Dewey, "The Assistance of Destitute Convalescent and Recovered Patients, Discharged from Hospitals for the Insane," *Proc. of NCCC* (Portland, Ore., 1905), pp. 339–43.

6. Alexander Johnson, *Adventures in Social Welfare, Being Reminiscences of Things, Thoughts and Folks during Forty Years of Social Work* (Fort Wayne, Ind.: Fort Wayne Printing Co., 1923), pp. 377ff.

7. SCAA *Annual Report* (1905), p. 25.

8. Homer Folks, "A Year's Work in Aftercare of the Insane," p. 5, paper delivered before the National Conference on June 19, 1907, HFC; Johnson, *Adventures in Social Welfare,* pp. 377–78.

9. Folks, "A Year's Work," p. 5; *Proc. of NCCC* (Philadelphia, 1906), p. 55; SCAA *Annual Report* (1906), p. 2; SCAA *Minutes,* Nov. 17, 1911.

10. Homer Folks, "Aftercare of the Insane," p. 140, address delivered before the Quarterly Conference of Superintendents and Managers of State Hospitals, New York, Sept. 25, 1913, in Homer Folks, *Public Health and Welfare: The Citizens' Responsibility—Selected Papers of Homer Folks,* ed. Savel Zimand (New York: Macmillan, 1958), pp. 138–45.

11. See John C. Burnham, "Psychiatry, Psychology and the Progressive Movement," *American Quarterly,* XII (Winter 1960), 457–65.

12. SCAA *Annual Report* (1906), p. 2; Folks, "A Year's Work," p. 7; New York *Evening Post,* June 19, 1907.

13. New York *Sun,* Dec. 29, 1907; SCAA *Minutes,* Nov. 17, 1911.

14. Clifford Beers, *A Mind That Found Itself* (New York: Doubleday, Doran, 1931), pp. 286, 325. Also see Nina Ridenour, *Mental Health in the United States: A Fifty Year History* (Cambridge: Harvard University, 1961), p. 5.

15. Ridenour, *Mental Health,* pp. 47, 55; Livingston Farrand to Clifford Beers, April 25, 1908, quoted in Beers, *A Mind That Found Itself,* p. 279.

16. Folks, "A Year's Work," pp. 1–2.

17. Homer Folks to Mayor George B. McClellan, Jr., May 28, 1906, New York City Municipal Archives, New York; New York *Tribune,* May 16, 1904; *Proc. of NCCC* (Philadelphia, 1906), pp. 49–56.

18. Homer Folks, "The Influences of Education on Public Health," pp. 4–5, address delivered at Columbia University, New York, May 3, 1909, HFC. Actually, a broad social hygiene movement had originated in 1901

when a Committee of Seven of the New York Medical Society delivered an important report on the subject of venereal disease. In 1905 the American Society of Social and Moral Prophylaxis was organized, and by 1912 eighteen social hygiene associations had been formed in American cities and states.

19. See Homer Folks, *Outline of a Plan for Beginning Practical Work in the State of New York for the Prevention of Insanity* (New York: SCAA Pub. No. 117, 1910), or "The Prevention of Insanity," *Review of Reviews*, XLIII (May 1911), reprinted in Folks, *Public Health and Welfare*, pp. 92–104.

20. Homer Folks, *Why Should Anyone Go Insane?* (New York: SCAA Pub. No. 121, 1911), p. 6.

21. Ridenour, *Mental Health*, pp. 122–23; Homer Folks, "The New York Campaign for the Prevention of Insanity," *Survey*, XXV (Nov. 12, 1910), 265.

22. SCAA *Minutes*, Feb. 25, May 3, 1910. This was the third state mental hygiene society to be formed.

23. Folks, "The New York Campaign," p. 268; Folks, "The Prevention of Insanity," pp. 91–102. Folks asked, "Who can doubt that if these facts [regarding the causes of insanity] were generally known to the public, as they are known to physicians familiar with mental disease, they would have a profound effect upon the conduct of the average man?"

24. Homer Folks to Dr. Albert Shaw, Dec. 23, 1910, Albert Shaw Papers, New York Public Library, New York; Homer Folks, "The Prevention of Insanity," p. 95; SCAA *Annual Report* (1910), p. 3.

25. Folks, "The Prevention of Insanity," p. 103; *S.C.A.A. News*, Nov. 12, 1912, p. 6.

26. See Homer Folks, "State Hospitals at the Parting of the Ways" (1913), in Folks, *Public Health and Welfare*, pp. 122–30.

27. Beers, *A Mind That Found Itself, passim*; Richard H. Shryock, *The Development of Modern Medicine* (New York: Knopf, 1947), pp. 376–77.

28. SCAA *Annual Report* (1923), pp. 58–59.

29. There is no one generally accepted definition of feeble-mindedness. However, there is agreement that the term contains three essential and interrelated concepts: (1) marked limitation or deficiency of intelligence, frequently associated with other shortcomings of personality, which is due to (2) lack of normal development, rather than to mental disease or deterioration, and which manifests itself in (3) social and economic incompetence. See Stanley P. Davies, *Social Control of the Mentally Deficient* (New York: Crowell, 1930), pp. 1–2, 339.

30. Davies, *Social Control*, pp. 67, 84–85.

31. Homer Folks, "Report of the Committee on the Mentally Defective and Their Relation to the State," *Proceedings of the New York State Conference of Charities and Correction* (Albany: NYSCCC, 1912), pp. 172–79 (hereafter cited as *Proc. of NYSCCC*). Also, Homer Folks, "The State as Eugenist," p. 2, second Kennedy Lecture, delivered April 7, 1913, New York School of Philanthropy, HFC.

32. For an excellent history of the eugenics movement in America see Mark H. Haller, "American Eugenics: Hereditarian Social Thought, 1870–1930" (Ph.D. dissertation, University of Wisconsin, 1959). Also see Rudolph J. Vecoli, "Sterilization: A Progressive Measure?," *Wisconsin Magazine of History*, XLIII, No. 3 (Spring 1960), 190–202; Davies, *Social Control*, p. 99; Ridenour, *Mental Health*, p. 49. Present-day thought lacks confidence in sterilization as a measure of social control. It is unlikely to reduce the number of mentally deficient in succeeding generations, and it is no substitute for constructive training and community programs in the present.

33. In New York State the law was contested in several of the courts and repealed by an act of the legislature on May 19, 1920.

34. Folks, "The State as Eugenist," pp. 2, 7, 10; Folks, "Report of the Committee on the Mentally Defective," p. 174.

35. Folks, "The State as Eugenist," *passim*. The New York *Times* of April 9, 1913, reported, "The urgent need of more thorough segregation of the feebleminded was the chief point made yesterday by Folks when he appeared as one of the Kennedy lecturers." Also see *S.C.A.A. News*, April 1914, p. 1.

36. Davies, *Social Control*, pp. 123, 125, 182–85; Homer Folks, "Continuation of a Discussion of Paper by Professor H. S. Jennings, 'Health Progress and Race Progress,'" Indianapolis, May 24, 1927, HFC.

37. A colony for the feeble-minded may be defined as any group of feeble-minded inmates living together under supervision outside a parent institution, while remaining under its jurisdiction, and contributing to a greater or lesser degree by labor to their support. Also see Jane Addams, *My Friend, Julia Lathrop* (New York: Macmillan, 1935), pp. 103–08.

38. See Davies, *Social Control*, pp. 184–201, 216–17.

39. *Ibid.*, pp. 256–57.

40. Folks, "Report of the Committee on the Mentally Defective," p. 175; *S.C.A.A. News*, Oct. 1925, p. 3; Homer Folks, "A State Mental Hygiene Program Through the School Period," p. 2, address delivered at the National Conference of Social Work, June 1922, HFC; Davies, *Social Control*, pp. 297–98.

41. New York *Times*, Jan. 2, 1922; *S.C.A.A. News*, April 1923, p. 2; New York *Times*, Feb. 19, 1923.

42. SCAA *Annual Report* (1923), p. 51; New York *Times,* Oct. 8, 1923; Ch. 591, New York State *Laws of 1923.*

43. See Homer Folks, "Some Financial Problems of Our State Institutions," *Proc. of NYSCCC* (1909), pp. 201–08; CAA *Minutes,* Dec. 20, 1912; *S.C.A.A. News,* May–June 1915, "Special Constitutional Convention Issue"; SCAA *Annual Report* (1923), p. 52.

44. SCAA *Annual Report* (1923), p. 52; John M. Glenn, Lilian Brandt, and F. Emerson Andrews, *Russell Sage Foundation* (2 vols., New York: Russell Sage Foundation, 1947), II, 456.

45. Homer Folks to Louisa Lee Schuyler, Oct. 17, 1923, HFC.

46. *S.C.A.A. News,* July 1923, p. 1.

47. Glenn, Brandt, and Andrews, *Russell Sage Foundation,* II, 455–56; SCAA *Annual Report* (1924), p. 47.

48. Interview with Mr. Stanley Davies, Oct. 17, 1962, White Plains, N.Y.

49. *Mental Hygiene Bulletin,* Nov. 1923, p. 49.

50. Quoted in SCAA *Annual Report* (1924), p. 48.

51. New York *Times,* May 19, 1927.

52. Homer Folks to Governor Franklin D. Roosevelt, March 21, 1929; Roosevelt to Folks, March 27, 1929, Franklin D. Roosevelt Papers, Roosevelt Library, Hyde Park, N. Y. (hereafter cited as FDR).

53. SCAA *Minutes,* April 19, 1929; *S.C.A.A. News,* April 1929, pp. 12–13; Homer Folks to Lt. Governor Herbert H. Lehman, May 20, 1929; Homer Folks to Franklin D. Roosevelt, June 28, 1929, June 26, 1930; Roosevelt to Folks, June 30, 1930, FDR; SCAA *Annual Report* (1931), p. 31; interview with Herbert H. Lehman, Dec. 11, 1962, New York City.

54. Ridenour, *Mental Health,* p. 32; *S.C.A.A. News,* June 1937, p. 1; Sept. 1939, p. 3; Feb. 1940, p. 4; SCAA *Minutes,* Nov. 16, 1939; SCAA *Annual Report* (1940), p. 16.

55. SCAA *Minutes,* Oct. 31, 1940; Folks, OHP, p. 91; *S.C.A.A. News,* Nov. 10, 1940, p. 4; SCAA *Annual Report* (1941), p. 20.

56. Homer Folks, Journal, Dec. 6, 1940; Nov. 30, 1942, HFC; *S.C.A.A. News,* Dec. 1942, p. 5; "Progress Report of the Temporary Commission on State Hospital Problems," Nov. 30, 1942, *passim,* HFC; *S.C.A.A. News,* Sept. 1944, p. 1; *Insulin Shock Treatment: A Study by the Temporary Commission on State Hospital Problems* (1944), *passim,* esp. pp. 78–81.

57. Deutsch, *The Mentally Ill,* p. 500.

58. Interview with Miss Katharine Ecob, Oct. 14, 1962, New York City; Ridenour, *Mental Health,* pp. 56–57.

59. Had Folks not encouraged her to seek official adoption of the plan, in all probability it would never have been carried out. Interview with Miss Katharine Ecob, Oct. 14, 1962, New York City.

60. *Ibid.; S.C.A.A. News,* March 1941, p. 4.

61. Interview with Miss Katharine Ecob, Oct. 14, 1962, New York City; SCAA *Annual Report* (1942), pp. 48–49.

62. Interview with Miss Katharine Ecob, Oct. 14, 1962, New York City; *S.C.A.A. News,* Nov. 1943, p. 1; SCAA *Annual Report* (1942), pp. 48–49; (1943), p. 20; (1944), p. 28.

63. SCAA *Minutes,* April 8, May 14, 1943; *S.C.A.A. News,* April 1943, p. 4; Nov. 1943, p. 1; Ridenour, *Mental Health,* pp. 57–58.

64. See Homer Folks, "The Tyranny of the Past and the Hope of the Future" (1943), in Folks, *Public Health and Welfare,* pp. 420–28.

65. The National Mental Health Act resulted largely from World War II, which turned up some very unpleasant health statistics, none more startling than those on mental and nervous diseases. Some 1,100,000 men were rejected for military duty because of mental or neurological disorders—by far the largest group of causes for rejection. Together with the rejectees for mental and educational deficiencies the staggering total came to 1,767,000 out of 4,800,000. In addition, of those inducted into the Army and subsequently given medical discharges, 40 per cent were dismissed for psychiatric disorders. By 1946, 60 per cent of all hospitalization under the Veterans Administration was for psychiatric disorders, at a cost of $40,000 or more per case. See *Senate Report on the National Mental Health Act, 79th Congress, 2nd Session,* Report No. 1353, pp. 2–3; also George W. Bachman, *Health Resources in the United States: Personnel, Facilities and Sources* (Washington: Brookings Institute, 1952), p. 143; *S.C.A.A. News,* May 1945, p. 1; SCAA *Annual Report* (1946), p. 20.

66. Interview with Dr. George Baehr, Oct. 5, 1962, New York City. As two experts have testified, Folks's influence on the mental health movement did not cease with the close of his active career. See, for example, Dr. George S. Stevenson, nationally known leader of the mental hygiene movement and consultant for the National Association for Mental Health, to Homer Folks, Feb. 4, 1957 (the author is indebted to Mrs. Lawrence Orton for allowing him to see this letter). William T. Beaty, executive director of the World Federation for Mental Health, to the author, Aug. 29, 1962.

8
SOCIAL THOUGHT

1. Almost every one of the more than twenty personal acquaintances of Folks that the author interviewed testified to this. The following list is only a sample: Dr. Nina Ridenour, Oct. 2, 1962, New York City; Miss Ruth

Taylor, Oct. 2, 1962, Hartsdale, N.Y.; Dr. George Baehr, Oct. 5, 1962, New York City; Miss Katharine Ecob, Oct. 14, 1962, New York City; Dr. Philip Klein, Nov. 11, 1962, White Plains, N.Y.

2. See above.

3. Interviews with Mr. and Mrs. Lawrence M. Orton, Oct. 2, Nov. 29, 1962, New York City; Mr. and Mrs. Savel Zimand, Oct. 25, Nov. 27, 1962, New York City; Mr. Leonard W. Mayo, Nov. 14, 1962, New York City; Hon. Herbert H. Lehman, Dec. 11, 1962, New York City.

4. Interview with Dr. Philip Klein, Nov. 11, 1962, White Plains, N.Y.

5. Interviews with Mrs. John A. Kingsbury, Dec. 6, 1962, New York City; Miss Katharine Ecob, Oct. 14, 1962, New York City.

6. Homer Folks to Harvey N. Ott, May 25, 1939, HFC.

7. Homer Folks to John A. Kingsbury, Sept. 20, 1911, HFC.   8. *Ibid.*

9. Homer Folks, Journal, June 14, 1911, HFC. The degree and citation are in the HFC.

10. *Proceedings of the National Conference of Charities and Correction* (St. Louis: NCCC, 1910), p. 661 (hereafter cited as *Proc. of NCCC*).

11. Telegram from Edward T. Devine to Homer Folks, May 24, 1910, HFC.

12. Telegram from Robert W. deForest to Homer Folks, May 25, 1910, HFC.

13. Rochester (N.Y.) *Democratic Chronicle,* May 27, 1910.

14. Interviews with Mr. and Mrs. Lawrence M. Orton, Oct. 2, 1962, New York City; Mr. and Mrs. Savel Zimand, Nov. 27, 1962, New York City; Dr. James E. Perkins, Oct. 1, 1962, New York City; Mr. Robert Barrie, Oct. 19, 1962, New York City. Mr. Folks used to say he did his "thinking" during the summer months. He had a study at the camp and he usually spent the early morning hours there where he wrote many of his addresses he presented during the year.

15. Interviews with Mrs. John A. Kingsbury, Dec. 6, 1962, New York City; Mr. Robert Barrie, Oct. 19, 1962, New York City.

16. Homer Folks to Louisa Lee Schuyler, July 14, 1925, HFC.

17. Homer Folks, "The Citizen's Interest in Public Charities," address delivered before the Society of the Genesee, New York City, Feb. 6, 1904, HFC; Homer Folks, "What the State Charities Aid Association Is, and What It Stands For," extracts of an address at the annual meeting of the SCAA, Feb. 2, 1909, HFC.

18. Edward T. Devine to Homer Folks, Dec. 8, 1939, HFC.

19. Folks, "Citizen's Interest in Public Charities," p. 4.

20. Homer Folks, "The Place of Philanthropy in Social Progress," p. 19,

address delivered before the Alumni Association of Albion College, June 26, 1894, HFC.

21. Homer Folks, "The Prevention of Insanity" (1911), in Homer Folks, *Public Health and Welfare: The Citizens' Responsibility—Selected Papers of Homer Folks,* ed. Savel Zimand (New York: Macmillan, 1958), p. 100.

22. Homer Folks, "What We Have Learned Since 1889" (1934), in Folks, *Public Health and Welfare,* p. 308.

23. Folks, "The Place of Philanthropy," p. 9.

24. Homer Folks, "Introductory Remarks" to the Kennedy Lectures delivered by Folks at the New York School of Philanthropy, March 31, 1913, HFC.

25. Folks, "The Place of Philanthropy," pp. 1, 4, 9. Folks was part of a progressive, not regressive, social movement. He and his colleagues did not look backward to a form of rugged agrarian individualism which they believed to be the backbone of the early American republic; there was no strong attempt to hold onto or restore the values of the agrarian past. They were, in fact, most concerned with improving urban-industrial life, and it was to a spirit of cooperation and the power of an expanding government that they turned for redress of grievances.

26. Philadelphia *North American,* May 13, 1906; Homer Folks, "Church and Charity," address delivered before the Park Avenue (N.Y.) Methodist Church, Nov. 7, 1901, HFC.

27. Folks, "The Place of Philanthropy," p. 11.

28. Folks, "Church and Charity," pp. 5–6.

29. Folks, "Citizen's Interest in Public Charities," p. 7; Brooklyn (N.Y.) *Citizen,* May 27, 1905; New York *Tribune,* May 29, 1905.

30. See Homer Folks, "Jungle Rule or Golden Rule?," address delivered before the Yonkers, N.Y., Tuberculosis and Health Association, Oct. 23, 1925, in Folks, *Public Health and Welfare,* pp. 243–57; New York *Times,* editorial, Oct. 4, 1925.

31. Folks, "Jungle Rule or Golden Rule?," p. 257.

32. Folks, "The Place of Philanthropy," p. 5.

33. Homer Folks to Albion Small, May 28, 1892; Homer Folks to Amos Warner, June 1, 1892; Homer Folks to J. Laurence Laughlin, Aug. 25, 1892; Homer Folks to Albion Small, Aug. 25, 1892, Feb. 27, 1893, HFC.

34. Homer Folks, "The Influence of Education on Public Health," p. 21, address delivered at Columbia University, May 3, 1909, HFC; also see Homer Folks, "Serving Through Legislation" (1909), in Folks, *Public Health and Welfare,* pp. 67–72.

35. *Proc. of NCCC* (Cincinnati, 1899), p. 349. Folks may have come into contact with James while he attended Harvard.

36. Folks, "The Place of Philanthropy," p. 9; Folks, "What We Have Learned Since 1889."

37. See Merle Curti, "Jane Addams on Human Nature," *Journal of the History of Ideas,* XXII, No. 2 (April–June 1961), 244.

38. Folks, "The Place of Philanthropy," p. 9.

39. Homer Folks to Mr. and Mrs. Lawrence M. Orton, April 4, 1925. The author is indebted to Mr. and Mrs. Orton for allowing him to see this letter.

40. Homer Folks, "Educational Aspects of Modern Philanthropy," un-dated manuscript in the HFC.

41. See Homer Folks, "College Graduates in Benevolent Work," address delivered at the International Congress of Charities, Correction and Philanthropy, Chicago, June 1893, in Folks, *Public Health and Welfare,* pp. 23–33.

42. Homer Folks, "Municipal Administration and Social Betterment, or, The Welfare of the Citizen the Chief Concern of the City," p. 2, lecture delivered at Cornell University, Oct. 9, 1905, HFC.

43. Homer Folks, "Municipal Administration and Social Betterment, Continued," p. 20, lecture delivered at Cornell University, Oct. 10, 1905, HFC.

44. Homer Folks, "Some Steps Toward the Millenium: Rational Governmental Development," sixth Kennedy Lecture delivered at the New York School of Philanthropy, May 5, 1913, HFC.

45. Folks, "Municipal Administration, Continued," *passim;* Yonkers (N.Y.) *Statesman,* June 17, 1937.

46. *S.C.A.A. News,* March–April 1916, p. 2.

47. Homer Folks, "The Failure of Government in America," p. 5, address delivered at Muhlenberg College, Allentown, Pa., Oct. 20, 1910, HFC.

48. *Ibid.,* p. 6.

49. Merle Curti, "American Philanthropy and the National Character," *American Quarterly,* X, No. 4 (Winter 1958), 436.

50. *Proc. of NCCC* (Cincinnati, 1899), p. 349; Homer Folks, "Making Relief Respectable" (1934), in Folks, *Public Health and Welfare,* pp. 284–301 (italics mine).

51. Arthur S. Link and William B. Catton, *American Epoch* (New York: Knopf, 1963), p. 72.

9
PUBLIC HEALTH—TUBERCULOSIS

1. Homer Folks, "Disease and Dependence," address delivered at the National Conference of Charities and Correction, Atlanta, 1903, in Homer Folks, *Public Health and Welfare: The Citizens' Responsibility—Selected Papers of Homer Folks,* ed. Savel Zimand (New York: Macmillan, 1958), pp. 39–45. Public health, by the way, according to a lengthy but one of the most widely accepted definitions, is "the science and the art of preventing disease, prolonging life, and promoting physical health and efficiency through organized community efforts for the sanitation of the environment, the control of community infections, the education of the individual principles of personal hygiene, the organization of medical and nursing service for the early diagnosis and preventive treatment of disease, and the development of the social machinery which will ensure to every individual in the community a standard of living adequate for the maintenance of health." See C. E. A. Winslow, *The Life of Hermann M. Biggs* (Philadelphia: Lea and Febiger, 1929), p. 345.

2. Homer Folks, "Points of Contact between the Health Officer and the Social Worker," address delivered before the Sociological Section of the American Public Health Association, Sept. 20, 1912, HFC.

3. The bacteriological origins of typhoid, leprosy, and malaria were discovered in 1880, of tuberculosis in 1882, of cholera in 1883, of diphtheria and tetanus in 1884, of plague in 1884, and dysentery in 1898. See Howard D. Kramer, "The Germ Theory and the Early Public Health Program in the United States," *Bulletin of the History of Medicine,* XXII, No. 3 (May–June 1948), 233–47; Frederick P. Gorham, "The History of Bacteriology and Its Contribution to Public Health Work," in *A Half Century of Public Health,* ed. Mazyck Ravenel (New York: American Public Health Association, 1921), pp. 66–93; James A. Tobey, *Public Health Law* (New York: Commonwealth Fund, 1947), pp. 1–14; Richard H. Shryock, "The Origins and Significance of the Public Health Movement in the United States," *Annals of Medical History,* I, No. 6, n.s. (Nov. 1929), 645–65. Also three biographies useful for understanding developments in public health and medicine in the latter nineteenth century are Winslow, *Hermann Biggs;* Simon and James T. Flexner, *William Henry Welch and the Heroic Age of Medicine* (New York: Viking, 1941); and James H. Cassedy, *Charles V. Chapin and the Public Health Movement* (Cambridge: Harvard University, 1962).

4. Cassedy, *Charles V. Chapin,* pp. 78ff.; Gorham, "The History of

Bacteriology," pp. 86ff.; Charles V. Chapin, "History of State and Municipal Control of Disease," in Ravenel, *A Half Century,* pp. 133–60; C. E. A. Winslow, *Conquest of Epidemic Disease* (Princeton: Princeton University, 1943), pp. 362–80; Chapin, *Sources and Modes of Infection* (New York: Wiley, 1910).

5. C. E. A. Winslow, *The Evolution and Significance of the Modern Public Health Campaign* (New Haven: Yale University, 1935), p. 36; Donald H. Fleming, *William H. Welch and the Rise of Modern Medicine* (Boston: Little, Brown, 1954).

6. Kramer, "The Germ Theory," p. 246.

7. Winslow, *Hermann Biggs,* pp. 120ff.

8. Homer Folks, "Public Health Work in the Prevention of Dependence" (1909), in Homer Folks, *Public Health and Welfare,* p. 83.

9. Homer Folks, "Points of Contact," p. 1.

10. Samuel Hopkins Adams, "Tuberculosis: The Real Race Suicide," *McClure's,* XXIV (Jan. 1905), 234–39; Lilian Brandt, "The Social Aspects of Tuberculosis Based on a Study of Statistics," in *A Handbook on the Prevention of Tuberculosis* (New York: Committee on the Prevention of Tuberculosis, Charity Organization Society of New York, 1903), pp. 36–38; Richard H. Shryock, *National Tuberculosis Association, 1900–1954* (New York: NTA, 1957), p. 63.

11. Shryock, *National Tuberculosis Association,* p. 61.

12. Edward T. Devine, *When Social Work Was Young* (New York: Macmillan, 1939), pp. 93–94.

13. Shryock, *National Tuberculosis Association,* pp. 65, 88–97.

14. Lilian Brandt, *A Directory of Institutions and Societies Dealing with Tuberculosis in the United States and Canada* (New York: Committee on the Prevention of Tuberculosis, Charity Organization Society of New York, 1904), p. 263.

15. Shryock, *National Tuberculosis Association,* p. 112.

16. *Ibid.,* p. 85.

17. Homer Folks, "Health as an Investment," *Transactions of the National Association for the Study and Prevention of Tuberculosis* (New York: NASPT, 1905), p. 39; Also see Chicago *Chronicle,* Washington *Post,* New York *Evening Post,* May 19, 1905; Homer Folks, Journal, May 18, 1905, HFC.

18. *Minutes* of the Meetings of the Board of Managers of the New York State Charities Aid Association, New York City, Nov. 9, 1906, May 17, 1907 (hereafter cited as SCAA *Minutes*).

19. See John M. Glenn, Lilian Brandt, and F. Emerson Andrews, *Russell Sage Foundation* (2 vols., New York; Russell Sage Foundation, 1947), I,

27, 30; Homer Folks, "The Reminiscences of Homer Folks," Oral History Project (Columbia University, 1949), p. 75 (hereafter cited as OHP). Immediately thereafter another $5,000 was given to the SCAA by the Russell Sage Foundation. Later, several $25,000 grants were made to the Association, all for the campaign against tuberculosis. Between 1907 and 1917 the largest single amount of money expended by the Foundation (approximately $230,000) went to the SCAA for this purpose.

20. George J. Nelbach, "The Early Days," address by the former executive secretary of the New York State Committee on Tuberculosis and Public Health at the Homer Folks Memorial Service, held on June 10, 1963, Hotel Statler-Hilton, New York City. The author is indebted to Mrs. Savel Zimand for giving him a copy of this address. Also see Homer Folks to John A. Kingsbury, Sept. 30, 1907, John A. Kingsbury Papers, Library of Congress, Washington, D.C.; interview with Mrs. John A. Kingsbury, Dec. 6, 1962, New York City.

21. Folks, OHP, pp. 43, 74; New York State Charities Aid Association *Annual Report* (1907), p. 2 (hereafter cited as SCAA *Annual Report*); Livingston Farrand, executive secretary of the National Association for the Study and Prevention of Tuberculosis, to Homer Folks, Oct. 30, 1907, HFC; SCAA *Minutes,* Nov. 8, 1907; Homer Folks, "A State Aroused: Effective Control of Tuberculosis in Small Cities and Rural Communities," *Charities,* XXI (Nov. 7, 1908), 229–32.

22. *Prevention of Tuberculosis: Handbook of the Campaign for the Prevention of Tuberculosis in New York State, Outside of New York City* (New York: SCAA Pub. No. 102, 1908), p. 7.

23. SCAA *Annual Report* (1908), p. 2; *Prevention of Tuberculosis,* pp. 7–9.

24. Nelbach, "The Early Days."

25. *Ibid.; Prevention of Tuberculosis,* p. 2.

26. Theodore Roosevelt to Homer Folks, Jan. 18, 1908, HFC.

27. *Prevention of Tuberculosis,* p. 9. The SCAA urged communities to institute the following to avoid any spreading of the disease: (1) notification and registration of all cases; (2) free bacteriological examination of sputum; (3) a free tuberculosis dispensary; (4) a visiting nurse service; (5) relief for the families of needy consumptives; (6) sanatorium treatment for incipient cases; (7) a hospital for advanced cases; (8) home care and medical supervision of cases that could not be removed to sanatoria and hospitals; (9) a suitable building code to prevent congestion in housing; (10) supervision of milk and other food supplies; and (11) an educational center for conducting a continuous campaign against the disease.

28. SCAA *Annual Report* (1908), p. 3; *Minute* of Tribute to Homer

Folks adopted by the Board of Directors of the New York State Committee on Tuberculosis and Public Health, Inc., March 14, 1963. The author is indebted to Mrs. Savel Zimand for letting him see this.

29. Henry D. Chadwick and Alton S. Pope, *The Modern Attack on Tuberculosis* (New York: Commonwealth Fund, 1942), pp. 10–11. Speaking of physicians' unwillingness to register tuberculosis cases, a concerned contemporary of Folks wrote, "The fault lies with the medical profession. . . . they have fought this progress with all their blind bitterness and prejudice; and their prejudice has been, and still is, one of the patent allies of the disease" (Adams, "Real Race Suicide," p. 237).

30. SCAA *Minutes,* May 22, 1908; SCAA *Annual Report* (1908), p. 6.

31. Ch. 351, New York State *Laws of 1908.*

32. Quoted in SCAA *Annual Report* (1908), p. 6.

33. Winslow, *Hermann Biggs,* pp. 209–10; Shryock, *National Tuberculosis Association,* pp. 103–12; Homer Folks, *County Hospitals for Tuberculosis* (New York: SCAA Pub. No. 109, 1909), pp. 1–4.

34. Folks, *County Hospitals,* p. 5.

35. Adams, "Real Race Suicide," p. 236.

36. Philip P. Jacobs, "Memorandum from P. P. Jacobs to P. P. Jacobs," National Tuberculosis Association Archives, New York City; Folks, OHP, pp. 77ff.; SCAA *Minutes,* March 19, 1909; SCAA *Annual Report* (1909), p. 3; Ch. 341, New York State *Laws of 1909.*

37. Folks, *County Hospitals,* pp. 9–10.

38. Folks, OHP, pp. 78–79; SCAA *Annual Report* (1910), p. 2.

39. Shryock, *National Tuberculosis Association,* pp. 107–08, 157.

40. Homer Folks, "Some Adverse Factors in the Tuberculosis Program" (1913), in Folks, *Public Health and Welfare,* pp. 131–37; Adolphus S. Knopf, *A History of the National Tuberculosis Association* (New York: NTA, 1922), p. 351; New York *Times,* Sept. 28, 1913; Chadwick and Pope, *The Modern Attack,* p. 4.

41. Ch. 323, New York State *Laws of 1914;* SCAA *Minutes,* April 17, 1914; Homer Folks, "Origin, Growth and Possible Developments of the Sanatorium Movement in New York State as a Whole," p. 6, address delivered at the annual conference of the State and Local Committees on Tuberculosis and Public Health of the State Charities Aid Association, May 24, 1944, HFC.

42. SCAA *Annual Report* (1917), p. 26; SCAA *Minutes,* May 21, 1917.

43. *S.C.A.A. News,* Feb. 1921, p. 4; SCAA *Annual Report* (1927), pp. 42–45; *S.C.A.A. News,* May 1933, p. 2; June 1933, p. 1.

44. James H. Cassedy, "Muckraking and Medicine: Samuel Hopkins Adams," *American Quarterly,* XVI, No. 1 (Spring 1964), 85–99.

45. Homer Folks, "Public and Private—And Both," *Survey,* LV (Nov. 1, 1925), 137–38; Folks, "A State Aroused," p. 230. In 1911 and 1912, *The Delineator* published a serial by Samuel Hopkins Adams (published in book form the following year), "The Health Master," which aimed to present, in fictional form, the "progressive specialized thought of modern medical science" pertaining to preventive medicine, pointing out to the public the emerging concept that the health officer was and should be a scientist, not merely a political hack or a tracker down of offensive odors.

46. Homer Folks, "Continuity and Growth of the State Department of Health" (1936), in Folks, *Public Health and Welfare,* pp. 312–13; Homer Folks, "The State as Life-Saver: Public Health," third Kennedy Lecture, delivered April 14, 1913, HFC; Folks, OHP, p. 49.

47. For the best account of Governor Sulzer's life see Jacob A. Friedman, *The Impeachment of Governor William Sulzer* (New York: Columbia University Studies in History, No. 444, 1939).

48. *Ibid.,* p. 268; Winslow, *Hermann Biggs,* p. 258; Henry Morganthau, *All in a Lifetime* (New York: Doubleday, Page, 1922), p. 170; Gregory Mason, "William Sulzer and Invisible Government," *Outlook,* CV (Oct. 18, 1913), 356–60.

49. Morganthau, *All in a Lifetime,* p. 163; Folks, "Continuity and Growth," p. 313; Folks, Journal, Dec. 23, 1912, HFC; Folks, OHP, p. 50; Folks, "Continuity and Growth," p. 313.

50. Folks, "Continuity and Growth," p. 314; Folks, OHP, pp. 50ff.; Morganthau, *All in a Lifetime,* p. 163; Winslow, *Hermann Biggs,* p. 252.

51. Interview with George J. Nelbach, Oct. 1, 1962, New York City; *S.C.A.A. News,* Jan. 1913, p. 1.

52. Winslow, *Hermann Biggs,* pp. 252–53; "The Progress of the World," *Review of Reviews,* XLVII (Feb. 1913), 142–43; Folks, Journal, Jan 10, 1913, HFC.

53. Folks, Journal, 1912–1919, Jan. 10, 1913, *HFC; S.C.A.A. News,* Feb.–March, 1913, p. 1.

54. Folks, Journal, Feb. 14–15, 1913, HFC; *Governor Sulzer's Message on Public Health with Report of Special Health Commission, Transmitted to the Legislature February 19, 1913* (Albany: Lyons, 1913), HFC.

55. *Minutes* of the Meetings of the New York State Public Health Council, March 13, 1914, New York State Department of Health, Albany, N.Y. (hereafter cited as PHC *Minutes*). Almost all legislation affecting matters of health in New York State after 1866 were exclusive of New York City.

This was true because since 1866 New York City had an economical and efficient public health department with a good sanitary code headed by a full-time commissioner reasonably free from political influence. See Howard D. Kramer, "Early Municipal and State Boards of Health," *Bulletin of the History of Medicine,* XXIV (Nov.–Dec. 1950), 503–29; Dr. Haven Emerson, "The Reminiscences of Dr. Haven Emerson," OHP, 1950, p. 75. Interview with Dr. Granville Larimore, deputy commissioner New York State Department of Health, Dec. 3, 1962, Albany, N.Y.

56. Interviews with Dr. Granville Larimore, Dec. 3, 1962, Albany, N.Y.; Dr. Hollis S. Ingraham, Commissioner of Health, New York State Department of Health, "Our Common Cause: The Health and Welfare of All," *S.C.A.A. Viewpoint,* XI (Spring 1964), 1.

57. The other six divisions were Sanitary Engineering, Laboratories and Research, Vital Statistics, Communicable Diseases, Publicity, and Education.

58. Winslow, *Hermann Biggs,* p. 253.

59. *S.C.A.A. News,* March 1913, p. 1.

60. Interview with George J. Nelbach, Oct. 1, 1962, New York City.

61. Quoted in *S.C.A.A. News,* Feb.–March 1913, p. 7. Similar excerpts from papers throughout the state are reprinted in this issue of the *News.*

62. Folks, Journal, March 25, 1913, HFC; Ch. 559, New York State *Laws of 1913; S.C.A.A. News,* May 1913, p. 1; Folks, "Continuity and Growth," pp. 313–14.

63. Winslow, *Hermann Biggs,* p. 254.

64. Morganthau, *All in a Lifetime,* p. 164; interviews with Dr. Granville Larimore, Dec. 3, 1962, Albany, N.Y.; George J. Nelbach, Oct. 1, 1962, New York City; Dr. George Baehr, Oct. 5, 1962, New York City.

65. George J. Nelbach to the author, Aug. 16, 1962. He said, "I know that to be the case, for I assisted him daily while both were in preparation."

66. Hermann M. Biggs, "Contribution to Public Health," in *Thirty Years of Service: A Tribute to Homer Folks* (New York: Klebold, 1923), p. 17.

67. PHC *Minutes, passim,* State Department of Health, Albany, N.Y.; interviews with Dr. Granville Larimore, Dec. 3, 1962, Albany, N.Y.; Dr. George Baehr, Oct. 5, 1962, New York City.

68. PHC *Minutes,* Dec. 2, 1913, State Department of Health, Albany, N.Y.

69. *Ibid.,* Sept. 30, Oct. 14, 1913.

70. Interview with Dr. Granville Larimore, Dec. 3, 1962, Albany, N.Y.; Folks, "Continuity and Growth," pp. 314–17.

71. Interview with Dr. Granville Larimore, Dec. 3, 1962, Albany, N.Y.

72. Folks, "Continuity and Growth," p. 317; Winslow, *Hermann Biggs,* p. 277; New York *Times,* April 12, 1915; SCAA *Annual Report* (1915), pp. 8off.

73. *S.C.A.A. News,* April 1915, p. 1.

74. SCAA *Minutes,* April 21, 1915; *S.C.A.A. News,* March 1915, *passim;* April 1915, p. 2.

75. Quoted in *S.C.A.A. News,* March 1915, pp. 7–8. Similar excerpts from newspapers throughout the state can be found in this issue of the *News.*

76. *S.C.C.A. News,* April 1915, p. 3.

77. Folks made this statement in 1936; see "Continuity and Growth," p. 318. This, however, is still true today.

78. Biggs, "Contribution to Public Health," p. 17.

79. Winslow, *Hermann Biggs,* p. 200.

10
AMERICAN RED CROSS

1. Homer Folks, "Some Aspects Toward the Millennium," last Kennedy Lecture, delivered May 5, 1913, at the New York School of Philanthropy, HFC; Homer Folks, "War, Best Friend of Disease," *Harper's Magazine,* CXL (March 1920), 457; Homer Folks, "What We Have Learned Since 1889" (1934), in Homer Folks, *Public Health and Welfare: The Citizens' Responsibility—Selected Papers of Homer Folks,* ed. Savel Zimand (New York: Macmillan, 1958), pp. 302–10.

2. Folks, "What We Have Learned," p. 303; Folks, "War, Best Friend of Disease," p. 457; Homer Folks, "Civilization's Indictment of War," *Harper's Magazine,* CXL (Dec. 1919), 68. Also see John Haynes Holmes, "War and the Social Movement," *Survey* (Sept. 26, 1914), pp. 629–30.

3. *Minutes* of the Meetings of the Board of Managers of the New York State Charities Aid Association, New York City, March 25, April 18, 1917 (hereafter cited as SCAA *Minutes*); *S.C.A.A. News,* April 1917, p. 8.

4. *S.C.A.A. News,* June 1917, p. 6.

5. Richard H. Shryock, *National Tuberculosis Association, 1904–1954* (New York: NTA, 1957), p. 180. For the best account of American benevolence abroad during World War I see Merle Curti, *American Philanthropy Abroad: A History* (New Brunswick; N.J.: Rutgers University, 1963), Ch. 9, "The Great War," pp. 224–58.

6. G. R. Gaeddert, "The American National Red Cross in World War I, 1917–1918," *American Red Cross Monographs* (Washington: American

National Red Cross, 1950), IV, p. 393; Charles Hurd, *The Compact History of the American Red Cross* (New York: Hawthorn, 1959), p. 144.

7. Homer Folks, Journal, May 22, 1917, HFC; unsigned letter from the American Red Cross War Council to the United States State Department, June 16, 1917, American National Red Cross, Office of Research Information, Washington, D.C. (hereafter cited as ARC).

8. Editorial, *The Survey,* XXXVIII (July 1917), 353.

9. Mrs. Lawrence M. Orton to the author, April 13, 1964; Mrs. Savel Zimand to the author, Feb. 24, 1965.

10. Homer Folks to Evelyn Folks (his daughter), July 29, 1917. This and all subsequent letters cited in this chapter written by Folks from abroad, were in the possession of the late Mrs. Savel Zimand (Folks's daughter Gertrude), who worked in France during that period. The author is indebted to her for allowing him to quote them.

11. Actually great national crises have often sustained and refreshed reform impulses. Although such benefits certainly do not justify the enormous costs of war, within limits war has at times actually contributed to human betterment, especially in the fields of medical care, science, and public health. See Dr. Wilson G. Smillie, *Public Health: Its Promise for the Future* (New York: Macmillan, 1955), p. 277.

12. Homer Folks, *An International Adventure: What the American Red Cross is Doing for the Civilians of France, July 1917–May 1918* (Paris: American Red Cross, 1918), Introduction; Homer Folks to Evelyn Folks, July 29, 1917.

13. Foster Rhea Dulles, *The American Red Cross: A History* (New York: Harper, 1950), p. 175; Henry P. Davison, *The American Red Cross in the Great War* (New York: Macmillan, 1920), pp. 152–53; Homer Folks, "Report of the Director of the Department of Civil Affairs, American Red Cross in France," June 30, 1918, *passim,* ARC (hereafter cited as "Report").

14. Homer Folks to Evelyn Folks, July 29, 1917.

15. Homer Folks, "Six Months Report of the Director: Department of Civil Affairs: American Red Cross in France," Jan. 1918, p. 4, ARC.

16. Homer Folks to Maud Folks (his wife), Aug. 19, Aug. 26, Sept. 26, 1917; Ernest P. Bicknell, *With the Red Cross in Europe, 1917–1922* (Washington: American National Red Cross, 1938), p. 24; Dulles, *American Red Cross,* pp. 175–76.

17. Homer Folks to Maud Folks, Sept. 26, 1917.

18. Homer Folks to Maud Folks, Nov. 5, 1917.

19. Homer Folks to Maud Folks, Aug. 26, 1917.

20. Homer Folks to Maud Folks, Sept. 9, 1917.

21. Folks, *An International Adventure,* p. 26.

22. Folks, "Report," June 30, 1918, ARC.

23. *S.C.A.A. News,* Oct. 1917, p. 1; Gaeddert, "American Red Cross in World War I," p. 397.

24. Homer Folks, "The Call of the Perishing: An Account of Conditions Among Serbian Refugees in France and the Means of Relieving Them," Aug. 1, 1918, ARC.

25. Homer Folks, "Livingston Farrand: Work for Tuberculosis Control in France, 1917–1919," in *Memoriam, Livingston Farrand* (New York: Academy of Medicine, 1940), pp. 15–17; C. E. A. Winslow, *The Life of Hermann M. Biggs* (Philadelphia: Lea and Febiger, 1929), p. 310.

26. Hurd, *The Compact History,* p. 167; Gaeddert, "American Red Cross in World War I," p. 403; Davison, *American Red Cross in the Great War,* p. 157.

27. Quoted in Davison, p. 162.

28. Folks, *An International Adventure,* p. 17; Dulles, *American Red Cross,* p. 176.

29. Homer Folks to Maud Folks, Sept. 26, 1917; *S.C.A.A. News,* Nov. 1917, p. 1.

30. Homer Folks, "Remarks at the Opening of the Baby-Saving Show at Lyons, France," April 9, 1918, HFC; Davison, *American Red Cross in the Great War,* p. 171; Dulles, *American Red Cross,* p. 176.

31. Davison, *American Red Cross in the Great War,* p. 162.

32. Homer Folks to Maud Folks, Oct. 17, 1917; Homer Folks to Louisa Lee Schuyler, Nov. 15, 1917, HFC.

33. SCAA *Minutes,* Dec. 19, 1917; Homer Folks to Maud Folks, Oct. 30, 1917.

34. *S.C.A.A. News,* Oct. 1918, p. 2.

35. *Proceedings of the National Conference of Social Work* (Kansas City: NCSW, 1918), p. 648.

36. Hurd, *The Compact History,* p. 163; Dulles, *American Red Cross,* pp. 154, 177.

37. Hurd, *The Compact History,* p. 164.

38. Homer Folks to Henry P. Davison, Nov. 11, 1918, ARC.

39. *S.C.A.A. News,* Dec. 1918, p. 1; *American National Red Cross Bulletin,* Nov. 2, 1918, May 31, 1919, ARC; Robert E. Olds to Homer Folks, June 3, 1919, ARC.

40. Folks, "What We Have Learned Since 1889," p. 304.

41. Homer Folks to Dr. Hermann M. Biggs, Oct. 30, 1918, HFC.

42. *S.C.A.A. News,* March 1919, p. 4.

43. Homer Folks, *Journal of World War I Survey Mission, passim,* HFC.

44. Homer Folks to Maud Folks, Nov. 23, 1918.

45. Homer Folks to Maud Folks, Dec. 9, 1918.

46. Homer Folks, "The Human Costs of the War" (1919), in Folks, *Public Health and Welfare,* pp. 184–97; also see Homer Folks, *The Human Costs of the War* (New York: Harper, 1920), pp. 196–97; Folks, "Civilization's Indictment of War," p. 75; New York *Times,* June 19, 1919; Homer Folks, "Experiences Abroad, Showing the Relationship Between Tuberculosis and a General Health Program," *Proceedings of the National Tuberculosis Association* (New York: NTA, 1919), pp. 61–66; Dulles, *American Red Cross,* pp. 202–4.

47. Folks, "Experience Abroad," *passim.*

48. Hurd, *The Compact History,* pp. 172–73; Dulles, *American Red Cross,* pp. 195–98; Curti, *American Philanthropy,* Ch. 10, "The Aftermath," pp. 259–300.

49. New York *Times,* June 1, 1919; *S.C.A.A. News,* Nov. 1919, p. 1; Folks, "Civilization's Indictment of War," p. 26; Folks, "War, Best Friend of Disease," pp. 458–59; Folks, Journal, Sept. 22, 1919, HFC; Homer Folks to the Bureau of Personnel, American National Red Cross, April 26, 1919, ARC; Folks, *The Human Costs of the War,* p. 230; Homer Folks to Louisa Lee Schuyler, July 10, 1924, HFC.

50. Folks, *The Human Costs of the War; The Survey,* XLIV (June 22, 1920), 449.

51. *The Nation,* XI (Oct. 13, 1920), 411.

52. New York *Times Book Review,* XXV (July 25, 1920), 12.

53. Charles N. Arbuckle, minister, First Baptist Church, Newton Center, Mass., to Homer Folks, Dec. 15, 1920, HFC; interview with Philip Nelbach, executive secretary, National Citizens Committee for the World Health Organization, Inc., Oct. 1, 1962, New York City.

54. Hurd, *The Compact History,* pp. 163ff.; Marian B. Clausen, "The American Red Cross in Peace, 1919–1939," *American Red Cross Monographs* (Washington: American National Red Cross, 1950), V, Preface, pp. i, ii.

55. Dulles, *American Red Cross,* pp. 196, 217.

56. SCAA *Minutes,* Dec. 17, 1920; Homer Folks to Louisa Lee Schuyler, Nov. 8, 1920, HFC.

57. *Ibid.;* New York State Charities Aid Association *Annual Report* (1921), p. 31; Livingston Farrand to Homer Folks, Feb. 2, 1921, ARC.

58. Homer Folks to Livingston Farrand, Feb. 21, June 1, 1921, ARC; *S.C.A.A. News,* March 1921, p. 1; Folks, Journal, Feb. 3, 1921, HFC.

59. Kendall Emerson to Livingston Farrand, Feb. 26, 1921, ARC; Dulles, *American Red Cross,* p. 208.

60. Interview with Mr. Clyde E. Buckingham, director, Office of Re-

search Information, American National Red Cross, Washington, D.C., Dec. 17, 1962.

61. *Ibid.;* Kendall Emerson to Livingston Farrand, June 1, 1921, ARC.

62. Kendall Emerson to Livingston Farrand, June 2, 1921, ARC; Homer Folks to Livingston Farrand, July 5, 1921, Livingston Farrand Papers, Cornell University, Ithaca, N.Y.

63. Dulles, *American Red Cross,* p. 205.

64. Hurd, *The Compact History,* p. 180.

65. American National Red Cross *Bulletin of the Insular and Foreign Division, 15th Division,* II, No. 12 (Dec. 1919), 4, ARC.

66. Curtis E. Lehman, assistant chairman of the Central Committee, to Homer Folks, Sept. 5, 1919, ARC.

67. Homer Folks to Livingston Farrand, Oct. 21, 1919, ARC; SCAA *Minutes,* Oct. 29, 1919.

68. Mrs. William K. Draper, vice-chairman, New York County Chapter, American Red Cross, to members of the Executive Committee, Nov. 7, 1919, ARC.

69. SCAA *Minutes,* Nov. 17, 1919.

70. American National Red Cross, *Bulletin,* p. 4; Dulles, *American Red Cross,* pp. 219–20.

71. Homer Folks, "The First Years of Health Service," Atlantic Division, American National Red Cross, p. 1, ARC.

72. Selskar M. Gunn and Philip S. Platt, *Voluntary Health Agencies* (New York: Ronald, 1945), p. 249.

73. Homer Folks, "Bailey Burritt and Public Health," in *Better Times Health Issue in Honor of Bailey B. Burritt,* XXVI, No. 7 (Nov. 3, 1944), 9.

74. Homer Folk, "The East Harlem Health Center," *Hospital Social Service,* XVIII (1928), 204.

75. East Harlem Health Center Stationery Letterhead, HFC. Dr. Shirley W. Wynne was honorary chairman of the Center; Dr. James Alexander Miller, chairman; Folks, chairman of the Executive Committee; Bailey B. Burritt, chairman of the Council; and Kenneth D. Widdemer, chief executive officer.

76. At the Center the City Health Department maintained the tuberculosis, general, eye, and baby clinics. Among the other cooperating agencies were the American Social Hygiene Association, Association for the Prevention and Relief of Heart Disease, New York Committee on Dispensary Development, New York Mental Hygiene Committee, Henry Street Visiting Nurse Service, Maternity Center Association, New York Diet Kitchen Association, Babies Dairy Association, Catholic Charities, Charity Organi-

zation Society, and United Hebrew Charities. See New York *Times,* July 20, 1924; Folks, "East Harlem Health Center," p. 204.

77. Homer Folks, "Ten Years at East Harlem," remarks at the tenth anniversary celebration of East Harlem Health Center, Jan. 19, 1933, HFC.

78. New York *Times,* March 5, 1928.

79. Folks, "Bailey B. Burritt and Public Health," pp. 9–11.

80. New York City is now divided into thirty health districts, each one having its own center.

81. Dulles, *American Red Cross,* pp. 225, 230–31, 244.

II
MORE PUBLIC HEALTH

1. Domenico Gagliardo, *American Social Insurance* (New York: Harper, 1949), pp. 455–56; Clarke A. Chambers, *Seedtime of Reform: American Social Service and Social Action, 1918–1933* (Minneapolis: University of Minnesota, 1963), p. 157. It was in Germany that broad national programs of health insurance and industrial accident insurance were first inaugurated around 1883–1884. See Hans Rothfels, "Bismarck's Social Policy and the Problem of State Socialism in Germany," *Sociological Review,* XXX, (1938), 288–302.

2. Edward T. Devine, "The Outlook for the Future on Poverty and Disease," *Proceedings of the National Conference of Social Work* (Atlantic City: NCSW, 1919), pp. 173–77 (hereafter cited as *Proc. of NCSW*). Also see C. E. A. Winslow, "Poverty as a Factor in Disease," *ibid.,* pp. 153–56; Owen Lovejoy, "A War Program for Peace," *ibid.,* pp. 664–65; David M. Schneider and Albert Deutsch, *The History of Public Welfare in New York State, 1867–1940* (Chicago: University of Chicago, 1941), pp. 242–43.

3. Milton Terris, "Hermann Biggs' Contribution to the Modern Concept of the Health Center," *Bulletin of the History of Medicine,* XX, No. 3 (Oct. 1946), 393; Schneider and Deutsch, *History of Public Welfare,* p. 243; Chambers, *Seedtime of Reform,* p. 157; Abraham Epstein, *Insecurity: A Challenge to America* (New York: Smith and Haas, 1933), pp. 447–56; Barbara N. Armstrong, *Insuring the Essentials* (New York: Macmillan, 1932), p. 372.

4. *Minutes* of the Meetings of the Board of Managers of the New York State Charities Aid Association, New York City, Oct. 29, Nov. 19, 1919 (hereafter cited as SCAA *Minutes*).

5. SCAA *Minutes,* Feb. 18, 1920.

6. Homer Folks to Grace Abbott, Sept. 28, 1934, Grace Abbott Papers,

University of Chicago Library, Chicago, Ill.; Homer Folks, "Public Health vs. Public Welfare" (1937), in Homer Folks, *Public Health and Welfare: The Citizens' Responsibility—Selected Papers of Homer Folks,* ed. Savel Zimand (New York: Macmillan, 1958), pp. 351–62; Homer Folks, "Health is Social Security" (1943), *ibid.,* pp. 429–38; Homer Folks, "What Kind of Social Security?," in *S.C.A.A. News,* April 1943, pp. 1ff.; interview with Mr. and Mrs. Savel Zimand, Oct. 25, 1962, New York City.

7. Homer Folks, *The Distribution of the Costs of Sickness in the United States: The Burden of the Costs of Sickness and Who Bears It* (New York: SCAA Pub. No. 187, 1928).

8. SCAA *Minutes,* Dec. 21, 1928; *S.C.A.A. News,* Jan. 1929, p. 8.

9. Folks, *The Costs of Sickness,* pp. 26–27; New York *Times,* July 12, 1928.

10. Folks, *The Costs of Sickness,* p. 37.

11. I. S. Falk, Committee on the Costs of Medical Care, *Medical Care for the American People* (Chicago: University of Chicago, 1933); The President's Research Committee on Social Trends, *Recent Trends in the United States* (Washington: Government Printing Office, 1933), p. lvi; Haven Emerson, "Medical Care for All of Us: The Committee on the Costs of Medical Care Reports," *Survey,* LXVIII (Dec. 1, 1932), 629–32; Epstein, *Insecurity,* pp. 408–14.

12. *S.C.A.A. News,* April 1920, p. 3; May 1920, p. 5.

13. *Ibid.,* April 1920, p. 1; Terris, "Biggs' Contribution," pp. 394, 402–12; James H. Cassedy, *Charles V. Chapin and the Public Health Movement* (Cambridge: Harvard University, 1962), p. 178; C. E.A. Winslow, *The Life of Hermann M. Biggs* (Philadelphia: Lea and Febiger, 1929), pp. 348ff.

14. New York *Times,* March 26, 1920; SCAA *Minutes,* March 26, 1920.

15. Homer Folks to Dr. C. E. A. Winslow, April 3, 1920. (The author is indebted to Mrs. C. E. A. Winslow for allowing him to see the correspondence in her possession between Dr. Winslow and Folks. All correspondence between the two, unless otherwise noted, is in her possession.) Homer Folks to Dr. William H. Welch, April 3, 7, 1920, Welch Papers, Welch Memorial Library, Johns Hopkins University, Baltimore (hereafter cited as WHW).

16. Dr. C. E. A. Winslow to Homer Folks, March 23, 1931; *S.C.A.A. News,* May 1920, p. 6; Winslow, *Hermann Biggs,* p. 352.

17. Homer Folks to Louisa Lee Schuyler, April 15, 1920, HFC.

18. Terris, "Biggs' Contribution," p. 399; *S.C.A.A. News,* May 1921, p. 5.

19. Hermann M. Biggs, "Some Comments on the Purpose of the Pro-

posed (Sage) Health Center Bill (1920) and Some Reasons for Its Enactment," HFC; Terris, "Biggs' Contribution," pp. 400ff.; Winslow, *Hermann Biggs*, pp. 348–52.

20. *S.C.A.A. News*, May 1921, p. 5; Ch. 509, New York State *Laws of 1921*; SCAA *Annual Report* (1921), p. 20; Winslow, *Hermann Biggs*, p. 355; Homer Folks, "The County Health Unit: With Special Reference to Cattaraugus County," in *The New York State Department of Health Quarterly*, Oct. 1924, p. 102.

21. Ch. 662, New York State *Laws of 1923*; SCAA *Minutes*, Feb. 28, 1923.

22. Homer Folks to Louisa Lee Schuyler, May 11, 1923, HFC.

23. Dr. C. E. A. Winslow to Homer Folks, March 26, 1931.

24. See, for example, Richard Hofstadter, who in *The Age of Reform* (New York: Knopf, 1956), p. 273, states, "Participation in the war put an end to the Progressive movement."

25. C. E. A. Winslow, *Health on the Farm and in the Village* (New York: Macmillan, 1931), p. 37; John M. Glenn, Lilian Brandt, and F. Emerson Andrews, *Russell Sage Foundation* (2 vols., New York: Russell Sage Foundation, 1947), I, 13, fn.

26. Richard H. Shryock, *National Tuberculosis Association, 1904–1954* (New York: NTA, 1957), pp. 159, 167–70; *S.C.A.A. News*, Oct. 1924, p. 5; Dr. Donald Budd Armstrong to the author, Aug. 20, 1962.

27. SCAA *Minutes*, Nov. 18, 1921.

28. Homer Folks, "Bailey Burritt and Public Health," *Better Times*, XXVI, No. 7 (Nov. 3, 1944), 9–11; SCAA *Minutes*, April 21, May 23, 1921; *S.C.A.A. News*, June 1922, p. 1; Homer Folks, "What I Have Learned from the Health Demonstrations," HFC.

29. Interviews with George J. Nelbach, Oct. 1, 1962, New York City; Dr. George Baehr, Oct. 5, 1962, New York City; John A. Kingsbury, "Milbank Memorial Fund Demonstrations," *Proc. of NCSW* (Washington, 1923), pp. 48–49. According to Dr. Herman G. Weiskotten, former dean of Syracuse University Medical School and Syracuse Health Commissioner, "Were it not for [Folks's] . . . patience and personal diplomacy, the Milbank Memorial Fund Demonstration in Syracuse would never have succeeded. Early failures in [the] . . . proposed program never discouraged him. He merely sought out the obstacles to success and planned means of overcoming them" (Dr. Herman G. Weiskotten to the author, Sept. 10, 1962).

30. *S.C.A.A. News*, Feb. 1923, p. 1; SCAA *Annual Report* (1922), pp. 21–22; Winslow, *Health on the Farm*, pp. 39, 236.

31. *S.C.A.A. News*, July 1926, pp. 3–4.

32. *S.C.A.A. News*, Dec. 1926, p. 9.

33. *Ibid.* 34. *S.C.A.A. News,* April 1929, p. 6.

35. Winslow, *Health on the Farm* (Cattaraugus County Demonstration); C. E. A. Winslow, *A City on a Hill* (New York: Donan, 1934) (Syracuse Demonstration); and C. E. A. Winslow and Savel Zimand, *Health Under the "El"* (New York: Harper, 1937) (Belleville-Yorkville Demonstration).

36. Folks, "What I Have Learned," *passim*; Homer Folks, *The Organization of the Syracuse and Cattaraugus County Health Demonstrations* (New York: SCAA Pub. No. 170, 1925).

37. Winslow, *Health on the Farm,* pp. 17–19, 224; *City on a Hill,* p. 358; Winslow and Zimand, *Under the "El,"* pp. 183–85; Folks, "What I Have Learned," p. 11; *S.C.A.A. News,* Dec. 1928, p. 2.

38. Winslow and Zimand, *Under the "El,"* p. 196; Winslow, *Health on the Farm,* pp. 22–23; Winslow, *City on a Hill,* Foreword, p. ix.

39. Homer Folks, "Health and Welfare" (1925), in Folks, *Public Health and Welfare,* pp. 217–32.

40. Homer Folks, "Tuberculosis: Going But Not Gone Yet," *Review of Reviews,* LXXV (Feb. 1927), 197–99; New York *Times,* Jan. 25, 1925; Folks, "Health and Welfare," p. 223; Homer Folks, "The Next Ten Years," address delivered in Syracuse, N.Y., June 1, 1927, HFC.

41. Homer Folks, "A Modern Public Health Program," address delivered before the Pennsylvania Tuberculosis Society, Jan. 20, 1937, HFC; Homer Folks, "Next Steps in Public Health," in *The Government of the City of New York* (New York: Constitutional Convention Commission, 1915), pp. 50–53.

42. New York *Times,* May 9, 1925; *S.C.A.A. News,* Jan. 1926, p. 4.

43. SCAA *Annual Report* (1927), p. 48; (1931), p. 25; Lee K. Frankel, *The Five Year Diphtheria Campaign* (New York: SCAA, 1931).

44. *S.C.A.A. News,* Feb. 1941, p. 3. By 1945 there were only two deaths from diphtheria in New York State (outside New York City). The death rate was 0.03 (quoted in *S.C.A.A. News,* May 1941, p. 2).

45. Homer Folks, "The Next To Go," address delivered to the Westchester County Tuberculosis and Public Health Association of the SCAA, April 10, 1934, HFC.

46. Homer Folks, "The Millennium—Why Not?," *Progress,* II, No. 2 (Feb. 1913), 33–36.

47. Folks, "The Next to Go," *passim;* SCAA *Minutes,* Jan. 21, 1932; *S.C.A.A. News,* Feb. 1932, p. 1. In 1933 there were 68,000 cases of syphilis reported as compared to only 17,500 cases of tuberculosis.

48. Homer Folks, "Citizens Support in Syphilis Control" (1936), in Folks, *Public Health and Welfare,* pp. 327–36.

49. SCAA *Annual Report* (1938), p. 14; *S.C.A.A. News,* Jan. 1938, p. 1.

50. *S.C.A.A. News,* March 1938, p. 4; Homer Folks, "The Administration of Public Health," (1944), HFC; SCAA *Annual Report* (1942), p. 1.

51. Homer Folks to Governor Alfred E. Smith, Feb. 14, 15, 1927, Alfred E. Smith Papers, New York State Library, Albany, N.Y.; *S.C.A.A. News,* April 1927, p. 3.

52. Interview with Dr. James E. Perkins, Oct. 1, 1962, New York City.

53. Governor Franklin D. Roosevelt to Homer Folks, April 15, 1930; Folks to Roosevelt, April 23, 1930, Franklin D. Roosevelt Papers, Roosevelt Library, Hyde Park, N.Y. (hereafter cited as FDR); *S.C.A.A. News,* May 1930, p. 16; SCAA *Annual Report* (1930), p. 39.

54. *S.C.A.A. News,* March 1931, *passim;* Homer Folks, "Organizing for Health," radio address over station WEAF, New York City, Oct. 10, 1932, HFC; *Public Health in New York State,* Report of the New York State Health Commission (Albany: State Department of Health, 1931); Homer Folks, "The Reminiscences of Homer Folks," Oral History Project (Columbia University, 1949), pp. 83–84. The commission submitted its final report in the spring of 1932. See *S.C.A.A. News,* April 1932, p. 1.

55. *S.C.A.A. News,* March 1931, p. 8.

56. Homer Folks to Dr. C. E. A. Winslow, Feb. 24, 1931.

57. Dr. C. E. A. Winslow to Homer Folks, March 3, 1931.

58. *S.C.A.A. News,* April 1931, p. 1; Dr. James Quinlivan to the author, July 23, 1963. Dr. Quinlivan wrote: "New York State [still] does not have any legislation making county health departments mandatory. . . . As yet the opportune moment for introducing this legislation has not arrived, so it is nothing more than a hope at this time. There are now 21 county health departments in New York State." Also see Dr. Haven Emerson, *Local Health Units for the Nation* (New York: Commonwealth Fund, 1945), pp. 204–14.

59. Dr. Thomas Parran, Jr., to Governor Herbert H. Lehman, Dec. 11, 1935, HFC.

60. Ch. 753, New York State *Laws of 1936;* interview with Governor Herbert H. Lehman, Dec. 11, 1962, New York City; New York *Herald Tribune,* New York *Times,* May 29, 1936; *S.C.A.A. News,* June 1936, p. 1.

61. There is an entire scrapbook of congratulatory messages in the HFC.

62. New York *Times,* New York *Herald Tribune,* New York *Evening Post,* July 10, 1936; Homer Folks, Journal, July 9, 1936, HFC.

63. Homer Folks, "Response at the Dedication of the Homer Folks

Tuberculosis Hospital" (1936), in Folks, *Public Health and Welfare,* pp. 322–24.

64. *Minutes* of the Board of Directors of the National Tuberculosis Association, Executive Committee, Jan. 8, 1916, National Tuberculosis Association Archives, New York City (hereafter cited as *NTA Minutes*); Shryock, *National Tuberculosis Association,* p. 174.

65. Homer Folks, "Interstate Factors in the Tuberculosis Problem," *Proceedings of the National Tuberculosis Association* (1916), pp. 305–11; *S.C.A.A. News,* May 1916, p. 3.

66. See, for example, Dr. Reginald Atwater to Homer Folks, Feb. 1, 1938; Dr. George Baehr to Homer Folks, Feb. 5, 1938; Dr. Thomas Parran to Homer Folks, Feb. 7, 1938; Dr. Frank G. Boudreau to Homer Folks, Feb. 2, 1938; Dr. Kendall Emerson to Homer Folks, Feb. 3, 1938, HFC.

67. Homer Folks, "An Outline of a Suggested Nation-Wide Federal, State, Local, Program to Prevent Tuberculosis," HFC; *S.C.A.A. News,* June 1938, p. 1.

68. *NTA Minutes,* Feb. 11, 1939; SCAA *Annual Report* (1939), p. 20.

69. New York *Times,* June 21, 1938; *NTA Minutes,* June 22, 1938.

70. Gagliardo, *American Social Insurance,* pp. 460ff.; Frank J. Bruno, *Trends in Social Work, 1874–1956* (New York: Columbia University, 1957), p. 313.

71. *S.C.A.A. News,* June 1944, p. 1; Sept. 1944, p. 1.

72. Homer Folks to John A. Kingsbury, June 6, 1930, HFC. The last two laws Folks helped draft became effective in New York State on Jan. 1, 1947. One of the measures authorized a new statewide program for the eradication of tuberculosis and the expansion and improvement of city and county health departments. The other removed the "means test" from the county and state tuberculosis hospital laws. Thereafter, tuberculosis care was based entirely on need for services; the ability to care for all finally became the goal of New York's anti-tuberculosis program. See SCAA *Minutes,* Feb. 8, April 12, 1946; *S.C.A.A. News,* April 1946, p. 4; Jan. 1947, p. 1.

73. SCAA *Annual Report* (1946), pp. 7–8.

74. To reflect a wider concern with all lung-damaging ailments, after several decades as the State Committee on Tuberculosis and Public Health, in 1963 the fifty-six-year-old committee changed its name to the New York State Tuberculosis and Respiratory Disease Association, Inc. In addition to a wider program in the field of chronic respiratory disease—such as chronic bronchitis and emphysema—increasing emphasis was put on the eradication rather than the control of tuberculosis, through optimum treatment, largely through chemotherapy.

75. According to Dr. C. E. A. Winslow, "When we pay tribute to the

State of New York for its unquestioned leadership in public health . . . on this Continent, we are really paying tribute to the State Charities Aid Association and to Homer Folks, the greatest statesman in public welfare in our generation." See "Buttressing Democracy by Citizen Service," in *S.C.A.A. News,* May 1942, pp. 12–13. In 1951 Folks was elected an Honorary Fellow of the New York Academy of Medicine. A year later the New York State Public Health Association presented him with its first annual Hermann M. Biggs Memorial Award. To fill the need for a special tribute to those who made valuable contributions outside the scientific field, in 1952 the National Tuberculosis Association established the Will Ross Medal, and Homer Folks was selected as the first recipient of that honor.

12
SOCIAL SECURITY

1. Clarke A. Chambers, "Creative Effort in an Age of Normalcy, 1918–1933," in *The Social Welfare Forum* (New York: Columbia University, 1961), p. 253. For a fuller treatment of the subject by the same author see *Seedtime of Reform: American Social Service and Social Action, 1918–1933* (Minneapolis: University of Minnesota, 1963). While talking about reformers in general, rather than merely social workers, Arthur S. Link made this same point several years before Chambers. See "What Happened to the Progressive Movement in the 1920s?," *American Historical Review,* LXIV, No. 4 (July 1959), 833–51. Also see Nathan Edward Cohen, *Social Work in the American Tradition* (New York: Dryden, 1958), pp. 138, 154; Frank J. Bruno, *Trends in Social Work, 1874–1956* (New York: Columbia University, 1957), pp. 297–300.

2. Homer Folks, "Our Duty to the Children of Europe," *Proceedings of the National Conference of Social Work* (Milwaukee: NCSW, 1921), p. 77 (hereafter cited as *Proc. of NCSW*). Folks pointed to the fact that voluntary benevolent associations such as the American Public Health Association, the National Conference, the New York State Charities Aid Association, the American Prison Association, and others were organized shortly after a period of apathy in post Civil War America.

3. Homer Folks, "Some Thoughts on a Seventieth Birthday" (1937), in Homer Folks, *Public Health and Welfare: The Citizens' Responsibility—Selected Papers of Homer Folks,* ed. Savel Zimand (New York: Macmillan, 1958), p. 343; interview with Miss Katharine Ecob, Oct. 15, 1962, New York City.

4. Homer Folks, "Prevention Succeeds," presidential address before the National Conference of Social Work, Washington, D.C., May 1923, in

Folks, *Public Health and Welfare*, p. 220; *S.C.A.A. News*, July 1922, p. 4; New York *Times*, June 29, 1922.

5. Homer Folks, "Teamwork in Social Welfare," address delivered before the New York State Conference of Social Work, Troy, N.Y., Nov. 16, 1927, HFC.

6. Homer Folks, "Social Engineering," address delivered before the Council of Social Agencies, Ithaca, N.Y. Nov. 7, 1928, HFC.

7. *Ibid.*

8. Homer Folks, "What the State Charities Aid Association Is," extracts of an address delivered at the 1909 annual meeting of the SCAA, HFC; "The State Charities Aid Association as a Health Agency," address delivered in Rochester, N.Y., Nov. 24, 1922, HFC; "Abstract of an Address by Homer Folks at the 1925 S.C.A.A. Annual Meeting," HFC.

9. Folks, "Social Engineering," *passim;* Chambers, "Creative Effort," pp. 266–67; Graham Taylor to Homer Folks, March 17, 1937, HFC. Tenement house reformers also thought of themselves as social engineers. See Roy Lubove, *The Progressives and the Slums: Tenement House Reform in New York City, 1890–1917* (Pittsburgh: University of Pittsburgh, 1962), *passim.*

10. *S.C.A.A. News,* Dec. 1925, p. 11; New York State Charities Aid Association *Annual Report* (1926), p. 34 (hereafter cited as SCAA *Annual Report*); *Minutes* of the Meetings of the Board of Managers of the New York State Charities Aid Association, New York City, Feb. 19, 1926 (hereafter cited as SCAA *Minutes*).

11. *S.C.A.A. News,* March 1927, p. 2; Feb. 1928, pp. 1–2; April 1928, pp. 3–6; Feb. 1929, p. 1; March 1929, pp. 6–7; SCAA *Minutes,* Jan. 31, 1928; John M. Glenn, Lilian Brandt, and F. Emerson Andrews, *Russell Sage Foundation* (2 vols., New York: Russell Sage Foundation, 1947), II, 455.

12. Quoted in *S.C.A.A. News,* May 1929, p. 1; Judge Peter Cantline to the author, Oct. 15, 1962; New York *Times,* Feb. 23, 1928; Homer Folks, "1930 Annual Meeting," HFC.

13. David M. Schneider and Albert Deutsch, *The History of Public Welfare in New York State, 1867–1940* (Chicago: University of Chicago, 1941), pp. 286–87.

14. Ch. 565, New York State *Laws of 1929; S.C.A.A. News,* July 1929, p. 4.

15. Homer Folks, "The Next Step in Welfare Legislation," address delivered in New York, Jan. 16, 1929, HFC.

16. Abraham Epstein, *Insecurity: A Challenge to America* (New York: Smith and Haas, 1933), pp. 532–33; Chambers, *Seedtime of Reform,* pp. 163–67.

17. Schneider and Deutsch, *History of Public Welfare,* p. 345. Actually, an old age pension bill had been drawn up and introduced in the legislature in 1927, but it failed in that and the following session.

18. SCAA *Minutes,* Nov. 15, 1929; Folks, "1930 Annual Meeting," HFC (italics mine).

19. Folks, "1930 Annual Meeting"; *S.C.A.A. News,* Feb. 1930, p. 5.

20. Ch. 38, New York State *Laws of 1930; S.C.A.A. News,* Dec. 1929, p. 7; Schneider and Deutsch, *History of Public Welfare,* pp. 346–49.

21. That same year Arkansas and Massachusetts also passed laws setting no maximum pensions.

22. *S.C.A.A. News,* March 1930, p. 3; SCAA *Minutes,* Feb. 21, 1930.

23. New York *Times,* Dec. 22, 1930; New York *Sun,* Dec. 23, 1930; Schneider and Deutsch, *History of Public Welfare,* p. 346.

24. Folks, "Prevention Succeeds," p. 207.

25. Interview with Mr. Stanley P. Davies, Oct. 17, 1962, White Plains, N.Y.

26. New York *Times,* Nov. 10, 1930.

27. Schneider and Deutsch, *History of Public Welfare,* pp. 297, 302–03; *S.C.A.A. News,* Dec. 1930, p. 1.

28. Homer Folks to Governor Franklin D. Roosevelt, Dec. 2, 1930, Franklin D. Roosevelt Papers, Roosevelt Library, Hyde Park, N.Y. (hereafter cited as FDR); SCAA *Minutes,* Dec. 13, 1930; *S.C.A.A. News,* Dec. 1930, p. 1.

29. *S.C.A.A. News,* Feb. 1931, p. 1; SCAA *Annual Report* (1931), pp. 13–14; SCAA *Minutes,* Dec. 13, 1930; *S.C.A.A. News,* March 1931, p. 3; *Work Relief: A Memorandum on Work as a Means of Providing Unemployment Relief* (New York: Joint Committee of the State Board of Social Welfare and the State Charities Aid Association, 1931); Schneider and Deutsch, *History of Public Welfare,* p. 305.

30. Homer Folks to Franklin D. Roosevelt, Feb. 19, 1931, FDR.

31. New York *Times,* Feb. 20, 1931; Homer Folks, "Remarks on an Adequate Program for a State and Local Public Welfare Administration," address delivered before the Connecticut Conference on Social Welfare, April 28, 1931, HFC.

32. See *S.C.A.A. News,* Aug. 1931, p. 1; SCAA *Annual Report* (1931), p. 15; Bernard Bellush, "Apprenticeship for the Presidency: Franklin D. Roosevelt as Governor of New York" (Ph.D. dissertation, Columbia University, 1950), p. ix (italics mine).

33. Quoted in Schneider and Deutsch, *History of Public Welfare,* p. 307; SCAA *Annual Report* (1931), p. 16.

34. Ch. 798, New York State *Laws of 1931*; Bruno, *Trends in Social Work*, pp. 302–03; Schneider and Deutsch, *History of Public Welfare*, p. 310; Frank Freidel, *Franklin D. Roosevelt: The Triumph* (Boston: Little, Brown, 1956), p. 221.

35. Schneider and Deutsch, *History of Public Welfare*, pp. 308–09, 311. Whether Folks was instrumental in Hopkins' appointment to TERA has not been ascertained. The possibility, however, is a very real one since Roosevelt did confer with Folks on this matter. Arthur P. Miles, *An Introduction to Public Welfare* (Boston: Heath, 1949), p. 215; Freidel, *Franklin D. Roosevelt*, p. 221.

36. *S.C.A.A. News*, Dec. 1931, p. 1.

37. Homer Folks to Franklin D. Roosevelt, Jan. 21, 1932, FDR; SCAA *Annual Report* (1932), p. 12.

38. Homer Folks to Franklin D. Roosevelt, Jan. 21, Feb. 2, 1932, FDR; *S.C.A.A. News*, Jan. 1932, p. 1; SCAA *Minutes*, Jan. 21, 1932.

39. Franklin D. Roosevelt to Homer Folks, Jan. 25, 1932, FDR; SCAA *Minutes*, Feb. 18, 1932; Homer Folks, Journal, Feb. 1932, *passim*, HFC; SCAA *Minutes*, March 17, 1932; Schneider and Deutsch, *History of Public Welfare*, p. 313.

40. *S.C.A.A. News*, March 1932, p. 1; SCAA *Annual Report* (1932), p. 10.

41. Homer Folks to Franklin D. Roosevelt, July 11, 1932, FDR; New York *Times*, Nov. 6, 1932; *S.C.A.A. News*, Sept. 1932, p. 1; Oct. 1932, p. 1; SCAA *Minutes*, Oct. 20, Nov. 17, 1932; SCAA *Annual Report* (1932), pp. 9–10.

42. New York *Times*, Oct. 9, 28, 1934; Oct. 21, 1935; SCAA *Minutes*, Oct. 24, 1935; *S.C.A.A. News*, Sept. 1933, p. 1; Nov. 1933, p. 10; Dec. 1933, p. 3; Sept. 1934, p. 1; Schneider and Deutsch, *History of Public Welfare*, pp. 338–39.

43. Homer Folks, "Public Relief as a Social Policy," address delivered before the National Conference of Social Work, Detroit, June 13, 1933, HFC; Homer Folks, "Making Relief Respectable" (1934), in Folks, *Public Health and Welfare*, pp. 284–301; New York *Times*, March 24, 1934; SCAA *Annual Report* (1931), p. 18; *S.C.A.A. News*, Jan. 1934, p. 1.

44. Homer Folks, "Memo of Remarks at the Annual Meeting of the New York State Welfare Officers," June 28, 1934, HFC.

45. New York *Times*, New York *Tribune*, Dec. 12, 1933; New York *Times*, March 14, 1934; *S.C.A.A. News*, Nov. 1933, p. 2; SCAA *Minutes*, Nov. 16, 1933.

46. Homer Folks, "Trends in Home Relief for the Future," Dec. 11,

1933, HFC; New York *Times,* March 14, 1934; SCAA *Annual Report* (1934), pp. 13–14; *S.C.A.A. News,* March 1934, p. 3; Schneider and Deutsch, *History of Public Welfare,* p. 33.

47. SCAA *Minutes,* Jan. 19, 1933; *S.C.A.A. News,* Jan. 1933, p. 1.

48. *S.C.A.A. News,* Jan. 1933, p. 2.

49. Schneider and Deutsch, *History of Public Welfare,* pp. 321ff. Some people contend, and it can be argued, that the RFC was the first federal relief bill. This act, however, attempted to evade the question of federal aid through a subterfuge—by providing federal-state *loans* instead of grants-in-aid. The RFC made available $300,000,000 for loans to the states for "relief and work relief to the needy and distressed." The act, though, made careful provision for the repayment of these loans, although later Congress passed another act providing that the loans need not be repaid. For an excellent discussion of relief and the RFC see Edith Abbott, *Public Assistance: American Principles and Politics* (Chicago: University of Chicago, 1941), pp. 666–69.

50. Schneider and Deutsch, *History of Public Welfare,* p. 322; Abbott, *Public Assistance,* pp. 671–72.

51. *S.C.A.A. News,* Jan. 1935, p. 1; Schneider and Deutsch, *History of Public Welfare,* pp. 353ff.; Edwin E. Witte, *The Development of the Social Security Act* (Madison: University of Wisconsin, 1962), pp. 41ff.; Joseph C. Dougherty, Jr., "The Genesis of the Social Security Act of 1935" (Ph.D. dissertation, Georgetown University, 1955), pp. 95–169.

52. Bruno, *Trends in Social Work,* p. 309; Dougherty, "The Genesis," p. 227; Robert H. Bremner, *From the Depths: The Discovery of Poverty in the United States* (New York: New York University, 1956), pp. 263–64; Schneider and Deutsch, *History of Public Welfare,* pp. 353ff. Needless to say, the Social Security Act was patterned on the experience of other earlier, successful, experiments in federal-state cooperation, such as the first federal child labor law (1916) and the Sheppard-Towner Act (1921), both of which showed how the states and federal government could work together for social welfare under a grant-in-aid program. See Helen R. Wright, "Three Against Time: Edith and Grace Abbott and Sophonsiba Breckenridge," *Social Service Review,* XXVIII (March 1954), 41–53.

53. Witte, *Development of Social Security Act,* pp. 173–89. The whole matter of health insurance was included in the original assignment and a separate report was made on it, one which recommended a health insurance bill. Because it was known that the medical profession's objections couldn't be overcome, introduction of health insurance was postponed for the sake of passing the social security bill.

54. Quoted in Arthur M. Schlesinger, Jr., *The Crisis of the Old Order* (Boston: Houghton Mifflin, 1957), p. 25.

55. *S.C.A.A. News,* Sept. 1934, p. 4; SCAA *Annual Report* (1934), p. 15; Schneider and Deutsch, *History of Public Welfare,* pp. 338–39; interview with Mr. Hugh R. Jackson, former executive secretary of the Wardwell Commission, Oct. 3, 1962, New York City; SCAA *Annual Report* (1936), pp. 17–18; SCAA *Minutes,* Jan. 16, 1936; *S.C.AA. News,* Jan. 1936, p. 1.

56. *S.C.A.A. News,* Jan. 1936, p. 1.

57. Schneider and Deutsch, *History of Public Welfare,* pp. 338–39; SCAA *Minutes,* April 16, May 21, 1936; SCAA *Annual Report* (1936), pp. 17–19. In 1946 the Ostertag Act, which Folks helped draft, was enacted. This act, which went into effect on Jan. 1, 1947, amended the Social Welfare Law to provide for a county-unit system of public welfare. City and town public welfare agencies were eliminated. See *S.C.A.A. News,* Jan. 1947, p. 1.

58. *S.C.A.A. News,* Dec. 1937, p. 1; May 1938, p. 1. See Article VIII, Sections 3, 4, 5, and 6; SCAA *Annual Report* (1938), pp. 9–11; Schneider and Deutsch, *History of Public Welfare,* p. 364.

59. Stephen Smith, "The History of Public Health," in *A Half Century of Public Health,* ed. Mazyck P. Ravenel (New York: American Public Health Association, 1921), p. 2.

60. *S.C.A.A. News,* March 1937, p. 1; New York *Times,* Feb. 19, 1937. Earlier, congratulatory telegrams sent to Folks from President Roosevelt and Chief Justice Hughes were read aloud to those attending the dinner.

61. For example, see Mr. V. C. Branhan to Homer Folks, Feb. 17, 1937; Mr. I. S. Falk to Homer Folks, Feb. 12, 1937, HFC. Also see *S.C.A.A. News,* March 1937, p. 3; New York *Times,* New York *Herald Tribune,* Feb. 19, 1937.

62. Folks, "Some Thoughts on a Seventieth Birthday," pp. 338–44; New York *Times,* New York *Herald Tribune,* Feb. 19, 1937.

63. New York *Herald Tribune,* Feb. 19, 1937.

13
STATESMAN EMERITUS

1. *Minutes* of the Meetings of the Board of Managers of the New York State Charities Aid Association, New York City, Oct. 31, 1940 (hereafter cited as SCAA *Minutes*); Homer Folks to Dr. H. M. Cassidy, Aug. 24, 1941, HFC.

2. New York *Times,* New York *Herald Tribune,* Yonkers (N.Y.)

Herald Statesman, Oct. 17, 1940. Also see William Chadbourne to Homer Folks, Oct. 8, 1940; Hermann Hagedorn to Homer Folks, Oct. 8, 24, 1940, HFC.

3. New York State Charities Aid Association *Annual Report* (1940), p. 14 (hereafter cited as SCAA *Annual Report*).

4. *S.C.A.A. News,* May 1942, p. 3.

5. Homer Folks, "The S.C.A.A. and the Defense of Democracy," in SCAA *Annual Report* (1940), p. 8.

6. *Ibid.,* p. 10; Also see Homer Folks, "The S.C.A.A. Faces the War," or "The S.C.A.A. Takes Another Look," in *S.C.A.A. News,* Oct. 1941, p. 1; Homer Folks, "The Central Purpose of the S.C.A.A.," address delivered at the seventieth anniversary meeting of the SCAA, New York City, May 1942, reprinted in Homer Folks, *Public Health and Welfare: The Citizens' Responsibility—Selected Papers of Homer Folks,* ed. Savel Zimand (New York: Macmillan, 1958), pp. 410–19.

7. Folks, "S.C.A.A. Takes Another Look," p. 1.

8. Folks, "The Central Purpose," p. 412; SCAA *Annual Report* (1942), pp. 16–17; (1945), p. 5.

9. SCAA *Minutes,* Nov. 8, 1946, Jan. 10, Feb. 14, 1947; New York *Herald Tribune,* Feb. 21, 1947.

10. In the HFC there is a scrapbook full of newspaper clippings and personal notes and messages on Folks's retirement.

11. *Health News,* March 1947, n.p., HFC.

12. *New York Medicine,* April 5, 1947, n.p., HFC.

13. New York *Sun,* Feb. 21, 1947; New York *Times,* Feb. 22, 1947.

14. New York *PM,* Feb. 21, 1947.

15. Editorial, "Homer Folks, Statesman Emeritus," *American Journal of Public Health,* XXXVII (May 1947), 570–71.

16. Many people expressed this feeling to the author in personal interviews: for example, Miss Katharine F. Lenroot, Oct. 1, 1962, New York City; Dr. Philip Klein, Nov. 11, 1962, White Plains, N.Y.; Miss Ruth Taylor, Oct. 2, 1962, Hartsdale, N.Y.

17. I am indebted to Mr. and Mrs. Savel Zimand for allowing me to see their folder full of letters, notes, and telegrams of condolence, as well as tributes and resolutions on Mr. Folks's death. Because of a newspaper strike, none of the New York City newspapers ran an obituary. Hundreds of other newspapers throughout the country, however, had lengthy ones and, in many cases, even articles, on his death. See for example Yonkers (N.Y.) *Herald Statesman,* Feb. 14, 15, 1963.

18. Karl deSchweinitz, "The Past as a Guide to the Function and Pattern

of Social Work," in *Frontiers for Social Work,* ed. William Wallace Weaver (Philadelphia: University of Pennsylvania, 1960), pp. 82, 84.

19. Sickness still is the most persistent, serious, and uncertain social hazard confronting all Americans. Although probably more amenable to prevention and cure than any other social peril, it continues to be the major cause of poverty and thus the leading reason why people seek assistance. Illness is of public as well as of private interest, and health, like education, is a national asset; it should, therefore, be the concern of all. One of the major tasks Americans face today, then, is that of providing free adequate health facilities and services to all who may need them; Medicare or any other voluntary or compulsory contributory scheme for distributing among many some of the monetary losses that would otherwise be experienced by a few after they become ill is no adequate substitute for this.

20. Interviews with George J. Nelbach and Dr. James E. Perkins, Oct. 1, 1962, New York City; Dr. Frank G. Boudreau, Dec. 12, 1962, New York City.

21. Yonkers (N.Y.) *Herald Statesman,* Feb. 21, 1947. Also see Homer Folks, "Statement on 'The Place of the Social Worker in Reconstruction Work in Europe,'" Memorandum from Commissioner to Europe, Robert E. Olds, to Heads of Departments and Field Units in Europe, Feb. 1921, American National Red Cross, Office of Research Information, Washington, D.C.

22. Interviews with Miss Ruth Taylor, Oct. 2, 1962, Hartsdale, N.Y.; Miss Katharine F. Lenroot, Oct. 1, 1962, New York City.

23. Interviews with Miss Ruth Taylor, Oct. 2, 1962, Hartsdale, N.Y.; Mr. Robert Osborn and Mr. George J. Nelbach, Oct. 1, 1962, New York City; Miss Katharine Ecob, Oct. 14, 1962, New York City; Dr. Nina Ridenour, Oct. 2, 1962, New York City.

24. Interviews with Mr. Robert Osborn and Mr. George J. Nelbach, Oct. 1, 1962, New York City; Dr. Philip Klein, Nov. 11, 1962, White Plains, N.Y.

25. Interviews with Mr. Leonard W. Mayo, Nov. 14, 1962, New York City; Mr. Stanley P. Davies, Oct. 17, 1962, White Plains, N.Y.

26. John A. Kingsbury, "Homer Folks as a Teacher," in *Thirty Years of Service: A Tribute to Homer Folks* (New York: Klebold, 1923), p. 32; interviews with Mr. Robert Osborn and Mr. Lowell Iberg, Oct. 1, 1962, New York City; Miss Ruth Taylor, Oct. 2, 1962, Hartsdale, N.Y.; Mrs. George H. Laws to the author, Aug. 20, 1962.

27. "S.C.A.A. as a Training School," in *Milestone 55: Some of the More Important Activities of the State Charities Aid Association During the 55th*

Year of its History (New York: SCAA Pub. No. 185, 1927), pp. 66–67. For example, some of the people who began their careers with the SCAA were John A. Kingsbury, secretary of the Milbank Memorial Fund; Bailey B. Burritt, general director, New York Association for Improving the Condition of the Poor; Ruth Taylor, Commissioner of Public Welfare, Westchester County, N.Y.; Louise Strachen, director of health education, National Tuberculosis Association; Jane Allen, general director, National Organization for Public Health Nurses; Lillian Quinn, director, Joint Vocational Service, Russell Sage Foundation; Philip P. Jacobs, publicity director, National Tuberculosis Association; and Stanley P. Davies, executive director, Community Service Society of New York. The list could be extended indefinitely.

A great many others who never worked directly for him nevertheless expressed the feeling that Folks served as an inspiration and a potent influence on their lives. For example, Morris A. Jacobs, New York City Commissioner of the Department of Hospitals; Roger N. Baldwin, reformer; Maxwell Hahn, vice-president, the Field Foundation; George J. Hecht, publisher, *Parent's Magazine;* Dr. Hollis Ingraham, Deputy Commissioner, New York State Department of Health; Dr. James E. Perkins, managing director, National Tuberculosis Association; Dr. Leona Baumgartner, New York City Commissioner of Health. Again, innumerable others could be listed.

28. Actually, three of Folks's friends and admirers provided me with this information about his critics (interviews with Miss Ruth Taylor, Oct. 2, 1962, Hartsdale, N.Y.; Dr. Frank G. Boudreau, Dec. 12, 1962, New York City; Mr. Hugh R. Jackson, Oct. 3, 1962, New York City).

29. Even his most affectionate admirers, including his daughter, Mrs. Savel Zimand, agreed on this point.

30. A copy of the citation can be found in the HFC.

BIBLIOGRAPHICAL ESSAY

IN VIEW of the fact that the text of this work has been extensively documented, it seems unnecessary to list each item separately in a conventional bibliography. Rather, it would seem more desirable to indicate in an essay the general character of the sources, designating those that proved most useful, secondary and primary. Most of these sources have been cited; some have not. All have been helpful.

No one has written a full-length account of Homer Folks's life. Nor are there any documented and comprehensive accounts of his activities in any of the areas included in this study. While secondary accounts of some of the relevant fields do exist, they all fail to adequately describe and evaluate Folks's contributions to them.

The best account of his life is an eighteen-page biographical sketch written by Mr. Savel Zimand, Folks's son-in-law. It appears in the introduction to Homer Folks's *Public Health and Welfare: The Citizens' Responsibility—Selected Papers of Homer Folks,* edited by Savel Zimand (New York, 1958). This work contains forty-nine of Folks's papers written between 1891 and 1946, most of which were previously unpublished. It is the best single source of his published writings. Aside from brief newspaper items, Anna Liebowitz's "Homer Folks: A Study of His Professional Growth in Terms of His Contributions to the Field of Social Work and the Milieu in Which He Developed" (Master's essay, New York [now Columbia University] School of Social Work, 1950), is the only other account of his life and work. Written before the Folks Papers were available, this seventy-page study is, at best, a sketchy chronicle.

The basic source for this study is the Homer Folks Collection at the Columbia University School of Social Work in New York City. The Folks Papers include memorabilia of many kinds, photographs, numerous interesting scrapbooks (which contain a wealth of newspaper clippings relating to Folks), diaries, journals, medals, citations, certificates for distinguished service and outstanding accomplishments, an abundance of material on Folks's high school and college years (including notebooks, school certificates, compositions, term papers), some correspondence, manuscript copies of articles and addresses, and copies of Folks's published books, *The Care of Destitute, Neglected and Delinquent Children* (New York, 1902) and *The Human Costs of the War* (New York, 1920). His correspondence for the years 1904 through 1917, inclusive, is missing while, for the years after 1917 it is brief and, on the whole, insignificant. The high school and college items, the manuscript copies of Folks's articles and addresses, and the diaries and journals are most important. The collection has not been indexed but is organized and arranged satisfactorily. It also contains a large number of books, pamphlets, annual reports, and other publications of public and private agencies. No account of Homer Folks's life can be written without close scrutiny of this collection.

Only slightly less important than the Homer Folks Papers are the New York State Charities Aid Association *Annual Reports, Minutes* of the Meetings of the Board of Managers, *News,* and its other publications. This material is located at the State Charities Aid Association's offices in the United Charities Building in New York City. Since no history of the Association exists, these sources provide the only record of its activities. Whereas the Folks Papers are especially valuable for the development of his thought, this material is indispensable for an understanding of Folks's influence on social reform and legislation in New York State and the nation; both are vital for a study of his career. Needless to say, however, these sources, like most of the other primary ones used for this study, are unavoidably biased; the reader is therefore cautioned. On the other hand, unfortunately, they are the only sources available for a study of this nature.

Other manuscript collections contain some correspondence and related material. Unfortunately, most have little that is very useful. Folks wrote few letters; when possible, he preferred to communicate orally. To him, the telephone was more useful than the mail, and his important communications were face to face. Since most of his associates were also situated in the United Charities Building, he did not have to write many letters. The letters he did write were, on the whole, not very communicative. Nevertheless, I found several items of interest and importance in various collections. The Dr. Albert Shaw Papers (New York Public Library) yielded useful correspondence from Folks relating to the State Charities Aid Association's campaign for the prevention of insanity. The Lillian D. Wald Collection (New York Public Library) contains correspondence between Wald and others that points out the esteem in which Folks was held by his colleagues. Folks's role in the development of special classes for mentally retarded children in New York State is revealed in correspondence in the John H. Finley Papers (New York Public Library). The Herbert H. Lehman Papers (New York Public Library) contain a great many letters from Folks, which, although in large measure are perfunctory, illuminate the important role he played as an unofficial advisor to the Governor for many years. The same is true for the Alfred E. Smith Papers (State Library at Albany) and the Franklin D. Roosevelt Papers (Hyde Park, N.Y.). The Smith Papers have several helpful items on the 1923 bond issue campaign and the proposed development of county health units. The Roosevelt Papers are most useful for tracing Folks's part in the 1930 bond issue campaign, the two joint surveys of New York State's fifty-nine cities, and the subsequent bond issue campaigns to raise money for state aid to unemployment relief. Some correspondence on the anti-tuberculosis movement and Folks's 1911 European trip is in the John A. Kingsbury Papers (Library of Congress). The Grace Abbott Papers (University of Chicago) contain letters from Folks that are important for understanding his views on health and social insurance. The Livingston Farrand Collection (Cornell University) has correspondence on appropriating the proceeds from the 1923 bond issue, and a few items on Red Cross activities. The Dr. William H. Welch Collection (Johns Hopkins University) has several important letters from Folks pertaining to various public health matters. Finally, the Benjamin B. Lindsey Papers (Library of Congress) has an interesting exchange of letters between Lindsey and Folks relating to the juvenile court and probation movement in the early twentieth century.

In addition, Mrs. Lawrence M. Orton (Folks's daughter Evelyn) and Mr. Savel Zimand (husband of the late Gertrude Folks Zimand, his other daughter) possess many items of interest. Most important are personal letters written by Folks to his family from France during World War I, letters written by others to Folks at the time of his retirement and during the latter years of his life, and, finally, letters of condolence at the time of his death in February 1963. Last, Mrs. C. E. A. Winslow made available to me a large and important exchange of correspondence between her husband and Folks, which was helpful in understanding Folks's role in New York State public health activities in the 1920s, especially the attempted development of state health centers.

Many of Folks's letters are in the Mayors' Papers located at the New York City Municipal Archives. Except for those dealing with the creation of the Municipal Lodging House, however, most of them are relatively unimportant. The hundreds of thousands of items for each of New York City's mayors are poorly organized and difficult to use; for this reason the Folks letters are not worth locating.

Some public agencies and one quasi-public one have large amounts of very useful material. For example, the quasi-public American Red Cross in Washington, D.C., has copies of all the reports Folks wrote while he served as Director of the Department of Civil Affairs in France during World War I. Red Cross files also contain extremely important correspondence, reports, and bulletins in regard to Folks's postwar Red Cross activities— child welfare work abroad and health center activities at home. Another item located at the Red Cross is a collection of carefully documented mimeographed monographs on various aspects of the organization's history. Most profitable for this study are G. R. Gaeddert's "The History of the American Red Cross in World War I, 1917–1918" (Washington, D.C., 1950) and Marian B. Clausen's "The American Red Cross in Peace, 1919–1939" (Washington, D.C., 1950).

Two other public agencies have important and otherwise unaccessible unpublished material. The New York State Department of Health has several folders of items on Folks's career and relations with that department. More important, however, are the records of the New York State Public Health Council, which meaningfully reflect Folks's part in developing that historic body. The Children's Bureau, Department of Health, Education, and Welfare, Washington, D.C., has important material that illuminates the part Folks played in helping to create the bureau and develop its future policy.

On the other hand, the archives of voluntary agencies contain little of use for this study. Unfortunately, over the years most of the organizations with which Folks was associated, such as the National Association for Mental Health, the Community Service Society, Russell Sage Foundation, and the American Social Health Association, destroyed most items of interest. Only recently have they begun to preserve materials useful for students of history. The National Tuberculosis Association and the Community Council of Greater New York (formerly the Welfare Council) do however have much important information relating to Folks's career. The *Minutes* of the meetings of the former organization's Board of Directors are helpful in tracing Folks's relation to the national association and his views on federal assistance to the anti-tuberculosis movement. The latter organization has a great deal of information on the part Folks played in creating New York City's Welfare Council and in shaping its subsequent development. Although an account of this is not included in the study, it nevertheless aided in understanding Folks's thought.

While few unpublished materials of voluntary organizations were used for this study, their publications, reports, bulletins, and pamphlets, as well as those of public agencies, were helpful. A few examples of these are:

Handbook on the Prevention of Tuberculosis (Charity Organization Society of New York, 1903); Lilian Brandt, *Directory of Institutions and Societies Dealing With Tuberculosis in the United States and Canada* (Charity Organization Society of New York, 1904); Margaret Rich, *Josephine Shaw Lowell* (Community Service Society, 1954); *The Best Administration New York Ever Had* (Citizens' Union, 1903); *The Department of Public Charities of the City of New York* (City Club of New York, 1903); Lee K. Frankel, *In the Early Days of Charities* (National Conference of Jewish Social Service, 1930); *Work Relief: A Memorandum on Work as a Measure of Providing Unemployment Relief* (New York State Charities Aid Association and the State Department of Social Welfare, 1931). *The Proceedings of the National Conference of Charities and Correction* (later Social Work, then Social Welfare), of the *New York State Conference of Charities and Correction,* and the *Transactions of the National Association for the Study and Prevention of Tuberculosis* (later National Tuberculosis Association) also yielded rich fruit. They were especially valuable for tracing the evolution among social workers from a preoccupation with relief to a concern for prevention and social action.

Published and unpublished memorial addresses furnished an unusually fertile source of information for the study. For example, the unpublished addresses delivered at the Homer Folks Memorial Service (June 10, 1963, New York) were helpful in evaluating Folks's career, especially his early efforts to prevent tuberculosis. *Memorial Addresses, George Herbert Palmer, 1842–1933* (Cambridge, Mass., 1935) provides useful information for understanding one of the more important influences on Folks's life. Various activities that occupied Folks's attention are clarified in *Solomon Lowenstein Memorial Meeting* (New York, 1942) and in *In Memoriam, Livingston Farrand* (New York, 1940). In addition, privately published pamphlets are also helpful. Most of these are in the Homer Folks Collection and consist of such materials as *Thirty Years of Service: A Tribute to Homer Folks* (New York, 1923) and *Thirty Years of Service: Tributes to James E. West* (New York, 1941).

Government documents and publications were not widely used in the study. I occasionally consulted the *Congressional Record,* the *Proceedings* of the White House Conferences on Children, and the New York State Board of Charities *Annual Reports.* More important were the New York State *Laws* and reports of numerous state commissions. Representatives of the latter class of material are *Public Health in New York State: Report of the New York State Health Commission* (Albany, 1931) and *Insulin Shock Therapy: A Study by the Temporary Commission on State Hospital Problems* (Albany, 1944).

Along with the Homer Folks Papers and the State Charities Aid Association material, personal interviews provided a major source of information for this work. These talks were profitable in amplifying what Folks did, why he took certain actions, and what their importance and limitations were in the eyes of some of the participants. All the people I spoke with provided me with knowledge otherwise unobtainable, such as clues to Folks's character and personality. Most rewarding were long conversations with Mr. and Mrs. Savel Zimand (Oct. 25, Nov. 27, 1962, and July 14, 1964, New York City) and Mr. and Mrs. Lawrence M. Orton (Oct. 2 and Nov. 29, 1962, New York City). They of course know more about Homer Folks than anyone else and were extremely frank in their discussions with me. Next to them, Mr. George J. Nelbach, long-time friend and assistant to Folks, as well as former executive director of the State Committee on Tuberculosis and Public Health of the State Charities Aid Association, helped to solidify my thinking on various aspects of Folks's life and career, in an interview in New York City on Oct. 1, 1962. Mr. Nelbach has an amazing memory for people, places, and events that were vital in Folks's life. Like Nelbach, Mr. Robert Osborn (Oct. 1, 1962, New York City), executive director of the New York State Tuberculosis and Respiratory Disease Association, Inc., Mr. Stanley P. Davies (Oct. 17, 1962, White Plains, N.Y.), former executive director of the State Committee on Mental Hygiene of the SCAA, and Mr. Hugh R. Jackson (Oct. 3, 1962, New York City), president of the Better Business Bureau of New York City, all former employees of Folks's and leading State Charities Aid Association figures, were extremely helpful in providing general information on a wide range of topics. Dr. Nina Ridenour (Oct. 2, 1962, New York City), secretary of the Ittleson Foundation, and Miss Katharine Ecob (Oct. 14, 1962, New York City), former secretary of the State Committee on Mental Hygiene of the SCAA, were especially helpful in regard to Folks's mental hygiene work. Dr. George Baehr (Oct. 5, 1962, New York City), chairman of the Public Health Council, Dr. James E. Perkins (Oct. 1, 1962, New York City), managing director of the National Tuberculosis Association, and Dr. Frank G. Boudreau (Dec. 12, 1962, New York City), former executive director of the Milbank Memorial Fund, were particularly informative on Folks's public health work. His endeavors on behalf of child welfare were stressed by Miss Katharine F. Lenroot (Oct. 1, 1962, New York City), former chief of the U.S. Children's Bureau, and Miss Ruth Taylor (Oct. 2, 1962, Hartsdale, N.Y.), former Commissioner of Public Welfare, Westchester County, N.Y. Mrs. John A. Kingsbury (Dec. 6, 1962, New York City), widow of the former secretary of the SCAA's Committee on the Prevention of Tuberculosis, took time to recall incidents regarding her husband's association with Folks. She also provided valuable insights into Folks's character and relations with other social workers. Mr. Robert Barrie (Oct. 19, 1962, New York City), director, Division of Health and Welfare, Board of National Missions, United Presbyterian Church, U.S.A., mainly discussed Folks's summer activities, and Mr. Leonard W. Mayo (Nov. 14, 1962, New York City), executive director of the Association for the Aid of Crippled Children, talked with me at length about Folks's legislative work. Dr. Philip Klein (Nov. 11, 1962, White Plains, N.Y.), longtime faculty member of the Columbia University School of Social Work, expressed some judgments on Folks's historical significance, while Dr. Granville Larimore (Dec. 3, 1962, Albany, N.Y.), Deputy Commissioner of Health, New York State Department of Health, provided me with information on Folks's work with and relation to the State Department of Health. Hon. Herbert H. Lehman (Dec. 11, 1962, New York City), former Governor and U.S. Senator, recalled with great gusto the many ways in which Folks helped him while he occupied the executive chair at Albany, as well as the incidents relating to the decision in 1936 to name one of the state's tuberculosis sanatoria the Homer Folks Tuberculosis Hospital. Finally, Mr. Clyde E. Buckingham (Dec. 17, 1962, Washington, D.C.), director, Office of Research Information, American Red Cross, helped me gain a better understanding of Red Cross activities and Folks's part in the development of that organization.

In addition to these and other personal interviews, numerous letters to the author provided useful information. The Oral History Project at Columbia University was also very valuable. The typescript copies made from recorded interviews hold a great deal of background material on reform and social conditions in New York throughout Folks's career. The contributions of Homer Folks (1949), Lawrence Veiller (1949), Dr. Haven Emerson (1950), Robert S. Binkerd (1949), Francis R. Stoddard (1949), Roger N. Baldwin (1954), William J. Schieffelin (1949), and Laurence A. Tanzer (1949) are all important and are cited in several chapters. Numerous others, however, including Bruno Lasker (1956), Louis H. Pink (1949), Henry Bruere (1949), Lawson Purdy (1948), William H. Allen (1950), C. C. Burlingham (1949), Genevieve Earle (1950), and Allen Wardwell (1952), are also relevant.

Newspapers and periodicals, especially those containing articles by Folks, are important. Perhaps it bears repeating that there are several scrapbooks in the Folks Collection full of newspaper and magazine clippings relating to Folks. In addition, at various points in the study I used the files of New York City newspapers, especially the *Times, Daily Tribune, Evening Post, Herald,* and the *Herald Tribune.* Periodicals of a general nature most frequently cited include *Outlook, Annals of the American Academy of Political and Social Science, Review of Reviews, The Nation,* and *Harper's Magazine.* More valuable, however, are articles found in periodicals devoted to special interests. In this category those that deserve special mention are such journals as *Commons, Charities and Commons, Charities, Charities Review, Survey, Social Service Review, Municipal Affairs, Parent's Magazine, Better Times,* and the *American Journal of Public Health.*

There are many published diaries, letters, autobiographies, and reminiscences of social workers, public health and welfare officials, and agents of public and private organizations. While, like all the other sources, they must be used with care, they are an important source of information. Jane Addams' *The Second Twenty Years at Hull House* (New York, 1930) is most important for a discussion of social work in the early twentieth century, the first White House Conference on Dependent Children, and the relation between social workers and the Progressive Party in 1912. Clifford Beers's *A Mind That Found Itself* (New York, 1931) is the best source for an understanding of the origins of the national mental hygiene movement. Ernest P. Bicknell's *The American Red Cross in the Great War* (New York, 1920) and *With the Red Cross in Europe, 1917–1922* (Washington, D.C., 1938) are important for understanding that organization's overseas work. Edward T. Devine's *When Social Work Was Young* (New York, 1939) is especially helpful with regard to New York City tenement house reform and the early anti-tuberculosis movement. The best source of information on the Municipal Assembly fight over revision of New York's tenement house code is P. Tecumseh Sherman's *Inside the Machine: Two Years in the Board of Aldermen, 1898–1899* (New York, 1901). Fred S. Hall's *Forty Years, 1902–1942: The Work of the New York Child Labor Committee* (New York, 1958) presents a clear picture of child labor reform in New York. Ben B. Lindsey's *The Dangerous Life* (New York, 1931) illuminates the beginning of the juvenile court movement in the United States. Henry Morganthau's *All in A Lifetime* (New York, 1922) gives a vivid picture of Governor Sulzer and the way in which Folks and other social workers went about rewriting the state's public health laws during his administration. The best picture of the State Charities Aid Association's early work and successful establishment of the Bellevue Training School for Nurses is found in Abby Howland Woolsey's *A Century of Nursing, With Hints Toward the Organization of a Training School and Florence Nightingale's Historic Letter on the Bellevue School, September 18, 1872* (New York, 1916).

The following works are also helpful in many ways: Charles S. Bernheimer, *Half a Century of Community Service* (New York, 1948); Benjamin O. Flower, *Progressive Men, Women, and Movements of the Past Twenty-Five Years* (Boston, 1914); Raymond B. Fosdick, *Chronicle of a Generation* (New York, 1958); Alexander Johnson, *Adventures in Social Welfare, Being Reminiscences of Things, Thoughts and Folks During Forty Years of Social Work* (Fort Wayne, Ind., 1923); George Herbert Palmer, *Autobiography of a Philosopher* (Boston, 1930); Theodore Roosevelt, *The Letters of Theodore Roosevelt,* selected and edited by Elting E. Morison (8 vols., Cambridge, Mass., 1951–1954); Lincoln Steffens, *Autobiography* (New York, 1931) and *The Letters of Lincoln Steffens,* edited by Ella Winter and Granville Hicks (2 vols., New York, 1938); Oswald Villard Garrison, *Fighting Years: Memoirs of a Liberal Editor* (New York, 1939); and Everett P. Wheeler, *Sixty Years of American Life: Taylor to Roosevelt, 1850–1910* (New York, 1917).

In addition to the autobiographical information listed above, biographical portraits of three associates of Folks drawn by lifetime friends contain primary source material of immense importance for this study. They are Jane Addams' *My Friend, Julia Lathrop* (New York, 1935), Josephine Goldmark's *Impatient Crusader: Florence Kelley's Life Story* (Urbana, Ill., 1953), and Dr. C. E. A. Winslow's *The Life of Hermann M. Biggs* (Philadelphia, 1929). The Addams book is most useful for its accounts of the creation of the Children's Bureau and certain aspects of the mental hygiene crusade. The Goldmark book is most helpful in its discussions of the child labor and baby-saving movements. Winslow's account of Biggs is the best volume written on New York State's public health movement. Several other biographies are also useful for understanding the public health movement and evaluating Folks's contributions to it. They are James H. Cassedy's *Charles V. Chapin and the Public Health Movement* (Cambridge, Mass., 1962), Donald H. Fleming's *William H. Welch and the Rise of Modern Medicine* (Boston, 1954), and Robert L. Duffus's *Lillian Wald: Neighbor and Crusader* (New York, 1938). Louise Ware's *Jacob A. Riis: Police Reporter, Reformer, Useful Citizen* (New York, 1938) pictures many of the reform movements with which Folks was associated in New York City before the turn of the century, and Hermann Hagedorn's *Leonard Wood: A Biography* (2 vols., New York, 1931) presents background material for a better understanding of Folks's Cuban welfare work. Claude G. Bower's *Beveridge and the Progressive Era* (New York, 1932) is particularly illuminating on the early movement for federal child labor legislation.

Three other secondary works—historical accounts of a great philanthropic foundation, a public, and a private agency—are very useful. These are John M. Glen, Lilian Brandt, and F. Emerson Andrews, *Russell Sage Foundation, 1907–1946* (2 vols., New York, 1947); Richard H. Shryock,

National Tuberculosis Association, 1904–1954 (New York, 1957); and Dorothy E. Bradbury, *Five Decades of Action For Children: A History of the Children's Bureau* (Washington, D.C., 1962). Three others, however, are even more important. Frank J. Bruno's *Trends in Social Work, as Reflected in the Proceedings of the National Conference of Social Work, 1874–1956* (New York, 1957) is a summary of social workers' thoughts between the years indicated in the title. It is conveniently arranged in a topical and chronological fashion and, next to the *Proceedings* themselves, the best such account. David M. Schneider and Albert Deutsch's *The History of Public Welfare in New York State, 1867–1940* (Chicago, 1941) is an invaluable guide (and the only one) to New York State's developments in that field. It is almost entirely a descriptive account, however. Edith Abbott's *Public Assistance: American Principles and Policies* (Chicago, 1940) is the best source for a detailed (and documented) historical discussion of the administration and theory of public relief in America.

By nature of the relation between the authors and the topics considered, several important secondary accounts in the field of public health may almost be regarded as primary works. These include *A Half Century of Public Health,* edited by Dr. Mazyck P. Ravenel (New York, 1921); Dr. C. E. A. Winslow, *Health on the Farm and in the Village* (New York, 1931), and *A City on a Hill* (New York, 1943); and Winslow and Savel Zimand, *Health under the 'El'* (New York, 1937).

Many other secondary accounts give attention to developments in social work and public health and welfare. The most useful general accounts for this study are Robert Bremner, *From the Depths: The Discovery of Poverty in the United States* (New York, 1956) and *American Philanthropy* (Chicago, 1960); Clarke A. Chambers, *Seedtime of Reform: American Social Service and Social Action, 1918–1933* (Minneapolis, 1963); Merle Curti, *American Philanthropy Abroad: A History* (New Brunswick, N.J., 1963); and Arthur P. Miles, *An Introduction to Public Welfare* (Boston, 1949). For interesting interpretive accounts of social work in America see Reinhold Niebuhr, *The Contribution of Religion to Social Work* (New York, 1932), and Nathan Edward Cohen, *Social Work in the American Tradition* (New York, 1958). There are many histories of the public health movement. Among the best known and most important are Dr. C. E. A. Winslow's *The Conquest of Epidemic Disease* (Princeton, 1943) and *The Evolution and Significance of the Modern Public Health Campaign* (New Haven, 1935). Important, and related to these, are Dr. Henry D. Chadwick and Alton S. Pope's *The Modern Attack on Tuberculosis* (New York, 1942), Dr. Haven Emerson's *Local Health Units for the*

Nation (New York, 1945), Dr. Wilson G. Smillie's *Public Health: Its Promise For the Future* (New York, 1955), and James A. Tobey's *Public Health Law* (New York, 1947). An interesting early account of one phase of the campaign against child labor is Edward N. Clopper's *Child Labor in City Streets* (New York, 1912). For an understanding of the treatment and care of the mentally deficient, as well as of the mental hygiene movement, consult Stanley P. Davies, *Social Control of the Mentally Deficient* (New York, 1930), Albert Deutsch, *The Mentally Ill in America: A History of Their Care and Treatment From Colonial Times* (New York, 1962), and Dr. Nina Ridenour, *Mental Health in the United States: A Fifty Year History* (Cambridge, Mass., 1961).

Several good secondary accounts of the Red Cross are at hand. They include Foster Rhea Dulles, *The American Red Cross: A History* (New York, 1950), and Charles Hurd, *The Compact History of the American Red Cross* (New York, 1959). Roy Lubove's *The Progressives and the Slums: Tenement House Reform in New York City, 1890–1917* (Pittsburgh, 1962) is an excellent account of that subject while interesting vignettes of important social workers are painted by Emma O. Lundberg in *Unto the Least of These* (New York, 1947). Several works contain relevant material on New York's municipal reform movement. The most helpful ones are Roy V. Peel, *The Political Clubs of New York City* (New York, 1935), Frederick Shaw, *The History of the New York City Legislature* (New York, 1954), Frank Mann Stewart, *A Half Century of Municipal Reform: The History of the National Municipal League* (Berkeley, 1950), and Beatrice Webb, *American Diary, 1898,* edited by David Shannon (Madison, 1963).

Several primary articles are particularly profitable. They include: Francis G. Peabody, " 'Going Slow' in Social Reform," *The Cambridge Magazine,* Feb. 1896, pp. 23–25, and "The Approach to Social Work," in *Social Problems and Social Policy,* edited by James Ford (New York, 1923); Samuel H. Adams, "Guardians of the Public Health," *McClure's,* XXXI (July 1908), 241–52, and "Tuberculosis: The Real Race Suicide," *McClure's,* XXIV (Jan. 1905), 234–49; Robert W. deForest, "Twenty-Five Years and After: The Anniversary Conference Last Week of the New York Charity Organization Society," *Charities and Commons,* XI (Nov. 30, 1907), 1113–46; Edith Abbott, "Social Insurance and Social Security," *Social Service Review,* VIII, No. 3 (Sept. 1934), 537–40, and "Grace Abbott —A Sister's Memories," *Social Service Review,* XIII, No. 3 (Sept. 1939), 351–407; Grace Abbott, "Recent Trends in Mothers' Aid," *Social Service Review,* VIII, No. 2 (June 1934), 191–211; Raymond B. Fosdick, "Public

Health and the Future," *American Journal of Public Health,* XXXVIII (Jan. 1948), 185–89; and Dr. Thomas Parran, "Surmounting Obstacles to Health Progress," *ibid.,* pp. 168–72.

Although there is no book on the entire child labor movement or the National Child Labor Committee, there are a great many articles that illuminate both. Among the most helpful are the following: Samuel McCune Lindsay, "Child Labor, a National Problem," *Annals of the American Academy of Political and Social Science,* XXVII, No. 2 (March 1906), 73–78; Edith Abbott, "Early History of Child Labor," *American Journal of Sociology,* XIV (July 1908), 15–37; Dorothy Bromley, "The New Move to End Child Labor," *Current History,* XXXVIII (Aug. 1933), 564–70; Elizabeth Brandeis, "Labor Legistlation," in *History of Labor in the United States,* edited by John R. Commons (4 vols., New York, 1918–1935), III, 399–456; Courtenay Dinwiddie, "The Present Status of Child Labor," *Social Service Review,* XIII, No. 3 (Sept. 1939), 431–39; Grace Abbott, "Federal Regulation of Child Labor, 1906–1938," *ibid.,* pp. 409–30; Richard B. Sherman, "The Rejection of the Child Labor Amendment," *Mid-America,* XLV, No. 1 (Jan. 1963), 3–17; and John Braeman, "Albert J. Beveridge and the First National Child Labor Bill," *Indiana Magazine of History,* LX (March 1964), 1–36.

Other useful and provocative articles are these: Aaron Abell, "The Catholic Church and Social Problems in the World War I Era," *Mid-America,* XXX, No. 3 (July 1948), 139–51; Vaughn D. Bornet, "The Manuscripts of Social Welfare," *The American Archivist,* XXIII, No. 1 (Jan. 1960), 33–48; Charles O. Burgess, "The Newspaper as Charity Worker: Poor Relief in New York, 1893–1894," *New York History,* XLIII, No. 3 (July 1962), 249–68; John C. Burnham, "Psychiatry, Psychology and the Progressive Movement," *American Quarterly,* XII (Winter 1960), 457–65; Clarke A. Chambers, "Creative Effort in an Age of Normalcy, 1918–1933," in the *Social Welfare Forum* (New York, 1961), pp. 252–71, and "Social Service and Social Reform: A Historical Essay," *Social Service Review,* XXXVII, No. 1 (March 1963), 76–90; Merle Curti, "American Philanthropy and the National Character," *American Quarterly,* X, No. 4 (Winter 1958), 420–37, and "Jane Addams on Human Nature," *Journal of the History of Ideas,* XXII, No. 2 (April–June 1961), 240–53; Allen Davis, "The Social Workers and the Progressive Party, 1912–1916," *American Historical Review,* LXIX, No. 3 (April 1964), 671–88, and "Settlement Workers in Politics, 1890–1914," *The Review of Politics,* XXVI, No. 4 (Oct. 1964), 505–17; Karl deSchweinitz, "The Past as a Guide to the Function and Pattern of Social Work," in *Frontiers for Social Work,* edited by William Wallace Weaver (Philadelphia, 1960); Jurgen Herbst, "Francis

Greenwood Peabody: Harvard's Theologian of the Social Gospel," *Harvard Theological Review*, LIV (Jan. 1961), 45–69; Donald Fleming, "Social Darwinism," in *Paths of American Thought*, edited by Arthur M. Schlesinger, Jr., and Morton White (Boston, 1963), pp. 123–46; Arthur S. Link, "What Happened to the Progressive Movement in the 1920's?," *American Historical Review*, LXIV, No. 4 (July 1959), 833–51; Roy Lubove, "Lawrence Veiller and the New York State Tenement House Commission of 1900," *Mississippi Valley Historical Review*, XLVII, No. 4 (March 1961), 659–77, "The New York Association for Improving the Condition of the Poor: The Formative Years," *New York Historical Society Quarterly*, XLIII, No. 3 (July 1959), 307–37, and "The Progressives and the Prostitute," *Historian*, XXIV (May 1962), 308–30; Lloyd C. Taylor, "Josephine Shaw Lowell and American Philanthropy," *New York History*, (Oct. 1963), 336–64; and Rudolph J. Vecoli, "Sterilization: A Progressive Measure?," *Wisconsin Magazine of History*, XLIII, No. 3 (Spring 1960), 190–202.

There are several excellent and helpful articles on the public health movement. Most pertinent are James H. Cassedy, "Muckraking and Medicine: Samuel Hopkins Adams," *American Quarterly*, XVI, No. 1 (Spring 1964), 85–99; Howard D. Kramer's "The Beginnings of the Public Health Movement in the United States," *Bulletin of the History of Medicine*, XXI, No. 3 (May–June 1947), 352–76, "The Germ Theory and the Early Public Health Program in the United States," *ibid.*, XXII, No. 3 (May–June 1948), 233–47, and "Early Municipal and State Boards of Health," *ibid.*, XXIV, No. 6 (Nov.–Dec. 1950), 503–29; Richard H. Shryock, "The Origins and Significance of the Public Health Movement in the United States," *Annals of Medical History*, I, No. 6, N.S. (Nov. 1929), 645–65; and Milton Terris, "Hermann Biggs' Contribution to the Modern Concept of the Health Center," *Bulletin of the History of Medicine*, XX, No. 3 (Oct. 1946), 387–412.

Finally, I profited enormously from reading unpublished Master's and Ph.D. theses, several of which, I might add, have since been published. Included among these are Albert Fein, "New York City Politics From 1897–1903: A Study in Political Party Leadership" (Master's essay, Columbia University, 1954); Mark H. Haller, "American Eugenics: Heredity and Social Thought, 1870–1930" (Ph.D. dissertation, University of Wisconsin, 1959), recently published as *Eugenics* (New Brunswick, N.J., 1963); George W. Knerr, "The Mayoral Administration of William L. Strong (Ph.D. dissertation, New York University, 1957); Miriam Z. Langsam, "Children West: A History of the Placing Out System of the New York Children's Aid Society, 1853–1890" (Master's essay, University of Wisconsin, 1961), recently published as *Children West* (Madison, 1964); Daniel Levine, "Variety in Reform Thought: Social Assumptions of American Reformers" (Ph.D. dissertation, Northwestern University, 1961), recently published as *Varieties of Reform Thought* (Madison, 1964); Jeremy Felt Pollard, "The Regulation of Child Labor in New York State, 1886–1942, With Emphasis Upon the New York Child Labor Committee" (Ph.D. dissertation, Syracuse University, 1959), recently published as *Hostages of Fortune* (Syracuse, N.Y., 1965); Henry Jacob Silverman, "American Social Reformers in the Late Nineteenth and Early Twentieth Century" (Ph.D. dissertation, University of Pennsylvania, 1963); Louise Caroll Wade, "Graham Taylor, Social Pioneer: 1851–1938" (Ph.D. dissertation, University of Rochester, 1954), recently published as *Graham Taylor* (Chicago, 1964); and Ned Weinberg, "The Federal Child Labor Amendment—A Study in Pressure Politics" (Ph.D. dissertation, Cornell University, 1942).

These examples give some indication of the varied and abundant materials, secondary and primary, on which this study rests.

INDEX

Unless otherwise noted, all bills, statutes, committees, commissions, and departments are in New York State.